Wildlife of North America

UNIVERSITY PRESS OF FLORIDA

Florida A&M University, Tallahassee
Florida Atlantic University, Boca Raton
Florida Gulf Coast University, Ft. Myers
Florida International University, Miami
Florida State University, Tallahassee
University of Central Florida, Orlando
University of Florida, Gainesville
University of North Florida, Jacksonville
University of South Florida, Tampa
University of West Florida, Pensacola

University Press of Florida

Gainesville

Tallahassee

Tampa

Boca Raton

Pensacola

Orlando

Miami

Jacksonville

Ft. Myers

Wildlife of North America

A Naturalist's Lifelist

- ☐ Mammals
- ☐ Birds
- ☐ Reptiles
- ☐ Amphibians
- ☐ Freshwater Fishes
- ☐ Butterflies
- ☐ Dragonflies and Damselflies

WHIT BRONAUGH

Copyright 2006 by Whit Bronaugh
Printed in the United States of America on acid-free paper
All rights reserved

11 10 09 08 07 06   6 5 4 3 2 1

A record of cataloging-in-publication data is available from the Library of Congress.
ISBN 0-8130-3012-9

All photographs are copyright by Whit Bronaugh:
Dall's Sheep, *Ovis dalli*, page i
Eastern Tailed-Blue, *Everes comyntas*, page ii
Gophersnake, *Pituophis catenifer*, page ii
American Alligator, *Alligator mississippiensis*, page ii
Red-shouldered Hawk, *Buteo lineatus*, page ii
Eastern Fox Squirrels, *Sciurus niger*, page iii
Widow Skimmer, *Libellula luctuosa*, pages x and 395
Black-tailed Jackrabbit, *Lepus californicus*, page 83
Snowy Egret, *Egretta thula*, page 128
Long-nosed Leopard Lizard, *Gambelia wislizenii*, page 207
Cope's Gray Treefrog, *Hyla chrysoscelis*, page 238
Fountain Darter, *Etheostoma fonticola*, page 263
Monarch, *Danaus plexippus*, page 337

The University Press of Florida is the scholarly publishing agency for the State
University System of Florida, comprising Florida A&M University, Florida Atlantic
University, Florida Gulf Coast University, Florida International University, Florida State
University, University of Central Florida, University of Florida, University of North
Florida, University of South Florida, and University of West Florida.

University Press of Florida
15 Northwest 15th Street
Gainesville, FL 32611-2079
http://www.upf.com

North American Lifelist

of

_____

For my brother, John Hutchcraft Bronaugh (1959–2004)

What's in a Name? That which we call a rose
By any other name would smell as sweet.
Shakespeare, *Romeo and Juliet*, 1595

Man: Hello, my boy. And what is your dog's name?
Boy: I don't know. We call him Rover.
New Scientist, 1964

If you do not know the species, you know nothing.
Michael Mares and Janet Braun, 2000

Contents

Preface

I have loved being out in nature for as long as I can remember but the details of natural history did not grab my attention until I participated in a university field ecology course in Africa. I had grown up in central Kentucky where heavily manicured horse farms limited the opportunity to see much wildlife. Suddenly, in the savannas of Kenya and the bush veld of Botswana, I was overwhelmed by a diversity of large mammals unparalleled anywhere in the world since the Pleistocene. The experience transformed me into a sponge for natural history knowledge. But it was the birds, with their conspicuous variety in color, form, pattern, and behavior, that really got my attention.

So I became a birder, complete with a rapidly growing lifelist. I continued to identify and be interested in mammals, reptiles, and amphibians but only on a just-happened-to-see-them basis. Since I have only rarely been a fisherman, freshwater fish remained all but invisible. And I lumped butterflies and dragonflies with other insects into one category: bird food.

About the time I had accumulated what might generously be called a semi-expert knowledge of North American birds, my lifelist stalled around the 500 mark. A few new ones continued to trickle in each year but most of the birds on my "unseen list" required large amounts of effort, luck, and/or expense to see. I figured I would meet them in due time and continued to derive great joy from observing "old friends." But, as any birder will tell you, there *is* something special about seeing a new species or, as one ornithologist I know calls them, "steak dinner birds." After a particularly long drought in new acquaintances I thought, why limit myself to the birds?

I began flipping through my other field guides and soon realized what I had been missing by viewing the natural world through a feather filter. At first, the new morphological terminology (nasolabial groove, discal cell, nuchal shield, et cetera), not to mention the inconspicuousness of most non-avian vertebrates, was a bit daunting. Then there was the extreme variation in many reptile, amphibian, and butterfly species. For example, the dorsal stripe of the Northwestern Gartersnake may be yellow, orange, red, blue, white, faint, broken, or absent! And some groups, like the skipper butterflies (278 species in the United States and Canada) and the minnows (257 species), make the birder's LBJs (little brown jobs) seem like child's play. But gradually I was able to add a few date/location notes into the margins of my field guides.

Then I had the idea for this book. I wanted a single place to record *all* my lifelist additions. I also remembered how a bird lifelist had been a useful learning tool. It separated, and reinforced, what I knew from what I had yet to learn. But most of all, it was a source of inspiration. When I added the first warbler to my lifelist, a Wilson's in the Mummy Range of Colorado, I saw there were about 50 other species of warbler that I suddenly wanted to know more about. What were their names? Where were they found? How do you differentiate between the Mourning and the MacGillivray's? Eventually I was naming new birds in the field without having to first consult my field guide.

When I started keeping a lifelist of non-avian wildlife I was likewise inspired. Suddenly, I found myself looking under rocks and logs for salamanders (or anything else that might crawl out), making nocturnal visits to frog ponds, even using an old butterfly net to catch, identify, and release minnows, sculpins, and darters. Of course I still keep an ear and eye out for the odd bird. And it has been a blast! Now there is no "down" time as there is with just birds who are often quiet in midday, mostly diurnal, hard to observe in the rain, and, for many species, completely absent for more than half the year. By expanding my taxonomic horizons I can look for mammals and snakes on dry nights and amphibians on wet ones. Butterflies, dragonflies, and lizards are usually most active in the warmth of midday. Fish can be observed anytime of the day and, barring impenetrable ice, anytime of the year. Many of these creatures can be carefully captured for close examination before release. Better yet, with close-focusing binoculars they can be observed just like birds.

I now spend a lot of time experiencing nature in ways I would miss if I only had eyes for birds, or any other single group of animals. I don't just go birding anymore. Or mammaling. Or butterflying. I go *wildlifing*.

I conceived this book because it was something I wanted to have myself. But when I saw what the concept of a lifelist for all vertebrates, butterflies, and dragonflies did to inspire my own learning, I began to hope it could do the same for others. For too long the more conspicuous and charismatic birds and larger mammals have stolen the spotlight. Among the lesser-known species are some beautiful creatures. The intricate color patterns of darters, with names like Rainbow, Gilt, Harlequin, Firebelly, Tangerine, Candy, Christmas, and Splendid, make the plumage of warblers look mundane. And the exquisite abstract designs on butterfly wings simply defy description. It is time for naturalists to become more aware, more knowledgeable, and more appreciative of all our fellow beings, whether they are covered in hair, feathers, scales, exoskeleton, or bare skin. After all, none of our wildlife species lives in isolation. The prey of some ground-feeding birds is also the prey of frogs, salamanders, lizards, snakes, and shrews. Kingfishers, herons, and water snakes all eat small fish. Burrowing Owls live in old burrows made by prairie dogs, foxes, badgers, armadillos, and tortoises.

For me, the biggest reward of wildlifing is how much I've learned and continue to learn about natural history. For instance, did you know that the Amazon Molly (a fish) and 10 North American species of whiptail lizard consist entirely of females? Or that several species of horned lizard defend themselves by squirting blood from their eyes? Or that some shrews eat more than their weight each day, their hearts may beat 1,200 times per minute when excited, and a few species (*Blarina*) are the only mammals with a poisonous bite? So, load up your field guides, get out into the field to look for animals you have never heard of before, and uncountable and wondrous discoveries will be yours.

It is my fervent hope that this book will contribute to a greater awareness, appreciation, respect, and understanding of North American biodiversity, and that this will translate into increased protection and living space for all forms of wildlife.

Acknowledgments

A child's interest in nature is innate but it must be nurtured if it is to grow. I want to thank my mother, Ann Hutchcraft Bronaugh, for providing me with the perfect childhood where an old field, patches of woods, small and large creeks, a pond, climbing trees, and weedy fence rows were all within my home range, which I was free to explore. My love and understanding of nature was always enhanced by my many cherished outdoor experiences with my brother John, and my three "blood" brothers, Davis Buckner, Dan Patrick, and Mark Wells. When I was 12, my mother sent me on a YMCA canoe trip in Canada that sparked my lifelong relationship with wilderness. The flames were fanned by Tom Grunwald, a teacher who led teenagers on annual canoe trips in Quetico Provincial Park, and once to Hudson Bay. "Grunner" was also the original inspiration for many other wilderness experiences, especially the greatest outdoor adventure of my life: an 80-day, 1,100 mile canoe expedition my brother and I made from Yellowknife, Northwest Territories, via the Back River, to the Arctic Ocean.

During my college and graduate school years, I learned from and was inspired by many naturalists and biologists. In particular I would like to remember Terry Erwin, Dave Freddy, Dale Hein, Steve Juliano, Jim Karr, Ted Parker, Dave Pearson, Ron Ryder, Ann Rypstra, and Clive Walker.

The taxonomic and nomenclatural information in this book is the culmination of work done by thousands of biologists from Carolus Linnaeus to today's active researchers. I thank them all, especially the authors of the many field guides that are never very far from my reach. For specific taxonomic and nomenclatural questions for which the current literature, or my interpretation of it, was inadequate, I have relied on many scientists who graciously answered my questions and/or reviewed portions of the manuscript: Roland Kays, DeeAnn Reeder, and Don Wilson (mammals); Ralph Axtell, Brian Crother, Harry Greene, Richard Highton, Chris Phillips, and David Wake (reptiles and amphibians); Brooks Burr, Joe Nelson, Larry Page, Frank Pezold, and Stephen Walsh (freshwater fishes); Chuck Crumly, Joseph Dudley, Ernest Lundelius Jr., Larry Martin, Jim Mead, Gary Morgan, Eric Scott, David Steadman, Hugh Wagner, and Richard White (fossil vertebrates); George Austin, Jeffrey Glassberg, John Calhoun, Mike Quinn, Mark Salvato, Dale Schweitzer, and Bob Snetsinger (butterflies); Sid Dunkle and Dennis Paulson (dragonflies and damselflies). Nicole Capuano improved my understanding of NatureServe data, on which the maps were based, and Susan Heisey helped to create the actual maps.

I am grateful to Louise Bronaugh, Mal Frisbie, Tom Hall, and, especially, Dan Patrick for reviewing large portions of the manuscript. I thank my high school writing teachers for their instruction and for letting me write about the same topic over and over again (I'm still doing it!). I owe a special thanks to my sister, Ann Andrews, for teaching me how to write in the first place.

I will forever be indebted to my editor, John Byram, for believing in this book and shepherding it through its many stages. Thanks to Michele Fiyak-Burkely, Nevil Parker, Gillian Hillis, and anyone else at the University Press of Florida who had a hand in the production, distribution, and marketing of this book. I thank copy editor Beth McDonald for improving my grammar, and Jody Larson for proofreading the text.

In a work of this much detail, there are bound to be errors, all of which are my responsibility. I have striven to be perfect but I am, after all, only *Homo sapiens*.

From initial concept to the actual book you now hold in your hands, there could have been many different paths, each with its own unique set of acknowledgments. But every one of them would have said the following. I could not have written this book without the love, encouragement, and support of my wife, Louise, and my son, Gavin.

Checklist of North American Orders and Families

In the order and family checklists below, totals of non-annual visitors, marine visitors, and alien species are given in the headings. However, the living species column includes only the regular native fauna. Also indicated are the number of additional native species of a given family that have become extinct (†) or extirpated (ø) in historic times, or extinct (†P) or extirpated (øP) at the end of the Pleistocene. Page numbers refer to the beginning of a particular family in the regular native lifelists.

Class Mammalia: Mammals Species: 524 total, 444 extant regular native, 2 extirpated (0 Recent, 2 end-Pleistocene), 49 extinct (3 Recent, 46 end-Pleistocene), 1 non-annual visitor, and 28 alien.

Order	Living Species	Family		Living Species	Extinct Species	Page
☐ Didelphimorphia	1	☐ Didelphidae	Opossums	1		83
☐ Proboscidea	0	☐ Mammutidae	Mastodonts	0	1†P	83
		☐ Elephantidae	Elephants, Mammoths	0	3†P	83
☐ Sirenia	2	☐ Dugongidae	Dugongs	0	1†	83
		☐ Trichechidae	Manatees	1		84
☐ Cingulata	1	☐ Dasypodidae	Armadillos	1		84
		☐ Pampatheriidae	Pampatheres	0	1†P	84
		☐ Glyptodontidae	Glyptodonts	0	1†P	84
☐ Pilosa	0	☐ Mylodontidae	Grazing Ground-Sloths	0	1†P	84
		☐ Megatheriidae	Browsing Ground-Sloths	0	2†P	84
		☐ Megalonychidae	Flat-footed Ground-Sloths	0	1†P	84
☐ Primates	1	☐ Hominidae	Great Apes and Humans	1		85
☐ Rodentia	214	☐ Aplodontiidae	Sewellels	1		85
		☐ Sciuridae	Squirrels	67		85
		☐ Castoridae	Beavers	1	1†P	90
		☐ Heteromyidae	Pocket Mice, Kangaroo Rats	39		90
		☐ Geomyidae	Pocket Gophers	18		93
		☐ Dipodidae	Jumping Mice	4		94
		☐ Cricetidae	New World Mice, Rats, Voles	83		95
		☐ Erethizontidae	New World Porcupines	1		101
		☐ Caviidae	Capybaras, Cavies	0	2†P	101
☐ Lagomorpha	20	☐ Ochotonidae	Pikas	2		101
		☐ Leporidae	Hares, Rabbits	18	1†P	101
☐ Soricomorpha	45	☐ Soricidae	Shrews	38		103
		☐ Talpidae	Moles	7		105
☐ Chiroptera	46	☐ Phyllostomidae	New World Leaf-nosed Bats	4		106
		☐ Mormoopidae	Leaf-chinned Bats	1		106
		☐ Molossidae	Free-tailed Bats, Mastiff Bats	7		107
		☐ Vespertilionidae	Vesper Bats	34		107

☐ Carnivora	54	☐ Felidae	Cats	7	4†P 110
		☐ Canidae	Wolves, Foxes, Coyotes	9	1†P, 1øP 111
		☐ Ursidae	Bears	3	3†P 111
		☐ Otariidae	Eared Seals	4	112
		☐ Odobenidae	Walruses	1	112
		☐ Phocidae	Hair Seals	9	1† 112
		☐ Mustelidae	Weasels	11	1† 113
		☐ Mephitidae	Skunks	5	1†P 114
		☐ Procyonidae	Raccoons, Coatis	3	115
☐ Perissodactyla	2	☐ Equidae	Horses	2	5†P 115
		☐ Tapiridae	Tapirs	0	2†P 115
☐ Artiodactyla	12	☐ Tayassuidae	Peccaries	1	2†P 116
		☐ Camelidae	Camels, Llamas	0	3†P 116
		☐ Cervidae	Deer	5	5†P 116
		☐ Antilocapridae	Pronghorn	1	3†P 117
		☐ Bovidae	Bovids	5	3†P, øP 117
☐ Cetacea	49	☐ Balaenidae	Right Whales	2	118
		☐ Balaenopteridae	Rorquals	6	118
		☐ Eschrichtiidae	Gray Whales	1	119
		☐ Delphinidae	Dolphins, Killer Whales	21	119
		☐ Monodontidae	White Whales, Narwhals	2	120
		☐ Phocoenidae	Porpoises	2	121
		☐ Physeteridae	Sperm Whales	3	121
		☐ Ziphiidae	Beaked Whales	12	121

Class Aves: Birds Species: 956 total, 715 extant regular native, 3 extirpated (2 Recent, 1 end-Pleistocene), 22 extinct (5 Recent, 17 end-Pleistocene), 197 non-annual visitors, and 19 alien.

Order	Living Species	Family		Living Species	Extinct Species	Page
☐ Anseriformes	52	☐ Anatidae	Ducks, Geese, Swans	52	1†, 2†P	128
☐ Galliformes	19	☐ Cracidae	Currassows, Guans	1		132
		☐ Phasianidae	Partridges, Grouse, Turkeys	12	1†P	132
		☐ Odontophoridae	New World Quail	6		133
☐ Gaviiformes	5	☐ Gaviidae	Loons	5		133
☐ Podicipediformes	7	☐ Podicipedidae	Grebes	7		134
☐ Procellariiformes	27	☐ Diomedeidae	Albatrosses	3		134
		☐ Procellariidae	Shearwaters, Petrels	17		135
		☐ Hydrobatidae	Storm-Petrels	7		136
☐ Pelecaniformes	16	☐ Phaethontidae	Tropicbirds	2		137
		☐ Sulidae	Boobies, Gannets	3		137
		☐ Pelecanidae	Pelicans	2		137
		☐ Phalacrocoracidae	Cormorants	6		137
		☐ Anhingidae	Darters	2		138
		☐ Fregatidae	Frigatebirds	1		138
☐ Ciconiiformes	20	☐ Ardeidae	Bitterns, Herons, Egrets	12		138
		☐ Threskiornithidae	Ibises, Spoonbills	4		139
		☐ Ciconiidae	Storks	1	1†P	139
		☐ Teratornithidae	Teratorns	0	3†P	139
		☐ Cathartidae	New World Vultures	3	1†P	140
☐ Phoenicopteriformes	1	☐ Phoenicopteridae	Flamingos	1	1†P	140
☐ Falconiformes	31	☐ Accipitridae	Hawks, Kites, Eagles	24	5†P	140

Class Reptilia: Reptiles

Species: 354 total, 315 extant regular native, 4 extinct (0 Recent, 4 end-Pleistocene), 1 extirpated (Pleistocene), 0 non-annual visitors, and 34 alien.

Order or Suborder	Living Species	Family		Living Species	Extinct Species	Page
☐ Amphisbaenia	1	☐ Rhineuridae	North American Worm Lizards	1		207
☐ Sauria	112	☐ Iguanidae	Iguanid Lizards	2		207
		☐ Polychrotidae	Anoles	1		207
		☐ Phrynosomatidae	Spiny Lizards	43		207
		☐ Crotaphytidae	Collared and Leopard Lizards	8		210
		☐ Gekkonidae	Geckos	2		211
		☐ Eublepharidae	Banded Geckos	4		211
		☐ Xantusiidae	Night Lizards	5		212
		☐ Teiidae	Whiptails, Racerunners	22		212
		☐ Scincidae	Skinks	14		214
		☐ Anniellidae	North American Legless Lizards	1		215
		☐ Anguidae	Alligator and Glass Lizards	9		215
		☐ Helodermatidae	Venomous Lizards	1		216
☐ Serpentes	143	☐ Boidae	Boas, Pythons	3		216
		☐ Leptotyphlopidae	Threadsnakes	3		216
		☐ Colubridae	Colubrid Snakes	115		216
		☐ Elapidae	Coralsnakes, Seasnakes	4		225
		☐ Viperidae	Vipers, Pit Vipers	18		225
☐ Crocodylia	2	☐ Alligatoridae	Alligators, Caimans	1		226
		☐ Crocodylidae	Crocodiles	1		226
☐ Testudines	57	☐ Kinosternidae	Mud and Musk Turtles	10		227
		☐ Chelydridae	Snapping Turtles	2		227
		☐ Emydidae	Box and Water Turtles	33		228
		☐ Testudinidae	Tortoises	3	4†P, 1øP	230
		☐ Cheloniidae	Seaturtles	5		231
		☐ Dermochelyidae	Leatherback Seaturtles	1		231
		☐ Trionychidae	Softshells	3		231

Class Amphibia: Amphibians

Species: 279 total, 274 extant regular native, 1 extinct (1 Recent, 0 end-Pleistocene), 0 non-annual visitors, and 4 alien.

Order	Living Species	Family		Living Species	Extinct Species	Page
☐ Anura	95	☐ Ascaphidae	Tailed Frogs	2		238
		☐ Rhinophrynidae	Burrowing Toads	1		238
		☐ Scaphiopodidae	Spadefoots	7		238
		☐ Leptodactylidae	Neotropical Frogs	5		239
		☐ Bufonidae	True Toads	22		239
		☐ Hylidae	Treefrogs	27		241
		☐ Microhylidae	Narrow-mouthed Frogs	3		243
		☐ Ranidae	True Frogs	28	(1†)	243
☐ Urodela	179	☐ Cryptobranchidae	Hellbenders	1		245
		☐ Sirenidae	Sirens	4		245
		☐ Salamandridae	Newts	6		245
		☐ Proteidae	Mudpuppies, Waterdogs	5		246
		☐ Amphiumidae	Amphiumas	3		246

☐ Ambystomatidae	Mole Salamanders	14		247
☐ Dicamptodontidae	Pacific Giant Salamanders	4		248
☐ Rhyacotritonidae	Torrent Salamanders	4		248
☐ Plethodontidae	Lungless Salamanders	138		248

Freshwater Fishes (Class Cephalaspidomorphi: Lampreys, Class Chondrichthyes: Cartilaginous Fishes, Class Osteichthyes: Bony Fishes) Species: 944 total: 819 extant regular native, 17 extinct (17 Recent, 0 end-Pleistocene), 46 marine visitors, and 62 alien.

Order	Living Species	Family		Living Species	Extinct Species	Page
☐ Petromyzontiformes	18	☐ Petromyzontidae	Lampreys	18		263
☐ Myliobatiformes	1	☐ Dasyatidae	Whiptail Stingrays	1		264
☐ Acipenseriformes	9	☐ Acipenseridae	Sturgeons	8		264
		☐ Polyodontidae	Paddlefishes	1		265
☐ Lepisosteiformes	5	☐ Lepisosteidae	Gars	5		265
☐ Amiiformes	1	☐ Amiidae	Bowfins	1		266
☐ Hiodontiformes	2	☐ Hiodontidae	Mooneyes	2		266
☐ Anguilliformes	1	☐ Anguillidae	Freshwater Eels	1		266
☐ Clupeiformes	9	☐ Engraulidae	Anchovies	1		266
		☐ Clupeidae	Herrings, Shads	8		266
☐ Cypriniformes	326	☐ Cyprinidae	Minnows	257	5†	267
		☐ Catostomidae	Suckers	69	2†	285
☐ Characiformes	1	☐ Characidae	Characins	1		290
☐ Siluriformes	40	☐ Ictaluridae	North American Catfishes	40	1†	290
☐ Esociformes	8	☐ Esocidae	Pikes	4		293
		☐ Umbridae	Mudminnows	4		294
☐ Salmoniformes	40	☐ Osmeridae	Smelts	5		294
		☐ Salmonidae	Trouts, Salmons	35	2†	294
☐ Percopsiformes	9	☐ Percopsidae	Trout-perches	2		297
		☐ Aphredoderidae	Pirate Perches	1		297
		☐ Amblyopsidae	Cavefishes	6		297
☐ Gadiformes	2	☐ Gadidae	Cods	2		298
☐ Mugiliformes	1	☐ Mugilidae	Mullets	1		298
☐ Atheriniformes	4	☐ Atherinopsidae	New World Silversides	4		298
☐ Beloniformes	1	☐ Belonidae	Needlefishes	1		299
☐ Cyprinodontiformes	58	☐ Aplocheilidae	Rivulines	1		299
		☐ Fundulidae	Topminnows	27	1†	299
		☐ Poeciliidae	Livebearers	13	2†	301
		☐ Goodeidae	Goodeids	3	1†	302
		☐ Cyprinodontidae	Pupfishes	14	1†	302
☐ Gasterosteiformes	5	☐ Gasterosteidae	Sticklebacks	4		303
		☐ Syngnathidae	Pipefishes	1		304
☐ Scorpaeniformes	29	☐ Cottidae	Sculpins	29	1†	304
☐ Perciformes	248	☐ Moronidae	Temperate Basses	4		306
		☐ Centrarchidae	Sunfishes, Basses	31		306
		☐ Percidae	Perches, Darters	189	1†	309
		☐ Sciaenidae	Drums, Croakers	1		322
		☐ Elassomatidae	Pygmy Sunfishes	6		323
		☐ Cichlidae	Cichlids	1		323
		☐ Embiotocidae	Surfperches	1		323
		☐ Eleotridae	Sleepers	3		323
		☐ Gobiidae	Gobies	12		324
☐ Pleuronectiformes	1	☐ Achiridae	American Soles	1		324

Class Insecta: Insects
Order Lepidoptera: Butterflies

Species: 736 total, 585 extant regular native, 1extinct (1Recent, 0 end-Pleistocene), 1 extirpated, 144 non-annual visitors, and 5 alien.

Family	Living Species	Subfamily		Living Species	Extinct Species	Page
☐ Papilionidae	23	☐ Parnassiinae	Parnassians	3		337
		☐ Papilioninae	Swallowtails	20		337
☐ Pieridae	54	☐ Pierinae	Whites	21		339
		☐ Coliadinae	Sulphurs	33		340
☐ Lycaenidae	112	☐ Miletinae	Harvesters	1		343
		☐ Lycaeninae	Coppers	16		343
		☐ Theclinae	Hairstreaks	61		344
		☐ Polyommatinae	Blues	34	1†	348
☐ Riodinidae	16	☐ Riodininae	Metalmarks	16		351
☐ Nymphalidae	163	☐ Libytheinae	Snouts	1		352
		☐ Heliconiinae	Heliconians, Fritillaries	34		352
		☐ Nymphalinae	True Brushfoots	59		355
		☐ Limenitidinae	Admirals, Allies	13		359
		☐ Charaxinae	Leafwings	4		360
		☐ Apaturinae	Emperors	3		360
		☐ Satyrinae	Satyrs	46		360
		☐ Danainae	Monarchs	3		364
☐ Hesperiidae	217	☐ Pyrrhopyginae	Fiertips	1		364
		☐ Pyrginae	Spread-wing Skippers	77	1ø	364
		☐ Heteropterinae	Skipperlings	5		370
		☐ Hesperiinae	Grass-Skippers	121		370
		☐ Megathyminae	Giant-Skippers	13		379

Order Odonata: Dragonflies and Damselflies
Species: 451 total, 442 extant regular native, 0 extinct, 8 non-annual visitors, and 1 alien.

Suborder	Living Species	Family		Living Species	Extinct Species	Page
☐ Zygoptera	131	☐ Calopterygidae	Broad-winged Damsels	8		395
		☐ Lestidae	Spreadwings	19		395
		☐ Platystictidae	Shadowdamsels	1		397
		☐ Protoneuridae	Threadtails	3		397
		☐ Coenagrionidae	Pond Damsels	100		397
☐ Anisoptera	311	☐ Petaluridae	Petaltails	2		404
		☐ Aeshnidae	Darners	38		405
		☐ Gomphidae	Clubtails	100		407
		☐ Cordulegastridae	Spiketails	9		414
		☐ Macromiidae	Cruisers	9		415
		☐ Corduliidae	Emeralds	50		416
		☐ Libellulidae	Skimmers	103		420

List of Symbols

*   at some risk of global extinction (vulnerable, imperiled, or critically imperiled)

ø   extirpated from North America since Columbus

øP   extirpated from North America during end-Pleistocene or Holocene up to Columbus

†?   possibly extinct since Columbus

†   extinct since Columbus

†P   extinct during end-Pleistocene or Holocene up to Columbus

Introduction

Scope of the Book

This book lists all the native, accidental, and alien species of mammals, birds, reptiles, amphibians, freshwater fishes, butterflies, dragonflies, and damselflies in North America north of Mexico, a total of 4,244 species. According to recent findings, turtles and crocodilians are not true reptiles, but for convenience this book follows the traditional concept of reptile that includes them. Fishes that occur in inland saline waters (for example, Salt Creek in Death Valley, and Salton Sea, California) and marine fishes that enter freshwater are included. The geographic area covered is the same as the American Birding Association's "ABA area," which includes ocean regions within 200 miles of land, or half the distance to a neighboring country, whichever is less. Thus, Greenland, Bermuda, and the Bahamas are excluded. The main list also includes those species known or thought to have become extinct since the arrival of humans in North America 13,000 years ago. These species are included to give a more complete picture of the North American fauna and to remind us of what we have already lost. Alien species are not native to North America but have been intentionally or accidentally introduced from other parts of the world and are now maintaining viable populations in the North American wild without direct human assistance.

Marine mammals, pelagic birds, seaturtles, and the Yellow-bellied Seasnake are included, but marine fishes that never enter freshwater are not. (The marine fishes, along with mollusks, corals, crustaceans, and other important marine fauna, will be included in the forthcoming *Marine Animals of North America: A Lifelist for Naturalists, Divers, Snorkelers, and Beach Combers.*) The term "wildlife" should not be limited to vertebrates (or even animals) but with over 3,000 species of vertebrates in the area covered, space considerations quickly become limiting. However, to represent the non-vertebrate fauna, and to recognize and encourage the rapidly growing interest in them, I have included the butterflies, dragonflies, and damselflies as well.

Scientific and English Names

The scientific name of an organism consists of two Latinized and italicized names. The first is the genus, which is always capitalized. The second name, the specific epithet, is never capitalized and never appears without the genus name. Scientific nomenclature is a universal language, recognized and used by scientists and naturalists of all languages and nationalities. However, that does not mean that scientific names are permanent. Zoological systematics and nomenclature are in a constant state of flux as new discoveries are made in the field, laboratory, and museum. You may be surprised that, even in North America, completely new species are still being discovered, each requiring its own unique name. Taxonomic revisions may move a species into a different genus or family, split one species into two or more new ones, or lump two or more species together under the same name. For example, in 1983 the American Ornithologists' Union (AOU) decided that the previously recognized Brown-capped Rosy-Finch (*Leucosticte australis*), Gray-crowned Rosy-Finch (*Leucosticte tephrocotis*), and Black Rosy-Finch (*Leucosticte atratus*) were actually subspecies of an Asian bird called the Rosy Finch (*Leucosticte arctoa*). Ten years later, the AOU split them back into the original four species. There is evidence to suggest that the Red Crossbill should be split into as many as nine different species. Based on molecular genetic studies, the Slimy Salamander has been split into 13 different species. However, such changes are not always universally accepted among taxonomists. Some proposed name changes in the scientific literature are accepted or rejected relatively quickly while others remain controversial and unresolved for many years.

Stability in English names is also a much desired yet elusive goal. English names must often change to reflect changes in the scientific names with which they are paired. Many species also have different English names depending on the location or the author of your field guide. Confusion is not limited to within a class, or even phylum, of organisms. Depending on where you are, the name "gopher" can refer to ground squirrels (*Spermophilus*), tortoises (*Gopherus*), a frog (*Rana capito*), or pocket gophers (Geomyidae). The Southeastern Pocket Gopher (*Geomys pinetis*) is locally called a salamander. Even within the most recent lists of standardized English names used for this book, the White, Cuban, and Banded peacocks are butterflies; the Black, Smallmouth, and Bigmouth buffaloes are fish; the Ringtail (*Bassariscus astutus*) is a mammal but 6 species of dragonfly (*Erpetogomphus*) have the group name of ringtail; the 3 sylphs and 29 emeralds are dragonflies, but among neotropical hummingbirds there are also 3 sylphs and 24 emeralds; the Coppery Emerald of this book is a dragonfly (*Somatochlora georgiana*), but it is also a hummingbird (*Chlorostilbon russatus*) of South America; the Slaty Skimmer (*Libellula incesta*) is a dragonfly, but the Black Skimmer (*Rynchops niger*) is a bird; and "darter" can refer to 177 species of North American fishes (*Ammocrypta*, *Crystallaria*, *Etheostoma*, *Percina*), an Old World bird related to our Anhinga, and a number of European dragonflies (*Sympetrum*).

Many animals are so obscure that the determination of a suitable English name is primarily left to the scientists and conservationists who work with them. Well-known species that have small ranges seem to have less confusion or controversy surrounding their English name. But the English names of many widespread species vary considerably depending on one's location, profession, personal preference, or choice of field guide. The Puma has been known by no less than 40 English names including Mountain Lion, Panther, Cougar, Painter, Catamount, Deer Cat, Mountain Devil, King Cat, Silver Lion, and Mountain Screamer. While most of those names are nearly or completely out of use today, Mountain Lion, Puma, and Cougar have all been used in recent field guides.

One of the most problematic examples, at least from the perspective of English speakers on both sides of the Atlantic, is that of *Cervus elaphus*. English-speaking Europeans call this animal Red Deer, but most North Americans know it as Elk, the name English-speaking Europeans use for *Alces*, the genus North Americans call Moose! Wapiti (Shawnee for "white rump") is the alternative, less confusing, and more appropriate name for North American *Cervus elaphus*, but it almost never seems to be used except as an alternative name!

In spite of some persistent problems, attempts to standardize English names have improved the situation tremendously over years past. Thus, few birders, if any, still use the names Bog-pumper (American Bittern), Fly-up-the-creek (Green Heron), Twixt-hell-and-the-white-oak (Chuck-will's-widow), or Timberdoodle (American Woodcock). In an effort to bring stability and consistency to both scientific and English names, a number of checklists have been published by organizations dedicated to the study of the different animal groups in this book. Though not yet perfect or stable, these lists have caused the problems listed above to be the exception rather than the rule.

Here are the primary sources for the scientific and English names used in this book:

Mammals

For Recent mammals I follow *Mammal Species of the World* (Wilson and Reeder 2005), a product of the Checklist Committee of the American Society of Mammalogists. This is the reference (actually an earlier draft of it) followed by Kays and Wilson (2002) in their recent Princeton Field Guide to the *Mammals of North America*. For alien species not in Kays and Wilson (2002), I follow the most recent Checklist of North American Mammals from the Museum of Texas Tech University (Baker et al. 2003a). The taxonomy and nomenclature of Baker et al. (2003a) is very close to that of Wilson and Reeder (2005), and in a few cases, which should not cause any confusion, I used an English name from Baker et al. (2003a).

I have made two important, and to some, unusual, departures from most checklists and field guides for mammals. I have put Modern Humans in their proper place in the animal world (between sloths and rodents), and I have included extinct mammals that were present in North America when Modern Humans first arrived (see Extinct Species). For extinct end-Pleistocene mammals I mainly used Kurtén and Anderson (1980) and Anderson (1984), as amended by references cited in Extinct Species.

Birds

I follow the American Ornithologists' Union *Check-list of North American Birds*, 7th edition (AOU 1998, as amended by supplements: AOU 2000; Banks et al. 2002, 2003, 2004, 2005) for taxonomy and nomenclature, and the *American Birding Association Checklist: Birds of the Continental United States and Canada* (ABA 2002, and supplements: Robbins et al. 2003, 2004) for determination of introduced and accidental species. For extinct end-Pleistocene birds I followed Steadman and Martin (1984), and subsequent papers cited in Extinct Species.

Reptiles and Amphibians

Except for my inclusion of two unisexual *Ambystoma* biotypes (see page 48 in this book), I follow the checklist by Crother, et al. (2000, as amended by Crother et al. 2003 and, based on more recent research, the Committee on Standard English and Scientific Names) approbated by the Society for the Study of Amphibians and Reptiles, the American Society of Ichthyologists and Herpetologists, and the Herpetologists' League. I used *Pleistocene Amphibians and Reptiles in North America* (Holman 1995) for extinct end-Pleistocene reptiles and amphibians.

Freshwater Fishes

I follow the American Fisheries Society's *Common and Scientific Names of Fishes from the United States, Canada, and Mexico*, 6th edition (Nelson et al. 2004), with a few modifications based on Page and Burr (forthcoming).

Butterflies

I follow the North American Butterfly Association's *Checklist and English Names of North American Butterflies* (North American Butterfly Association 2001, as amended by Caterino et al. 2003).

Dragonflies and Damselflies

I follow the checklist by Paulson and Dunkle (1999) as amended on the website of the Dragonfly Society of the Americas (2005).

Overall, my goal has been to present what is most generally accepted by experts in their respective fields. Future editions of this book will include updated taxonomy and nomenclature. Meanwhile, between editions you may keep your list current by periodically visiting www.wildlifelist.org. If your field guide is newer than your edition of this book, the website should explain most of the differences you may find. If your field guide is older, but still recent, most of the differences between it and this book are described in the appendix.

Following a collection of lists from different sources inevitably leads to some inconsistencies in form or spelling (for example, Paiute Dancer and Piute Ground Squirrel; Blackchin Shiner and Black-chinned Hummingbird; Saltmarsh Harvest Mouse and Salt Marsh Skipper; Northern Pygmy Clubtail and Northern Pygmy-Owl), but I have chosen to preserve most of these differences here (even though I prefer a more standard nomenclature). My one major departure from this policy is to capitalize English names of all species (currently it is not conventional to capitalize the English names of mammals and fishes). I do this for consistency of style within this book, because it is the convention followed by most field guides, and because it leads to less confusion. For example, there are 12 species of California chipmunks but only one California Chipmunk (*Tamias obscurus*). A cave salamander is any of a number of salamander species that spend part or all of their lives in caves, but a Cave Salamander is *Eurycea lucifuga*. A pretty white shiner describes any of a number of minnows, but a pretty White Shiner is a particularly nice looking specimen of *Luxilus albeolus*, and a white Pretty Shiner might describe an albino specimen of *Lythrurus bellus*. And if capitalization of the English names of wildlife encourages greater respect for our fellow beings, so much the better.

I follow the Council of Biology Editors in not capitalizing animal group-names when used with two or more species, or general geographic features when multiple place names are listed. Examples are Acadian and Least flycatchers; Garden and Lesser slender salamanders; and Duck and Tennessee rivers.

The criteria for the order in which species are listed vary among the major groups, but are usually consistent with the standardized references for those groups. All orders and families are in phylogenetic order, as are the genera and species of birds and butterflies. The mammals, reptiles, amphibians, freshwater fishes, dragonflies, and damselflies are listed in alphabetical order, within their respective family, by genus, then species.

Wildlifing: Finding, Identifying, and Observing Wildlife

Many people are attracted to birding because birds are often both obvious and easy to observe. The same can be said for some mammals, lizards, butterflies, and dragonflies because, like most human observers, they are diurnal and not shy. But where are all those hundreds of species of small mammals, snakes, frogs, salamanders, and fishes? How do you find them and, when you do, how do you observe and identify them?

First, start with the introductory sections of your field guides. There you will find out why, for example, you have perhaps rarely or never seen any of the 179 species of salamanders in North America: they are mostly nocturnal and silent, often only active during rainy periods, and otherwise hidden beneath rocks, logs, moss, or other objects. To find them you need to become nocturnal yourself, be prepared to get a little wet, or look under rocks, logs, and other forest debris.

Going out with someone knowledgeable about wildlife will shortcut the path to finding and identifying fauna. Many parks and preserves have naturalists who offer scheduled field trips. Conservation groups, like the National Audubon Society and its local chapters, do the same. Take a class from a local college, nature center, or natural history institute (often associated with national parks). Join a Christmas or breeding bird count, a Fourth of July butterfly count, or a spring frog count. Reflecting the more inclusive nature of this book, some naturalists are organizing "biodiversity days" or "bioblitzes," where they try to find and identify as many species as possible, regardless of the taxon.

When it comes to identification, do not let the diversity intimidate you. If you are already an experienced birder or butterflier, remember what it was like when you tried to identify your first sparrow or skipper. The details may be different but the methodology is similar for squirrels, snakes, salamanders, suckers, and skimmers. One main difference you should be aware of, especially if you are mainly used to birds and larger mammals, is that many of the species in other groups can be highly variable in their appearance. Morphology, the form and structure of the animal, is often more important than color or pattern.

Many of these animals can be captured and held long enough to, for example, count the labial scales on a gartersnake, compare the relative positions of the dorsal and pelvic fins on a minnow, or check the shape of the parotoid gland on a toad. But with the recent development of high quality, close-focusing binoculars, "in the hand" characteristics are rapidly becoming "field marks." My binoculars allow me to focus at ten power on an animal less than six feet from my eyes! With close-focusing binoculars you *can* count the labial scales on a gartersnake, compare the relative positions of the dorsal and pelvic fins on a minnow, or check the shape of the parotoid gland on a toad, all without capturing the animal and causing undue stress. You may "miss" a few that way but you would probably miss just as many with pursuit and capture. You will also discover the joys of observing behaviors other than the "predator" avoidance you would see if you tried to catch them. There are now field guides that emphasize the use of binoculars to identify and observe butterflies (Glassberg 1999, 2001), dragonflies (Dunkle 2000), and freshwater fishes (Smith 1994). I have found that close-focusing binoculars work just as well for many small mammals, frogs, aquatic salamanders, lizards, turtles, and snakes.

Binoculars are also helpful when the specimen is in hand because, when turned around backwards, they make great high-powered magnifying glasses. Just hold your subject very close to one eyepiece while you look through the opposite front lens. With this technique, you can even compare the genitalia and tiny markings of damselflies, and thereby identify the species, not just the genus.

If your wildlifing experience has been limited to certain taxa, you may find sensitizing your taxonomic radar to all the species in this book a bit overwhelming. Use the maps in your national field guides to make a list of just the species found in your immediate area or destination, or, better yet, buy a state or regional field guide. This will narrow your focus and be especially helpful when identifying species of large confusing groups like the skippers or minnows. Spend time casually flipping through your field guides to build familiarity not only with the species but also with how they are arranged in the book. At first, concentrate on what separates the higher taxa like orders, families, and genera. Aside from helping you to quickly minimize the choices when identifying a species in the field, all this "homework" will be especially helpful in organizing the field guide you gradually create in your head. The field marks of 100 species are much easier to remember if divided into categories of genus, family, and order. But in the field, remember to concentrate on the animal as long as possible, and take detailed notes, before consulting your field guide. Your experience observing wildlife will be your greatest reward, as well as your best teacher. Soon you'll be on your way to observing hundreds of unique species of wildlife, from the 1/2-inch Western Pygmy-Blue to the 100-foot Blue Whale.

Conservation

For most readers, this section is preaching to the choir. Obviously, an animal's welfare is more important than filling in a space in this book. I am reminded of the story of the rarely seen Black Rail that was unwittingly trampled to death by overzealous birders. Sometimes wildlife is better off remaining unobserved. Usually the animal's behavior will let you know if restraint is in order. Be especially careful not to be intrusive during the breeding season or other stressful periods such as late winter when animals' fat reserves may be at their lowest.

As you learn about wildlife whose habits are unfamiliar to you, you should become aware of their particular vulnerabilities. Use your binoculars or spotting scope whenever possible to minimize harassment or handling of the animals. In John James Audubon's day, shotguns were a primary tool used in the observation of birds. The field guides of Roger Tory Peterson and others helped make the transition from guns to binoculars. Today, a similar movement, from insect nets to binoculars, is underway in the observation of butterflies and dragonflies. Binoculars are also useful in the observation of other forms of wildlife, even fish. However, this is not to say that collecting animals for scientific study is bad. On the contrary, scientific collections are a vital tool for scientific research as well as conservation. Most of the information in your field guides relating to identification, including the paintings, drawings, and range maps, was obtained from museum specimens. And voucher specimens have been instrumental in documenting the decline of many species, which can lead to their legal protection and efforts to improve their chances of survival.

For a number of small creatures, like many fish, reptiles, and amphibians, you may need to temporarily capture the animal to make a positive identification. Make sure you abide by the rules and regulations of state, provincial, and federal wildlife agencies regarding capture and holding of wild species. In many states, you must have a fishing license or some other permit even if you are capturing and releasing minnows. More important, before capturing any animal, check your field guides to follow safe handling techniques, both for you and for the animal. For example, when handling salamanders keep your hands and the animal moist and cool, and make sure your hands are free of harmful chemicals such as insect repellant, sun tan lotion, or skin toxins from other amphibians. If you temporarily hold fish in a mini-aquarium or water-filled plastic bag for identification, take care to replace the water frequently so the oxygen level does not drop too low. If you have never tried to identify a *Notropis* shiner you will be surprised at how long it can take; do not let the fish be a casualty of your indecision. Never hold lizards or salamanders by the tail because it may break off, a self-inflicted amputation intended to allow the animal to escape, leaving the predator (you!) with just the still wriggling tail. This makes the animal more vulnerable to predation and food shortages until it can regrow a new tail. The bottom line is to learn the animal's needs, as well as its behavior in captivity, beforehand, to keep both observer and the observed happy and safe. And, of course, always return animals to their actual homes, not merely similar habitat where escape routes, food sources, and their conspecific neighbors are unfamiliar to them.

Care of the animal means care of the habitat. Replace overturned rocks, logs, leaf litter, et cetera, as close as possible to their original positions to conserve microhabitats. Think twice about rolling a boulder, especially on a steep slope, that may be too heavy to replace properly. How would you feel if a giant ripped off the roof of your house and dropped it back on crooked so that gaps sucked out the cozy warm air and let in the wind and rain? Try to search in areas with little human traffic to minimize and disperse disturbance.

Above all, be particularly aware of threatened and endangered species. These are indicated in this book as well as in many field guides. Contact the U.S. Fish and Wildlife Service, the Canadian Wildlife Service, or your state/provincial wildlife agency for further information. Generally, these animals should be viewed only from a non-threatening distance or under the guidance of wildlife officials or researchers. For some species such as the Kirtland's Warbler and Whooping Crane, special guided tours have been set up to allow wildlifers to observe the animals without risking the future of the species. If you do happen upon an endangered species on your own, especially in an area where it is unexpected, be sure to inform those associated with the conservation and recovery of the species.

Final Advice

The activity of pursuing wildlife for the sole reason of checking them off one's lifelist and recording them in this book is, to me, a benign if unfulfilling pastime at best. Once, while guiding a particularly obsessive but unappreciative lister in Peru, I excitedly pointed out a beautiful Paradise Tanager with its turquoise breast, apple green face, black wings and tail, and scarlet and yellow rump. With no small amount of impatience and disdain he said, "I already saw that one in Ecuador." Sure, he had probably *looked* at one in Ecuador, but I doubt if he really *saw* it, and certainly he did not *observe* it or make any meaningful connection with it. And in any case, he had not seen *this* Paradise Tanager.

So, if I may be so bold, do not take listing so seriously that it becomes the only goal. Observe the behavior of wildlife, note aspects of their natural history. Let your desire to see new species cause you to ask questions about biodiversity, biogeography, ecology, behavior, and conservation. Why are there so many darters? Why do we have only one species of dipper, and why is it not found in the mountain streams of the Appalachians? How did pupfish get to those desert springs? What are the food plants of swallowtail butterflies? How do butterflies spend the winter? How did unisexual species of whiptail lizards evolve? Why is the Indiana Myotis rare and endangered but the closely related Little Brown Myotis one of the most common and widespread bats in North America?

Think how your knowledge might benefit wildlife conservation. Share your expertise with others. Seek to understand and discover. Skim through your field guides and you will probably be surprised at how much basic natural history remains unknown. In the 1996 *National Audubon Society Field Guide to North American Reptiles and Amphibians*, the breeding habits of 27 of our salamander species are listed as poorly known, uncertain, or unknown. The same can be said of the early life stages of many of our butterflies, dragonflies, and small, non-avian vertebrates. Extend your observations beyond mere identification and you might make an important discovery. You will also make a stronger, more meaningful connection with a unique part of the natural world.

Finally, and most important, never get too used to the brilliant red of a cardinal, the antics of a squirrel, or the marvel of animal flight. Treat each encounter with wildlife as a unique privilege. Maintain a child's curiosity and sense of wonder and you will be greatly rewarded by your exploration of nature.

How to Use This Book

This book has two different checklists. First, beginning on page xvii, is a list of orders and families, presented in phylogenetic order, each with the number of regularly occurring native species north of Mexico. This gives an overall view of the diversity of our fauna. The second list, starting on page 83, and detailed below, is the lifelist section that forms the bulk of the book and has an entry for each species of North American wildlife. The lifelist is divided into the following five classes of vertebrates and two orders of insects: mammals, birds, reptiles, amphibians, freshwater fishes, butterflies, and dragonflies/damselflies.

Species Lifelist

Each species listing includes the English name, scientific name, a checkbox, conservation status, and space to record the date and location of your first sighting of that species. Where applicable, each of the seven major wildlife groups (vertebrate classes or insect orders) is further divided into three lists: (1) regular natives, (2) non-annual visitors, and (3) aliens.

Regular Natives

First is the list of all regularly occurring native species, which includes year-round residents, seasonal breeders, winter residents, and regular visitors or migrants. This is the true North American fauna. Species that are at some risk of extinction are marked with an asterisk (*) according to the ranking system of the Natural Heritage Network, The Nature Conservancy, and the Association for Biodiversity Information (see NatureServe 2005 or Stein et al. 2000 for further information). Included are all species that are globally critically imperiled (G1), imperiled (G2), or vulnerable (G3). The Natural Heritage Network system is biologically more appropriate and accurate than the U.S. Endangered Species List, which only includes those species that have been *legally* recognized as endangered or threatened via a bureaucratic and political process. Species that are possibly extinct are indicated with a dagger and question mark (†?). Those marked with a dagger (†) are presumed to be extinct. Species that are known or thought to have become extinct at the end of the Pleistocene (shortly after humans invaded North America) or at sometime from then until Columbus, are labeled †P. Extant species that have been extirpated from North America are indicated by the symbol ø (since Columbus), or øP (end-Pleistocene to Columbus). All species that are now extinct, possibly extinct, or missing are also summarized in Extinct Species.

Non-annual Visitors

The second section within each major animal group is a list of species that naturally occur in North America but not on a regular basis—often quite rarely. These include birds, bats, butterflies, or dragonflies, because their ability to fly makes them capable of traveling far beyond the normal range of their species. Also included in this category are a number of marine fishes that rarely enter freshwater. None of these species are a significant part of our fauna although their occurrence in our area, whether the result of an adventurous individual or a storm blowing migrants off course, is natural. Some, such as the Wandering Albatross, Hairy-legged Vampire Bat, White-dotted Cattleheart, and Sooty Saddlebags, have only been recorded once, while others, like the Fork-tailed Flycatcher, are seen almost annually. Field guides variously refer to these animals as accidental, casual, vagrant, rare visitor, or stray, but the definition of these terms varies with the field guide author. My goal here is to separate those species that visit so rarely and in such low numbers that few would treat them as a normal and significant part of the North American fauna. Rather than subjectively distinguish among different degrees of rarity or occurrence I use one category: non-annual visitors.

This part of the list includes all birds considered by the American Birding Association (2002; Robbins et al. 2003) to be casual (code 4), accidental (code 5), origin hypothetical, or no longer possible to find (code 6), with the exception of formerly resident or annual visitors that are now extinct, probably extinct, or extirpated. I give the benefit of the doubt to Worthen's Sparrow, treating it as an extirpated regular native, although evidence supporting this view is more suggestive than substantial. The only record of Worthen's Sparrow north of Mexico is from Grant County, New Mexico, in June 1884, but today the species is known to move beyond its Mexican breeding range only in winter. That bird, which became the type specimen of the species, may have been a stray from Mexico, but it seems more likely that there was a small population in New Mexico that was soon extirpated by the overgrazing happening at the time (ABA 2002). I also include all marine mammals in the regular native list even though some, such as Fraser's Dolphin and Perrin's, Ginkgo-toothed, and Pygmy beaked whales, have only been recorded a few times. Their apparent rarity may be an artifact of their secretive nature, deep-water proclivities, and the paucity of observers who could identify them.

Over 140 Mexican and Caribbean butterflies have been observed just north of the southern U.S. border, on an apparently less than annual basis, but their status in our area is not always precisely known. Some species listed in this book as non-annual visitors may sometimes breed in our area, or at least be consistently or even commonly observed, for several years before retreating south again, or escaping our notice. Others, especially those only recorded once, may have escaped from butterfly houses or other breeders, come north with human assistance (in fruit shipments, for example), or been based on mislabeled specimens. Alternatively, there may be some species on the non-annual visitor list that are actually rare residents, but have escaped observation on a yearly basis. The non-annual list includes an additional 14 species documented on the North American Butterfly Association's website since the publication of their 2001 checklist.

Alien Species

Aliens are those non-native species that have been accidentally or intentionally introduced through human action but are now maintaining viable populations without direct human assistance. They are listed separately to maintain the ecological, evolutionary, and biogeographical integrity of the native species list, and to emphasize their status as unwelcome and often harmful interlopers in North America. While the impact of some alien species on our native fauna has been relatively minor, as a whole they are a major problem. In fact, according to The Nature Conservancy, alien species (including invertebrates, plants, and pathogens) are second only to habitat destruction in the degree to which they threaten the survival of our native wildlife. Due to the continent-wide coverage of this book, species like the House Finch, Bullfrog, and Channel Catfish, which are native in one part of North America but introduced in others, are not included in the lists of alien species. However, on a regional basis, if they are not native to a given area, they should certainly be treated the same as alien species from outside our continent, because they can be just as destructive to native fauna.

One caveat to this treatment of alien species concerns the reintroduction of end-Pleistocene species (or their close representatives) eliminated by human activities. The pristine balance of nature, as observed by the first European explorers in North America, is a myth, at least as far as the megafauna and associated predators, scavengers, and commensals are concerned. We may not be able to replace the actual species or subspecies that were present but, from an ecological and evolutionary perspective, the wild places of North America would be more truly North American with close relatives of the recently lost megafauna, than without. I am one of the few but growing number of people (Martin and Burney 1999; Flannery 2001; Donlan et al. 2005) who dream of cheetahs once again giving a reason for Pronghorns to keep up their speed. Our dense boreal forests and second growth woods would benefit from elephants doing the work that mammoths and mastodons did for millions of years until just a short time ago. Camels, llamas, capybaras, tapirs, and lions would also fill long established North American niches, only recently made vacant. These re-introductions would also improve the prospects for Gray Wolves, California Condors, Jaguars, and who knows what other species of plants and animals that have suffered at the loss of most of our native megafauna. Of course, we also have to make sure that we lose no more of what we have, and bring back much, in terms of population numbers, of what we have lost more recently.

Obviously, re-wilding North America to this extent will be a long, uphill process, but it is one that, unwittingly, we began 400 years ago when early European explorers and pioneers brought horses back to North America. Horses originated in North America 45 million years ago and have been here ever since, except for the human-caused hiatus of about 10,000 years that ended sometime around AD 1600 when they became reestablished in the wild. Even though these horses were a different species from the original natives, they quickly filled the void. By 1900 some two million wild horses covered much of the United States and the prairie regions of Canada. Horses are more native to North America than Moose, Elk, Grizzly Bears, and Humans, all of which first migrated from Asia in the late Pleistocene. At that time there were three to five species of horses present. The Feral Horse and Feral Ass (wild burro) should be seen as the best we can do at replacing them. Thus, I treat both these animals as reintroduced natives (in genus, if not species) rather than aliens. The Mountain Goat has been reintroduced to the southern Rocky Mountains as a replacement for the extinct, and possibly conspecific, Harrington's Mountain Goat, hunted to extinction 11,000 years ago.

Making an Entry

When you observe a species of wildlife for the first time, enter the date and location in the space provided. On the second line of each entry you can list memory joggers such as habitat, weather, subspecies, your companions at the time, behavior, identification marks observed, personal impressions, and date and location for subsequent sightings if the species is particularly rare or difficult to find or observe. If you see an animal not listed in this book because of more recent taxonomic changes or discoveries, record your observation in one of the blank entries at the end of each major group. Many of our rare species, especially those found only in extreme southern California, Arizona, New Mexico, Texas, and Florida, are more common and easier to see in Mexico or the West Indies. Whether you choose to "count" wildlife you see outside U.S. and Canadian borders is, of course, entirely up to you. Obviously, limiting the coverage of this book to species within political boundaries is, to say the least, biogeographically arbitrary, but any southern biogeographic boundary of North America is ambiguous when so many different taxa are considered.

Some animals are so secretive and difficult to see that you may want to record when you identify them by sound (calls of rails, owls, frogs, et cetera) or sign (tracks of large cats, mole excavations). For other species that are either so inaccessible (subterranean salamanders and fishes) or rare and endangered that observing them in the wild would be dangerous for either you or the animal, you may want to record when you have seen them in zoos, aquariums, or other controlled situations.

Obviously, you cannot observe living specimens of truly extinct species unless we are someday able to resurrect them from preserved DNA. But you can still record your observations of museum specimens or, if you are lucky, fossil specimens in the field. You could even spend time in the species' former habitat imagining their presence. Watch a Pronghorn and imagine the American Cheetah. While sitting under an Osage-orange tree, picture the fruit being eaten by a Columbian Mammoth.

The bottom line is, this is your book. If you want to compare your lifelist to that of others, you can follow the listing rules of an organization like the American Birding Association. But you can also make up your own guidelines, or ignore rules altogether.

Feel free to enter and/or count any experience you have in which you make a meaningful connection with a species of wildlife.

Finding a Species Listing

If you have any trouble finding a particular species in the lifelist section, most species can be quickly found using the English name index. English names with more than one word where the last word is not a group name, such as Gila Monster and Mourning Cloak, are indexed according to the entire name. Thus, *Heloderma suspectum* is listed in the English index under "Gila Monster," not "Monster, Gila." To simplify the index, unhyphenated multiple-word group names, such as ground squirrels, are listed under the larger group name, that is, squirrels.

In some cases, an English group name covers many species of different genera or even families. For example, there are 177 species of darters spread among four genera. Under the group name salamander you will find 155 species represented in 16 genera and four families! Even if you have located the correct genus, you may be faced with as many as 144 species, as in the darter genus *Etheostoma*. (Incidentally, the world's largest vertebrate genus is *Eleutherodactylus*, the rainfrogs. Only six species of *Eleutherodactylus* occur in our area, but the total number of species in this genus, found mostly in the Neotropics, is over 700 and still growing!) However, the species in most of the large genera in this book are listed alphabetically in the main list, making them easy to find. Only birds and butterflies are listed in phylogenetic order, and their largest genera are only 21 species (*Dendroica*) and 25 species (*Papilio*), respectively.

If you still have a problem locating your species, your best bet is to use the scientific name index. Although genera are listed, a given species is indexed according to its species name (specific epithet) because that part of the name is more unique than the genus name. There are 144 species that share the genus name *Etheostoma*, but the maximum number of species (in this book) that share the same specific epithet is only 11, as in the case of *elegans*. The specific epithet is also usually more stable than the genus of a species. For example, in 1758 Carolus Linnaeus described the Loggerhead Seaturtle as *Testudo caretta*. It has since been called *Chelonia caretta*, *Thalassochelys caretta*, and now, *Caretta caretta*.

Most name changes will involve the English name or the genus name, rarely both. In all these cases, looking up the specific epithet will usually solve the problem. For example, say you have just observed for the first time a dragonfly with a white abdomen and large black-and-white patches on the wings. According to your field guide it is called a Desert Whitetail (*Libellula subornata*). When you go to record your sighting in this book you do not find it with other *Libellula* species. The reason is that recent studies have shown that it belongs in a separate genus *Plathemis*, along with the Common Whitetail. Without knowing this change, your solution is to look up the specific name, *subornata*, in the scientific name index. There you will find "*subornata, Plathemis*" referring you to page 425 where you will find the Desert Whitetail, your latest life species.

Now say you are paddling quietly along the edge of a calm, shallow river lined with trees when a startled turtle slips off a slanting tree trunk and lands in your canoe (it can happen!). Never without your field guide to reptiles, you easily identify it as a Common Musk Turtle, the first you have ever seen. Later, when you want to record this life event, you cannot find Common Musk Turtle in this book. Again, using the scientific name index, *odoratus, Sternotherus* will lead you to your species, now called Stinkpot.

If your species has been moved to a different genus, and under its specific epithet in the index you find more than one genus name, you can quickly eliminate most of them by looking at the letter code following each genus (M = Mammal, B = Bird, R = Reptile, A = Amphibian, F = Fish, L (for Lepidoptera) = Butterfly, D = Dragonfly or Damselfly). For example, under the specific name *elegans* in the scientific name index there are 11 genera listed, but as you can see by their associated letter codes, only one is a mammal, three are reptiles, four are birds, and three are fishes.

In the rare case where you are unsure or unsuccessful, it may be that your latest life species has had its specific epithet changed, been lumped with another species, or otherwise declared invalid. When in doubt, go to the appendix where most recent taxonomic and nomenclatural changes are explained. In fact, reviewing the appendix is a good idea anyway because it will alert you to new species and split species not found or treated as such in your field guide. For each recently described species, or subspecies elevated to full species status, that is not found in recent field guides, the appendix provides diagnostic characters and geographic range. You may be surprised to see that this includes over 100 species, mostly mammals, reptiles, amphibians, and freshwater fishes, not covered by current field guides. To stay completely current, visit www.wildlifelist.org where the lists in this book are continually updated, allowing you to accurately keep track of over 4,200 species of North American wildlife, from Arctic Foxes to Zigzag Darners.

Biodiversity and Zoogeography
of North America

The current species composition and distribution of the North American fauna is the result of a complex mixture of geological, ecological, evolutionary, climatological, historical, and other factors. It is like a multidimensional jigsaw puzzle whose solution is compounded by pieces that are missing (extinct or extirpated), altered (reduced ranges and populations), or in the wrong box (introduced species). Even so, zoogeographers have discovered some patterns that can help us make sense of how the 3,594 regularly occurring native species of wildlife in this book are distributed in North America.

This chapter is offered as a counterbalance to the reductionism inherent in making a list of species that encourages the observation of the natural world from just the single species perspective. Whenever you observe one strand or node in the web of life it is always enlightening to step back and take a look at the whole web to better understand how it is put together. What follows is a brief summary of our knowledge of the North American fauna, a comparison with the world fauna, the major patterns that influence the zoogeography and diversity of our fauna, and the specific patterns and highlights that characterize each of the seven major groups of wildlife covered. Keep in mind that "North America" in this book refers to the continent north of Mexico, and, unless noted otherwise, only the native extant vertebrates, butterflies, and odonates (dragonflies and damselflies) are considered. For this chapter, alien and accidental species are usually excluded from consideration because we are concentrating on broad, natural patterns of the regularly occurring native North American fauna.

Some of the statistics used, such as the number of mammal species in a given state, come from sources (mainly NatureServe 2005) based on taxonomies slightly different from what I used in the species lists. However, those differences are too small to affect the overall patterns presented here. Also, the number of species in a given genus or family depends on the current knowledge and, to a certain degree, opinions of biologists. I have used exact numbers but you should view them not as immutable facts but rather as a snapshot of our current knowledge and taxonomic judgment of North American biodiversity. Likewise, expect small changes in future descriptions of species diversity in a given geographic area due to new discoveries and actual changes in the distribution of species.

Our Knowledge of North American Biodiversity

North America has one of the best-surveyed faunas in the world. Compared to tropical areas it has far fewer species and far more taxonomists. Of course, many of the species in this book were known and named by Native Americans for at least 13,000 years, possibly longer. Unfortunately, most of this lore has been lost or ignored by Western science although a number of our official "English" names for wildlife species are partially or wholly derived from Native American animal names or other words. Some examples in this book are Jaguar, Collared Peccary, California Condor, Smooth-billed Ani, Diamond-backed Terrapin, Massasauga, Yonahlossee Salamander, Junaluska Salamander, Muskellunge, Cui-ui, Apache Skipper, Sachem, Aztec Dancer, and Comanche Skimmer. Latinized versions of Native American words are also used in some scientific names.

The modern scientific naming of North American wildlife began with Carolus Linnaeus, the creator of modern nomenclature and classification, in 1758 in the 10th edition of his *Systema Naturae*. In this and subsequent works Linnaeus described 307 currently recognized regular native North American species (42 mammals, 204 birds, 24 reptiles, 1 amphibian, 14 freshwater fishes, 18 butterflies, and 4 dragonflies). By 1810, the year Alexander Wilson observed over two billion passenger pigeons in one flock, and the year after Charles Darwin was born, scientists had described only 564 vertebrates in North America, just 22 percent of the total. But by the time the Darwin and Wallace papers on natural selection were read before the Linnaean Society, in 1858, taxonomy was in its heyday. By then 1,382 vertebrates (54%) still considered valid had been described. On average, throughout the 1800s, 150 new species of North American vertebrate were described each decade. Much of this discovery was the result of the establishment of the Smithsonian Institution and other museums, and major expeditions, like that of Lewis and Clark, to the western half of the continent. The zenith decade was the 1850s when 38 mammals, 60 birds, 85 reptiles, 34 amphibians, 119 freshwater fishes, 56 butterflies, and 40 odonates were described.

By the time the last wild passenger pigeon was shot, in 1900, the known North American vertebrate fauna consisted of 2,016 species (78%). The pace of discovery slowed considerably after that with most of the remaining unknown animals being much harder to detect, owing to their close similarity to known species, or their secretive habits. From 1900 to 1953, when the molecular structure of DNA was revealed, only 247 new vertebrates were added to the list. But, after a time of rapid developments in molecular biology, the study of DNA and other molecular characters would bring about a resurgence in discovery by allowing scientists to tease apart many cryptic species and establish more accurate phylogenetic relationships. Consequently, more North American vertebrates (297) were described in the second half of the 1900s than in the first half (228; see fig. 1).

As might be expected by the differences in popularity and ease of observation or capture, the pace of scientific discovery and description of birds was much faster than that for the other animal groups. In fact, 95 percent of the currently known North American avifauna had been described by 1869, long before the same level of knowledge was acquired for mammals (1930), butterflies (1944), reptiles (1973), odonates (1981), freshwater fishes (1992), and amphibians (2000).

The golden age of Natural History in North America is now long past but the discovery of new species is certainly not over. Since the beginning of 1990, 6 mammals,

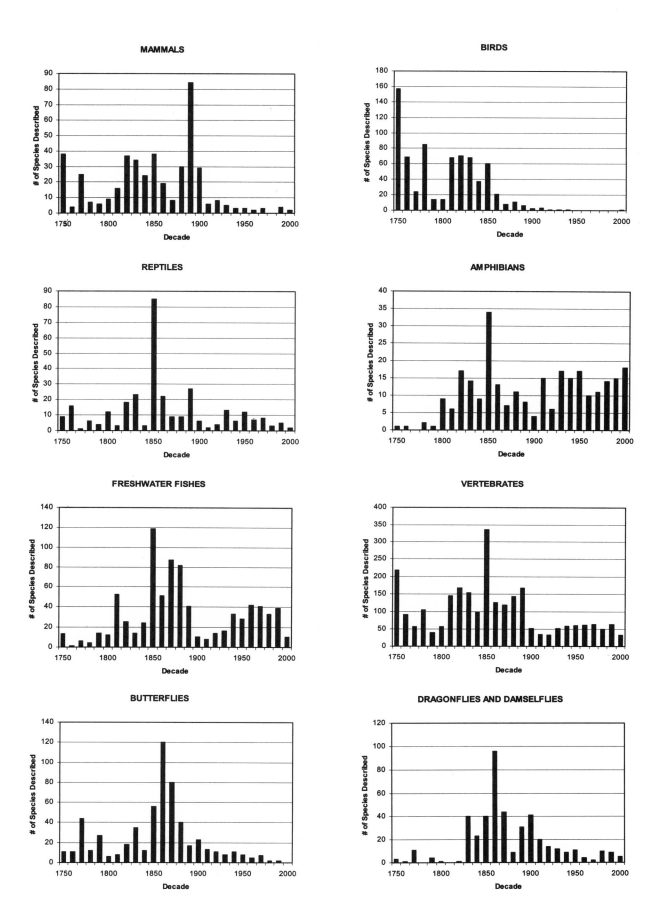

Figure 1. Number of currently recognized regular native species described per decade for North American mammals, birds, reptiles, amphibians, freshwater fishes, vertebrates (excluding marine fishes), butterflies, and dragonflies and damselflies. Note different scales for species numbers.

Table 1. New Species from North America North of Mexico Described Since 1990 with Year of Description

Mammals

Sonoma Tree Vole	*Arborimus pomo*	1991
Pygmy Beaked Whale	*Mesoplodon peruvianus*	1991
Appalachian Cottontail	*Sylvilagus obscurus*	1992
Alaska Tiny Shrew	*Sorex yukonicus*	1997
Perrin's Beaked Whale	*Mesoplodon perrini*	2002
Cockrum's Desert Shrew	*Notiosorex cockrumi*	2003

Birds

Gunnison Sage-Grouse	*Centrocercus minimus*	2000

Reptiles

Escambia Map Turtle	*Graptemys ernsti*	1992
Pascagoula Map Turtle	*Graptemys gibbonsi*	1992
Little White Whiptail	*Aspidoscelis gypsi*	1993
Pai Striped Whiptail	*Aspidoscelis pai*	1993
Colorado Checkered Whiptail	*Aspidoscelis neotesselata*	1997
Bezy's Night Lizard	*Xantusia bezyi*	2001
Slowinski's Cornsnake	*Pantherophis slowinskii*	2002

Amphibians

Cascade Torrent Salamander	*Rhyacotriton cascadae*	1992
Columbia Torrent Salamander	*Rhyacotriton kezeri*	1992
Barton Springs Salamander	*Eurycea sosorum*	1993
Ramsey Canyon Leopard Frog	*Rana subaquavocalis*	1993
San Gabriel Mountains Slender Salamander	*Batrachoseps gabrieli*	1996
Blue Ridge Dusky Salamander	*Desmognathus orestes*	1996
Southern Zigzag Salamander	*Plethodon ventralis*	1997
Hell Hollow Slender Salamander	*Batrachoseps diabolicus*	1998
Gregarious Slender Salamander	*Batrachoseps gregarius*	1998
Sequoia Slender Salamander	*Batrachoseps kawia*	1998
Kings River Slender Salamander	*Batrachoseps regius*	1998
Catahoula Salamander	*Plethodon ainsworthi*	1998
Wandering Salamander	*Aneides vagrans*	1999
Northern Ravine Salamander	*Plethodon electromorphus*	1999
Shenandoah Mountain Salamander	*Plethodon virginia*	1999
Salado Salamander	*Eurycea chisholmensis*	2000
Georgetown Salamander	*Eurycea naufragia*	2000
Jollyville Plateau Salamander	*Eurycea tonkawae*	2000
Blue Ridge Gray-cheeked Salamander	*Plethodon amplus*	2000
Cheoah Bald Salamander	*Plethodon cheoah*	2000
South Mountain Gray-cheeked Salamander	*Plethodon meridianus*	2000
Northern Gray-cheeked Salamander	*Plethodon montanus*	2000
Gabilan Mountains Slender Salamander	*Batrachoseps gavilanensis*	2001
San Simeon Slender Salamander	*Batrachoseps incognitus*	2001
Santa Lucia Mountains Slender Salamander	*Batrachoseps luciae*	2001
Lesser Slender Salamander	*Batrachoseps minor*	2001
Austin Blind Salamander	*Eurycea waterlooensis*	2001
Kern Plateau Salamander	*Batrachoseps robustus*	2002
Dwarf Black-bellied Salamander	*Desmognathus folkertsi*	2002
Cumberland Dusky Salamander	*Desmognathus abditus*	2003
Chamberlain's Dwarf Salamander	*Eurycea chamberlaini*	2003
Big Levels Salamander	*Plethodon sherando*	2004
Scott Bar Salamander	*Plethodon asupak*	2005

continued

Table 1.—*Continued*

Freshwater Fishes

Orangefin Shiner	*Notropis ammophilus*	1990
Holiday Darter	*Etheostoma brevirostum*	1991
Tallapoosa Darter	*Etheostoma tallapoosae*	1991
Yazoo Shiner	*Notropis rafinesquei*	1991
Umpqua Chub	*Oregonichthys kalawatseti*	1991
Alabama Sturgeon	*Scaphirhynchus suttkusi*	1991
Vermilion Darter	*Etheostoma chermocki*	1992
Relict Darter	*Etheostoma chienense*	1992
Crown Darter	*Etheostoma corona*	1992
Barrens Darter	*Etheostoma forbesi*	1992
Guardian Darter	*Etheostoma oophylax*	1992
Egg-mimic Darter	*Etheostoma pseudovulatum*	1992
Spring Pygmy Sunfish	*Elassoma alabamae*	1993
Warrior Darter	*Etheostoma bellator*	1993
Lipstick Darter	*Etheostoma chuckwachatte*	1993
Coastal Darter	*Etheostoma colorosum*	1993
Tuskaloosa Darter	*Etheostoma douglasi*	1993
Etowah Darter	*Etheostoma etowahae*	1993
Frecklebelly Darter	*Percina stictogaster*	1993
Tombigbee Darter	*Etheostoma lachneri*	1994
Duskytail Darter	*Etheostoma percnurum*	1994
Alabama Darter	*Etheostoma ramseyi*	1994
Yazoo Darter	*Etheostoma raneyi*	1994
Palezone Shiner	*Notropis albizonatus*	1994
Rocky Shiner	*Notropis suttkusi*	1994
Pearl Darter	*Percina aurora*	1994
Coal Darter	*Percina brevicauda*	1994
Cherokee Darter	*Etheostoma scotti*	1995
Southern Logperch	*Percina austroperca*	1995
Buffalo Darter	*Etheostoma bison*	1997
Brook Darter	*Etheostoma burri*	1997
Golden Darter	*Etheostoma denoncourti*	1997
Highland Rim Darter	*Etheostoma kantuckeense*	1997
Shawnee Darter	*Etheostoma tecumsehi*	1997
Mobile Logperch	*Percina kathae*	1997
Gulf Logperch	*Percina suttkusi*	1997
Southeastern Blue Sucker	*Cycleptus meridionalis*	1999
Rush Darter	*Etheostoma phytophilum*	1999
Shoal Bass	*Micropterus cataractae*	1999
Blue Ridge Sculpin	*Cottus caeruleomentum*	2000
Laurel Dace	*Phoxinus saylori*	2001
Orangetail Shiner	*Pteronotropis merlini*	2001
Santa Cruz Pupfish	*Cyprinodon arcuatus*	2002
Headwater Darter	*Etheostoma lawrencei*	2002
Corrugated Darter	*Etheostoma basilare*	2003
Chickasaw Darter	*Etheostoma cervus*	2003
Stone Darter	*Etheostoma derivativum*	2003
San Felipe Gambusia	*Gambusia clarkhubbsi*	2003
Piebald Madtom	*Noturus gladiator*	2004

Butterflies[a]

Coppermine Sulphur	*Colias johanseni*	1990
Heather Blue	*Agriades cassiope*	1998

continued

Dragonflies and Damselflies

Spot-winged Meadowhawk	*Sympetrum signiferum*	1991
Tamaulipan Clubtail	*Gomphus gonzalezi*	1992
Southern Snaketail	*Ophiogomphus australis*	1992
Wisconsin Snaketail	*Ophiogomphus susbehcha*	1993
Jane's Meadowhawk	*Sympetrum janeae*	1993
Leonora's Dancer	*Argia leonorae*	1994
Pima Dancer	*Argia pima*	1994
Sabino Dancer	*Argia sabino*	1994
Dashed Ringtail	*Erpetogomphus heterodon*	1994
Yaqui Dancer	*Argia carlcooki*	1995
Broad-tailed Shadowdragon	*Neurocordulia michaeli*	2000
Cream-tipped Swampdamsel	*Leptobasis melinogaster*	2002
Interior Least Clubtail	*Stylogomphus sigmastylus*	2004
Ouachita Spiketail	*Cordulegaster talaria*	2004
Sioux Snaketail	*Ophiogomphus smithi*	2004

a. Opler and Warren (2003) list four other species of butterflies described since 1990 that have not yet been accepted by the North American Butterfly Association Checklist Committee.

1 bird, 7 reptiles, 33 amphibians, 49 freshwater fishes, 2 butterflies, and 15 odonates have been described for the first time and are currently recognized (table 1). Even our nascent century (starting from January 1, 2000) has already seen the description of at least 38 new species in North America, and more are on the way. Note that these figures do not include "new" species that were formerly recognized subspecies, now elevated to full species status. Of course some, or possibly many, of these recently described species may eventually be demoted to subspecies status if the "lumpers" regain their dominance over the "splitters." But few zoologists, if any, would say that discovery is finished. While very few forms immediately recognizable to the average naturalist have not been described, there is still much potential for the discovery of cryptic species. These are groups of two or more species that are genetically distinct but nearly, or completely, indistinguishable on the basis of their external morphology, behavior, or ecology. In the last few decades, molecular genetic methods, such as protein electrophoresis, DNA hybridization, and, more recently, comparison of nuclear and mitochondrial nucleotide sequences, have become the primary means of discovering and separating cryptic species.

The rate of adding new species as well as the total number of species currently recognized have also been greatly influenced by a change in our concept of what a species is. All species concepts attempt to divide the complex reality of continuous genetic variation into discrete taxonomic units (species). The problem is where to draw the line. The traditional approach uses the Biological Species Concept: Species are "groups of actually or potentially interbreeding natural populations that are reproductively isolated from other such groups" (Mayr 2001).

Some biologists prefer the Evolutionary Species Concept: "A species is a single lineage of ancestral descendant populations of organisms which maintains its identity from other such lineages and which has its own evolutionary tendencies and historical fate" (Wiley 1978).

Still others prefer one of the variations of the Phylogenetic Species Concept, such as this one by Wheeler and Platnick (2000): A species is "the smallest aggregation of (sexual) populations or (asexual) lineages diagnosable by a unique combination of character states."

And others adopt any of two dozen other concepts (see Coyne and Orr 2004). Fortunately, most species in this book would be recognized as species by most taxonomists, no matter which species concept they used. As Darwin (1859) wrote in *On the Origin of Species*, "No one definition has satisfied all naturalists; yet every naturalist knows vaguely what he means when he speaks of a species." However, there are still many cases where the difference between one taxonomist's species and another taxonomist's subspecies is the species concept used. The Evolutionary Species Concept tends to recognize more species than the Biological Species Concept, while the Phylogenetic Species Concept would recognize even more. Overall, the current trend favors more splitting, so even without the discovery of new species whose populations were unknown to scientists, checklists and field guides will continue to expand for a while as more subspecies are elevated to full species, and more previously known populations are described as new species.

Future editions of this book will contain new species that are identifiable in the field without resorting to molecular genetic methods or relying solely on geography. Some of these species will consist of populations we were already aware of but did not realize were different species. Ornithologists have long known that sage-grouse occurred in the Gunnison Basin of southwest Colorado, but it wasn't until 2000 that those populations were described as a separate full species (Gunnison Sage-Grouse). Before that, the most recently discovered non-pelagic North American bird was the Dusky Flycatcher, first described in 1939.

Most undiscovered, non-cryptic species of North America will probably be those that are so secretive and/or have such tiny ranges that they have heretofore been overlooked. The Ramsey Canyon Leopard Frog, of the Huachuca Mountains in Arizona, was already down to less than 150 adults when it was first described in 1993. Usually, frogs draw attention to themselves with their mating calls, but this species always gives its snorelike call from about three feet under water, making it inaudible above the surface. We would still not know of the Blanco Blind Salamander if a work crew excavating a Texas spring in 1951 had not bothered to notify scientists of a strange subterranean salamander they found. Everything we do know about it comes from the one surviving specimen from 1951; none have been found since. The Pygmy Sculpin, described in 1968, is fairly common throughout its range, but its entire range consists of one spring, Coldwater Spring in Calhoun County, Alabama. The existence of the Pigeon Mountain Salamander was first revealed in 1988. It is abundant where it lives, but it only lives around two areas of limestone outcroppings between elevations of 720 and 1,640 feet on the east side of Pigeon Mountain in the northwestern corner of Georgia. The Broad-tailed Shadowdragon, a dragonfly of Maine and New Brunswick, hides in forest shadows by day and flies only after sunset for less than 40 minutes. It was described in 2000. The Dwarf Black-bellied Salamander, described in 2002, is identifiable in the field but is known only from two tributaries of the Nottely River in Union County, Georgia.

The combination of new species concepts, molecular techniques, and greater effort by taxonomists has created an explosion of new species, particularly among salamanders and freshwater fishes. Since 1990 at least 32 new species of salamanders have been described in North America, and the number of species waiting to be described or elevated from subspecies rank may be as many as 40 or more (R. Highton, pers. comm.). The same period has seen the description of 49 new species of North American freshwater fishes, including 34 darters. It has been estimated that between 28 and 75 more darter species will be added to the list in the near future (Ceas and Burr 2002). Clearly, our faunal lists are not yet complete. Your field guides are still works in progress.

Comparison of North American and World Faunas

Whenever the biodiversity of a given place is mentioned, especially if it is a proposed or protected natural area, some variation of the phrase, "one of the most biologically rich areas on the planet," is usually included. Quite often this is a case of promotion getting in the way of accuracy. In fact, for most major groups of organisms, nowhere in North America comes close to the biodiversity of the lowland tropics. North America represents 13 percent of the earth's land surface and it harbors only about 6 percent of the earth's vertebrates (discounting marine fishes; see table 2), while tropical forests cover just 6 percent of the earth's land but support something over 50 percent of the world's vertebrates. However, change "biologically rich" to "biologically unique" and most natural areas, including the continent as a whole, would certainly qualify.

About half of the 3,594 extant regular native species in this book are endemic to North America. Our fauna is much less unique at higher taxonomic levels with just 13 families and one order found nowhere else. However, North America stands out in other ways. Here we can boast the most diverse temperate freshwater ecosystem in the world. The Tennessee-Cumberland watershed represents the height of this diversity with one of its tributaries, the Duck River, containing at least 84 species of freshwater fish, more than twice the number in all of Great Britain. The continental United States is also number one in the world for freshwater mussels, freshwater crayfishes, freshwater snails, caddisflies, mayflies, and stoneflies.

Table 2. Total Numbers of Species for the World, and Extant Regular Native and Endemic Species of North America, North of Mexico

Taxon	World	North America	North America (% of World)	North American Endemic Species
Mammals	5,416	444	8.2	200
Birds	9,721	715	7.4	52
Reptiles	8,240	315	3.8	135
Amphibians	6,016	274	4.6	233
Freshwater Fishes	11,300	819	7.2	696
All Vertebrates[a]	40,623	2,567	6.3	1,316
Butterflies	17,500	585	3.3	209
Odonata	5,574	442	7.9	266
Totals	63,697	3,594	5.6	1,791

Sources for world species: Wilson and Reeder, 2005; Dickinson 2003; Uetz 2005; AmphibiaWeb 2006; Page and Burr, forthcoming; Robbins and Opler 1997; Schorr et al. 2004.
a. Exclusive of marine fishes.

North America also has a great diversity of salamanders with about one-third of the world's species. Globally, salamanders make up only about 9 percent of all amphibian species but they account for 65 percent of the amphibian fauna of North America. The 51 species of non-marine turtles found north of Mexico represent 17 percent of the world's total. The United States has about 7 percent of the world's freshwater fishes, ranking seventh among the world's countries but first among temperate countries. Other outstanding features of North American biodiversity include 114 species of gymnosperms (second only to China), 4,000 endemic plants, and 1,791 endemic vertebrates.

Origins of the North American Fauna

If you go back far enough in time, about 3.5 billion years ago, all life on Earth can be traced to its origin in a single common ancestor. Since then life has evolved prolifically according to changes in geography, climate, geology, and the biotic environment, as constrained by the genetic histories of each given lineage. At the same time, the extinction and dispersal of species have greatly complicated the biogeographical picture. The movement of the tectonic plates carrying continents and islands had many long-lasting effects on the current North American fauna. When continents join, faunas mix, and some species successfully colonize new areas while others become extinct due to new competition, predation, disease, or other impacts of the invading species. When continents separate, faunas become isolated and may evolve in different directions. Changes in sea level and temperature, climate, soil type, and other abiotic factors can be the doom or boom of a given lineage, depending on the genetic tools it has inherited. All these factors have combined in countless ways to produce our current set of species. From our present day perspective, however, the North American fauna has been most heavily influenced by past associations with Eurasia and South America, the impact of the Chicxulub Asteroid, and the independent evolution of lineages within the continent. Much of the discussion below is based on Brown and Lomolino (1998), Flannery (2001), and Stein et al. (2000).

The Chicxulub Asteroid Impact

Today's North American fauna has been shaped by myriad events, but the most influential, by far, is that horrific day, 65 million years ago, when a six-mile-wide asteroid weighing one quadrillion tons (the equivalent of 11 billion aircraft carriers) screamed into Earth's atmosphere at 300,000 miles per hour. One second later it slammed into the north shore of the Yucatan Peninsula, near present-day Chicxulub, creating a crater over 100 miles wide and up to three miles deep. The impact released the energy equivalent of 100 million hydrogen bombs. The asteroid struck at a northbound angle that caused North America to receive the brunt of the impact and subsequent devastation. The sky became incandescent as ejecta from the blast fell back into the atmosphere. Soon the skies turned black with the soot of continent-wide forest fires. A 3,000-foot tsunami pulverized the shores of the Gulf of Mexico.

Every living thing within 300 miles of ground zero was completely obliterated. Trees were flattened all across the continent of North America. The immediate effects of the impact decreased with distance but for life as a whole on planet earth, the worst was yet to come. For the next few months the earth was as dark as a cloudy, moonless night. Photosynthesis ceased and the temperature plummeted. When the dust settled and the sunlight returned, the vast amount of carbon dioxide released from the impact caused a 15-degree global warming that lasted many centuries. Sulfuric and nitric acid rained from the sky. The result for life on earth was catastrophic: 75 percent of the world's species became extinct, including all of the dinosaurs that had ruled the earth for 150 million years. On land, no animal over 50 pounds was left alive.

But in the wake of disaster lay opportunity for the survivors. Crocodiles, turtles, anguid lizards, a few mammals, and many of the fishes and amphibians survived the impact, by virtue of their aquatic or burrowing habits. As living conditions improved, survivors from other regions less affected by the impact moved in. Freed from ecological constraints such as competition and predation, some lineages rapidly proliferated and radiated to inherit the new world. In particular, mammals and birds came to dominate. Without the Chicxulub Asteroid, few, if any, of the mammals and birds listed in this book would have evolved, including humans.

Interchanges with Eurasia

The incompleteness of the fossil record causes much debate about the origin of many faunal groups but, overall, North American wildlife has many more affinities with Eurasia than with other regions of the world. This is due to the ancient connection with Europe in the Permian supercontinent of Pangea, and a number of subsequent connections with both western Europe, via the Greenland-Scotland Ridge, and northeastern Asia, including the latest formation of the Beringian land bridge during the last ice age. Thus, North America and Eurasia share a large number of their orders and families, many of their genera, and some of their species, as a comparison of North American and Eurasian field guides will show. When European naturalists first explored North America, much of the fauna was vaguely, if not specifically, familiar to them, especially among the mammals and birds. The biotic exchanges, of course, went in both directions but, possibly due to the much larger landmass of Eurasia, the Eurasian species, more often than not, supplanted the North American natives. During the Pliocene, 5–1.8 million years BP, two-thirds of all North American mammal genera were of Eurasian origin. More invasions occurred during the 20 or so interglacial periods of the Pleistocene (1.8 million to 10,000 years BP). Some of the many surviving Eurasian invaders include bison, deer, cats, and humans.

Today, two-thirds of North America's mammal families, and around 40 percent of its genera, are Holarctic (also distributed in Eurasia). For birds, about 74 percent of North American families and 46 percent of the genera are Holarctic. Among both classes there are many shared species, a number of which have completely or nearly circumboreal or circumpolar distributions, including Polar Bear, Caribou, Arctic Fox, Herring Gull, Great Gray Owl, and Common Raven.

Butterflies first arose during the mid Cretaceous (about 80–100 million years BP) when the major continents were still attached. Not surprisingly, North America taxa shared with Eurasia today include all butterfly families except the metalmarks (Riodinidae), 15 of the 24 North American subfamilies, and about 15 percent of the genera. Odonates (dragonflies and damselflies) evolved even earlier, some 300 million years ago in the Carboniferous period. Ten of the 12 families of North American odonates are at least in part Holarctic, as well as about 28 percent of the odonate genera. The petaltail, spiketail, cruiser, and emerald families are strictly of temperate origin. The northern distributions and flight capabilities of some butterflies and odonates probably explain most of the shared genera. There are over 30 species of Holarctic butterflies including Old World Swallowtail, Mourning Cloak, Red Admiral, Painted Lady, two parnassians, and several sulphurs, blues, fritillaries, alpines, arctics, and skippers. Holarctic odonates include Treeline Emerald, Four-spotted Skimmer, Black Meadowhawk, and Wandering Glider.

For reptiles, amphibians, and freshwater fishes, the Atlantic, Pacific, and Arctic Oceans, and the high latitude of the past Beringian and North Atlantic land bridges, have been a more formidable barrier. Most of the lineages that are Holarctic today tend to be the ancient and/or higher taxa such as families and orders, which date back to continental connections. Examples include mudpuppies, lungless salamanders, ranid frogs, toads, boid and colubrid snakes, geckos, bowfins, minnows, sturgeons, and pikes. The only Holarctic species of cold-blooded vertebrates are anadromous fishes like salmons, smelts, lampreys, sturgeons, and a few northern obligate freshwater fishes, like the Longnose Sucker, Alaska Blackfish, Burbot, and Northern Pike, which have survived since the land bridges were sundered.

The East Asia Disjunction

One particularly interesting, and ancient, connection with Eurasia concerns the American Alligator, Paddlefish, and Hellbender of the eastern United States. Their only close relatives are the Chinese Alligator (*Alligator sinensis*), Chinese Swordfish (*Psephurus gladius*), Chinese Giant Salamander (*Andrias davidianus*), and Japanese Giant Salamander (*Andrias japonicus*). There are also over 100 plant genera, including tuliptree (*Liriodendron*), hickory (*Carya*), ginseng (*Panax*), and jack-in-the-pulpit (*Arisaema*), that have a similar disjunct distribution. The favored explanation is that these lineages have survived since the middle Tertiary when North America, Europe, and Asia were connected and covered by a huge swath of temperate deciduous forest. Since then, this biota has been largely eliminated in western North America by a Pliocene drying trend, while many European extinctions occurred during the Pleistocene when species were trapped between the advancing glaciers and the east-west oriented Alps, Pyrenees, and Mediterranean Basin.

The Great American Biotic Interchange

Since the late Cretaceous 75 million years ago, South America has been relatively close to North America but the two continents have only been connected for the last three million years (since the late Pliocene). During South America's isolation there were several periods of three to six million years where the continents were close enough that some organisms could survive the crossing, probably most often by island hopping, to invade the other continent. In between these periods were long stretches of time, up to 25 million years, when dispersals would have been limited to rare instances involving flying birds, butterflies, bats, and odonates, or very durable animals like turtles that could survive long rafting trips on floating flood debris. All that changed three million years ago when the Isthmus of Panama formed and allowed the Great American Biotic Interchange to take place.

Only a few of the extant North American mammals are descendants of lineages that evolved in South America. They include the North American Porcupine, Virginia Opossum, and Nine-banded Armadillo. The now extinct North American glyptodonts, capybaras, and giant ground sloths (see Extinct Species) also originated in South America (Marshall 1985).

More than anything else, the character of the North American avifauna is set apart from that of Eurasia by the neotropical migrants. Compared to mammals, bird families of South America were more successful invaders of North America (Vuilleumier 1985). They include hummingbirds, tyrant flycatchers, vireos, wood-warblers, emberizids (sparrows and towhees), cardinalids (cardinals, grosbeaks, and buntings), blackbirds and orioles, and tanagers. These groups make up almost all the neotropical migrants that now breed in North America. The South American teratorns, *Milvago* caracaras, and the huge, predatory, flightless terrorbirds (*Titanis*) also came to North America but have since become extinct.

Even more successful invaders of the north were the South American reptiles and amphibians (Vanzolini and Heyer 1985). Most of North America's snakes, and all the iguanid lizards, *Bufo* toads, treefrogs, leptodactylid frogs, and narrow-mouthed toads are ultimately from South American lineages. Most of these groups first moved into Central America where they radiated and then spread north. The *Anolis* lizards and *Eleutherodactylus* frogs came to North America via the West Indies and Florida. The teiid lizards have the curious history of originating in North America in the Cretaceous, spreading to South America in the Paleocene, then becoming extinct in North America (along with the dinosaurs when the Chicxulub asteroid struck), and later, returning to North America in the form of our present-day racerunners and whiptails (*Aspidoscelis*).

Because of the necessity of freshwater connections, few freshwater fishes from South American lineages have reached farther north than central Mexico. The exceptions are the Mexican Tetra, which extends north into Texas and New Mexico, and the Rio Grande Cichlid, restricted to the Rio Grande system of Mexico and Texas (Miller 1966).

Given the flight capabilities of butterflies and odonates, immigration between North and South America probably occurred many times, in both directions, before the continents were connected. Of the butterfly families, only the metalmarks definitely originated in South America although many other genera, especially along the southern U.S. border, presumably evolved in the Neotropics. Eight of the 12 odonate families now in North America have ties to the tropics. About 35 genera are presumed to be of tropical origin, with a few more distributed in both temperate and tropical regions (D. Paulson, pers. comm.).

North American Lineages

Overwhelmingly, North America is a land of immigrants. Many species and genera evolved here, but most of the faunal families now present originated elsewhere. The few North American families that may have originated here and survive today include squirrels, canids, horses, camels, pronghorns, snapping turtles, whiptail lizards, amphiumas, mole salamanders, torrent salamanders, American giant salamanders, lungless salamanders, Pirate Perch, mooneyes, trout-perches, cavefishes, sunfishes, and pygmy sunfishes. The origins of bird families are especially difficult to determine because of the paucity of fossils; the hollow and fragile bones of birds were built for flight, not fossilization. But DNA studies have so far shown that only the grouse (Tetraoninae) and New World quail (Odontophoridae) may be endemic to North America, although some researchers give the latter a South American origin.

Zoogeographic Patterns of North America

North America's proximity to Asia, via Alaska and past Bering land bridges, its flirtation and final joining with South America, and the lesser influence of the West Indian lineages, were all important in the current makeup of the North American fauna. Western Alaska, southern Florida, the Mexican border, and, to a lesser extent, the entire boundary of North America, will always be a magnet to naturalists hoping to see accidental birds, bats, butterflies, odonates, and other normally extralimital species. But the combination of North America's large size, diversity of land forms and climates, and relative spatial and temporal isolation has had an even greater impact on the uniqueness and diversity of our wildlife, at least at the species level. Together, these factors have been paramount in the evolution of 1,791 species that are not normally or naturally found elsewhere. Within North America the diversity of any given taxon has been augmented or limited by some subset of the following.

Continental Factors

When considering any given ecosystem or taxonomic group, larger geographic areas tend to have more species. This is the species-area relationship, one of the few real laws in ecology. With 13 percent of the world's land surface, over 7.5 million square miles,

North America's size alone would predict a high level of biodiversity. However, a major mitigating factor is the location of North America in the higher latitudes. Within most taxa, the number of species decreases with distance from the equator. This greatly diminishes the area effect in most of Canada and Alaska, which, together, are one and one-half times bigger than the contiguous United States, but support less than half as many species. In fact, Canada and Alaska support only about 235 vertebrate, butterfly, and odonate species that do not also occur south of Canada. The latitudinal gradient also accounts for the southern states generally having the highest diversity, especially Florida and the states bordering Mexico. Our southern border happens to just overlap the northern extension of many species more typical of Mexico and Central America. If history had caused the U.S.-Mexican border to average 100 miles further north, we would have about 250 fewer species on our list.

A large percentage of the zoogeographical patterns and biodiversity of North America can be traced to variations in the physical environment. In terrestrial habitats, climate and soil type are paramount, while temperature is a principle factor in freshwater. North America has a long, varied, and active geologic past creating diverse soils, mountain ranges, plains, river systems, lakes, and other land forms which, combined with ocean currents, the jet stream, and prevailing winds, have given rise to a wide range of physical conditions to which different species have adapted. The distribution of land animals is especially affected by the moisture gradient; more species occupy wetter climates and habitats. In most of our desert areas, the presence of oases, riparian habitats, and mountains accounts for much of the regional biodiversity. The diversity of physical environments determines the diversity of vegetation associations to which our fauna are adapted. North America is blessed with 10 of the world's 14 biome types (Udvardy 1975). On a much finer scale, in the United States alone, The Nature Conservancy has identified over 4,500 unique vegetation associations and estimates a final total of over 7,000 (Stein et al. 2000). This makes fertile ground for faunistic diversity.

The wildlife of North America is the product of the entire history of life with all its major and minor extinction events, adaptive radiations and other evolutionary processes, and range expansions and contractions. But much of the current distribution of our fauna, as well as the origin of some of our species, can be attributed to the influence of the Pleistocene ice ages and the fact that we are now in an interglacial period. A mere 18,000 years ago, during the most recent glacial maximum, an ice sheet up to three miles thick covered almost all of Canada and, in the east, the United States south to the Ohio River. As the glaciers retreated, the climate warmed, sea levels rose, biomes moved north 10–20° latitude, deserts became drier, state-sized lakes shrank, disappeared, or moved, and watersheds merged and split. All these changes may have driven a few species to extinction, but most responded by moving to new latitudes or elevations or wherever their required habitat led them. Thus, the general distribution of fauna today (minus modern human impacts) has only characterized North America for about the last 10,000 years or so.

Regional and Ecological Factors

Geographic barriers promote speciation by isolating populations that are then able to diverge genetically. Mountain ranges separate lowland species and lowlands separate mountain species. Many of the 60 or more vertebrates endemic to California can be attributed to much of that state being surrounded by ocean and high mountains. The limits of watersheds are particularly effective at promoting species divergence in aquatic organisms because gene flow is eliminated completely. Geographic barriers that facilitated the formation of species alive today may or may not still exist. For example, a number of Baja California–southwestern U.S. species pairs of mammals and reptiles were probably split by the Gulf of California three million years ago when it extended much farther north. But one million years ago the Gulf of California receded to about its present limit, allowing the species pairs to meet or overlap in range (Riddle et al. 2000a).

Mountains generate much regional biodiversity by repeating the latitudinal life zones along an elevational gradient. On most mountain ranges there is a corresponding species gradient with the most species at low elevations and a declining diversity with an increase in elevation. An exception to this pattern occurs on desert peaks where the drastic moisture gradient partially offsets the elevation gradient to cause the highest biodiversity to be at middle elevations.

Another isolating mechanism is the creation of geographic and habitat islands. Most of our marine islands are too close to the mainland to have generated many new endemic species. Through a process called the rescue effect, the proximity of mainland populations allows sufficient immigration, and thus gene flow, to prevent genetic divergence. However, some islands in the Bering Sea are farther out than most, and the mobility or behavior of some species may reduce the incidence of immigration. In any case, the isolation has been sufficient for the evolution of 12 species that are restricted to North American marine islands: Pribilof Island Shrew, Saint Lawrence Island Shrew, Insular Vole (Hall and Saint Matthew Islands), and Unalaska Collared Lemming (Umnak and Unalaska Islands), all of the Bering Sea; Vancouver Island Marmot and Vancouver Lamprey from Vancouver Island; Beach Vole (Muskeget Island, Massachusetts); and from the Channel Islands of California, the Island Fox, Island Scrub-Jay, Island Night Lizard, Channel Islands Slender Salamander, and Avalon Scrub-Hairstreak. Formerly, the Channel Islands also supported the endemic but now extinct Channel Islands Pygmy Mammoth.

Habitat islands have been more important than geographic islands in the generation of isolated species and the distribution patterns of others. Some species, like the Panamint Alligator Lizard and Palmer's Chipmunk, may evolve in mountain habitats called sky islands because they are surrounded by dry lowlands. There are many species of minnows, suckers, pupfishes, killifishes, livebearers, and sculpins whose current distribution, and possibly evolution, are due to the breakup and shrinkage of the great Pleistocene lakes into scattered "islands" of freshwater and saltwater in a sea of desert. Other habitats that exist in island form, like limestone caves, bogs, stranded remnants of the Pleistocene environment, and small watersheds, often have species restricted to within their boundaries.

On a seasonal basis, real or apparent biodiversity of a given area is greatly affected by the migration, hibernation, aestivation, and other seasonal behaviors of wildlife. In the far north, only a few animals are active all year. The rest head south, hibernate, or overwinter in some non-adult stage. At lower latitudes, bird diversity peaks with the spring and fall migrations, especially along the major flyways and at important staging grounds. The adult stages of many of our butterflies and odonates are restricted to a few weeks each year. Shifts in weather patterns and food availability may cause sudden invasions of otherwise rare species.

While physical and vegetational attributes of the environment may determine the potential distribution of wildlife, a given species' actual range may be smaller due to competition, predation, parasitism, symbiotic relationships, or other ecological inter- actions with other animals. It is no coincidence that many closely related species, like the Black-capped and Carolina chickadees, and many sibling species of salamanders, have generally parapatric (abutting) ranges with little or no overlap where hybrids are limited. Most aquatic frogs and salamanders are kept out of larger streams by predatory fishes. The Snail Kite is restricted to the distribution of apple snails, its primary, or only, prey. Black-footed Ferrets cannot live without prairie-dogs.

Human Factors

Today, it would be difficult to find a species in this book whose range or population has not been affected by human impacts to some degree. In the last 13,000 years, most of the 100 extinctions and extirpations of North American vertebrates were probably caused, directly or indirectly, by human activities. The Nature Conservancy estimates that up to 40 percent of our native freshwater fishes are endangered or already extinct. Around 1,200 native plants and animals of North America are currently officially en- dangered. However, reliable estimates, unaffected by the politics and economics that have mired the Endangered Species Act, place the true number of North American endangered species and subspecies closer to 16,000 (Wilcove 1999).

The primary threat for over 90 percent of endangered species is habitat loss or deg- radation. In the conterminous United States today, as much as 58 percent of the natural vegetation has been converted to agriculture or development, or has been otherwise significantly altered (Stein 2000). This figure would be far greater if not for mountains and deserts. Noss et al. (1995) determined that 27 ecosystem types have lost over 98 percent of their area due to modern human impacts. A World Wildlife Fund study (Ricketts et al. 1999) found that 69 of 76 ecoregions have less than 40 percent of their original area, and 67 of them are in critical, endangered, or vulnerable condition. As the habitat goes, so goes the wildlife. The impact on wildlife has been even greater due to the fragmentation of many of these remaining habitats into small, isolated areas. This process generally increases the odds of local extinction and decreases the odds of natural repopulation through immigration. The introduction of alien species, pollu- tion, and overexploitation are other major human factors that have caused significant range collapse and population decline in many species.

Mammals

We're animals. We're born like every other mammal and we live our whole lives around disguised animal thoughts.

BARBARA KINGSOLVER

If all the beasts were gone, men would die from a great loneliness of spirit.

CHIEF SEATTLE

In spite of the loss of most of North America's megafauna, the current mammalian fauna is a fascinating mix of species with interesting and sometimes unusual or unique adaptations. The Pronghorn is the fastest long-distance runner in the world, and the fastest running animal in North America. It can maintain a speed of 45 mph for a distance of over four miles, and has a top speed of over 60 mph. The Mexican Free-tailed Bat, whose range includes the southern half of the United States, holds the world record for colony size of any mammal (unless you count the Tokyo metropolitan area). The colony in Bracken Cave, Texas, has an estimated 20 million individuals. The Meadow Vole can begin to breed when only one month old, and may produce up to 17 litters of 3 to 10 pups in one year. This remarkable fecundity makes it the most prolific mammal on Earth as well as the most abundant mammal in North America (when at the peak of their two- to five-year population cycle). The Arctic Fox has such efficient insulating fur that it doesn't shiver until the temperature reaches -94°F! The Great Sperm Whale has the largest brain of any known animal, can stay submerged for over an hour, and can reach depths of over 6,000 feet. By living off their fat, hibernating pregnant Polar Bears go for eight months without eating or drinking. Grasshopper mice are predators, complete with large home ranges, complex social and courtship behaviors, territorial marking, the ability to communicate with a "howling" vocalization, and specialized predatory techniques that allow them to kill kangaroo rats larger than themselves. The California Ground Squirrel is the only animal known to signal in infrared. It increases the temperature in its tail when taunting rattlesnakes (but not when taunting gopher snakes, which cannot sense infrared).

In North America, we have the opportunity to observe 444 native mammal species, of which 200 are found exclusively north of Mexico. They range in size from the tiny American Pygmy Shrew, one of the smallest of the world's mammals, weighing less than two dimes, to the 100-foot, 150-ton Blue Whale, the largest animal in the history of the world. North America's largest land mammal is the American Bison (weighing up to one ton), although just 13,000 years ago about 13 other mammals were as big or bigger, including the mastodon, two mammoths, and a three-ton ground sloth.

As with most places in the world, the most diverse mammal group is the rodent order comprising just under half (214) of North America's mammalian species. Next are the carnivores with 54 species, followed by cetaceans (49), bats (46), and insectivores (45). Nearly two-thirds of our mammal species fall into one of six families: Cricetidae (New World mice and rats, 83 species), Sciuridae (squirrels, 67), Heteromyidae (pocket mice and kangaroo rats, 39), Soricidae (shrews, 38), Vespertilionidae (vesper bats, 34), and Delphinidae (dolphins, 21). The three most diverse genera are *Sorex* shrews (31),

MAMMALS

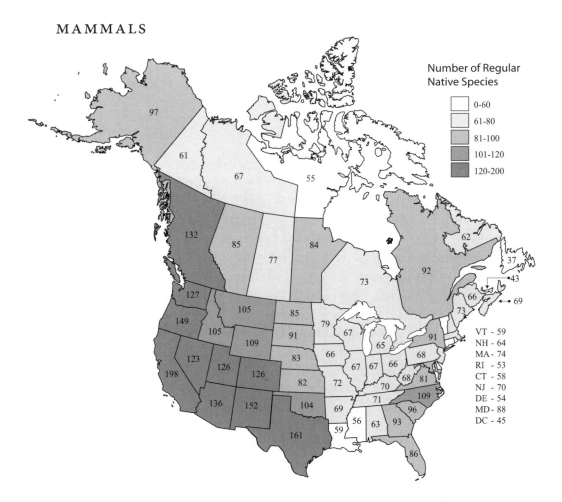

Tamias chipmunks (22), and *Spermophilus* ground squirrels (21). Of the 12 occurring orders of mammals, three (opossums, armadillos, and manatees) are represented in North America by only one extant species. Twelve mammal families are currently represented in North America by only one species: Virginia Opossum, West Indian Manatee, Nine-banded Armadillo, Modern Human, Sewellel, American Beaver, North American Porcupine, Peters's Ghost-faced Bat, Walrus, Collared Peccary, Pronghorn, and Gray Whale. However, had the Pleistocene megafauna survived the invasion of humans, four of those families would have multiple species (beavers, pronghorns, peccaries, and armadillos), while three other families would still be present with just one species each (Northern Glyptodont, Steller's Seacow, American Mastodon). Only the family Aplodontiidae (Sewellel) is endemic north of Mexico. The sole surviving member of the family Antilocapridae, the Pronghorn, is nearly endemic with a range that extends a little into northern Mexico.

At least 45 species of mammals have ranges that, at some latitudes, are transcontinental. Ten (Little Brown Myotis, Hoary Bat, Modern Human, American Beaver, North American Deermouse, Common Muskrat, North American Porcupine, Gray Wolf, Red Fox, and American Black Bear) are also found from south of the Mexican border to the Arctic treeline or beyond. Other than the Modern Human, the Hoary

Bat is our most widespread, non-marine mammal. This migratory, insectivorous bat is found from Hudson Bay to Patagonia, and on many Pacific and Atlantic islands including Hawaii. The Puma ranges from western Canada to Tierra Del Fuego at the southern tip of South America. Six of our whales (Northern Minke, Blue, Fin, Humpback, Killer, and Great Sperm) are distributed worldwide from tropical to polar seas. On the other end of the range-size spectrum are the 17 or so mammals, mostly shrews and rodents, whose range covers only a few counties at most. The Beach Vole has the smallest range of any North American mammal (or warm-blooded vertebrate). It is confined to Muskeget Island, a one-square-mile sandy island west of Nantucket Island, Massachusetts. Close behind are the endangered Saltmarsh Harvest Mouse of San Francisco Bay and, in the Bering Sea, the Pribilof Island Shrew, restricted to Saint Paul Island, and the Insular Vole of Hall and Saint Matthew islands.

At the scale of states and provinces, the latitudinal species gradient is apparent primarily in the west. Overall, the pattern is somewhat obscured by the inclusion of marine mammals for coastal areas. But even among non-marine mammals the gradient is not particularly steep because all mammals can thermoregulate, allowing 72 non-marine species (11 shrews, 4 lagomorphs, 15 carnivores, 30 rodents, 7 ungulates, and 5 bats) to inhabit North America north of 60° latitude. Eleven marine mammals and 21 non-marine mammals only occur north of the southern Canadian border. Regionally the Pacific Coast and the southwest are the most diverse with California (198), Texas (161), New Mexico (152), Oregon (149), and Arizona (136) ranking highest. These states benefit from their southern border regions and, for California, Oregon, and Texas, their marine fauna. All western states have over 100 species of mammals, while all eastern states have fewer than 100 species. Most eastern states have very similar sets of species while the species composition of western states is more varied, owing to the more diverse habitats and greater number of geographic barriers.

California also has, by far, the most endemic mammals (18) due to its geographic barriers of ocean, desert, and mountains. Alaska is the surprising second with eight mammals only found there. Texas has three endemic mammals, Washington, Oregon, Florida, and New Mexico have two, and Idaho, Nevada, Massachusetts, Utah, British Columbia, and the Yukon Territory each have one. Canada claims seven endemic species (Gaspé Shrew, Maritime Shrew, Arctic Hare, Vancouver Island Marmot, and Ungava, Ogilvie Mountains, and Richardson's collared lemmings).

No marine mammals are endemic to North America north of Mexico although the Northern Elephant Seal, Guadalupe Fur Seal, and Hubbs's Beaked Whale are generally found only along the west coast and Baja California. However, that is not surprising because most marine mammals have very large ranges. North American waters and coasts harbor 56 percent of the world's marine mammal species.

To the naturalist who contemplates the North American fauna broadly from both a geographic and temporal perspective, the most glaring feature is the paucity of large mammals. When humans first came here, North America rivaled the Serengeti Plains of Africa in its abundance and diversity of megafauna, large predators, and associated scavengers. Gone from North America are about 45 species of megafauna including ground-sloths, mastodons, mammoths, horses, tapirs, camels, llamas, shrub-oxen, glyptodonts, and seven predators bigger than a Gray Wolf (see Extinct Species). The magnitude of this loss of diversity is much greater than it first appears because it also meant the loss of 11 of North America's 53 mammal families. Even before the devastating impact of modern agriculture, roadways, and urbanization, North America was already significantly altered by the elimination of many large animals and their predators. In historic times we have only lost another three species, the Caribbean Monk Seal, Sea Mink, and Steller's Seacow, the latter having already been extirpated from North America in the late Pleistocene or early Holocene. However, the ranges and populations of many other species have been greatly reduced, most notably those of the Gray Wolf, Puma, American Bison, prairie-dogs, Black-footed Ferret, Grizzly Bear, Elk, and Pronghorn. On a species-wide basis, The Nature Conservancy lists 47 mammals as vulnerable, 15 as imperiled, and 11 as critically imperiled.

Birds

In a world that seems so very puzzling is it any wonder birds have such appeal? Birds are, perhaps, the most eloquent expression of reality.
ROGER TORY PETERSON

Without birds, where would we have learned that there can be song in the heart?
HAL BORLAND

Birds are the most visible part of the animal spectrum; with their varied colors and forms and ability to fly and sing, it is no wonder that so many people are drawn to them. For many who previously had little biological training or experience with nature, birds served as their introduction to the natural world. For those who have yet to become birders, appreciation of the beauty and gracefulness of birds is enough to get started, but equally enticing are the myriad adaptations and abilities of our truly fine-feathered friends. For example, the hearing of Great Gray Owls is so acute and directionally attuned that they can locate and capture rodents hidden under snow cover. The 1/7-ounce Ruby-throated Hummingbird flies nonstop across the Gulf of Mexico at 75 wing beats per second. Bar-tailed Godwits fly 7,000 miles nonstop across the Pacific Ocean (Alaska to New Zealand) in six days, losing half their body weight in the process. Arctic Terns commute 25,000 miles each year, from the Arctic to Antarctica and back again. Phalaropes swim in tight circles to create a vortex that brings small invertebrate prey to the surface. Poorwills go into torpor (a state of inactivity with greatly reduced body temperature, heart rate, and breathing rate) for days at a time during southwestern winters when few flying insects are out. Anna's Hummingbirds become torpid on a nightly basis during cold periods to prevent overnight starvation. During New England winters, tiny Golden-crowned Kinglets are able to find and consume up to three times their body weight in food (mostly geometrid or "inchworm" caterpillars) and maintain their body temperature of 111°F even when ambient temperatures are well below zero. In the breeding season, Red-eyed Vireos sing their song as many as 22,000 times a day.

North America currently supports 715 living regular native bird species, another 197 non-annual visitors, and 19 established exotics. Flight allows birds to migrate or roam large distances so that most of our species are also found outside North America for at least part of the year. This leaves the surprisingly low number of about 52 species that are endemic north of Mexico. These endemics are dominated by the emberizid sparrows (10 species) and the generally non-migratory grouse (9), woodpeckers (8), jays and crows (8), and chickadees and titmice (5). Only about 15 birds are restricted to the lower 48 states and none are exclusive to Canada.

With wingspans of 9 feet, our largest birds are the California Condor and American White Pelican. The Bald Eagle, Magnificent Frigatebird, and Sandhill Crane have wingspans of 7 1/2 feet. From tip of bill to tip of tail, our longest birds are American White Pelican (62"), Trumpeter Swan (60"), Tundra Swan (52"), and Whooping Crane (52"). The Trumpeter Swan is also our heaviest bird at up to 38 pounds. Our smallest birds, by any measurement, are the tiny bundles of energy we call hummingbirds. The Calliope Hummingbird is the ultimate featherweight of North America, reaching a length of only 3 1/4 inches (including bill and tail!) and weighing only 1/8 ounce (less than two dimes). Over 30 of our songbirds, from 13 different families, are less than 5 inches long. The Winter Wren, Black-tailed Gnatcatcher, and Golden-crowned Kinglet barely reach 4 inches.

The North American avifauna is dominated by the songbirds (Passeriformes, 305 species), shorebirds (Charadriiformes, 131), and waterfowl (Anseriformes, 52). The most diverse families include the waterfowl (Anatidae, 52), wood-warblers (Parulidae, 50), emberizid finches (Emberizidae, 50), sandpipers (Scolopacidae, 50), gulls and terns (Laridae, 46), and tyrant-flycatchers (Tyrannidae, 35). The only monotypic bird families in North America are Aramidae (Limpkin) and Peucedramidae (Olive Warbler). Another 14 species are the sole extant, regular native representative of their respective family in North America: Plain Chachalaca, Anhinga, Magnificent Frigatebird, Wood Stork, Greater Flamingo, Barn Owl, Elegant Trogon, Horned Lark, Verdin, Bushtit, Brown Creeper, American Dipper, Wrentit, and Phainopepla. North America has no endemic orders or families of birds. The current classification includes only 7 genera with more than 10 species: *Dendroica* wood-warblers (21), *Larus* gulls (19), *Calidris* sandpipers (17), *Vireo* vireos (14), *Sterna* terns (13), *Anas* ducks (12), and *Empidonax* flycatchers (11).

Other than deep inside caves or deep underwater, birds can be found anywhere within North America, even to the North Polar region, far out at sea, and thousands of feet in the air. Many birds have very large ranges, exemplified by the Peregrine Falcon, Osprey, Barn Owl, Great Egret, Glossy Ibis, and, recently, Cattle Egret. These birds are nearly worldwide in their distributions and breed on every continent except Antarctica. About 200 bird species in North America have ranges that reach from coast to coast, and around 300 have ranges (including migration and winter range) that stretch from Canada to Mexico or farther south. Availability of food and/or physiological limitations forces many of our birds south for the winter (or north for the summer). But some are capable of living year round at all extremes of our climate. The Great Horned Owl is a permanent resident continent-wide from treeline in Alaska and Canada to tropical rainforest in southern Peru.

Very few birds are naturally restricted to small areas. Most of the range of the Brown-capped Rosy-Finch is in Colorado, and most of the range of Abert's Towhee is

BIRDS

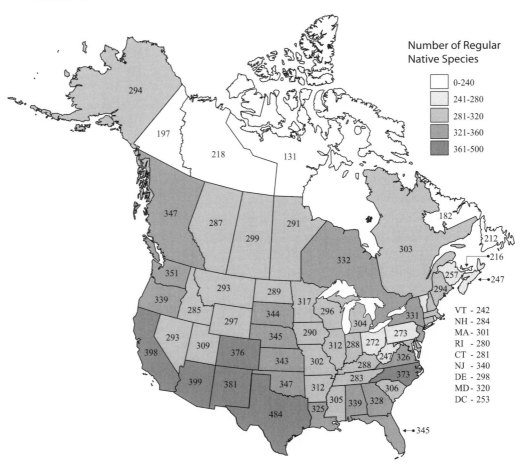

in Arizona. As a breeder, Kirtland's Warbler is mainly confined to Michigan, the Golden-cheeked Warbler breeds only in Texas, and the Bristle-thighed Curlew breeds only in Alaska. Only four birds are endemic to a single state. MacKay's Bunting breeds on Alaskan islands in the Bering Sea and winters on the west coast of Alaska (a few accidentals have been reported from as far south as Oregon). The Florida Scrub-Jay is endemic to Florida, and California has sole claim to the Island Scrub-Jay, only found on Santa Cruz Island, and to the Yellow-billed Magpie.

Not surprisingly, the most diverse states are crowded along or near the southern U.S. border, especially in the Southwest. Texas, with its unique combination of western, eastern, Mexican, coastal, and pelagic species has by far the greatest diversity with 484 regular native birds, followed by Arizona (399), California (398), New Mexico (381), Colorado (376), and North Carolina (373). On the West Coast, Washington (351) and British Columbia (347) make it into the top 10 because of their many migrant and pe-lagic species. Considering its latitude, Alaska (294) has a high bird diversity but it ben-efits from numerous visiting and breeding Siberian species. There is a noticeable drop in diversity from southern border states to adjacent states to the north, and from the southern provinces to the northern territories and Nunavut. Otherwise, bird diversity

is fairly even across the continent. For example, 27 states and provinces fall between 280 and 310 species.

This apparent evenness of bird diversity is an artifact of several factors including the great mobility of birds, large ranges for most species, and the lumping of breeding, wintering, and migrating species into one number. Birds are by far the most mobile animals, so their patterns of diversity and distribution are constantly changing, mostly in regular patterns associated with the seasons, longer-term weather patterns, and fluctuating food supplies. About 70 percent of North America's birds are long distance migrants. In the far north, local bird diversity peaks during the breeding season, but for most parts of North America the peak occurs during spring and fall migration. For any given location, most birds will be present only part of the year as breeders, migrants, or winter residents. Bird diversity is particularly boosted in Atlantic and Pacific coastal states and provinces due to the many migrant and pelagic species. In the far north, summer bird diversity is greatly augmented by the many breeding waterfowl and shorebirds, many of which stay only for a matter of weeks. Compared to other vertebrates, birds are particularly dominant in the far north, at least during the breeding season. Of the 2,522 species of regular native vertebrates north of Mexico, 28 percent (715) are birds. But in Canada north of the 60th parallel, the 238 species of birds make up 63 percent of the total vertebrate fauna (375). Even on Ellesmere Island, just a "day's drive" from the North Pole, you could find up to 40 species of birds in the breeding season.

If only breeding birds are considered (Robbins et al. 1986), the region of highest diversity shifts to southeastern Canada and New England, mainly due to the breeding ranges of many neotropical migrants. In fact, the diversity gradient in the east is inverted, making the Florida Peninsula less diverse than more northern states of the eastern United States. However, during the winter, the normal latitudinal diversity gradient suddenly becomes very pronounced. Along the southern tier of states, and extending up the milder coastal areas, over 100 species may winter in a given area. Winter diversity rapidly tapers off to less than 40 species in southern Canada. About 32 species (mostly grouse, owls, woodpeckers, corvids, chickadees, and finches) have populations that spend the winter north of 60° latitude. About 20 of these species are year-round residents up to the northern treeline. In the winter north of treeline, the only land birds you are likely to find are Snowy Owl, Rock Ptarmigan, Willow Ptarmigan, Gyrfalcon, Common Raven, and, amazingly, the tiny Hoary Redpoll.

Although they are not part of the regular North American avifauna, the 197 species of non-annual visiting birds (including occasional breeders) must be mentioned because of the intense interest in them by birders. With birding hotlines, cell phones, GPS, digital cameras, and e-mail, birders can now learn of rarities within minutes of the first sighting and have an excellent chance of chasing them down. These days, if a rare bird hangs around for a while, hundreds of birders, including many from out of state, will travel to add it to their lifelist. There are 715 regular native birds in North America, plus about 20 established alien species, but over 20 birders, at least, have seen more than 800 species of birds north of Mexico, and at least two birders have seen 850! When accidental species are added to the regular natives, the North American list is 912 species, and the California and Texas lists grow to 613 and 612, respectively. Arizona's list grows to 524, New Mexico increases to 505, and Alaska, because of its proximity to Asia, comes in fifth with 494. In most states and provinces you have the chance to see up to 100 or more additional bird species that occur there on a less than annual basis.

The border regions of North America, including the Atlantic and Pacific coasts, are the prime areas for seeing visitors from Eurasia, Mexico, the Caribbean, and far out at sea. But given the power of flight and the vagaries of weather, many of the birds on the non-annual visitor list could show up anywhere. A Xantus's Hummingbird, normally a resident in Baja California, once spent 10 months in British Columbia. Long-tailed Jaegers, normally an arctic or pelagic species, have been recorded in nearly every state. And the accidental list keeps growing. In the last few years the following species have been added: Bermuda Petrel, Fea's/Zino's Petrel, Bulwer's Petrel, Galapagos/Hawaiian Petrel, Chinese Pond-Heron, Common Redshank, Greater Sandplover, Band-tailed Gull, Kelp Gull, Stygian Owl, Piratic Flycatcher, Mangrove Swallow, Yellow-browed Warbler, Orange-billed Nightingale-Thrush, and Yellow-throated Bunting.

Unfortunately, North America has lost more bird species than any other continent. Since the arrival of Columbus, we have caused the extinction of the Labrador Duck, Great Auk, Passenger Pigeon, Carolina Parakeet, Bachman's Warbler, and probably the Eskimo Curlew. The Gray-crowned Yellowthroat and probably Worthen's Sparrow have been extirpated. But at least 18 other species were eliminated when the first humans came to the New World, as shown in Extinct Species. Meanwhile, habitat loss in the last few centuries has drastically reduced the populations of most species and put many on the fast track to oblivion. The California Condor and Whooping Crane are still hanging by a thread with about 200 individuals each, although that is a significant recovery from lows of 22 and 18, respectively. Currently, the Ivory-billed Woodpecker persists only in our faith in a few lucky observers and the grainy images of a video. The Nature Conservancy considers a total of 50 North American bird species to be at some degree of risk (27 vulnerable, 14 imperiled, and 9 critically imperiled).

Reptiles

Precisely the least, the softest, lightest, a lizard's rustling, a breath, a flash, a moment— a little makes the way of the best happiness.
FRIEDRICH NIETZSCHE

In the parched path
I have seen the good lizard
(one drop of crocodile)
meditating.
FEDERICO GARCÍA LORCA, *THE OLD LIZARD*

Most of the quotes I have seen about reptiles, especially snakes, had less to do with their actual qualities than with human superiority, fear, and ignorance. But once their undeserved reputation is cast aside, the beauty of reptiles is revealed and their amazing

REPTILES

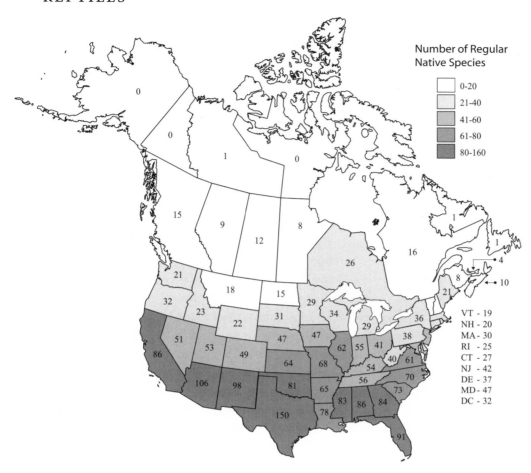

abilities and behaviors can be discovered. For example, ten of the whiptail lizards are unisexual species consisting entirely of females. Reproduction takes place by parthenogenesis, the development of an unfertilized egg into a female clone. Some of the seven species of horned lizards have the bizarre defensive behavior of squirting blood from their eyes at would-be predators. Geckos, represented in our area by six species, are famous as a group for their vocalizations, nocturnal habit, and ability to scale windows and cross ceilings. Tortoises live to 50 years or more. Threadsnakes have vestigial eyes and spend most of their time underground where, protected by covering themselves with a cloacal discharge, they feed on termites and the larvae and pupae of ants. The Gila Monster is one of only two venomous lizards in the world. Hog-nosed snakes eat toads by using powerful hormones to counteract the toad's skin toxins and puncturing inflated toads with a specialized tooth at the back of each upper jaw.

North America has 315 species of living native reptiles, of which 135 are endemic. Our largest reptiles are the familiar American Crocodile and American Alligator, the latter of which may reach 19 feet in length. Crocodilians arose during the Triassic, along with many dinosaur groups, but they survived the impacts of the Chicxulub

Asteroid and have out-lasted dinosaurs by 65 million years and counting. Less often seen but equally impressive is the Leatherback Seaturtle, the largest turtle in the world, which may reach 9 feet in length and weigh up to one ton. The Eastern Indigo Snake is our largest snake with a record total length of slightly over 8 1/2 feet. Our smallest reptile is the tiny Reef Gecko that grows to a maximum length of 2 1/4 inches, including the inch-long tail. Black-headed snakes, wormsnakes, and threadsnakes are usually pencil thin and less than a foot long. The smallest of all are the Florida Crowned Snake, Flat-headed Snake, and Mexican Black-headed Snake, none of which exceed 10 inches in length.

Overall, the reptiles of North America exhibit a strong latitudinal diversity gradient. The top ten states in reptile diversity include all eight southern boundary states plus Oklahoma and Georgia. Texas, with 150 species, is far ahead of the rest, which range from Arizona (106) to Louisiana (78). The northern tier states range from 36 species (New York) to 15 species (North Dakota), while all of Canada and Alaska have only 43 species. One reptile, the Common Gartersnake, barely ranges into the Northwest Territories. Alaska, Nunavut, and the Yukon Territory have no reptiles.

The North American turtle fauna consists of 57 species with 37 found nowhere else. Included are six of the seven species of marine turtles, four of which have nested on our beaches. Diamond-backed Terrapins inhabit brackish and salt waters of coastal marshes of the Gulf and Atlantic states from Texas to Massachusetts. The other 50 species include three tortoises (*Gopherus*) and two box turtles (*Terrapene*), which are generally terrestrial, and 45 species of freshwater turtles (Kinosternidae and Emydidae), mostly found in the eastern United States and concentrated in the Gulf states where each state has between 26 and 31 species. Only nine freshwater turtles reach into southern Canada.

Seven freshwater turtle species are endemic to a single state. Cagle's and Texas map turtles, and Texas River Cooter are restricted to Texas; the Peninsula and Suwannee cooters are found only in Florida; Alabama claims the Flattened Musk Turtle; and Mississippi is the exclusive home of the Yellow-blotched Map Turtle.

The Alligator Snapping Turtle, endemic to southeastern United States, weighs up to 300 pounds and is one of the largest freshwater turtles in the world. It often lies on the bottom of a river or lake with its mouth open, wriggling a small, pink, wormlike appendage to lure its fish prey. The only other member in its family (Chelydridae) in North America is the smaller Snapping Turtle that is found from Canada to Ecuador. The most diverse group of turtles in North America is the genus of map turtles (*Graptemys*), which has 14 species. They occur primarily in lakes and rivers of the midwestern and southeastern United States, with eight of the species restricted to just one or two river systems that empty into the Gulf of Mexico. Two species, Escambia and Pascagoula map turtles, were not described until 1992.

The Florida Worm Lizard is now treated as the only living member of the endemic family Rhineuridae, and it is the only North American representative of the suborder Amphisbaenia. This pink, shovel-nosed, legless reptile is found in Florida and extreme southern Georgia where it spends most of its life underground.

True lizards are well represented in North America by 112 species, 37 of them endemic. Their highest diversity is found in the deserts of the southwestern states, where Arizona and Texas represent the peak with 46 species each, while only six lizards reach into southern Canada: both short-horned lizards, Northern Alligator Lizard, Prairie Skink, Five-lined Skink, and Western Skink.

Seventy percent of our lizards are in one of three families: Phrynosomatidae (spiny lizards, 43 species), Teiidae (whiptails, 22), and Scincidae (skinks, 14). These families also have the largest genera: whiptails (*Aspidoscelis*, 22), spiny lizards (*Sceloporus*, 20), and skinks (*Plestiodon*, 13). The Green Anole, the "chameleon" of pet stores because it can change color, is our sole representative of the diverse tropical genus *Anolis*, which numbers nearly 200 species. The Gila Monster of the southwest shares its family (Helodermatidae) with only one other species, the Mexican Beaded Lizard (*Heloderma horridum*) of western Mexico. The California Legless Lizard is a small, burrowing, snakelike lizard of California and Baja California. The only other member of its family (Anniellidae) is endemic to a small part of Baja California. Four other lizards without limbs, called glass lizards (*Ophisaurus*), are in the family Anguidae and are distributed primarily in the southeastern states.

At least 14 lizards are endemic to a single state. Endemic to California are the Blunt-nosed Leopard Lizard, Coachella Valley Fringe-toed Lizard, Panamint Alligator Lizard, Island Night Lizard (on three of the Channel Islands), and Sandstone Night Lizard (restricted to a 1.5 square mile area in Anza-Borrego Desert State Park). Arizona endemics include Arizona Striped, Pai Striped, and Red-backed whiptails, and Bezy's Night Lizard, just described in 2001. The Florida Scrub Lizard and Florida Sand Skink are found only in Florida, the Little White Whiptail and Southwestern Fence Lizard occur just in New Mexico, and the Colorado Checkered Whiptail is restricted to a few counties in southeastern Colorado.

North America has 143 species of snakes and can claim 59 of them exclusively. In terms of diversity the most successful snakes in North America are the gartersnakes (*Thamnophis*, 16 species), rattlesnakes (*Crotalus*, 13), black-headed snakes (*Tantilla*, 11), watersnakes (*Nerodia*, 10), and ratsnakes (*Pantherophis*, 9). Together, these five genera make up 42 percent of our snake fauna.

The Colubridae is, by far, the most diverse snake family in North America with 115 species. The pit vipers (Viperidae) come in at a distant second with 18 species, followed by the four species of coralsnakes and seasnakes (Elapidae). Two families of snakes, the threadsnakes (Leptotyphlopidae) and boas (Boidae), have just three representatives each in North America. The genus *Leptotyphlops* is one of the most diverse snake genera in the world with 92 species. The boas are primarily tropical and subtropical although one of our species, the Northern Rubber Boa, reaches into British Columbia. Our boas are generally less than three feet in length, but their tropical relatives (pythons and anacondas) are the largest snakes in the world.

Following the generalized latitudinal gradient of species diversity, snakes are more diverse in the southern tier of states. Each of the southeastern coastal states from Louisiana to South Carolina has 41 or 42 species, except Florida, which has 46. In the Southwest, Arizona (52) and New Mexico (47) benefit from about 15 snakes that are found nowhere else except south of the Mexican border. Texas, with its size, diverse climate and geography, and southern extensions, has 73 snake species, the most of any state. In contrast, all of Canada is home to a total of 26 species of snakes.

Gartersnakes are our most common snakes and are widely distributed from deep into Canada, coast to coast, and south to Costa Rica. The Common Gartersnake has the largest and most northern distribution of any North American reptile. Its range extends from the southern tip of Florida to just north of the 60th parallel into the Northwest Territories, as well as coast to coast.

The Saltmarsh Snake is restricted to coastal saline habitats from Texas to Florida, and a few other snakes, like the Cottonmouth, occasionally enter salt and brackish waters, but the Yellow-bellied Seasnake is our only truly marine snake. Although it just enters our area off the coast of southern California, it is the most widely distributed snake in the world, occurring throughout tropical and subtropical waters of the Indian and Pacific oceans.

Most of our snakes are relatively widespread within North America and/or into Mexico or further south. The Central American Indigo Snake, of southern Texas, occurs south all the way to Venezuela. Four of our snakes are endemic to a single state. The Brazos River and Concho watersnakes are each confined to their namesake river systems in central Texas. The Short-tailed Snake and Rim Rock Crowned Snake are restricted to portions of Florida, the latter species to less than 100 square miles in just two southern counties.

Missing from our reptile fauna are four species of tortoises that became extinct, plus one that was extirpated, soon after the first arrival of humans in North America (see Extinct Species). Their shells ranged in size from 10 inches to nearly 4 feet long. Fortunately, no other North American reptiles have become extinct since then, but today about 63 species (20%) are at some degree of risk: 35 vulnerable, 19 imperiled, and 9 critically imperiled. Habitat destruction and alteration, vehicles, and the good-snake-equals-dead-snake mentality are significant threats to at least 24 lizards, 17 snakes, the American Crocodile, and 21 turtles in North America.

Amphibians

Most amphibia are abhorrent because of their cold body, pale colour, cartilaginous skeleton, filthy skin, fierce aspect, calculating eye, offensive smell, harsh voice, squalid habitation, and terrible venom; and so their Creator has not exerted his powers [to make] many of them.
CAROLUS LINNAEUS, 1758

It's not easy being green.
KERMIT THE FROG

We have come a long way since Linnaeus named *Bufo marinus* (Cane Toad) in 1758. Worldwide, we have now described over 6,000 species (a number that climbs almost weekly) while attitudes toward amphibians have reached new levels of appreciation, although much of that was bought with the revelation of their recent declines. Unfortunately, amphibians take some effort to observe outside their hiding places because they are mostly nocturnal and/or fossorial, belying their sometimes high densities. But they are fascinating and endearing creatures when you get to know them.

Although we are all familiar with the process since childhood, it is something just short of a miracle that frogs and toads change from herbivorous, aquatic, water breathing tadpoles to predaceous, terrestrial, air breathing adults. The tailed frogs of the Pacific Northwest and northern Rockies are unique among anurans in that they have a copulatory organ (an everted cloaca). This is an adaptation to ensure fertilization in their fast-flowing stream habitat. The Grotto Salamander of the Ozarks moves from mountain brooks, as a larva, to caves, as an adult, where it soon loses its fins, pigment, and ability to see for the rest of its life. Several other subterranean salamanders rarely, if ever, see the light of day. The Cave Salamander can flick its tongue out to catch prey in just 5.5 milliseconds. Some northern frogs, including Gray Treefrog, Spring Peeper, Boreal Chorus Frog, and Wood Frog, spend the winter frozen solid, except for the inside of their cells, with no breathing and no heart beat. They are able to revive in the spring because, at the onset of freezing, they flush their cells with glucose, a natural antifreeze.

North America has 274 species of extant, native amphibians of which 233 (85%) are endemic. Amphibians are generally thought of as small, harmless creatures but a few are surprisingly large and intimidating. The Two-toed Amphiuma, an eel-like aquatic salamander with minute legs, can grow to a startling length of over 45 inches. The similarly shaped Three-toed Amphiuma and Greater Siren are nearly as long. Shorter but more monstrous and prehistoric looking is the 29-inch Hellbender, a denizen of rivers in the Ozarks and Appalachians. The Hellbender is the closest relative of the Japanese and Chinese giant salamanders (*Andrias*), the latter of which is the largest living amphibian in the world reaching a length of five feet! On land, the largest salamanders in North America, and the world, are the Tiger Salamander and Coastal Giant Salamander, both of which reach 13 inches in total length. Our largest anurans are the Cane Toad (9 1/2"), Bullfrog (8"), Colorado River Toad (7"), and Pig Frog (6 3/8"). The smallest amphibians in North America would hardly be morsels for these creatures. The Little Grass Frog of Florida and the Atlantic Coastal Plain is our smallest frog reaching a maximum snout-vent length of 11/16 inch. The Rio Grande Chirping Frog barely reaches 1 inch, and 14 other frogs are 1 1/2 inches or less. Our smallest salamanders are the San Marcos Salamander and Pygmy Salamander, both fully grown at 2 inches, including the tail.

The latitudinal diversity gradient for amphibians is particularly pronounced because of their inability to generate their own heat to avoid freezing. Thus, while each of the southern tier states, except dry Arizona and New Mexico, harbor over 50 species, only 45 amphibians (24 anurans and 21 salamanders) are found in all of Canada and Alaska. At the southern border of the Yukon, Northwest Territories, and Nunavut the amphibian diversity drops to seven species (six anurans and the Rough-skinned Newt), and only the Western Chorus Frog and the Wood Frog are found much farther north. The Wood Frog is the only amphibian to range north to timberline across Canada and Alaska, in places well above the Arctic Circle. Within the 48 states, amphibian diversity

AMPHIBIANS

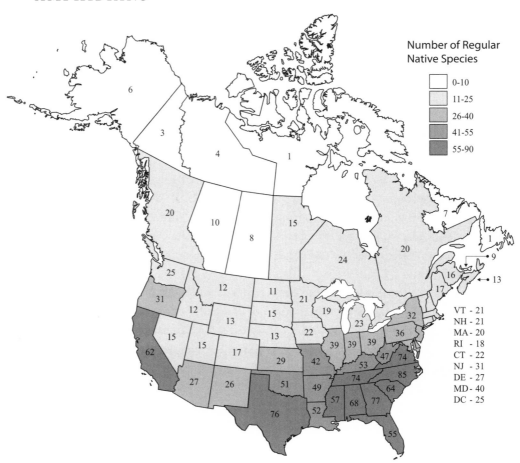

is skewed to the Southeast where eight states are in the top ten, led by North Carolina (85), Georgia (77), Tennessee (76), and Virginia (74). Outside this region, Texas (76) and California (62) stand out.

In general there are more species of salamanders than frogs in mountains and uplands, while the opposite is generally true in lowland regions, except the Atlantic and Gulf Coastal Plain where their numbers are about equal (Duellman and Sweet 1999). Regional centers of diversity include the Southern Appalachians, Allegheny Plateau, Gulf Coastal Plain, Southern Coastal Plain, Ozark and Ouachita mountains, and the Pacific Coast, Cascade, and Sierra Nevada ranges. The southern Appalachian region has the highest salamander diversity contributing greatly to North Carolina (55), Tennessee (53), Virginia (48), and Georgia (46) having the most species. Aquatic salamanders are most diverse in the Atlantic and Gulf lowlands and the Edwards Plateau of central Texas. The southeastern coastal plain also supports the highest diversity of mole salamanders (Ambystomatidae), true frogs (Ranidae), and treefrogs (Hylidae). Toads (Bufonidae) are most diverse in the southwestern United States where aquatic systems are isolated by dry deserts, leading to much speciation. The Pacific Northwest is noteworthy for its three endemic families: Ascaphidae (tailed frogs), Rhyacotritonidae (torrent salamanders), and Dicamptodontidae (giant salamanders).

Three families, the toads (Bufonidae), treefrogs (Hylidae), and true frogs (Ranidae), comprise 82 percent of the 95 species of anurans. The largest genera are true frogs (*Rana*, 29 species), true toads (*Bufo*, 22), chorus frogs (*Pseudacris*, 13), and treefrogs (*Hyla*, 10). The Mexican Burrowing Toad, which ranges into southern Texas, is the sole member of its family (Rhinophrynidae). North America is the exclusive home of the family Ascaphidae with two species of tailed frogs. The New World Leptodactylidae is the largest anuran family in the world with 1,268 species (and counting), but only five of them naturally occur north of Mexico.

Nearly two-thirds (60) of our anurans are endemic to North America, the remaining species having ranges that extend into Mexico. Only one amphibian, the Wood Frog, has a transcontinental range. Most of its distribution is in the north but it reaches from Alaska to Alabama. Four anurans (Plains Spadefoot, Western and Great Plains toads, and Pacific Treefrog) range from Canada to Mexico. Our most widespread species are the Wood Frog and Northern Leopard Frog.

Most eastern species of frogs have sizeable ranges with the exception of the Florida Bog Frog, endemic to two counties in western Florida. All other states with endemic anurans are in the West: California, Texas, and Nevada have two each, and Wyoming and Arizona each have one. The small ranges of several anurans have become dangerously smaller due to human impacts. The Relict Leopard Frog has been reduced to only a few sites; the Amargosa Toad is slowly recovering from a population low of just 30 adults; and the Wyoming Toad has only been saved from the fate of the Vegas Valley Leopard Frog by a captive-breeding and reintroduction program.

The origin of salamanders was recently pushed back at least 100 million years to the late Jurassic (165 million years ago) in Asia (Gao and Shubin 2001, 2003), but today their diversity is concentrated in North and Central America. The 179 species of North American salamanders belong to 9 of the world's 10 salamander families with lungless salamanders (Plethodontidae) comprising 77 percent (138 species). Plethodontids have been able to occupy terrestrial habitats because they can lay eggs in moist terrestrial environments and there is direct development. The largest genera are woodland salamanders (*Plethodon*, 55), brook salamanders (*Eurycea*, 25), slender salamanders (*Batrachoseps*, 19), dusky salamanders (*Desmognathus*, 19), and mole salamanders (*Ambystoma*, 14). North America claims three endemic salamander families: amphiumas (Amphiumidae), Pacific giant salamanders (Dicamptodontidae), and torrent salamanders (Rhyacotritonidae). The sirens (Sirenidae) and mole salamanders (Ambystomatidae) are nearly endemic, otherwise occurring only in Mexico. The family Proteidae consists of five North American species (Mudpuppy and waterdogs, *Necturus*), and one European species (the blind, subterranean Olm, *Proteus anguinus*). The Hellbender is our only species of the giant salamander family (Cryptobranchidae), which also contains the Japanese and Chinese giant salamanders. Cryptobranchids were recently discovered to be living fossils having changed little from an ancestor 165 million years old (Gao and Shubin 2003).

The most dramatic change in our understanding of salamander diversity is the result of recent taxonomic discoveries and revisions. As recently as 1990, only 135 species were recognized in North America. Today, the number is 179 with 29 of the additions being described since 1995.

The saltwater and desert barriers along the southern U.S. border have served to make the North American salamander fauna highly distinctive with 173 endemic species. The only species also found in Mexico are Lesser Siren, Black-spotted Newt, Tiger Salamander, Arboreal Salamander, Garden Slender Salamander, and Ensatina. A few species are widespread, most notably the Eastern Newt, Tiger Salamander, and Spotted Salamander, and the range of many species includes several states. But the habitat requirements, low dispersal rates, and consequently limited gene flow of many salamander species have resulted in a high degree of state endemism, especially compared to most other vertebrates. California stands out with 26 endemic species in six genera including 17 species of slender salamanders (*Batrachoseps*). Texas has 13 endemic salamanders, all in the genus *Eurycea*, followed by North Carolina (1 *Necturus*, 4 *Plethodon*) and Georgia (1 *Desmognathus*, 3 *Plethodon*). Nine other states have one to three endemics for a total of 63 salamander species restricted to one state. Several of these species have ranges that are little more than dots on a map because they are confined to a single mountain, spring, or cave system.

The northern plains and much of the Rocky Mountain and desert regions are a formidable challenge to salamanders. North Dakota, South Dakota, and Nebraska have just two species, and only the Tiger Salamander occurs in Wyoming, Colorado, Utah, and Arizona. Nevada has no salamanders. Surprisingly, in addition to the Tiger Salamander, New Mexico is home to an endemic *Aneides* (Sacramento Mountains Salamander) and an endemic *Plethodon* (Jemez Mountains Salamander), which are now roughly 600 and 1,000 miles, respectively, from their closest relatives.

Perhaps the most intriguing distribution of a salamander is that of the Ensatina. This species, the only member of its genus, occupies all the mountain regions surrounding the Central Valley of California forming a "ring species" in which interbreeding is rare or absent where the ends of the ring overlap in southern California. However, genetic studies have been interpreted by some taxonomists to warrant splitting the Ensatina into as many as 11 or more species.

Our amphibian fauna is still mostly intact with no end-Pleistocene extinctions, one definite recent extinction (Vegas Valley Leopard Frog), one recent extirpation (Tarahumara Frog, extirpated in 1983, reintroduced in 2004), and two species that are missing or possibly extinct (Catahoula Salamander and Blanco Blind Salamander). However, many others are endangered, and "amphibian" has almost become synonymous with "decline" in the last two decades. In modern times, worldwide, we have definitely lost 34 species, possibly another 134, and 1,856 species, nearly one-third of the world's total, are globally threatened (IUCN et al. 2004). Most of this loss has occurred in the past few decades. In North America, 109 amphibians (20 anurans, 89 salamanders) are globally at some risk of extinction: 43 vulnerable, 35 imperiled, 31 critically imperiled.

One Special Addition: Unisexual *Ambystoma* Biotypes

The above discussion does not account for unisexual *Ambystoma* biotypes, and they are currently not included in official species lists. In general, hybrids, the offspring of parents from different species, are usually evolutionary dead ends and therefore receive no species designation, governmental protection, or place in this book. I make an exception in the case of some unisexual mole salamanders because, although they are of hybrid origin and do not conform to any current species definition, they persist through successive generations as unique, identifiable, and sometimes common organisms. They are included within the Ambystomatidae in the lifelist section.

Unisexual *Ambystoma* reproduce through a process called gynogenesis in which females must mate with a male of a sexual species to stimulate the egg to divide and develop, but fertilization does not occur and no genes from the males are received by the offspring. They may also reproduce via hybridogenesis in which males of a sexual species do contribute one set of chromosomes to the female offspring, but when those female offspring produce eggs, the paternal chromosomes are deleted (to be replaced by mating with another male) and so are not passed on to the next generation. Unisexual *Ambystoma* biotypes are usually all-female populations that contain from two to five sets of genes derived from two or three of the following four species: Jefferson Salamander (*A. jeffersonianum*, genetic component designated by "J"), Blue-spotted Salamander (*A. laterale*, "L"), Small-mouthed Salamander (*A. texanum*, "T"), and Tiger Salamander (*A. tigrinum*, "Ti"). Some combinations were originally named as species, but most biologists now refer to them generally as biotypes and specifically by their genomic complements using the above abbreviations. For example, the biotype LTTTi has one set of genes from *A. laterale*, two sets from *A. texanum*, and one set from *A. tigrinum*.

However, most of the 20 or so unisexual *Ambystoma* biotypes are not known to represent ongoing lineages. For this reason I include only two forms in the lifelist section: JJL (formerly Silvery Salamander, *Ambystoma platineum*) and JLL (formerly Tremblay's Salamander, *Ambystoma tremblayi*), both of which comprise ongoing clonal lineages. As a whole, unisexual *Ambystoma* biotypes occur from northern Wisconsin southeast to extreme northern Kentucky, and northeast through the Great Lakes region to the Maritimes. For a more detailed discussion of unisexual *Ambystoma*, and descriptions and ranges of JJL and JLL, see Petranka (1998, 122–29).

Freshwater Fishes

I know the joy of fishes in the river through my own joy, as I go walking along the same river.
CHUANG TZU

I've been here three hours
Without one single bite.
There might be no fish . . .
. . . But, again,
Well, there might!
DR. SEUSS, *MCELLIGOT'S POOL*

For most people, our freshwater fishes are generally hidden unless we see them on the end of a fishing line, on a dinner plate, or in an aquarium. But a fascinating world awaits the patient, land-based observer and adventurous snorkeler or diver. Freshwater fish adaptations and behaviors are myriad and marvelous. The pupfishes, one of our most endangered groups of fishes, are able to withstand the most extreme environmental conditions. They can survive temperatures of 32–113°F, salinity over four times that of ocean water, and the lowest oxygen concentrations (0.13 mg/liter) tolerated by any obligate gill breathing fish. Madtoms, smaller versions of catfishes, have venomous spines. The Amazon Molly is an entirely female species, the apparent result of a hybridization event between Shortfin and Sailfin mollies. To procreate, an Amazon Molly must mate with a male of either parent species, although the sperm only stimulates the egg to develop and does not contribute genetic material to the offspring. Pacific salmon are able to avoid scores of wrong turns as they swim upstream as much as 1,000 miles to their home gravel bars. The Toothless and Widemouth blindcats, and four cavefishes, lack eyes and skin pigments, and live their entire lives in the perpetual darkness of subterranean waters. Bowfins, mudminnows, and gars can breathe air to supplant the gills in poorly oxygenated waters. Males of the Egg-mimic, Lollypop, Guardian, and Relict darters have egglike knobs on the tips of the second dorsal fin rays that lure females to the male's nesting territory because females prefer to spawn in a nest that already has eggs. The Cutlips Minnow, like some cichlids in Africa, has the specialized but somewhat gruesome feeding behavior of plucking out the eyes of other fishes. The Alaska Blackfish can survive being trapped in solid ice as long as its tissues do not freeze. The Borax Lake Chub lives in a spring-fed pond with natural arsenic levels 25 times the critical limit for human consumption.

The living native freshwater fishes of North America number 819 species, with another 46 marine species that sometimes enter freshwater, and 62 alien species introduced to freshwaters. However, new freshwater fish species are still being described nearly every year. At least 50 more species are known but not yet formally described, and more subspecies will be elevated to full species (Warren et al. 2000). The great majority (696, 85%) of our freshwater fishes are endemic, but this is not too surprising since most of our species are restricted to freshwater and North America is surrounded by ocean—except along the Mexican border which, other than the Rio Grande, is straddled by few watersheds and much desert. Mexico and the United States share just 82 species. Only a handful of obligate freshwater species are also native to parts of Eurasia. They include the Northern Pike, Longnose Sucker, and Burbot.

The largest freshwater fish in North America is the White Sturgeon, of California and the Pacific Northwest, which grows to an impressive 20 feet in length. Other giants of our lakes and rivers include the Atlantic Sturgeon (14'), Alligator Gar (10'), Lake Sturgeon (9'), Green Sturgeon (7'), and Paddlefish (7'). The Longnose Gar, Striped Bass, Muskellunge, and Colorado Pikeminnow may grow to 6 feet. However, the size distribution of species is heavily weighted toward the small end. More than half (over 400) of our species reach a maximum length of 5 inches or less. Of those, about 180 species never exceed 3 inches, and about 30 are 2 inches or less. Most of these small fishes are minnows or darters, but the smallest of all are from three other families. The Pygmy Killifish (Fundulidae), Devils Hole Pupfish (Cyprinodontidae), and the Everglades, Okefenokee, Carolina, Bluebarred, and Spring pygmy sunfishes (Elassomatidae) are full grown at 1 1/4 inches. (The world's smallest adult fish, and vertebrate, is the recently described Stout Infantfish [*Schindleria brevipinguis*] from the Great Barrier Reef in Australia [Watson and Walker 2004]. Males are just a hair longer than 1/4 inch and weigh less than 1 milligram, about the weight of a mosquito!)

The minnow family (Cyprinidae) is by far the most diverse group of North American freshwater fishes with 257 species, or 31 percent of the ichthyofauna. It also happens to be the world's largest family of fishes, marine or freshwater, with over 2,100 species. Minnows are found throughout our continent, from isolated spring-fed desert lakes like Borax Lake, Oregon, where the Borax Lake Chub is the only fish in the lake, to the amazingly diverse rivers of the southeastern states, where up to 60 species of minnow may be found in one river system. The second most diverse family is the Percidae with 189 species, all but three of them darters. Many of these small fishes sport surprisingly intricate and brilliant color patterns of orange, red, green, and blue. All darters are confined to the Atlantic and Gulf drainages with the greatest diversity centered on Tennessee, which has over 100 species. The sucker family (Catostomidae) is a distant third in diversity with 69 species, although these bottom-feeders make up most of the fish biomass of many freshwater habitats. The darter genus *Etheostoma* is the most diverse vertebrate genus in North America with 137 species. Other large fish genera are the *Notropis* shiners and minnows (78), *Percina* darters (43), *Cottus* sculpins (28), *Noturus* madtoms (27), and *Fundulus* topminnows and killifish (25).

Thirteen of our fish families stand out because only one of the species in the family is found here, or the family is endemic to North America. Not including several introduced or predominantly marine species, there are nine families that are represented in North America by a single species. The Mexican Tetra (Characidae) and Rio Grande Cichlid (Cichlidae) are our only members of their mostly tropical families that number over 800 and 700 species, respectively. The Burbot (Gadidae), Freshwater Drum (Sciaenidae), and Tule Perch (Embiotocidae) are the only obligate freshwater species of their respective families that occur in North America. American Eels (Anguillidae) breed in the Atlantic Ocean but spend most of their lives in North American brackish or freshwater as far inland as South Dakota. The unusual paddlefish is one of only two species of the Polyodontidae; the other one lives in the Yangtze River system in China. Two North American families are both monotypic and endemic to North America. The 5-inch Pirate Perch (Aphredoderidae) is unusual in that during its growth, the urogenital opening moves from the normal position forward to the throat region. The reason, discovered only recently (Fletcher et al. 2004), is that they enter narrow openings in underwater root masses headfirst to spawn. The Bowfin is the last living species of the ancient family Amiidae, as well as the order Amiiformes, which was once distributed on all continents except Antarctica and Australia. Five other families are endemic to North America: Hiodontidae (mooneyes, 2 species), Percopsidae (trout-perches, 2), Amblyopsidae (cavefishes, 6), Centrarchidae (sunfishes and basses, 31), and Elassomatidae (pygmy sunfishes, 6).

There are at least 138 species of freshwater fishes that are endemic to a single state or province. Currently, Texas has the most with 19, followed by California (18), Alabama (17), Tennessee (16), Nevada (12), Oregon (8), North Carolina (6), and 19 other states or provinces with one to four endemic species. The current rate of elevating subspecies

FRESHWATER FISHES

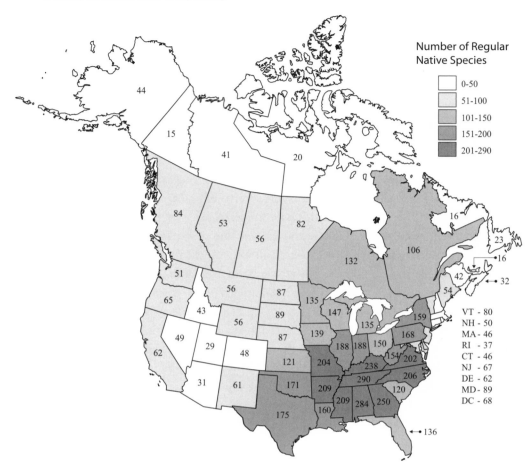

Number of Regular
Native Species

- 0-50
- 51-100
- 101-150
- 151-200
- 201-290

VT - 80
NH - 50
MA - 46
RI - 37
CT - 46
NJ - 67
DE - 62
MD- 89
DC - 68

to full species status, and of describing new species, will certainly increase these numbers. Many more freshwater fish species have ranges that happen to overlap political borders but are much smaller than an average-sized state. Bear Lake, which straddles the Idaho-Utah border, supports four endemic fishes (Bonneville Cisco, Bonneville Whitefish, Bear Lake Whitefish, and Bear Lake Sculpin). About 30 other species are confined to a single small lake, creek, spring, or cave system. Most of these are denizens of the small springs and lakes left over from the state-sized western lakes of the Pleistocene. In some cases, a species' entire range would fit in a large backyard. The Devils Hole Pupfish has one of the smallest natural ranges of any vertebrate in the world. The entire population of this tiny blue fish lives and breeds in a spring along a limestone shelf that is only 20 square meters, the size of a small patio. (The world record for vertebrates may belong to the Red-finned Blue-eye [*Scaturiginichthys vermeilipinnis*], which is restricted to an even smaller spring in Queensland, Australia.)

Most freshwater fishes of North America are restricted to one or the other side of the Continental Divide, usually within one major or minor river system. Some of our most widespread species, including the Lake Whitefish, Lake Trout, Northern Pike,

Lake Chub, and Longnose Sucker, have taken advantage of the huge expanses of similar aquatic habitats of Alaska and Canada. The Burbot has one of the largest ranges, which includes all of Canada and Alaska south to Oregon, southern Illinois, and northern New Jersey. The Fathead Minnow and Longnose Dace have extensive ranges that include Pacific, Atlantic, and Arctic drainages, the latter species extending from the Arctic Circle to Mexico.

The circumpolar Arctic Char has the most northern distribution of any North American freshwater fish, extending from New England, Alaska, and the northern mainland of Canada to the north end of Ellesmere Island, well above 80° latitude and less than 500 miles from the North Pole. In many lakes and streams of the northern islands it is the only fish present. The range of the Ninespine Stickleback extends somewhat farther south but may also reach as far north.

The current distribution of North American freshwater fishes can only be understood by considering the historical changes in geography. Flip through the range maps of your field guide and you will see that many species are restricted to single drainage systems but others have ranges that extend across watershed divides or are highly disjunct. Obviously, most fish cannot move over dry land, but a variety of geological events have allowed fishes to cross watershed boundaries. Quite often this occurs through a process called stream capture. A watershed divide is eroded away until the upper part of one stream, along with its fishes, begins to flow into the other, formerly separated stream. Fish can also disperse to other drainages during floods created by beaver dams, glacial ice dams, or rising lake waters from glacial melting. Some fishes, like certain trout and sculpins, are salt tolerant enough to have used marine or brackish waters to move to other freshwater systems. Within drainage systems, a fish's range may be restricted, or separated from a sister species, by habitat, interactions with other species, and physical barriers such as the Fall Line and other waterfalls. The Fall Line is a low line of cliffs separating the Appalachian Piedmont from the Coastal Plain, and it runs from New Jersey to Alabama.

The advance and retreat of Pleistocene continental glaciers have had a profound impact on fish distributions in North America. As the glaciers advanced, fish were eliminated from much of the northern half of the continent. As the glaciers receded, relatively rapid changes occurred in watershed boundaries, water levels, the size of lakes, and direction of flow. For example, glacial Lake Agassiz, which covered parts of Manitoba, Ontario, North Dakota, and Minnesota, was four times bigger than current Lake Superior, the world's largest lake today. Glaciers caused water from the Great Lakes region to flow into the Mississippi system, then the Susquehanna, then the Hudson, and finally the St. Lawrence, each change offering new opportunities for fishes to expand their ranges.

Some zoogeographic consequences of the ice ages and other geologic events are as follows (Briggs 1986). There is a strong distinction between fish faunas of either side of the Continental Divide with few species in both Pacific and Atlantic drainages. The eastern side has four times as many species as the west, largely due to the greater stability and size of the Mississippi Basin and its north-south orientation, which allowed northern species an easy retreat from the Pleistocene glaciers. Almost all localized endemics, including troglodytic fishes, are found in unglaciated areas. Many of the localized endemic fishes of the West probably had much larger ranges during the ice age when vast lakes filled many intermountain basins. Since then, most of the water has evaporated or retreated underground, and a number of fish species have been isolated in small pools and springs.

There is a well-defined latitudinal gradient of species in the East, but this pattern is obscured in the West by the scarcity of aquatic habitats in the Southwest. Thus, most western states have fewer species than the southwestern and south-central Canadian provinces. In the entire Canadian Arctic Archipelago, a combined landmass twice the size of Texas, there are only eight species of native fishes. All of mainland Canada and Alaska, with half the land area of North America, harbors only 180 species (23%) and only 10 are endemic. In contrast, the greatest concentration of diversity occurs in the Georgia-sized Tennessee-Cumberland River System, which supports 230 species, over 29 percent of all freshwater fishes in North America. Other regions of high species diversity and endemism are the Ozark Plateau and Ouachita Mountains, northern California–southern Oregon, the confluence region of the Rio Grande and Rio Pecos, and the southern Atlantic Coastal Plain. Among the states and provinces, eight southeastern states rank above all others in fish species diversity. Tennessee has the most native freshwater fishes with 290 species, followed by Alabama (284), Georgia (250), Kentucky (238), Mississippi (209), Arkansas (209), North Carolina (206), Missouri (204), and Virginia (202). Outside of the glaciated areas, Arizona and Utah tie for the least diversity with 28 species, and no western state has more than 70.

As far as we know, pre-Columbian humans in North America did not cause the extinction of any freshwater fish. However, since the 1800s we have lost at least 17 species, more than all the recently extinct mammals, birds, reptiles, and amphibians combined. Most of them were known only from a single spring, lake, or stream, although many widespread species are now endangered. Over the next few decades, freshwater fishes will probably comprise the majority of North American vertebrate extinctions. They are under siege and losing to the human impacts of canal and dam building, channelization, introduction of alien species, pollution, sedimentation, lowering of water tables, changes in water flow, and destruction of wetlands and stream banks. As a result, 105 species are vulnerable, 65 are imperiled, and 91 are critically imperiled. That represents an alarming 33 percent of our fish species whose survival is in jeopardy.

Butterflies

"Just living is not enough," said the butterfly. "One must have sunshine, freedom, and a little flower."
HANS CHRISTIAN ANDERSEN

Happiness is a butterfly, which, when pursued, is always just beyond your grasp, but which, if you will sit down quietly, may alight upon you.
NATHANIEL HAWTHORNE

What is not to like about animals that seem lighter than air, are incapable of harm, and reflect all the colors of the rainbow in a kaleidoscope of intricate and beautiful designs?

Butterflies are like joy with wings. And their various behaviors are no less appealing. If we had not learned about it since childhood, the idea that caterpillars can rearrange themselves into butterflies would sound truly incredible. The Harvester is the only carnivorous butterfly in North America; its larvae feed on woolly aphids. Males of some butterflies locate females in their pupae by smell and wait for them to emerge so they can mate with them first. The caterpillars of some blues exude sweet honeydew that is consumed by attending ants that, in return, provide protection from predators. Each fall, after flying up to 2,000 miles or more, millions of Monarchs from central and eastern North America find their precise wintering site in central Mexico, even though none of them have ever been there before.

North America is currently blessed with at least 587 regularly occurring native butterflies, with another 140 or so subtropical species that cross our southern border with less than annual frequency. A majority of our butterflies are also found in Eurasia or south of the United States, leaving about 209 species that are endemic to North America north of Mexico.

Our smallest butterfly, the Western Pygmy-Blue, is also one of the smallest butterflies in the world with a maximum wingspan of just under 3/4 inch. About 25 other butterflies (8 hairstreaks, 6 blues, 3 metalmarks, and 8 skippers) have wingspans of less than 1 inch. Our largest butterflies, the Eastern Tiger, Giant, and Two-tailed swallowtails, can exceed 6 inches in wingspan.

Nearly 85 percent of North American butterflies are in three families: Hesperiidae (skippers, 217 species), Nymphalidae (brushfoots, 163), and Lycaenidae (gossamerwings, 112). At the subfamily level the greatest number of species are found in the Hesperiinae (grass-skippers, 121), Pyrginae (spread-wing skippers, 77), Theclinae (hairstreaks, 61), Nymphalinae (true brushfoots, 59), and Satyrinae (satyrs, 46). There are no endemic or monotypic families or subfamilies in North America, but the Harvester (Miletinae), American Snout (Libytheinae), and Dull Firetip (Pyrrhopyginae) are our only representatives of their subfamilies. The parnassians (Parnassiinae), emperors (Apaturinae), and monarchs (Danainae) each have just three species north of Mexico, and the leafwings (Charaxinae) have four. *Amblyscirtes* (roadside-skippers) is currently the most diverse genus with 22 species. Nine other genera have more than 15 species: *Papilio* swallowtails (17), *Colias* sulphurs (18), *Lycaena* coppers (16), *Satyrium* hairstreaks (17), *Callophrys* hairstreaks and elfins (17), *Chlosyne* checkerspots and patches (18), *Erynnis* duskywings (17), and *Hesperia* skippers (17).

As with many other animals, the distribution of many butterflies is delimited by major mountain ranges, deserts, arctic treeline, the boreal forests, and the edges of the eastern deciduous forests. The northern limit of freezing temperatures determines how far north many subtropical butterflies occur and explains why they are often present in some places in some (non-freezing) years and not in others. Because the southern boundary of the United States is very near the freezing temperature line, many subtropical butterflies occur in our area only as non-annual visitors. Some of these species may be common in some years and completely absent in others, while others have only been recorded once or a handful of times. Summer and spring temperatures and precipitation are likely important factors limiting the flight period or range of many

BUTTERFLIES

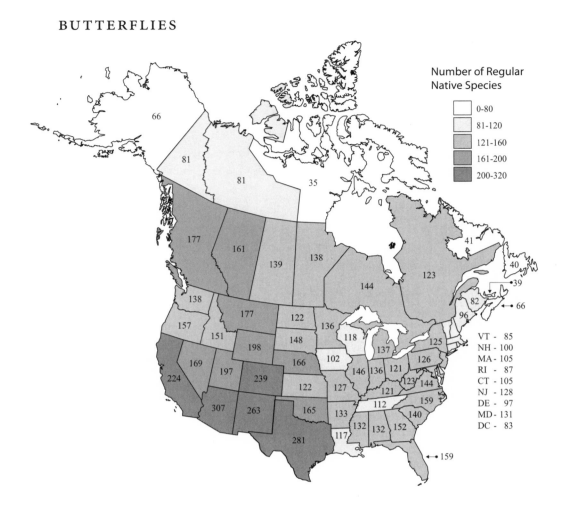

species depending on their individual requirements or tolerances. Specialized habitats such as alpine tundra or bogs, distribution of host plant species, and human alteration or destruction of habitat also shape and restrict the distribution of butterflies. Locally, the population of some butterfly species may fluctuate greatly, even becoming temporarily extinct, because of fire, rainfall patterns, floods, and other temporary disturbances.

Over 60 butterflies have transcontinental ranges, at least at certain latitudes. Some of our most widespread species include Checkered White, Clouded Sulphur, Orange Sulphur, Gray Hairstreak, Spring Azure (but this may represent a complex of species), Mourning Cloak, Red Admiral, Painted Lady, Monarch, Common Checkered-Skipper, and Common Sootywing. The Mourning Cloak is resident nearly everywhere but the central Arctic and peninsular Florida. From its winter range south of freezing temperatures, the Painted Lady each year re-colonizes the entire continent to just north of the 60th parallel, with some even reaching northern Greenland and Iceland. It is the world's most cosmopolitan butterfly, occurring on all continents except Australia and Antarctica.

While a larger number of species have state-sized ranges, only nine are endemic to a single state or province. The Coppermine Sulphur, described in 1990, is, so far, known only from the type locality of Barnard Harbor, 70 miles north of Coppermine, Nunavut. It is one of the few terrestrial animals, and the only species in this book besides the Alaska Marmot, that is only found north of the Arctic Circle. The Florida Leafwing is endemic to southern Florida. The other seven state endemic butterflies are restricted to small areas of California: Sierra Sulphur, Avalon Scrub-Hairstreak, Veined Blue, San Emigdio Blue, Heather Blue, Xerces Blue (extinct), and Unsilvered Fritillary. The Avalon Scrub-Hairstreak is our only insular endemic butterfly and is confined to Santa Catalina Island. Another 23 species are nearly state endemics, with the majority of them also occurring primarily in California.

Most of our butterflies live through freezing winters by hibernating in the egg, larva, pupa, or adult stage, depending on the species. A high level of glycerol in the blood and the conversion of water to a colloid allow them to survive in spite of air temperatures that plummet below -40°F. Arctic and alpine species often have a two-year life cycle to compensate for the short summer. These adaptations have allowed butterflies to inhabit nearly all vegetated areas of the Arctic. Nearly 100 species are found in Alaska and the northern territories of Canada. At least 18 species are year-round residents in the Canadian arctic islands. They include 4 sulphurs, 7 fritillaries, 2 alpines, 3 arctics, the Arctic Blue, and the American Copper. The ranges of the Arctic Blue, Hecla Sulphur, American Copper, Polaris Fritillary, and Arctic Fritillary extend to the northern part of Ellesmere Island, just 500 miles from the North Pole!

The ability of many butterflies to survive in northern latitudes lessens the slope of the latitudinal species gradient in the West, and practically eliminates it in the East. Southern Canadian provinces have butterfly faunas comparable, in number of species, to the eastern states. Four of the top five states for butterfly diversity share a border with Mexico: Arizona leads with 307 species, followed by Texas (281), New Mexico (263), and California (224). Otherwise, the Rocky Mountain region represents the peak of North American butterfly diversity, led by Colorado (239), Wyoming (198), Utah (197), Montana (177), British Columbia (177), and Nevada (169).

Butterflies generally require smaller patches of habitat than vertebrates, so all the native species, as far as we know, probably survived the original human invasion of North America, as well as the subsequent changes wrought by Native Americans and several hundred years of European presence. But by the twentieth century, urban and agricultural development had pushed some butterflies onto that slippery slope of population decline to extinction. The Xerces Blue disappeared in 1943 after its required habitat was covered by the growth of San Francisco. Thankfully, no other butterfly species have been so completely lost but too many are on the brink. Some, like the Florida populations of Schaus's Swallowtail and Miami Blue, are just a hurricane away from oblivion. In the United States, Mitchell's Satyr is the only full species on the federal endangered species list, although 21 subspecies of butterfly are listed. On a global basis The Nature Conservancy lists 74 North American species as vulnerable, 19 as imperiled, and 8 as critically imperiled. Even more are listed when only the U.S. or Canadian populations are considered.

Dragonflies and Damselflies

Deep in the sun-searched growths the dragonfly
Hangs like a blue thread loosened from the sky.

DANTE GABRIEL ROSSETTI, *SILENT NOON*

You hail from Dream-land Dragon-fly?
A stranger hither? So am I,
And (sooth to say) I wonder why
We either of us came!

AGNES M.F.R. DARMESTETER, *TO A DRAGON-FLY*

Dragonflies and damselflies (order Odonata) are like birds and butterflies in that they can be easy to observe, they often possess bright colors and attractive markings, and they exhibit a variety of fascinating behaviors. Like nighthawks, shadowdragons are crepuscular, generally flying only during twilight, usually for less than an hour each day. The Alabama Shadowdragon flies for only 10 to 20 minutes each day, just before nightfall. Female Slaty Skimmers can lay over 2,000 eggs in one session. In the far north, the life cycle of darners may last up to six years. In the Dragonhunter and some other clubtails, for reasons unknown, the male abdominal appendages punch holes in the female's head while in the mating position. Some whiteface males (*Leucorrhinia*) hold rival males in tandem until their mate has finished laying eggs. The Wandering Glider, sometimes called the Globe Skimmer, is the only worldwide dragonfly, found on all continents except Europe and Antarctica. Often with the help of storms, they are capable of crossing oceans on multi-day flights, and have occupied many oceanic islands where they may represent the entire odonate fauna.

The Odonata are one of the most ancient insect groups, having evolved during the Carboniferous period some 300 million years ago. Some Paleozoic ancestors of today's dragonflies were the largest flying insects ever. The Permian species *Meganeuropsis permiana* had a wingspan of 28 inches! Sadly, the days of truly giant dragonflies are long gone, but some of our living species are still among the largest of North American insects. Our largest odonate is the Giant Darner of the southwestern United States with a body length of 4.3 inches and a 5-inch wingspan. Our smallest dragonfly is the Elfin Skimmer, a mere 0.8 inches long. A number of bluets and forktails are about the same length but have slimmer bodies.

Today, North America has 442 species of odonates (131 damselflies, 311 dragonflies), with about 60 percent of them endemic. Canada has 198 species (55 damselflies, 143 dragonflies) but only the Canada Whiteface and Muskeg Emerald are endemic. Our odonates are dominated by three large families that represent over two-thirds of the species: Coenagrionidae (pond damsels, 100 species), Gomphidae (clubtails, 100), and Libellulidae (skimmers, 103). Twelve genera have ten or more species while over one-third of all species are in just five genera: *Gomphus* (clubtails, 38), *Enallagma* (bluets, 36), *Argia* (dancers, 30), *Somatochlora* (emeralds, 26), and *Libellula* (skimmers, 18).

North America has no endemic odonate families. The tropical family Platystictidae was unknown in North America until 1996 when the Desert Shadowdamsel was first

ODONATES

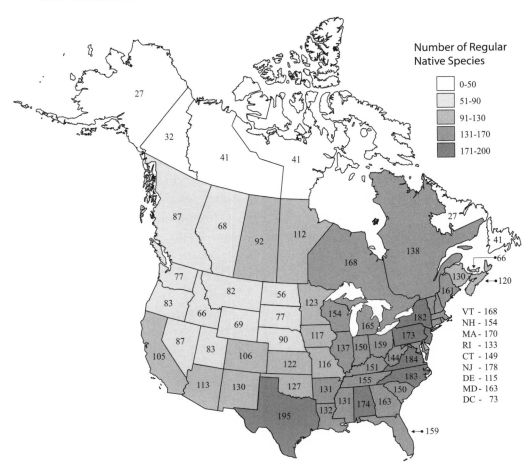

Number of Regular
Native Species

- 0-50
- 51-90
- 91-130
- 131-170
- 171-200

VT - 168
NH - 154
MA - 170
RI - 133
CT - 149
NJ - 178
DE - 115
MD - 163
DC - 73

observed in Arizona. The tropical family Protoneuridae is represented here by just three species of threadtails, which only range into Texas. With fossils dating to the Jurassic (195–136 million years ago), the Petaluridae are the most primitive of the living dragonflies. They are represented by 11 species scattered around the Pacific Rim but only two, the Gray and Black petaltails, are found in North America.

Odonates are found throughout North America except for most of the lands north of treeline. All species need water for breeding and the larval stage, and adults are most conspicuous near water, but adults can also be seen feeding far from water sources. Some species are both migratory and very widespread. The Common Green Darner normally ranges from Honduras to southern Canada, has naturally established itself in Hawaii, and has strayed to Britain and the east coast of Asia. Several other darners range from the United States to Argentina, while others are circumboreal. About 3 spreadwings, 6 pond damsels, 7 darners, 10 emeralds, and 7 skimmers have ranges that extend to or near the northern treeline. The Treeline Emerald has the most northern distribution of our dragonflies, being found across northern Eurasia, Alaska, Yukon, and the Northwest Territories, generally within 60 miles of treeline. About 54 North American odonates (2 broad-winged damsels, 5 spreadwings, 12 pond damsels, 10 darners, 5 emeralds, and 20 skimmers) have transcontinental distributions.

Not counting tropical and subtropical species whose ranges barely extend north of the Mexican border, few North American odonates have very small ranges. A handful of dragonflies, mostly clubtails, have ranges smaller than an average-sized state. Only six species are endemic to a single state. The Purple Skimmer, Tawny Sanddragon, and Westfall's Clubtail are only in Florida, the San Francisco Forktail and Exclamation Damsel are only in California, and the Tennessee Clubtail is restricted to Tennessee. The Ouachita Spiketail is known only from Arkansas but it was not described until 2004 so it may have been overlooked in nearby states.

The spreadwing, pond damsel, broad-winged damsel, petaltail, darner, and skimmer families are fairly evenly distributed throughout North America. The majority of spiketails, clubtails, and cruisers are found in the eastern and central portions of the continent, while the emerald family has a primarily eastern and northern distribution.

The latitudinal gradient of odonate diversity is broadly evident in North America. Texas, with the most species (195), has over twice as many species as Montana (82), which has twice as many species as the Northwest Territories (41). However, unlike other animal groups, it is not the southern border states that dominate odonate diversity, but rather the southeast and east coast states. After Texas comes Virginia (184), North Carolina (183), New York (182), New Jersey (178), Alabama (174), Pennsylvania (173), and Massachusetts (170). Tiny Vermont has more species (168) than any of the remaining states. West of the Great Plains, only New Mexico (130) has more odonates than Rhode Island (133) or Delaware (115). With the exception of these two smallest states, every state east of the Mississippi has as many or more species than any state west of the Mississippi, other than Texas.

No North American dragonflies or damselflies have been extirpated or become extinct due to human activities although the Hine's Emerald is a federally listed endangered species, and The Nature Conservancy considers 52 species to be in some degree of risk: 32 vulnerable, 15 imperiled, and 5 critically imperiled. However, accurate population estimates and trends are lacking for a majority of odonates (see Dunkle 2004).

Extinct Species

*The annihilation of a multitude of species has already been effected, and will continue to
go on hereafter, in a still more rapid ratio, as the colonies of highly civilized nations spread
themselves over unoccupied lands.*

GEOLOGIST CHARLES LYELL, 1859

We have an opportunity unique to our generation: to halt a mass extinction.

REED NOSS

Over the history of life on earth the rate of speciation has usually equaled or exceeded
the rate of extinction. This trend has been upset to varying degrees by a wide variety
of disturbances. An island volcano explodes. A land bridge connects long separated
continents and separates long connected oceans. Weather patterns and ocean currents
shift. Continental glaciers advance or retreat. Such events may trigger a short period of
accelerated extinction followed by a longer period of normal extinction and, perhaps
accelerated, speciation until the previous level of biodiversity is restored or surpassed.
Sometimes the disturbance is so catastrophic that major portions of the world's flora
and fauna are lost forever, and the recovery time can be several million years. Earth
has experienced five of these mass extinctions. They happened at or near the end of
the Ordovician (440 million years ago), Devonian (365 mya), Permian (245 mya), Triassic (210 mya) and Cretaceous periods (66 mya). An asteroid has been implicated in
the Permian extinction, which wiped out as much as 96 percent of all marine species.
Another asteroid caused the Cretaceous extinction that ended the dominance of the
dinosaurs (at least the non-avian variety), the marine ammonites, and half of the other
species in the world.

The background, or natural rate of extinction for a given family or order of organisms has been estimated at somewhere around a few species each million years. In the
continental United States alone, we have eliminated forever probably six species of
birds in the last few hundred years. Add Hawaii and the total number of globally extinct birds rises to 22. For the whole biosphere since 1500, human activities have caused
the extinction of at least 128 species of birds, 119 of which were restricted to islands as
permanent residents or breeders (BirdLife International 2000). Include the impact of
the first humans to inhabit the islands of the Pacific 30,000 to 1,000 years ago, and the
number of globally extinct birds soars to as many as 8,000 (Steadman 1995), including
an estimated 2,000 species of flightless rails! If that figure is close to the truth, then
humans have already caused the extinction of nearly half of all the Recent bird species
of the world. For vertebrates since AD 1600 the figures are at least 23 extinctions in the
continental United States, and 39 including Hawaii. Worldwide in the same period we
have lost at least 88 mammals (MacPhee and Flemming 1999), 100 reptiles, and possibly 134 amphibians, while up to 1,800 species of freshwater fishes are either seriously

endangered or already extinct. Add the loss of plants and invertebrate animals in the last 400 years and the number of recent extinctions is 1,140, about 1,000 times the normal background rate of extinction (Stolzenburg 1996). And these are just the known ones. Many places, especially in tropical forests, are losing thousands of species before most are even described. Human activities have caused the highest rate of extinction, about 30,000 species/year, since the dinosaurs disappeared 65 million years ago.

Today we may be experiencing a sixth mass extinction for which there is no asteroid to blame. We are the smoking gun. In fact, humans share the same lethal characteristics of large asteroid strikes: our impact on wildlife can be evolutionarily sudden, unpredictable, and catastrophic. The Earth's biodiversity may recover but not for several million years, at least.

In AD 77 Pliny the Elder made the earliest known documentation of a human caused extinction (Parejko 2003). He described the disappearance of silphium, a medicinal plant of the Mediterranean. About the same time, Europeans became aware that they had eliminated the Lion from their continent. But the extinction of the Dodo (*Raphus cucullatus*) in the late 1600s may have marked the first time humans were broadly aware of their own culpability in the disappearance of a species (Quammen 1996). While that was a historically important insight it did little to prevent human-caused extinctions over the next several centuries. There are many reasons for this but certainly a major one is that, all too often, the past is soon forgotten while the blighted present becomes the new standard by which future changes are judged.

Only 150 years ago Passenger Pigeons darkened the sky with flocks numbering in the billions while brightly colored Carolina Parakeets decorated trees year-round as far north as Wisconsin and New York. And yet I would guess that not many birders could recite all the important field marks of either species. Field guides usually leave them out because we cannot see them any more. But if we knew what to look for, we might see the ecological impact of their absence. I think all field guides and checklists should include species that have become extinct due to human activity since the time of Columbus, but preferably, as I have done in this book, since at least 46,000 years ago when Modern Humans first eliminated species in Australia. The more we are reminded of them, the more complete will be our ecological and biogeographical understanding of the North American fauna, and, more important, the more strongly we will act to protect what precious little we have left.

Table 3 lists all the mammals, birds, amphibians, freshwater fishes, and butterflies that are known to have become extinct in the continental United States and Canada since the arrival of Columbus. Also included are some species that have not been observed in many years, or after recent intensive searches, and are possibly already extinct. Note that the list does not include extinct subspecies or most of the species in danger of extinction. According to NatureServe (2004) about 710 (20%) of the extant regular native species in this book are globally vulnerable (363 species), imperiled (183), or critically imperiled (164). These at-risk species include 73 mammals (16%), 50 birds (7%), 63 reptiles (20%), 109 amphibians (40%), 261 freshwater fishes (33%), 101 butterflies (17%), and 52 dragonflies and damselflies (12%).

Table 3. Recently (Since AD 1492) Extinct (†) or Probably/Possibly Extinct (†?) Species of North America, North of Mexico

English Name	Scientific Name	Status	Date Last Reported
MAMMALS			
Steller's Seacow	*Hydrodamalis gigas*	†	1768 (Russia)
Caribbean Monk Seal	*Monachus tropicalis*	†	1952
Sea Mink	*Neovison macrodon*	†	1860–1920
BIRDS			
Labrador Duck	*Camptorhynchus labradorius*	†	1878
Eskimo Curlew	*Numenius borealis*	†?	1982
Great Auk	*Pinguinus impennis*	†	1844
Passenger Pigeon	*Ectopistes migratorius*	†	1914
Carolina Parakeet	*Conuropsis carolinensis*	†	1918
Bachman's Warbler	*Vermivora bachmanii*	†	1962
AMPHIBIANS			
Vegas Valley Leopard Frog	*Rana fisheri*	†	1942
Catahoula Salamander	*Plethodon ainsworthi*	†?	1964
Blanco Blind Salamander	*Eurycea robusta*	†?	1951
FRESHWATER FISHES			
Thicktail Chub	*Gila crassicauda*	†	1957
Pahranagat Spinedace	*Lepidomeda altivelis*	†	1938
Phantom Shiner	*Notropis orca*	†	1975
Clear Lake Splittail	*Pogonichthys ciscoides*	†	1970
Las Vegas Dace	*Rhinichthys deaconi*	†	1940
Snake River Sucker	*Chasmistes muriei*	†	1927
Harelip Sucker	*Moxostoma lacerum*	†	1893
Scioto Madtom	*Noturus trautmani*	†	1957
Deepwater Cisco	*Coregonus johannae*	†	1955
Shortnose Cisco	*Coregonus reighardi*	†	1985
Whiteline Topminnow	*Fundulus albolineatus*	†	1889
Amistad Gambusia	*Gambusia amistadensis*	†	1973
San Marcos Gambusia	*Gambusia georgei*	†	1983
Ash Meadows Poolfish	*Empetrichthys merriami*	†	1948
Santa Cruz Pupfish	*Cyprinodon arcuatus*	†	1971
Utah Lake Sculpin	*Cottus echinatus*	†	1928
Maryland Darter	*Etheostoma sellare*	†	1986
BUTTERFLIES			
Xerces Blue	*Glaucopsyche xerces*	†	early 1940s

Happily, reports of the extinction of one bird and two freshwater fishes were exaggerated, although all three species remain vulnerable. Stunningly, the Ivory-billed Woodpecker was possibly rediscovered in 2004 in the swamps of Arkansas, over 60 years after the last confirmed sighting. The Blackfin Cisco is apparently alive in Lake Nipigon (Turgeon et al. 1999). The Miller Lake Lamprey, presumed endemic to Miller Lake, Oregon, where it was eradicated in the 1950s by the state of Oregon (because it preyed on introduced trout!), was recently found in several streams northwest of Upper Klamath Lake (Lorion et al. 2000). Also, there are no recently extinct or missing reptiles, dragonflies, or damselflies, although the possibility remains that a species became extinct before it was ever discovered. The Catahoula Salamander (*Plethodon ainsworthi*) is known from only two specimens collected near Bay Springs, Mississippi, in 1964. At that time the specimens were misidentified as the Slimy Salamander (*Plethodon glutinosus*), an error not discovered until 1991. It was finally described in 1998 after many fruitless searches for more specimens (Lazell 1998). Although hope remains, it was most likely wiped out by deforestation. Only one person, the late Jackson Harold Ainsworth, who collected it and for whom it is scientifically named, is known to have seen the Catahoula Salamander alive. The Santa Cruz Pupfish was not formally recognized as a full species until 2002, over 30 years after the last population was eaten by Largemouth Bass that were introduced for sport fishing. Given the very small ranges of a number of species, especially salamanders and freshwater fishes, and the widespread habitat destruction and alteration that has occurred since the European invasion, it seems likely that a few other species have slipped through the cracks into the oblivion of extinction before we ever knew them.

End-Pleistocene Extinctions

It may be asked why I insert the Mammoth [into a list of American mammals] as if it still existed? I ask in return, why I should omit it, as if it did not exist?
THOMAS JEFFERSON, 1787, *NOTES ON THE STATE OF VIRGINIA*

That we should live in a world without megafauna is an extreme aberration. It is a condition that has not existed for the last 250 million years of evolutionary history.
JOHN TERBORGH

We live on a continent of ghosts.
PAUL S. MARTIN

The state of Maryland has a road sign that says, "Maryland Wildlife—Watch For It." Also on the sign are two silhouettes of native wildlife, a White-tailed Deer and an American Black Bear. These are the largest native land mammals in Maryland, or anywhere else east of the Mississippi, with the exception of Moose in Canada and New England, and a few small populations of reintroduced Elk and American Bison. But if the megafauna (animals as big or bigger than a deer) of the Pleistocene had survived the invasion of North America by *Homo sapiens*, those Maryland road signs would need silhouettes of up to 20 or more mammal species of similar or larger size.

Imagine hiking the Appalachian Trail and meeting up with an American Mastodon or a three-ton Giant Ground-Sloth. On the Great Plains you could have seen herds of American Horses, American Camels, Flat-headed Peccaries, Large-headed Llamas, and Columbian Mammoths. In the swamps and marshes of the southeast there were 300-pound Giant Capybaras, 400-pound Giant Beavers, 700-pound Great Tapirs, and 2,000-pound armored Northern Glyptodonts. In the west your bird list would have had an extra nine species of raptors including the Giant Teratorn that had an estimated wingspan of 16 feet. And everywhere you would have had to watch your back for American Lions, American Scimitar-Cats, Northern Sabertooths, and Giant Short-faced Bears.

The thought of a North American landscape populated by these animals may sound exotic and in the same category of the unimaginable past as the age of dinosaurs. But all these animals and more were present in North America until just 13,000 years ago, just a few thousand years before humans invented agriculture. The next time you see a White-tailed Deer, remember that it browsed alongside American Mastodons and Giant Ground-Sloths. When you see a Pronghorn, remember the American Cheetah that once chased it down. When you see a Turkey Vulture wheeling about in the sky, remember that not long ago it had to share the spoils of a carcass with American Lions, Dire Wolves, Giant Teratorns and other now extinct avian scavengers. Nearly every species in this book that you can see today, including *Homo sapiens*, lived and evolved in the presence of the lost megafauna and their commensals listed below. Even in the backcountry of Yellowstone, with the survival of American Bison and Grizzly Bears, and the reintroduction of Gray Wolves, the presumption of a natural pristine environment is false. Most of the big and fierce species, as well as their ecological associations and impacts, are missing.

In all, at least 50 mammal, 17 bird, and 5 turtle species became extinct in North America around the end of the Pleistocene epoch just 13,000 years ago. The cause of these extinctions may never be known with certainty, but the preponderance of evidence puts the blame squarely on human actions. The following is a very brief summary of the arguments and facts that implicate human activity in most of the late Pleistocene extinctions of North America (Martin 1984; Steadman and Martin 1984; Diamond 1989; Martin 1990; Holman 1995; Martin and Steadman 1999; Flannery 2001).

1. Among late Pleistocene mammals, extinctions disproportionately occurred in the larger species. North America lost 34 genera of mammals over 100 pounds, but only three genera of smaller mammals.

2. Comparable extinctions of megafauna did not occur during or after any of the 20 or so other major climate changes of the Pleistocene. More genera of North American megafauna have become extinct in the last 13,000 years than in the previous four million years.

3. Since the mass extinction caused by the Chicxulub Asteroid 65 million years ago, most extinction episodes can be associated with a change in climate, but all these changes were major cooling events. The megafauna of North America diversified during the last (Wisconsinan) glacial age when the climate was colder and many habitats were more restricted by glaciation, but most of the megafauna became extinct when the climate had been warming for 8,000 years and the retreat of the continental glaciers was well under way.

4. During the late Pleistocene humans coexisted with and hunted large herbivorous mammals and land turtles in North America. Most late Pleistocene extinctions in North America occurred soon after the arrival of Clovis hunting technology. The fact that archaeological sites are associated with relatively

few of the megafauna species is explained by the relatively short time, perhaps 10 years, between the onset of hunting and the extirpation of megafauna in a given area.

5. There is a close correlation between the timing of the first invasion of humans and the extinction of megafauna in North and South America, Australia, Madagascar, and oceanic islands worldwide including Wrangel Island, the West Indies, islands of the Mediterranean, and New Zealand. These events happened at different times and are not correlated with consistent changes in geology or climate. For example, mammoths became extinct in North America around 13,000 BP but survived on Wrangel Island, north of Siberia, until humans arrived around 1700 BC (yes, mammoths were still alive while the pyramids were being built!); large flightless birds became extinct in Australia around 46,000 BP, shortly after humans arrived, but the large flightless moas in New Zealand survived until the first humans arrived 800 years ago; ground-sloths disappeared around 13,000 BP in North America, but not until 6250 BP in Cuba, shortly after the first humans arrived. This pattern probably began about two million years ago in Africa with the first extinction of the vulnerable giant tortoises at the hands of hominid ancestors. Since then, giant tortoises throughout the world have disappeared soon after humans arrived, with the exceptions of the practically uninhabitable Aldabra Island and the remote parts of the Galapagos Islands. The pace of megafauna extinction and depopulation picked up 46,000 years ago, after humans invaded Australia, and has continued into modern times with the huge toll taken on marine megafauna.

6. Compared to North and South America, Australia, and oceanic islands, few late Pleistocene extinctions of megafauna occurred in Eurasia and Africa, but that is where human hunters and megafauna have shared a long evolutionary history as predator and prey.

7. Large mammals that coexisted with humans in Asia and migrated with them into North America were more likely to survive. These immigrants, already adapted to human hunting, included Moose, Elk, bison, Dall's and Bighorn sheep, and Grizzly Bears. The largest surviving mammals that were in North America before humans are the American Black Bear and Mule Deer. The few extinctions that did occur in Eurasia (mammoths, elephants, temperate and wooly rhinoceroses, hippopotamuses, muskoxen, cave bears, giant deer) follow a different temporal pattern from North American extinctions (and from climate patterns) but one that matches the spread of human cultures.

8. The ranges of many surviving species, such as Jaguar, Nine-banded Armadillo, and Collared Peccary, retreated southward, the opposite of what would be expected during a warming trend.

9. Studies of the annual growth rings in the tusks of the last mammoths and mastodons show that these animals were well fed and had a frequency of breeding that matches that of African elephants when under heavy hunting pressure (Fisher 1996, 1997).

10. Dwarfing in many of the surviving large mammals of North America and Australia was correlated with the arrival of humans. Dwarfing can be caused by hunting pressure, when hunters target large individuals, but it would not be expected during a warming trend coupled with the elimination of many potential competitors.

11. Most other mammals and birds that also became extinct at the same time were either predators (large cats, canids, and bears), scavengers (teratorns and vultures), or commensals (vampire bats and mastodon-birds) of the large mammals that became extinct.

12. While few pre-Columbian Holocene extinctions occurred in North America, recent studies have shown that prehistoric hunters significantly depressed populations of mammals, fishes, and birds, especially the larger species. The abundance of large mammals and birds observed in the eighteenth and nineteenth centuries in California (and probably elsewhere) was apparently a rebound effect resulting from the severe sixteenth- or seventeenth-century crash in the population of native hunters (Broughton 2004), who were devastated by diseases introduced by Europeans.

13. With the exception of large land turtles, which would have been desirable and easy prey for humans, the late Pleistocene herpetofauna of North America was the same as that which we find today.

Some scientists are not convinced that humans were the primary cause of the end-Pleistocene extinctions (Grayson and Meltzer 2003). Instead, they usually implicate rapid climate change and the resulting shifts in the structure, composition, nutritional value, and geographic location and extent of different plant communities. No doubt such changes occurred, but to varying degrees, they had occurred many times before without the large-scale extinction of megafauna. The extinct species below had already survived up to 22 glacial advances and retreats, which should only have made them more resilient to such changes. Climate changes certainly affected the megafauna, perhaps making some species more vulnerable, but the human role in their extinction was paramount.

In any case, the North America we see today is missing a major portion of its megafauna and associated species. When an animal becomes extinct its ecological and evolutionary impacts disappear as well. The American Cheetah was probably the reason that Pronghorn can run so fast (Byers 1997). In fact, today the Pronghorn's speed is obsolete because its fastest (unmotorized) predator, the coyote, is 30 mph slower. The huge ground-sloths, mammoths, and mastodons must have had a tremendous effect on the vegetation and, therefore, other herbivores. A number of plants have been left with ecological anachronisms, adaptations designed for animals that have since become extinct, rendering the adaptations obsolete. Today, the seeds of Osage-orange (*Maclura pomifera*) and Coffeetree (*Gymnocladus dioica*) rot inside the fruit lying on the ground, undispersed, because mammoths and mastodons no longer eat them. Honeylocust (*Gleditsia triacanthos*) and Desert Gourds (*Cucurbita foetidissima*), are now mainly found in flood plains (even though they grow well on upland sites) because their megafauna dispersers are gone, leaving them dependent on the vagaries of floods to move them from their parent plant. The armaments of hawthorns (*Crataegus*), American Holly (*Ilex opaca*), yuccas (*Yucca*), and prickly pears (*Opuntia*), among others, were designed to repel or frustrate the megaherbivores (Barlow 2000). As you peruse the list and descriptions of extinct late Pleistocene species below, imagine not only what those animals must have been like, but more relevantly, how things are different today because of their absence.

A Bestiary of Extinct Fauna of the End-Pleistocene

The taxonomy of living animals is an imperfect, often subjective, and sometimes controversial field of study, but the taxonomy of extinct animals is even more problematic since paleontologists must also deal with the scant, fragmentary, and biased nature of their specimens. Some species, like several of the horses and passerine birds, have been described by a single tooth or bone fragment. Even with complete specimens, most of the soft anatomy, behavior, and external appearance must be left to speculation. The number of species in some groups may be reduced with future taxonomic revisions. Also, some species presumed to have become extinct at the end of the Pleistocene may prove to be conspecific with extant species. However, given the bias and chance associated with any particular species becoming fossilized and subsequently found by a paleontologist, there may be some extinct late Pleistocene species yet to be discovered. Recent discoveries include the Plains Deer, first found in 1991, and the Toronto Deer, which was unknown until 1982 when its fossil antlers were discovered during the excavation of a subway tunnel.

There is no official list of accepted fossil species of the North American Pleistocene. Most uncertainty or controversy in the scientific literature surrounds the taxonomic validity at the species level, especially when the fossil specimens are fragmentary or in polytypic genera (like *Bison* and *Equus*). The species and descriptions included below are primarily based on Kurtén and Anderson (1980), Anderson (1984), Steadman and Martin (1984), Holman (1995), and Hulbert (2001). Some extinct fossil species listed in these references have since been invalidated, as explained below. The range of each species is derived from late Pleistocene fossil sites. Of course, had the megafauna and associated species survived, their ranges today would reflect the current climate, distribution of plants and animals, and impacts of humans.

> Pleistocene epoch—1.6 million to 10,000 years ago
> Wisconsinan glacial age—80,000 to 10,000 years ago
> Holocene (Recent) epoch—10,000 years ago to the present

MAMMALS

Most differences between this list and that of Kurtén and Anderson (1980) are explained in the species accounts below. Five other species in Kurtén and Anderson have been deleted due to more recent findings. The Noble Marten, *Martes nobilis,* is now considered to be conspecific with the extant American Marten, *M. americana* (Youngman and Schueler 1991). The Sonoita Ringtail, *Bassariscus sonoitensis,* has been lumped with the extant Ringtail, *B. astutus* (Harris 1990). The River Cat, *Felis amnicola*, from Florida is now conspecific with the Margay, *Leopardus wiedii* (Werdelin 1985). The Fugitive Deer, *Sangamona fugitiva*, was apparently based on a mixture of White-tailed or Mule deer and Elk bones (Churcher 1984). And according to Guthrie (1990), reports of Yak, *Bos grunniens*, from the late Pleistocene in Alaska, were based on discolored bones of modern cattle that had become mixed with late Pleistocene fossils in recent garbage dumps.

Family Mammutidae: Mastodons

†P American Mastodon *Mammut americanum*

The American Mastodon was 9 feet high at the shoulder, about 14 feet long, and weighed up to 6 tons. It had a flat head held horizontally, a well-developed trunk, relatively straight tusks that grew up to 9 feet long, and was primarily a browser. It once roamed throughout North America with most fossils being found in the eastern United States.

Family Gomphotheriidae: Gomphotheres

†P Northern Gomphothere *Cuvieronius tropicus*

Compared to elephants, *Cuvieronius* gomphotheres had proportionally shorter limbs, a longer body, and a longer, more horizontal head with nearly straight tusks. During the Pleistocene, the genus primarily occurred in South and Central America, sometimes ranging north to the southern United States. The Northern Gomphothere was definitely in Florida as recently as 130,000 years ago, and survived in Central and South America up to the end of the Pleistocene. It was likely in Florida at the end of the Pleistocene as well, but the coastal savanna and scrub habitats that it favored were on land that is now as much as 300 feet deep in the Gulf of Mexico, making the discovery of its fossils rather difficult (Dudley 1996; Gary Morgan, pers. comm.). However, since direct evidence of Northern Gomphotheres occupying Florida at the end-Pleistocene is lacking, I do not include it in the lifelist section.

Family Elephantidae: Elephants and Mammoths

†P Columbian Mammoth *Mammuthus columbi*

Primarily a grazer in open areas from Alaska to Mexico, the Columbian Mammoth stood over 12 feet high at the shoulder and had inwardly curving tusks up to 13 feet long. It was one of the largest elephants ever, with some males weighing an estimated 13 tons. Some scientists treat Columbian Mammoths from the late Pleistocene of North America as a different species, Jefferson's Mammoth (*Mammuthus jeffersonii*).

†P Channel Islands Pygmy Mammoth *Mammuthus exilis*

Confined to the northern Channel Islands of California (Santa Cruz, Santa Rosa, and San Miguel), this mammoth was dwarfed by the limited food resources on the islands. It was four to eight feet at the shoulder and weighed 440 to 4,400 pounds. It was the only known dwarf form of a proboscidian in the New World (Roth 1996). Formerly treated as a subspecies of *M. columbi* or *M. jeffersonii*.

†P Woolly Mammoth *Mammuthus primigenius*

Compared to the Columbian Mammoth, the Woolly Mammoth was smaller and had shorter appendages, longer hair, and a more northern distribution. It inhabited the tundra steppe regions of Alaska, Canada, and the northeastern United States. Its eight-foot-long curved tusks were used to scrape snow and ice off the tundra vegetation. Though extinct in North America by the end-Pleistocene, Woolly Mammoths persisted on Wrangel Island, Russia, until 1700 BC.

Family Dugongidae: Dugongs and Seacows

†P Steller's Seacow *Hydrodamalis gigas*

A huge relative of the extant West Indian Manatee, this marine mammal reached lengths of up to 25 feet, weighed about 10 tons, and ranged over much of the Bering Sea and down the west coast of North America. Though huge, it was easy to kill and it may have been hunted by Paleo-Indians in the coastal waters of Alaska around the Bering Strait (Domning 1970). It was "discovered" by Russians in 1741 in its last stronghold, the Commander Islands of the western Bering Sea, but had been hunted to extinction by 1768.

Family Dasypodidae: Armadillos

†P Beautiful Armadillo *Dasypus bellus*

Ecological and morphological equivalent of the extant Nine-banded Armadillo (which has not been found in Pleistocene deposits) but twice its length (nearly four feet) and three times heavier (about 65 pounds). Its range extended from New Mexico, Missouri, and south of New York to Florida and Mexico. Human hunting pressure probably forced its retreat to Central America and caused the decline in body size. Lowered Native American populations caused by the European invasion released armadillos from significant human predation and have allowed them to expand northward to the limits of their endurance of winter and to slowly increase in body size. Someday they may return to the size of *Dasypus bellus* (Flannery 2001). This species is not in the lifelist section because it is probably conspecific with the Nine-banded Armadillo. Human hunting at the end-Pleistocene probably changed the distribution, behavior, and size of the Nine-banded Armadillo but did not cause its extinction.

Family Pampatheriidae: Pampatheres

†P Northern Pampathere *Holmesina septentrionalis*

Looking much like a very large armadillo, the Northern Pampathere was about three feet tall, six feet long, and weighed up to 600 pounds. Unlike armadillos, pampatheres were herbivorous. Their range extended from Kansas and North Carolina south to Texas and Florida.

Family Glyptodontidae: Glyptodonts

†P Northern Glyptodont *Glyptotherium floridanum*

A turtlelike mammal with very short and massive limbs, a heavy, thick tail, and a dome-shaped body covered by a rigid carapace of nearly 2,000 polygonal scutes. The pelvic girdle and many of the vertebrae were fused to the carapace, greatly limiting mobility. Total length was over six feet, height about four feet, and the larger males may have weighed a ton. Semiaquatic. It ranged across the Gulf and Atlantic coastal plains from Texas to South Carolina. Also known as Simpson's Glyptodont.

Family Mylodontidae: Grazing Ground-Sloths

†ᴘ Powerful Ground-Sloth *Paramylodon harlani*

A large and very robust ground-sloth of grasslands from Washington and California to Florida, up to 12 feet tall and weighing 3,500 pounds. It had a coat of shaggy, course hair covering skin that was embedded with small pebblelike bones called dermal ossicles that may have protected it from predators. It walked on the outside of its hind feet and the knuckles of its front feet. It was massive and powerfully built with a huge chest and forelimbs equipped with large claws that may have defended it against Sabertooths, American Lions, and Dire Wolves. Also known as Harlan's Ground Sloth. Formerly placed in the genus *Glossotherium*.

Family Megatheriidae: Browsing Ground-Sloths

†ᴘ Giant Ground-Sloth *Eremotherium laurillardi*

Largest North American ground-sloth of the late Pleistocene. It had a total length of about 18 feet and weighed more than three tons. It walked and stood on the sides of its hind feet and the knuckles of its front feet, and often sat propped against its massive tail, browsing shrubs and trees in savanna. Its remains have been found from South Carolina to Texas and south to Brazil. North American populations were formerly treated as Rusconi's Ground Sloth, *E. rusconi*.

†ᴘ Shasta Ground-Sloth *Nothrotheriops shastensis*

The smallest North American ground-sloth. It weighed up to 400 pounds and reached nine feet in length. Several well-preserved specimens, including skin and hair, have been recovered from dry southwestern caves. It had long, course, pale yellowish hair, a slender build, small head, and prehensile lips. It walked on the sides of its hind feet and the knuckles of its front feet and foraged on a wide variety of plant species and plant parts as evidenced by well-preserved 13,000-year-old dung. It ranged from southern Alberta to California, northern Mexico, and Texas.

Family Megalonychidae: Flat-footed Ground-Sloths

†ᴘ Jefferson's Ground-Sloth *Megalonyx jeffersonii*

A browsing forest dweller the size of an ox, up to nine feet in length, with long powerful claws. Its range included the West Coast, Alaska, Canada, and the rest of the continental United States except for deserts and the Rocky Mountains. Unlike the above ground-sloths, *Megalonyx* walked with the hind feet flat on the ground. First described by, and eventually named after, Thomas Jefferson during his term as Vice President. His description of this species, in a talk to the American Philosophical Society in 1797, was the beginning of vertebrate paleontology in the United States.

Family Castoridae: Beavers

†P **Giant Beaver** *Castoroides ohioensis*

The Giant Beaver was possibly the largest North American rodent of all time. It weighed about 400 pounds, measured over 7 1/2 feet in length and 3 feet in height at the shoulder, and had 4-inch incisors. Its narrow tail was flattened, like the living American Beaver, but it is not known whether the Giant Beaver built dams or lodges. It inhabited lakes, ponds, and swamps from Alaska south to Florida and east of Nebraska.

Family Caviidae: Capybaras and Cavies

†P **Florida Capybara** *Hydrochaeris holmesi*

Similar to the living Capybara (*Hydrochaeris hydrochaeris*) of South America, which is the largest living rodent (up to 110 pounds) and spends most of its time in aquatic or semiaquatic habitats. All records are from Florida. Also called Holmes's Capybara.

†P **Giant Capybara** *Neochoerus pinckneyi*

Much larger than the living Capybara of South America, the Giant Capybara was possibly as large as the Giant Beaver. Presumably it had similar habits and habitat preferences. Recorded from Texas, Florida, and South Carolina. Also called Pinckney's Capybara.

Family Leporidae: Hares and Rabbits

†P **Aztlan Rabbit** *Aztlanolagus agilis*

This unique rabbit was first described in 1986 (Russell and Harris) from fossils in New Mexico, west Texas, and northern Mexico. It was the size of smaller cottontails (*Sylvilagus*) but had the limb proportions, and presumably the running ability, of a jackrabbit (*Lepus*). The Aztlan Rabbit was one of the few small mammals to become extinct near the end of the Pleistocene and may have disappeared just before the arrival of the first humans in the New World.

Family Phyllostomidae: American Leaf-nosed Bats

†P **Stock's Vampire Bat** *Desmodus stocki*

This vampire bat weighed two to three ounces, about twice the weight of the living Common Vampire Bat (*D. rotundus*). It may have been dependant on the blood of the now extinct megamammals. Recorded from Pleistocene deposits in Florida, Texas, and California.

Family Felidae: Cats

†P **American Scimitar-Cat** *Homotherium serum*

The canines of the American Scimitar-Cat were much shorter than in the Northern Sabertooth but still long enough, at four inches, to protrude slightly from the closed mouth, and they were also serrated and laterally compressed. The American Scimitar-Cat had a long neck and long limbs and was large enough, up to 600 pounds, to prey on mammoth calves. It was less common than the Northern Sabertooth, but it had a range that extended from Alaska and the Yukon south to Oregon, Texas, and Florida. Also called Scimitar Cat.

†P American Cheetah *Miracinonyx trumani*

A larger version of the living African Cheetah (*Acinonyx jubatus*). The American Cheetah specialized in chasing down fleet-footed ungulates such as the pronghorns. Unlike its African relative, the American Cheetah had fully retractile claws and more powerful forelimbs. Its fossils have been found in Nevada, Wyoming, and Colorado. Formerly placed in the genus *Acinonyx*. Recent DNA studies suggest that the American Cheetah is more closely related to the Puma and Jaguarundi than the African Cheetah.

†P American Lion *Panthera atrox*

Up to 50 percent larger than the extant African Lion (*P. leo*), the American Lion may have exceeded 800 pounds. It probably hunted in prides and behaved much like its African relatives. Lions immigrated across Beringia during the Wisconsinan glacial period and spread south all the way to Peru, but they were absent from Florida and the forests of the eastern United States. Some scientists classify the American Lion as a subspecies of the African Lion.

†P Northern Sabertooth *Smilodon fatalis*

The size of a lion but with stockier forequarters, a bobbed tail, and serrated upper canines that protruded six inches from the skull. It was an ambush predator of large, slow-moving mammals. It probably did not use its canines for direct stabbing during an attack on prey because the risk of damage to the slender teeth would have been too great. Once the prey was knocked over or pulled down and held still by the powerful front legs, the canines may have been used to cause rapid and extensive damage to major blood vessels and the windpipe with a quick bite to the throat. Such a wound would lead to a quicker kill than the suffocating bite employed by lions (Turner 1997). The Northern Sabertooth ranged from southern Alberta to southern California, Texas, and Florida, and south to Peru. It may be conspecific with Southern Sabertooth (*Smilodon populator*) of South America.

Family Canidae: Wolves and Foxes

†P Dire Wolf *Canis dirus*

The Dire Wolf was the size of a large Gray Wolf but with a much heavier build (about 150 pounds), larger head, and more powerful jaws and dentition. It filled a hyena-like niche of hunter/scavenger and ranged from southern Alberta south throughout most of the United States to Peru. Its remains are closely associated with Northern Sabertooths whose large canines may have prevented efficient feeding, leaving much meat for scavenging Dire Wolves.

øP Dhole *Cuon alpinus*

The Dhole was present in North America, from Alaska to Mexico, only during the late Pleistocene. It had immigrated from Asia where it still survives from Siberia to Sumatra and Java. It is reddish tan with a bushy black tail and weighs 30 to 45 pounds. Dholes hunt in packs and can bring down large deer.

Family Ursidae: Bears

†P Lesser Short-faced Bear *Arctodus pristinus*

Shorter and several hundred pounds smaller than the Giant Short-faced Bear, the Lesser Short-faced Bear was omnivorous and lived in eastern North America from Pennsylvania to Florida and south into Mexico.

†P Giant Short-faced Bear *Arctodus simus*

The most powerful predator of the North American Pleistocene and the largest mammalian carnivore ever, weighing up to 1,800 pounds, about 30 percent larger than Grizzly Bears. Giant Short-faced Bears were much more carnivorous than other bears. They had long limbs for running down any large animal short of a healthy adult mammoth or mastodon. Their heads were short and wide, giving them a catlike face. They were 5 1/2 feet tall at the shoulder, and up to 11 feet tall when standing upright on the hind legs. More closely related to *Tremarctos* than *Ursus* bears. Found throughout North America from Alaska to Mexico but absent from Florida.

†P American Cave-Bear *Tremarctos floridanus*

Related to the extant Spectacled Bear (*Tremarctos ornatus*) of South America, but much larger, weighing up to 1,000 pounds, the American Cave-Bear was almost exclusively herbivorous. New Mexico to Kentucky and Florida, and south into Mexico. Also called Florida Cave Bear.

Family Mephitidae: Skunks

†P Short-faced Skunk *Brachyprotoma obtusata*

Resembling a small spotted skunk (*Spilogale*), the Short-faced Skunk lived in boreal habitats from Arkansas and Pennsylvania to Utah. An upper jaw from western Utah was described as coming from a separate species, *B. brevimala* (Heaton 1985).

Family Equidae: Horses

The true diversity of late Pleistocene horses in North America is unknown. Nearly 60 extinct fossil species have been described in our region, but most have been shown to be synonyms, placed in the wrong genus, or based on characters not unique to the type specimen. Here I follow Winans (1985, 1989) with suggestions by E. Lundelius (pers. comm.) and E. Scott (pers. comm.). However, probably the most accurate statement that can be made is that at the end of the Pleistocene there were several (at least three) species of *Equus* in North America, but there is no general agreement among paleontologists as to the exact number of species involved, or their correct names.

†P Stilt-legged Onager *Equus calobatus*

A large stilt-legged horse from Texas.

†P Mexican Horse *Equus conversidens*

The smallest horse of the late Pleistocene of North America. Occurred in western

North America from Alaska to Mexico. The Feral Ass is a rough equivalent of this species.

†P Pygmy Onager *Equus francisci*

A small stilt-legged horse known from the middle west of the United States and Mexico. Specimens from Wyoming of a similar but slightly smaller horse with different lower incisor morphology may represent an undescribed species.

†P Western Horse *Equus occidentalis*

A large stout-legged horse of the southwest differing from *E. scotti* in lower incisor morphology. The Feral Horse approximates this species.

†P American Horse *Equus scotti*

A large stout-legged horse that occurred throughout much of the contiguous United States and in Mexico. Also called Scott's Horse.

Family Tapiridae: Tapirs

†P Great Tapir *Tapirus haysii*

The largest tapir of the late Pleistocene of North America, weighing over 700 pounds. It has been found south of a line from northern Arizona to southern Indiana and North Carolina. May be conspecific with *T. veroensis*. Formerly called Cope's Tapir, *Tapirus copei*.

†P Vero Tapir *Tapirus veroenis*

About the size of the living tapirs of the Neotropics, but with a shorter muzzle. Eastern United States to California, south of the Wisconsinan ice sheet. California specimens were formerly called California Tapir, *Tapirus californicus* (Graham 2003).

Family Tayassuidae: Peccaries

†P Long-nosed Peccary *Mylohyus nasutus*

A long-legged peccary, weighing about 110 pounds, it lived throughout much of the eastern and central United States.

†P Flat-headed Peccary *Platygonus compressus*

One of the most abundant large mammals of the late Pleistocene of North America. The Flat-headed Peccary traveled in small herds and had long legs adapted for speed in open areas. It had a shoulder height of about 30 inches. It ranged throughout North America south of the Wisconsinan ice sheet to Mexico.

Family Camelidae: Camels and Llamas

†P American Camel *Camelops hesternus*

Probably similar to the extant Arabian Camel (*Camelus dromedarius*) with a single hump but with longer legs. It traveled in large herds over most of western North America from the Yukon to central Mexico. Also called Yesterday's Camel.

†P Large-headed Llama *Hemiauchenia macrocephala*

The Large-headed Llama was larger than the extant Llama (*Lama glama*) of South America, but similar in shape. It had long limbs for running in open grasslands where it grazed. It ranged from California to Florida.

†P Stout-legged Llama *Palaeolama mirifica*

The Stout-legged Llama's shorter limbs and dentition adapted it for browsing and grazing in more rugged areas. Its remains have been found in California, Texas, and Florida.

Family Cervidae: Deer

†P Plains Deer *Bretzia nebrascensis*

Known from two end-Pleistocene antlers that fork at the base. The anterior tine is up to 12 inches long and unbranched. The posterior tine, up to 18 inches long, flattens into a roughly triangular palm with four smaller tines projecting past the palm's end. Discovered in 1991. Known from Nebraska and South Dakota (Gunnell and Foral 1994).

†P Broad-fronted Moose *Cervalces latifrons*

Largest member of the deer family, the Broad-fronted Moose is of Eurasian origin. It was bigger than the extant Moose and had wider but more simply structured antlers. It was present in Alaska and the Yukon Territory during the late Pleistocene.

†P Stag-Moose *Cervalces scotti*

A mooselike deer slightly smaller than the Broad-fronted Moose but larger than the extant Moose. It had very complex, palmated antlers that spanned more than five feet. It inhabited muskegs of the central and eastern United States.

†P Mountain Deer *Navahoceros fricki*

The Mountain Deer was between a Mule Deer and Elk in size, and had stout limbs and three-tined antlers. It was adapted to the rugged terrain of the Rocky Mountains and ranged from Wyoming to Mexico.

†P Toronto Deer *Torontoceros hypogaeus*

A medium-sized deer, about the size of a Caribou, with heavy, unbranched, unpalmated antlers that were round in cross section, had tines, and were oriented almost horizontally from the skull. Described in 1982 from late Pleistocene deposits in Toronto, Canada (Churcher and Peterson 1982).

Family Antilocapridae: Pronghorns

†P Diminutive Pronghorn *Capromeryx minor*

A delicate little pronghorn of the late Pleistocene, it was about 22 inches high at the shoulder, weighed around 22 pounds, and had paired horn-cores. The forward prong was short and triangular in cross section while the rear prong was longer and circular in cross section. Diminutive Pronghorn fossils have been found in southern California, New Mexico, and Texas.

†P Conkling's Pronghorn *Stockoceros conklingi*

A medium-sized pronghorn, smaller than the living species but with heavier limbs adapted to its rugged terrain in New Mexico, Arizona, and Mexico. Its V-shaped horns had prongs of equal length. A slightly larger and more slender-boned version of Conkling's Pronghorn from Arizona, New Mexico, and Nebraska has been described as *Stockoceros onusrosagris*, but its status as a separate species has not been rigorously established.

†P Shuler's Pronghorn *Tetrameryx shuleri*

A four-horned pronghorn of Texas comparable in size to the extant Pronghorn. Its horn-cores were check mark shaped, when viewed from the side, with the forward prong half as long as the back one, and both round in cross section.

Family Bovidae: Bison, Sheep, and Allies

Bison **spp.**

Bison taxonomy is controversial. Some authors believe multiple species coexisted while others interpret differences in fossils as geographic and temporal variation in a single lineage that survives today as the familiar American Bison (*Bison bison*). If the latter is true, then humans (or any other factor) did not cause the extinction of a *Bison* species. However, through hunting pressure, humans probably contributed to the decrease in body size of Bison, and the change from long-horned, more solitary forms to the modern short-horned, herding form. No matter what taxonomy is employed, the *Bison* fauna of North America changed dramatically shortly after the first humans arrived. I am more convinced of the single lineage theory, and so do not list extinct forms in the main lifelist. However, since the issue is unresolved, and to convey how much *Bison* have changed since humans arrived, here are the three extinct species most often reported from the late Pleistocene.

†P Ancient Bison *Bison antiquus*

Slightly larger than the extant American Bison, had a more pronounced hump, and its horns were short and straight.

†P Steppe Bison *Bison priscus*

A large bison with horns three times longer than in the American Bison. The horns were relatively straight before curving up at the ends. The Steppe Bison came from Eurasia and spread from Alaska to Mexico during the late Pleistocene.

†P Giant Bison *Bison latifrons*

A very large bison weighing between 2,500 and 4,000 pounds with a horn span of over eight feet. It was once found throughout most of North America, south of glaciation.

†P Woodland Muskox *Bootherium bombifrons*

Taller and slimmer, but shorter in length than the extant Muskox, the Woodland Muskox weighed up to 900 pounds and had horns that were broadly fused at the base forming a flattened "helmet." It lived in warmer climates than Muskox, its fossils having been found in most unglaciated areas of North America except the southwest and extreme southeast. Specimens formerly known as *Symbos cavifrons* were found to be males of this species (McDonald and Ray 1989).

†P Shrub-Ox *Euceratherium collinum*

Nearly the size of American Bison but probably more closely related to Muskox, the Shrub-Ox had sheeplike horns probably used by males for head butting. It once occurred from Canada south to California, Mexico, and Maryland.

†P Harrington's Mountain Goat *Oreamnos harringtoni*

Similar to the extant Mountain Goat but about 25 percent smaller and with slightly longer and more strongly curved horns. Preserved hair indicates that it was white like its surviving relative, but with more brown hairs suggesting a dirty-white appearance. It lived in the Grand Canyon and cool mountain habitats during the late Pleistocene in Arizona, Nevada, and Mexico.

øP Saiga *Saiga tatarica*

A Eurasian invader during the late Pleistocene, the Saiga is still common in Siberia. In North America during the last two ice ages they inhabited Alaska and the Northwest Territories. Saiga are the size of a slender sheep with an inflated muzzle and short horns that bend backward. They are capable of speeds over 40 mph.

BIRDS

Excluded from this list are some named fossil bird species that have not been well substantiated (for example, *Cremaster*, *Henocitta*, *Neortyx*). Also excluded are some extant species whose mostly tropical ranges included Florida during the late Pleistocene. At that time, Florida had up to twice the land area due to lower sea levels, and change of habitat, rather than human hunting, seems the likely reason for the range retraction in species like Gray-breasted Crake (*Laterallus exilis*), Northern Jacana (*Jacana spinosa*), and Southern Lapwing (*Vanellus chilensis*).

Family Anatidae: Ducks, Geese, and Swans

†P American Pygmy-Goose *Anabernicula gracilenta*

Known from the late Pleistocene of California, Nevada, New Mexico, and Texas. Specimens from Fossil Lake, Oregon, have been treated as a separate species, *A. oregonensis* (Howard 1964).

†P Flightless Scoter *Chendytes lawi*

A flightless duck of the Pacific coast that ranged from southern California to southern

Oregon but probably bred on offshore islands. It is one of only two birds (see Lesser Turkey, below) known to become extinct in the pre-Columbian Holocene, that is, well after the last ice age and the first arrival of humans in North America, but before the first arrival of Europeans. It survived until at least 3780 years BP (Morejohn 1976). The Flightless Scoter would have been easy prey for early Native Americans, and its bones have been found in their middens. Its demise was probably swift and assured once Native Americans were able to travel to the breeding islands (Steadman and Martin 1984).

Family Phasianidae: Partridges, Grouse, Turkeys, and Old World Quail

†P Lesser Turkey *Meleagris crassipes*

The smallest *Meleagris* turkey, fossil or living. Males were as large as the extant female Wild Turkey but had proportionally larger legs. It ranged from northeastern Mexico to the Grand Canyon and became extinct between 6600 and 3300 BP (Rea 1980).

Family Ciconiidae: Storks

†P North American Stork *Ciconia maltha*

A stork known from the late Pleistocene of California, Idaho, Florida, and Cuba. Like the extant Woolly-necked Stork (*Ciconia episcopus*) of Africa and Asia, it may have fed on carrion of now extinct megafauna. There are seven extant species of *Ciconia* storks found in Eurasia, Africa, and South America.

Family Teratornithidae: Teratorns

†P Merriam's Teratorn *Teratornis merriami*

Teratorns (meaning "wonder birds") were scavenging and/or ground-hunting birds of small animals. They were capable of flight but were bigger than condors. Merriam's Teratorn had a wingspan of over 12 feet. It has been recorded in California and Florida.

†P Giant Teratorn *Teratornis incredibilis*

The largest known flying bird of North America with an estimated wingspan of up to 16 feet. It has been found in late Pleistocene deposits in Nevada.

†P Slender Teratorn *Cathartornis gracilis*

A teratorn from the late Pleistocene of Rancho La Brea, California.

Family Cathartidae: New World Vultures

†P La Brea Condor *Breagyps clarki*

Late Pleistocene sites of this long-beaked condor are in California, Nevada, and New Mexico. It was bigger than the extant California Condor, with a wingspan of about 10 feet. It probably fed on the softer parts of a carcass (Hertel 1994).

Family Phoenicopteridae: Flamingos

†P Playa Flamingo *Phoenicopterus minutus*

A small flamingo known from Manix Lake, California, and Fossil Lake, Oregon. The larger extinct Pleistocene flamingo, *P. copei*, may be conspecific with the extant Greater Flamingo (*P. ruber*). Flamingos would have been highly susceptible to nest predation and disturbance by early humans.

Family Accipitridae: Hawks, Kites, and Eagles

†P American Vulture *Neophrontops americanus*

Similar to the Egyptian Vulture (*Neophron percnopterus*), this scavenger has been recorded in southern California and New Mexico. Like the Black Vulture, it probably fed on smaller scraps of a carcass (Hertel 1994).

†P Errant Vulture *Neogyps errans*

Related to Old World vultures, *Neogyps* fossils have been found in California and Nevada. This large vulture probably fed primarily on the tougher parts of a carcass like the hide (Hertel 1994).

†P Long-legged Eagle *Wetmoregyps daggetti*

Known from southern California and Mexico. Possessed an elongated tibia and tarsus.

†P Woodward's Eagle *Amplibuteo woodwardi*

Known from the late Pleistocene of Rancho La Brea, California.

†P Northern Hawk-Eagle *Spizaetus grinnelli*

Recorded from California, Nevada, New Mexico, and Mexico. Larger than both extant species of *Spizaetus* in the New World. Specimens from Nevada and New Mexico have been treated as a separate species, *S. willetti* (Howard 1935).

Family Falconidae: Caracaras and Falcons

øP Yellow-headed Caracara *Milvago chimachima*

The late Pleistocene presence of the Yellow-headed Caracara in Florida is based on fossils formerly regarded as a separate species, *M. readei* (Emslie 1998). This scavenger currently ranges from Costa Rica to Argentina and is known to follow large mammals for the prey they disturb.

Family Phorusrhacidae: Terrorbirds

†P Titan Terrorbird *Titanis walleri*

There is some evidence that this formidable predator survived to the end-Pleistocene in coastal south Texas (Baskin 1995). Titan Terrorbirds stood over six feet tall, weighed well over 300 pounds, and had massive, foot-long hooked beaks and four-inch claws. They were flightless but their wings were not weak and vestigial like those of most flightless birds (and many earlier illustrations of *Titanis*). Instead, they were modified into powerful arms with grasping, three-fingered hands. *Titanis walleri* was originally described from fossils in Florida.

Family Icteridae: Blackbirds and Allies

Mastodon-birds may have been commensals of large mammals in ways similar to modern cowbirds (*Molothrus*), which follow large mammals for the insects they stir up, or the African oxpeckers (*Buphagus*), which feed on the external parasites (ticks and flies) and scabs of large mammals. Both species may be congeneric with extant *Molothrus* cowbirds. "Mastodon-bird" is an admittedly speculative name since it cannot be proved that these birds followed mastodons. However, they certainly did not follow cows.

†P California Mastodon-bird *Pandanaris convexa*

A mastodon-bird from Rancho La Brea, California. Fossils from the middle upper Pleistocene of Florida have been described as *Pandanaris floridana*, but may also represent this species.

†P New Mexico Mastodon-bird *Pyelorhamphus molothroides*

A mastodon-bird from the Organ Mountains of New Mexico.

TURTLES

Family Emydidae: Box and Water Turtles

†P Giant Box Turtle *Terrapene carolina putnami*

This subspecies of the extant Eastern Box Turtle (modern record length 8 1/2 inches) grew to almost 11 inches and lived in the southeastern United States.

Family Testudinidae: Tortoises

Hesperotestudo is an extinct genus of small to very large land tortoises that was endemic to North America and more closely related to the extant gopher tortoises (*Gopherus*) than to the giant-tortoises of the Galapagos, Seychelles, and Mascarene islands (Meylan and Sterrer 2000). Several species survived to the end of the Pleistocene when they would have been easy prey for Modern Humans.

†P North American Giant-Tortoise *Hesperotestudo crassiscutata*

The largest North American tortoise of the late Pleistocene in North America. It weighed up to 500 pounds and had a carapace nearly four feet long. Known from Illinois and Pennsylvania south to Texas and Florida.

†P Smooth-shelled Tortoise *Hesperotestudo equicomes*

This tortoise had a smooth shell over 13 inches long. Known from Kansas.

†P Rough-shelled Tortoise *Hesperotestudo incisa*

A small species from Florida with a rough, 10-inch shell.

†P **Plains Tortoise** *Hesperotestudo wilsoni*

A rough-shelled species with a 10-inch shell that occurred in Oklahoma, Texas, and New Mexico.

øP **Bolson Tortoise** *Gopherus flavomarginatus*

Although it has a carapace up to two feet long and can weigh over 100 pounds, this species was not known to scientists until the late 1950s. Today, it is endangered and confined to a few reserves in northern Mexico, but at the end of the Pleistocene it ranged into southwestern Texas (Van Devender and Bradley 1994). Like other *Gopherus* tortoises, it digs long burrows. Distinguished from living *Gopherus* species by marginal scutes of the carapace that are lighter (with yellow pigment) than the rest of the shell and dark areolae on the carapace scutes.

Species Lifelist

Class Mammalia: Mammals

Order Didelphimorphia: American Opossums

**Family Didelphidae: American Opossums
(North America: 1; World: 87)**

☐ Virginia Opossum   *Didelphis virginiana*   _____

_____

Order Proboscidea: Mastodons, Elephants, and Gomphotheres

Family Mammutidae: Mastodons (North America: 0; World: 0)

☐ American Mastodon   *Mammut americanum*   †P _____

_____

**Family Elephantidae: Elephants and Mammoths
(North America: 0; World: 3)**

☐ Columbian Mammoth   *Mammuthus columbi*   †P _____

_____

☐ Channel Islands   *Mammuthus exilis*   †P _____
Pygmy Mammoth

_____

☐ Woolly Mammoth   *Mammuthus primigenius*   †P _____

_____

Order Sirenia: Dugongs and Manatees

**Family Dugongidae: Dugongs and Seacows
(North America: 0; World: 2)**

☐ Steller's Seacow   *Hydrodamalis gigas*   ØP, † _____

_____

Family Trichechidae: Manatees (North America: 1; World: 3)

☐ West Indian Manatee   *Trichechus manatus*   *   _____

_____

Order Cingulata: Armadillos, Pampatheres, and Glyptodonts

Family Dasypodidae: Armadillos (North America: 1; World: 21)

☐ Nine-banded Armadillo   *Dasypus novemcinctus*   _____

_____

**Family Pampatheriidae: Pampatheres
(North America: 0; World: 0)**

☐ Northern Pampathere   *Holmesina septentrionalis*   †P _____

_____

Family Glyptodontidae: Glyptodonts (North America: 0; World: 0)

☐ Northern Glyptodont   *Glyptotherium floridanum*   †P _____

_____

Order Pilosa: Sloths

**Family Mylodontidae: Grazing Ground-Sloths
(North America: 0; World: 0)**

☐ Powerful Ground-Sloth   *Paramylodon harlani*   †P _____

_____

**Family Megatheriidae: Browsing Ground-Sloths
(North America: 0; World: 0)**

☐ Giant Ground-Sloth   *Eremotherium laurillardi*   †P _____

_____

☐ Shasta Ground-Sloth   *Nothrotheriops shastensis*   †P _____

_____

**Family Megalonychidae: Flat-footed Ground-Sloths
and Two-toed Sloths (North America: 0; World: 2)**

☐ Jefferson's Ground-Sloth   *Megalonyx jeffersonii*   †P _____

_____

Order Primates: Primates

**Family Hominidae: Great Apes and Humans
(North America: 1; World: 5)**

☐ Modern Human *Homo sapiens* _____

_____

Order Rodentia: Rodents

Family Aplodontiidae: Sewellels (North America: 1; World: 1)

☐ Sewellel *Aplodontia rufa* _____

_____

Family Sciuridae: Squirrels (North America: 67; World: 278)

☐ Harris's Antelope Squirrel *Ammospermophilus harrisii* _____

_____

☐ Texas Antelope Squirrel *Ammospermophilus interpres* _____

_____

☐ White-tailed Antelope
Squirrel *Ammospermophilus leucurus* _____

_____

☐ Nelson's Antelope Squirrel *Ammospermophilus nelsoni* * _____

_____

☐ Gunnison's Prairie-dog *Cynomys gunnisoni* _____

_____

☐ White-tailed Prairie-dog *Cynomys leucurus* _____

_____

☐ Black-tailed Prairie-dog *Cynomys ludovicianus* * _____

_____

☐ Utah Prairie-dog *Cynomys parvidens* * _____

_____

☐ Northern Flying Squirrel *Glaucomys sabrinus* _____

_____

☐ Southern Flying Squirrel   *Glaucomys volans*   _____

_____

☐ Alaska Marmot   *Marmota broweri*   _____

_____

☐ Hoary Marmot   *Marmota caligata*   _____

_____

☐ Yellow-bellied Marmot   *Marmota flaviventris*   _____

_____

☐ Woodchuck   *Marmota monax*   _____

_____

☐ Olympic Marmot   *Marmota olympus*   *   _____

_____

☐ Vancouver Island Marmot   *Marmota vancouverensis*   *   _____

_____

☐ Abert's Squirrel   *Sciurus aberti*   _____

_____

☐ Arizona Gray Squirrel   *Sciurus arizonensis*   _____

_____

☐ Eastern Gray Squirrel   *Sciurus carolinensis*   _____

_____

☐ Western Gray Squirrel   *Sciurus griseus*   _____

_____

☐ Mexican Fox Squirrel   *Sciurus nayaritensis*   _____

_____

☐ Eastern Fox Squirrel   *Sciurus niger*   _____

_____

☐ Uinta Ground Squirrel   *Spermophilus armatus*   _____

_____

☐ California Ground Squirrel *Spermophilus beecheyi*

_____

_____

☐ Belding's Ground Squirrel *Spermophilus beldingi*

_____

_____

☐ Idaho Ground Squirrel *Spermophilus brunneus* *

_____

_____

☐ Merriam's Ground Squirrel *Spermophilus canus*

_____

_____

☐ Columbian Ground Squirrel *Spermophilus columbianus*

_____

_____

☐ Wyoming Ground Squirrel *Spermophilus elegans*

_____

_____

☐ Franklin's Ground Squirrel *Spermophilus franklinii*

_____

_____

☐ Golden-mantled Ground Squirrel *Spermophilus lateralis*

_____

_____

☐ Mexican Ground Squirrel *Spermophilus mexicanus*

_____

_____

☐ Mohave Ground Squirrel *Spermophilus mohavensis* *

_____

_____

☐ Piute Ground Squirrel *Spermophilus mollis*

_____

_____

☐ Arctic Ground Squirrel *Spermophilus parryii*

_____

_____

☐ Richardson's Ground Squirrel *Spermophilus richardsonii*

_____

_____

☐ Cascade Golden-mantled   *Spermophilus saturatus*   _____
Ground Squirrel
                                                        _____

☐ Spotted Ground Squirrel   *Spermophilus spilosoma*   _____

                                                        _____

☐ Round-tailed Ground Squirrel   *Spermophilus tereticaudus*   _____

                                                        _____

☐ Townsend's Ground Squirrel   *Spermophilus townsendii*   _____

                                                        _____

☐ Thirteen-lined Ground Squirrel   *Spermophilus*   _____
                                    tridecemlineatus
                                                        _____

☐ Rock Squirrel   *Spermophilus variegatus*   _____

                                                        _____

☐ Washington Ground Squirrel   *Spermophilus*   *   _____
                                washingtoni
                                                        _____

☐ Alpine Chipmunk   *Tamias alpinus*   _____

                                                        _____

☐ Yellow-pine Chipmunk   *Tamias amoenus*   _____

                                                        _____

☐ Gray-footed Chipmunk   *Tamias canipes*   *   _____

                                                        _____

☐ Gray-collared Chipmunk   *Tamias cinereicollis*   _____

                                                        _____

☐ Cliff Chipmunk   *Tamias dorsalis*   _____

                                                        _____

☐ Merriam's Chipmunk   *Tamias merriami*   _____

                                                        _____

☐ Least Chipmunk   *Tamias minimus*   _____

                                                        _____

☐ California Chipmunk   *Tamias obscurus*   _____

_____

☐ Yellow-cheeked Chipmunk   *Tamias ochrogenys*   * _____

_____

☐ Palmer's Chipmunk   *Tamias palmeri*   * _____

_____

☐ Panamint Chipmunk   *Tamias panamintinus*   _____

_____

☐ Long-eared Chipmunk   *Tamias quadrimaculatus*   _____

_____

☐ Colorado Chipmunk   *Tamias quadrivittatus*   _____

_____

☐ Red-tailed Chipmunk   *Tamias ruficaudus*   _____

_____

☐ Hopi Chipmunk   *Tamias rufus*   _____

_____

☐ Shadow Chipmunk   *Tamias senex*   _____

_____

☐ Siskiyou Chipmunk   *Tamias siskiyou*   _____

_____

☐ Sonoma Chipmunk   *Tamias sonomae*   _____

_____

☐ Lodgepole Chipmunk   *Tamias speciosus*   _____

_____

☐ Eastern Chipmunk   *Tamias striatus*   _____

_____

☐ Townsend's Chipmunk   *Tamias townsendii*   _____

_____

☐ Uinta Chipmunk *Tamias umbrinus* _____

_____

☐ Douglas's Squirrel *Tamiasciurus douglasii* _____

_____

☐ Red Squirrel *Tamiasciurus hudsonicus* _____

_____

Family Castoridae: Beavers (North America: 1; World: 2)

☐ American Beaver *Castor canadensis* _____

_____

☐ Giant Beaver *Castoroides ohioensis* †P _____

_____

Family Heteromyidae: Pocket Mice and Kangaroo Rats (North America: 39; World: 60)

☐ Bailey's Pocket Mouse *Chaetodipus baileyi* _____

_____

☐ California Pocket Mouse *Chaetodipus californicus* _____

_____

☐ Chihuahuan Pocket Mouse *Chaetodipus eremicus* _____

_____

☐ San Diego Pocket Mouse *Chaetodipus fallax* _____

_____

☐ Long-tailed Pocket Mouse *Chaetodipus formosus* _____

_____

☐ Hispid Pocket Mouse *Chaetodipus hispidus* _____

_____

☐ Rock Pocket Mouse *Chaetodipus intermedius* _____

_____

☐ Nelson's Pocket Mouse   *Chaetodipus nelsoni*   _____

                                                                    _____

☐ Desert Pocket Mouse   *Chaetodipus penicillatus*   _____

                                                                    _____

☐ Baja California Pocket Mouse   *Chaetodipus rudinoris*   _____

                                                                    _____

☐ Spiny Pocket Mouse   *Chaetodipus spinatus*   _____

                                                                    _____

☐ Agile Kangaroo Rat   *Dipodomys agilis*   *   _____

                                                                    _____

☐ California Kangaroo Rat   *Dipodomys californicus*   _____

                                                                    _____

☐ Gulf Coast Kangaroo Rat   *Dipodomys compactus*   _____

                                                                    _____

☐ Desert Kangaroo Rat   *Dipodomys deserti*   _____

                                                                    _____

☐ Texas Kangaroo Rat   *Dipodomys elator*   *   _____

                                                                    _____

☐ Heermann's Kangaroo Rat   *Dipodomys heermanni* *   _____

                                                                    _____

☐ Giant Kangaroo Rat   *Dipodomys ingens*   *   _____

                                                                    _____

☐ Merriam's Kangaroo Rat   *Dipodomys merriami*   _____

                                                                    _____

☐ Chisel-toothed Kangaroo Rat   *Dipodomys microps*   _____

                                                                    _____

☐ San Joaquin Valley Kangaroo Rat   *Dipodomys nitratoides* *   _____

                                                                    _____

☐ Ord's Kangaroo Rat   *Dipodomys ordii* _____

_____

☐ Panamint Kangaroo Rat   *Dipodomys panamintinus* _____

_____

☐ Dulzura Kangaroo Rat   *Dipodomys simulans* _____

_____

☐ Banner-tailed Kangaroo Rat   *Dipodomys spectabilis* _____

_____

☐ Stephens's Kangaroo Rat   *Dipodomys stephensi*   * _____

_____

☐ Narrow-faced Kangaroo Rat   *Dipodomys venustus* _____

_____

☐ Mexican Spiny Pocket Mouse   *Liomys irroratus* _____

_____

☐ Dark Kangaroo Mouse   *Microdipodops megacephalus* _____

_____

☐ Pale Kangaroo Mouse   *Microdipodops pallidus*   * _____

_____

☐ White-eared Pocket Mouse   *Perognathus alticolus*   * _____

_____

☐ Arizona Pocket Mouse   *Perognathus amplus* _____

_____

☐ Olive-backed Pocket Mouse   *Perognathus fasciatus* _____

_____

☐ Plains Pocket Mouse   *Perognathus flavescens* _____

_____

☐ Silky Pocket Mouse   *Perognathus flavus* _____

_____

☐ San Joaquin Pocket Mouse *Perognathus inornatus* _____

_____

☐ Little Pocket Mouse *Perognathus longimembris* _____

_____

☐ Merriam's Pocket Mouse *Perognathus merriami* _____

_____

☐ Great Basin Pocket Mouse *Perognathus parvus* _____

_____

Family Geomyidae: Pocket Gophers (North America: 18; World: 40)

☐ Yellow-faced Pocket Gopher *Cratogeomys castanops* _____

_____

☐ Desert Pocket Gopher *Geomys arenarius* * _____

_____

☐ Attwater's Pocket Gopher *Geomys attwateri* _____

_____

☐ Baird's Pocket Gopher *Geomys breviceps* _____

_____

☐ Plains Pocket Gopher *Geomys bursarius* _____

_____

☐ Knox Jones's Pocket Gopher *Geomys knoxjonesi* * _____

_____

☐ Texas Pocket Gopher *Geomys personatus* _____

_____

☐ Southeastern Pocket Gopher *Geomys pinetis* _____

_____

☐ Central Texas Pocket Gopher *Geomys texensis* * _____

_____

☐ Botta's Pocket Gopher   *Thomomys bottae*   _____

_____

☐ Camas Pocket Gopher   *Thomomys bulbivorus*   *   _____

_____

☐ Wyoming Pocket Gopher   *Thomomys clusius*   *   _____

_____

☐ Idaho Pocket Gopher   *Thomomys idahoensis*   _____

_____

☐ Western Pocket Gopher   *Thomomys mazama*   _____

_____

☐ Mountain Pocket Gopher   *Thomomys monticola*   _____

_____

☐ Northern Pocket Gopher   *Thomomys talpoides*   _____

_____

☐ Townsend's Pocket Gopher   *Thomomys townsendii*   _____

_____

☐ Southern Pocket Gopher   *Thomomys umbrinus*   _____

_____

Family Dipodidae: Jumping Mice (North America: 4; World: 51)

☐ Woodland Jumping Mouse   *Napaeozapus insignis*   _____

_____

☐ Meadow Jumping Mouse   *Zapus hudsonius*   _____

_____

☐ Western Jumping Mouse   *Zapus princeps*   _____

_____

☐ Pacific Jumping Mouse   *Zapus trinotatus*   _____

_____

Family Cricetidae: New World Mice, Rats, and Voles
(North America: 83; World: 681)

☐ White-footed Vole   *Arborimus albipes*   * _____

_____

☐ Red Tree Vole   *Arborimus longicaudus* * _____

_____

☐ Sonoma Tree Vole   *Arborimus pomo*   * _____

_____

☐ Northern Pygmy Mouse   *Baiomys taylori*   _____

_____

☐ Nearctic Collared Lemming *Dicrostonyx groenlandicus* _____

_____

☐ Ungava Collared Lemming   *Dicrostonyx hudsonius*   _____

_____

☐ Nelson's Collared Lemming *Dicrostonyx nelsoni*   _____

_____

☐ Ogilvie Mountains   *Dicrostonyx nunatakensis* _____
   Collared Lemming

_____

☐ Richardson's Collared Lemming *Dicrostonyx richardsoni* _____

_____

☐ Unalaska Collared Lemming *Dicrostonyx unalascensis* _____

_____

☐ Sagebrush Vole   *Lemmiscus curtatus*   _____

_____

☐ Brown Lemming   *Lemmus trimucronatus*   _____

_____

☐ Insular Vole   *Microtus abbreviatus*   * _____

_____

☐ Beach Vole   *Microtus breweri*   * _____

_____

☐ California Vole   *Microtus californicus*   _____

_____

☐ Gray-tailed Vole   *Microtus canicaudus*   _____

_____

☐ Rock Vole   *Microtus chrotorrhinus*   _____

_____

☐ Long-tailed Vole   *Microtus longicaudus*   _____

_____

☐ Mexican Vole   *Microtus mexicanus*   _____

_____

☐ Singing Vole   *Microtus miurus*   _____

_____

☐ Montane Vole   *Microtus montanus*   _____

_____

☐ Prairie Vole   *Microtus ochrogaster*   _____

_____

☐ Tundra Vole   *Microtus oeconomus*   _____

_____

☐ Creeping Vole   *Microtus oregoni*   _____

_____

☐ Meadow Vole   *Microtus pennsylvanicus*   _____

_____

☐ Woodland Vole   *Microtus pinetorum*   _____

_____

☐ Water Vole   *Microtus richardsoni*   _____

_____

☐	Townsend's Vole	*Microtus townsendii*	
☐	Taiga Vole	*Microtus xanthognathus*	
☐	Western Red-backed Vole	*Myodes californicus*	
☐	Southern Red-backed Vole	*Myodes gapperi*	
☐	Northern Red-backed Vole	*Myodes rutilus*	
☐	Round-tailed Muskrat	*Neofiber alleni*	*
☐	White-throated Woodrat	*Neotoma albigula*	
☐	Bushy-tailed Woodrat	*Neotoma cinerea*	
☐	Arizona Woodrat	*Neotoma devia*	
☐	Eastern Woodrat	*Neotoma floridana*	
☐	Dusky-footed Woodrat	*Neotoma fuscipes*	
☐	Desert Woodrat	*Neotoma lepida*	
☐	White-toothed Woodrat	*Neotoma leucodon*	
☐	Big-eared Woodrat	*Neotoma macrotis*	

☐ Allegheny Woodrat   *Neotoma magister*   * _____

_____

☐ Mexican Woodrat   *Neotoma mexicana* _____

_____

☐ Southern Plains Woodrat   *Neotoma micropus* _____

_____

☐ Stephens's Woodrat   *Neotoma stephensi* _____

_____

☐ Golden Mouse   *Ochrotomys nuttalli* _____

_____

☐ Common Muskrat   *Ondatra zibethicus* _____

_____

☐ Chihuahuan Grasshopper Mouse   *Onychomys arenicola* _____

_____

☐ Northern Grasshopper Mouse   *Onychomys leucogaster* _____

_____

☐ Southern Grasshopper Mouse   *Onychomys torridus* _____

_____

☐ Coues's Rice Rat   *Oryzomys couesi* _____

_____

☐ Marsh Rice Rat   *Oryzomys palustris* _____

_____

☐ Texas Deermouse   *Peromyscus attwateri* _____

_____

☐ Brush Deermouse   *Peromyscus boylii* _____

_____

☐ California Deermouse   *Peromyscus californicus* _____

_____

☐ Canyon Deermouse   *Peromyscus crinitus*   _____

_____

☐ Cactus Deermouse   *Peromyscus eremicus*   _____

_____

☐ Northern Baja Deermouse   *Peromyscus fraterculus*   _____

_____

☐ Cotton Deermouse   *Peromyscus gossypinus*   _____

_____

☐ Saxicoline Deermouse   *Peromyscus gratus*   _____

_____

☐ Northwestern Deermouse   *Peromyscus keeni*   _____

_____

☐ White-footed Deermouse   *Peromyscus leucopus*   _____

_____

☐ North American Deermouse   *Peromyscus maniculatus*   _____

_____

☐ Black-eared Deermouse   *Peromyscus melanotis*   _____

_____

☐ Merriam's Deermouse   *Peromyscus merriami*   _____

_____

☐ Northern Rock Deermouse   *Peromyscus nasutus*   _____

_____

☐ White-ankled Deermouse   *Peromyscus pectoralis*   _____

_____

☐ Oldfield Deermouse   *Peromyscus polionotus*   _____

_____

☐ Pinyon Deermouse   *Peromyscus truei*   _____

_____

☐ Western Heather Vole   *Phenacomys intermedius*   _____

_____

☐ Eastern Heather Vole   *Phenacomys ungava*   _____

_____

☐ Florida Deermouse   *Podomys floridanus*   *   _____

_____

☐ Fulvous Harvest Mouse   *Reithrodontomys fulvescens*   _____

_____

☐ Eastern Harvest Mouse   *Reithrodontomys humulis*   _____

_____

☐ Western Harvest Mouse   *Reithrodontomys megalotis*   _____

_____

☐ Plains Harvest Mouse   *Reithrodontomys montanus*   _____

_____

☐ Saltmarsh Harvest Mouse   *Reithrodontomys raviventris**   _____

_____

☐ Arizona Cotton Rat   *Sigmodon arizonae*   _____

_____

☐ Tawny-bellied Cotton Rat   *Sigmodon fulviventer*   _____

_____

☐ Hispid Cotton Rat   *Sigmodon hispidus*   _____

_____

☐ Yellow-nosed Cotton Rat   *Sigmodon ochrognathus*   _____

_____

☐ Northern Bog Lemming   *Synaptomys borealis*   _____

_____

☐ Southern Bog Lemming   *Synaptomys cooperi*   _____

_____

Family Erethizontidae: New World Porcupines
(North America: 1; World: 16)

☐   North American Porcupine   *Erethizon dorsata*   _____

                                                         _____

Family Caviidae: Capybaras and Cavies
(North America: 0; World: 18)

☐   Florida Capybara   *Hydrochaeris holmesi*   †P _____

                                                         _____

☐   Giant Capybara   *Neochoerus pinckneyi*   †P _____

                                                         _____

Order Lagomorpha: Pikas, Hares, and Rabbits

Family Ochotonidae: Pikas (North America: 2; World: 30)

☐   Collared Pika   *Ochotona collaris*   _____

                                                         _____

☐   American Pika   *Ochotona princeps*   _____

                                                         _____

Family Leporidae: Hares and Rabbits
(North America: 18; World: 61)

☐   Aztlan Rabbit   *Aztlanolagus agilis*   †P _____

                                                         _____

☐   Pygmy Rabbit   *Brachylagus idahoensis*   _____

                                                         _____

☐   Antelope Jackrabbit   *Lepus alleni*   _____

                                                         _____

☐   Snowshoe Hare   *Lepus americanus*   _____

                                                         _____

☐   Arctic Hare   *Lepus arcticus*   _____

                                                         _____

☐   Black-tailed Jackrabbit   *Lepus californicus*   _____

                                                         _____

☐ White-sided Jackrabbit   *Lepus callotis*   * _____

_____

☐ Alaskan Hare   *Lepus othus*   _____

_____

☐ White-tailed Jackrabbit   *Lepus townsendii*   _____

_____

☐ Swamp Rabbit   *Sylvilagus aquaticus*   _____

_____

☐ Desert Cottontail   *Sylvilagus audubonii*   _____

_____

☐ Brush Rabbit   *Sylvilagus bachmani*   _____

_____

☐ Manzano Mountains Cottontail   *Sylvilagus cognatus*   _____

_____

☐ Eastern Cottontail   *Sylvilagus floridanus*   _____

_____

☐ Mountain Cottontail   *Sylvilagus nuttallii*   _____

_____

☐ Appalachian Cottontail   *Sylvilagus obscurus*   _____

_____

☐ Marsh Rabbit   *Sylvilagus palustris*   _____

_____

☐ Robust Cottontail   *Sylvilagus robustus*   * _____

_____

☐ New England Cottontail   *Sylvilagus transitionalis*   _____

_____

Order Soricomorpha: Shrews and Moles

Family Soricidae: Shrews (North America: 38; World: 376)

☐ Northern Short-tailed Shrew   *Blarina brevicauda*   _____

_____

☐ Southern Short-tailed Shrew   *Blarina carolinensis*   _____

_____

☐ Elliot's Short-tailed Shrew   *Blarina hylophaga*   _____

_____

☐ Everglades Short-tailed Shrew   *Blarina peninsulae*   _____

_____

☐ North American Least Shrew   *Cryptotis parva*   _____

_____

☐ Cockrum's Desert Shrew   *Notiosorex cockrumi*   _____

_____

☐ Crawford's Desert Shrew   *Notiosorex crawfordi*   _____

_____

☐ Glacier Bay Water Shrew   *Sorex alaskanus*   _____

_____

☐ Arctic Shrew   *Sorex arcticus*   _____

_____

☐ Arizona Shrew   *Sorex arizonae*   *   _____

_____

☐ Baird's Shrew   *Sorex bairdi*   _____

_____

☐ Marsh Shrew   *Sorex bendirii*   _____

_____

☐ Cinereus Shrew   *Sorex cinereus*   _____

_____

☐ Long-tailed Shrew   *Sorex dispar*   _____

_____

☐ Smoky Shrew   *Sorex fumeus*   _____

_____

☐ Gaspé Shrew   *Sorex gaspensis*   *   _____

_____

☐ Prairie Shrew   *Sorex haydeni*   _____

_____

☐ American Pygmy Shrew   *Sorex hoyi*   _____

_____

☐ Saint Lawrence Island Shrew   *Sorex jacksoni*   *   _____

_____

☐ Southeastern Shrew   *Sorex longirostris*   _____

_____

☐ Mount Lyell Shrew   *Sorex lyelli*   *   _____

_____

☐ Maritime Shrew   *Sorex maritimensis*   _____

_____

☐ Merriam's Shrew   *Sorex merriami*   _____

_____

☐ Dusky Shrew   *Sorex monticolus*   _____

_____

☐ Dwarf Shrew   *Sorex nanus*   _____

_____

☐ New Mexico Shrew   *Sorex neomexicanus*   *   _____

_____

☐ Ornate Shrew   *Sorex ornatus*   _____

_____

☐ Pacific Shrew   *Sorex pacificus*   *   _____

_____

☐ American Water Shrew   *Sorex palustris*   _____

_____

☐ Preble's Shrew   *Sorex preblei*   _____

_____

☐ Pribilof Island Shrew   *Sorex pribilofensis*   *   _____

_____

☐ Fog Shrew   *Sorex sonomae*   _____

_____

☐ Inyo Shrew   *Sorex tenellus*   *   _____

_____

☐ Trowbridge's Shrew   *Sorex trowbridgii*   _____

_____

☐ Tundra Shrew   *Sorex tundrensis*   _____

_____

☐ Barren Ground Shrew   *Sorex ugyunak*   _____

_____

☐ Vagrant Shrew   *Sorex vagrans*   _____

_____

☐ Alaska Tiny Shrew   *Sorex yukonicus*   _____

_____

Family Talpidae: Moles (North America: 7; World: 39)

☐ Star-nosed Mole   *Condylura cristata*   _____

_____

☐ American Shrew Mole   *Neurotrichus gibbsii*   _____

_____

☐ Hairy-tailed Mole   *Parascalops breweri*   _____

_____

☐ Eastern Mole   *Scalopus aquaticus*   _____

_____

☐ Broad-footed Mole   *Scapanus latimanus*   _____

_____

☐ Coast Mole   *Scapanus orarius*   _____

_____

☐ Townsend's Mole   *Scapanus townsendii*   _____

_____

Order Chiroptera: Bats

**Family Phyllostomidae: New World Leaf-nosed Bats
(North America: 4; World: 160)**

☐ Mexican Long-tongued Bat   *Choeronycteris mexicana*   _____

_____

☐ Stock's Vampire Bat   *Desmodus stocki*   †P   _____

_____

☐ Mexican Long-nosed Bat   *Leptonycteris nivalis*   * _____

_____

☐ Lesser Long-nosed Bat   *Leptonycteris yerbabuenae*   _____

_____

☐ California Leaf-nosed Bat *Macrotus californicus*   _____

_____

**Family Mormoopidae: Leaf-chinned Bats
(North America: 1; World: 10)**

☐ Peters's Ghost-faced Bat   *Mormoops megalophylla*   _____

_____

**Family Molossidae: Free-tailed and Mastiff Bats
(North America: 7; World: 100)**

☐ Wagner's Bonneted Bat   *Eumops glaucinus*   _____

_____

☐ Greater Bonneted Bat   *Eumops perotis*   _____

_____

☐ Underwood's Bonneted Bat   *Eumops underwoodi*   _____

_____

☐ Pallas's Mastiff Bat   *Molossus molossus*   _____

_____

☐ Pocketed Free-tailed Bat   *Nyctinomops femorosaccus* _____

_____

☐ Big Free-tailed Bat   *Nyctinomops macrotis*   _____

_____

☐ Mexican Free-tailed Bat   *Tadarida brasiliensis*   _____

_____

**Family Vespertilionidae: Vesper Bats
(North America: 34; World: 407)**

☐ Pallid Bat   *Antrozous pallidus*   _____

_____

☐ Rafinesque's Big-eared Bat *Corynorhinus rafinesquii*   *   _____

_____

☐ Townsend's Big-eared Bat   *Corynorhinus townsendii* _____

_____

☐ Big Brown Bat   *Eptesicus fuscus*   _____

_____

☐ Spotted Bat   *Euderma maculatum*   _____

_____

☐ Allen's Big-eared Bat   *Idionycteris phyllotis*   *   _____

_____

☐ Silver-haired Bat   *Lasionycteris noctivagans*   _____

_____

☐ Western Red Bat   *Lasiurus blossevillii*   _____

_____

☐ Eastern Red Bat   *Lasiurus borealis*   _____

_____

☐ Hoary Bat   *Lasiurus cinereus*   _____

_____

☐ Southern Yellow Bat   *Lasiurus ega*   _____

_____

☐ Northern Yellow Bat   *Lasiurus intermedius*   _____

_____

☐ Seminole Bat   *Lasiurus seminolus*   _____

_____

☐ Western Yellow Bat   *Lasiurus xanthinus*   _____

_____

☐ Southwestern Myotis   *Myotis auriculus*   _____

_____

☐ Southeastern Myotis   *Myotis austroriparius*   *   _____

_____

☐ California Myotis   *Myotis californicus*   _____

_____

☐ Western Small-footed Myotis   *Myotis ciliolabrum*   _____

_____

☐ Long-eared Myotis   *Myotis evotis*   _____

_____

☐ Gray Myotis   *Myotis grisescens*   *

_____

_____

☐ Keen's Myotis   *Myotis keenii*   *

_____

_____

☐ Eastern Small-footed Myotis   *Myotis leibii*   *

_____

_____

☐ Little Brown Myotis   *Myotis lucifugus*

_____

_____

☐ Dark-nosed Small-footed Myotis   *Myotis melanorhinus*

_____

_____

☐ Arizona Myotis   *Myotis occultus*   *

_____

_____

☐ Northern Myotis   *Myotis septentrionalis*

_____

_____

☐ Indiana Myotis   *Myotis sodalis*   *

_____

_____

☐ Fringed Myotis   *Myotis thysanodes*

_____

_____

☐ Cave Myotis   *Myotis velifer*

_____

_____

☐ Long-legged Myotis   *Myotis volans*

_____

_____

☐ Yuma Myotis   *Myotis yumanensis*

_____

_____

☐ Evening Bat   *Nycticeius humeralis*

_____

_____

☐ Western Pipistrelle   *Pipistrellus hesperus*

_____

_____

☐ Eastern Pipistrelle   *Pipistrellus subflavus*   _____

_____

Order Carnivora: Carnivores

Family Felidae: Cats (North America: 7; World: 40)

☐ American Scimitar-Cat   *Homotherium serum*   †P _____

_____

☐ Ocelot   *Leopardus pardalis*   _____

_____

☐ Margay   *Leopardus wiedii*   _____

_____

☐ Canadian Lynx   *Lynx canadensis*   _____

_____

☐ Bobcat   *Lynx rufus*   _____

_____

☐ American Cheetah   *Miracinonyx trumani*   †P _____

_____

☐ American Lion   *Panthera atrox*   †P _____

_____

☐ Jaguar   *Panthera onca*   * _____

_____

☐ Puma   *Puma concolor*   _____

_____

☐ Jaguarundi   *Puma yagouaroundi*   _____

_____

☐ Northern Sabertooth   *Smilodon fatalis*   †P _____

_____

Family Canidae: Wolves, Foxes, and Coyotes
(North America: 9; World: 35)

☐ Dire Wolf   *Canis dirus*   †P _____

_____

☐ Coyote   *Canis latrans*   _____

_____

☐ Gray Wolf   *Canis lupus*   _____

_____

☐ Red Wolf   *Canis rufus*   * _____

_____

☐ Dhole   *Cuon alpinus*   øP _____

_____

☐ Gray Fox   *Urocyon cinereoargenteus*   _____

_____

☐ Island Fox   *Urocyon littoralis*   * _____

_____

☐ Arctic Fox   *Vulpes lagopus*   _____

_____

☐ Kit Fox   *Vulpes macrotis*   _____

_____

☐ Swift Fox   *Vulpes velox*   * _____

_____

☐ Red Fox   *Vulpes vulpes*   _____

_____

Family Ursidae: Bears (North America: 3; World: 8)

☐ Lesser Short-faced Bear   *Arctodus pristinus*   †P _____

_____

☐ Giant Short-faced Bear   *Arctodus simus*   †P _____

_____

☐ American Cave-Bear   *Tremarctos floridanus*   †P _____

_____

☐ American Black Bear   *Ursus americanus* _____

_____

☐ Grizzly Bear   *Ursus arctos* _____

_____

☐ Polar Bear   *Ursus maritimus* _____

_____

Family Otariidae: Eared Seals (North America: 4; World: 16)

☐ Guadalupe Fur Seal   *Arctocephalus townsendi*   * _____

_____

☐ Northern Fur Seal   *Callorhinus ursinus*   * _____

_____

☐ Steller's Sealion   *Eumetopias jubatus*   * _____

_____

☐ California Sealion   *Zalophus californianus* _____

_____

Family Odobenidae: Walruses (North America: 1; World: 1)

☐ Walrus   *Odobenus rosmarus* _____

_____

Family Phocidae: Hair Seals (North America: 10; World: 19)

☐ Hooded Seal   *Cystophora cristata* _____

_____

☐ Bearded Seal   *Erignathus barbatus* _____

_____

☐ Gray Seal   *Halichoerus grypus* _____

_____

☐ Ribbon Seal   *Histriophoca fasciata*   _____

_____

☐ Northern Elephant Seal   *Mirounga angustirostris*   _____

_____

☐ Caribbean Monk Seal   *Monachus tropicalis*   †   _____

_____

☐ Harp Seal   *Pagophilus groenlandicus*   _____

_____

☐ Spotted Seal   *Phoca largha*   _____

_____

☐ Harbor Seal   *Phoca vitulina*   _____

_____

☐ Ringed Seal   *Pusa hispida*   _____

_____

**Family Mustelidae: Weasels and Allies
(North America: 12 World: 59)**

☐ Sea Otter   *Enhydra lutris*   _____

_____

☐ Wolverine   *Gulo gulo*   _____

_____

☐ North American River Otter   *Lontra canadensis*   _____

_____

☐ American Marten   *Martes americana*   _____

_____

☐ Fisher   *Martes pennanti*   _____

_____

☐ Ermine   *Mustela erminea*   _____

_____

☐ Long-tailed Weasel   *Mustela frenata*

☐ Black-footed Ferret   *Mustela nigripes*   *

☐ Least Weasel   *Mustela nivalis*

☐ Sea Mink   *Neovison macrodon*   †

☐ American Mink   *Neovison vison*

☐ American Badger   *Taxidea taxus*

Family Mephitidae: Skunks (North America: 5; World: 12)

☐ Short-faced Skunk   *Brachyprotoma obtusata* †P

☐ American Hog-nosed Skunk   *Conepatus leuconotus*

☐ Hooded Skunk   *Mephitis macroura*

☐ Striped Skunk   *Mephitis mephitis*

☐ Western Spotted Skunk   *Spilogale gracilis*

☐ Eastern Spotted Skunk   *Spilogale putorius*

**Family Procyonidae: Raccoons and Allies
(North America: 3; World: 14)**

☐ Ringtail   *Bassariscus astutus*   _____

_____

☐ White-nosed Coati   *Nasua narica*   _____

_____

☐ Northern Raccoon   *Procyon lotor*   _____

_____

Order Perissodactyla: Horses, Tapirs, and Rhinos

Family Equidae: Horses and Asses (North America: 2; World: 8)

☐ Feral Ass   *Equus asinus*   _____

_____

☐ Feral Horse   *Equus caballus*   _____

_____

☐ Stilt-legged Onager   *Equus calobatus*   †P _____

_____

☐ Mexican Horse   *Equus conversidens*   †P _____

_____

☐ Pygmy Onager   *Equus francisci*   †P _____

_____

☐ Western Horse   *Equus occidentalis*   †P _____

_____

☐ American Horse   *Equus scotti*   †P _____

_____

Family Tapiridae: Tapirs (North America: 0; World: 4)

☐ Great Tapir   *Tapirus haysii*   †P _____

_____

☐ Vero Tapir   *Tapirus veroenis*   †P _____

_____

Order Artiodactyla: Even-toed Ungulates

Family Tayassuidae: Peccaries (North America: 1; World: 3)

☐ Long-nosed Peccary *Mylohyus nasutus* †P _____

_____

☐ Collared Peccary *Pecari tajacu* _____

_____

☐ Flat-headed Peccary *Platygonus compressus* †P _____

_____

**Family Camelidae: Camels and Llamas
(North America: 0; World: 4)**

☐ American Camel *Camelops hesternus* †P _____

_____

☐ Large-headed Llama *Hemiauchenia macrocephala* †P _____

_____

☐ Stout-legged Llama *Palaeolama mirifica* †P _____

_____

Family Cervidae: Deer (North America: 5; World: 51)

☐ Moose *Alces americanus* _____

_____

☐ Plains Deer *Bretzia nebrascensis* †P _____

_____

☐ Broad-fronted Moose *Cervalces latifrons* †P _____

_____

☐ Stag-Moose *Cervalces scotti* †P _____

_____

☐ Elk *Cervus elaphus* _____

_____

☐ Mountain Deer *Navahoceros fricki* †P _____

_____

☐ Mule Deer *Odocoileus hemionus* _____

_____

☐ White-tailed Deer *Odocoileus virginianus* _____

_____

☐ Caribou *Rangifer tarandus* _____

_____

☐ Toronto Deer *Torontoceros hypogaeus* †P _____

_____

Family Antilocapridae: Pronghorn (North America: 1; World: 1)

☐ Pronghorn *Antilocapra americana* _____

_____

☐ Diminutive Pronghorn *Capromeryx minor* †P _____

_____

☐ Conkling's Pronghorn *Stockoceros conklingi* †P _____

_____

☐ Shuler's Pronghorn *Tetrameryx shuleri* †P _____

_____

Family Bovidae: Bison, Sheep, and Allies
(North America: 5; World: 143)

☐ American Bison *Bison bison* _____

_____

☐ Woodland Muskox *Bootherium bombifrons* †P _____

_____

☐ Shrub-Ox *Euceratherium collinum* †P _____

_____

☐ Mountain Goat *Oreamnos americanus* _____

_____

☐ Harrington's Mountain Goat   *Oreamnos harringtoni*   †P _____

_____

☐ Muskox   *Ovibos moschatus*   _____

_____

☐ Bighorn Sheep   *Ovis canadensis*   _____

_____

☐ Dall's Sheep   *Ovis dalli*   _____

_____

☐ Saiga   *Saiga tatarica*   ØP _____

_____

Order Cetacea: Whales, Dolphins, and Porpoises
Family Balaenidae: Right Whales (North America: 2; World: 4)

☐ Bowhead   *Balaena mysticetus*   * _____

_____

☐ North Atlantic Right Whale   *Eubalaena glacialis*   * _____

_____

Family Balaenopteridae: Rorquals (North America: 6; World: 7)

☐ Northern Minke Whale   *Balaenoptera acutorostrata*   _____

_____

☐ Sei Whale   *Balaenoptera borealis*   * _____

_____

☐ Bryde's Whale   *Balaenoptera edeni*   _____

_____

☐ Blue Whale   *Balaenoptera musculus*   * _____

_____

☐ Fin Whale   *Balaenoptera physalus*   * _____

_____

☐ Humpback Whale   *Megaptera novaeangliae*   * _____

_____

Family Eschrichtiidae: Gray Whales (North America: 1; World: 1)

☐ Gray Whale   *Eschrichtius robustus*   _____

_____

**Family Delphinidae: Marine Dolphins
(North America: 21; World: 34)**

☐ Long-beaked
Common Dolphin   *Delphinus capensis*   _____

_____

☐ Short-beaked
Common Dolphin   *Delphinus delphis*   _____

_____

☐ Pygmy Killer Whale   *Feresa attenuata*   _____

_____

☐ Short-finned Pilot Whale   *Globicephala
macrorhynchus*   _____

_____

☐ Long-finned Pilot Whale   *Globicephala melas*   _____

_____

☐ Risso's Dolphin   *Grampus griseus*   _____

_____

☐ Fraser's Dolphin   *Lagenodelphis hosei*   _____

_____

☐ Atlantic White-sided Dolphin   *Lagenorhynchus acutus*   _____

_____

☐ White-beaked Dolphin   *Lagenorhynchus albirostris* _____

_____

☐ Pacific White-sided Dolphin   *Lagenorhynchus
obliquidens*   _____

_____

☐ Northern Right Whale Dolphin   *Lissodelphis borealis*   _____

_____

☐ Killer Whale   *Orcinus orca*   _____

_____

☐ Melon-headed Whale   *Peponocephala electra*   _____

_____

☐ False Killer Whale   *Pseudorca crassidens*   _____

_____

☐ Pantropical Spotted Dolphin   *Stenella attenuata*   _____

_____

☐ Clymene Dolphin   *Stenella clymene*   _____

_____

☐ Striped Dolphin   *Stenella coeruleoalba*   _____

_____

☐ Atlantic Spotted Dolphin   *Stenella frontalis*   _____

_____

☐ Spinner Dolphin   *Stenella longirostris*   _____

_____

☐ Rough-toothed Dolphin   *Steno bredanensis*   _____

_____

☐ Bottlenose Dolphin   *Tursiops truncatus*   _____

_____

Family Monodontidae: Belugas and Narwhals
(North America: 2; World: 2)

☐ Beluga   *Delphinapterus leucas*   _____

_____

☐ Narwhal   *Monodon monoceros*   _____

_____

Family Phocoenidae: Porpoises (North America: 2; World: 6)

☐ Harbor Porpoise   *Phocoena phocoena*   _____

_____

☐ Dall's Porpoise   *Phocoenoides dalli*   _____

_____

Family Physeteridae: Sperm Whales (North America: 3; World: 3)

☐ Pygmy Sperm Whale   *Kogia breviceps*   _____

_____

☐ Dwarf Sperm Whale   *Kogia sima*   _____

_____

☐ Great Sperm Whale   *Physeter catodon*   *   _____

_____

Family Ziphiidae: Beaked Whales (North America: 12; World: 21)

☐ Baird's Beaked Whale   *Berardius bairdii*   _____

_____

☐ Northern Bottlenose Whale   *Hyperoodon ampullatus*   _____

_____

☐ Sowerby's Beaked Whale   *Mesoplodon bidens*   *   _____

_____

☐ Hubbs's Beaked Whale   *Mesoplodon carlhubbsi*   *   _____

_____

☐ Blainville's Beaked Whale   *Mesoplodon densirostris*   _____

_____

☐ Gervais's Beaked Whale   *Mesoplodon europaeus*   *   _____

_____

☐ Ginkgo-toothed Beaked Whale   *Mesoplodon ginkgodens*   _____

_____

☐ True's Beaked Whale   *Mesoplodon mirus*   *   _____

_____

☐ Perrin's Beaked Whale   *Mesoplodon perrini*   _____

_____

☐ Pygmy Beaked Whale   *Mesoplodon peruvianus*   _____

_____

☐ Stejneger's Beaked Whale   *Mesoplodon stejnegeri*   *   _____

_____

☐ Cuvier's Beaked Whale   *Ziphius cavirostris*   _____

_____

NON-ANNUAL VISITORS
Family Phyllostomidae: New World Leaf-nosed Bats

☐ Hairy-legged Vampire Bat   *Diphylla ecaudata*   _____

_____

ALIEN MAMMALS
Family Cercopithecidae: Old World Monkeys

☐ Japanese Macaque   *Macaca fuscata*   _____

_____

☐ Rhesus Macaque   *Macaca mulatta*   _____

_____

Family Leporidae: Hares and Rabbits

☐ European Hare   *Lepus europaeus*   _____

_____

☐ European Rabbit   *Oryctolagus cuniculus*   _____

_____

Family Sciuridae: Squirrels

☐ Red-bellied Squirrel   *Sciurus aureogaster*   _____

_____

Family Cricetidae: New World Mice, Rats, and Voles

☐ European Bank Vole   *Clethrionomys glareolus*

_____

_____

Family Muridae: Mice, Rats, and Voles

☐ House Mouse   *Mus musculus*

_____

_____

☐ Brown Rat   *Rattus norvegicus*

_____

_____

☐ House Rat   *Rattus rattus*

_____

_____

Family Myocastoridae: Nutrias

☐ Nutria   *Myocastor coypus*

_____

_____

Family Felidae: Cats

☐ Feral Cat   *Felis catus*

_____

_____

Family Canidae: Wolves, Foxes, and Coyotes

☐ Feral Dog   *Canis familiaris*

_____

_____

Family Mustelidae: Weasels and Allies

☐ European Ferret   *Mustela putorius*

_____

_____

Family Suidae: Pigs and Hogs

☐ Wild Boar/Feral Pig   *Sus scrofa*

_____

_____

Family Cervidae: Deer

☐ Chital   *Axis axis*

_____

_____

☐ Common Fallow Deer   *Dama dama*

☐ Sika Deer   *Cervus nippon*

☐ Sambar   *Cervus unicolor*

Family Bovidae: Bison, Sheep, and Allies

☐ Barbary Sheep   *Ammotragus lervia*

☐ Blackbuck   *Antilope cervicapra*

☐ Feral Cattle   *Bos taurus*

☐ Nilgai   *Boselaphus tragocamelus*

☐ Feral Goat   *Capra hircus*

☐ Ibex   *Capra ibex*

☐ Himalayan Tahr   *Hemitragus jemlahicus*

☐ Gemsbok   *Oryx gazella*

☐ European Mouflon Sheep   *Ovis aries*

ADDITIONAL SPECIES

☐ _____ _____ _____

_____

☐ _____ _____ _____

_____

☐ _____ _____ _____

_____

☐ _____ _____ _____

_____

☐ _____ _____ _____

_____

☐ _____ _____ _____

_____

☐ _____ _____ _____

_____

☐ _____ _____ _____

_____

☐ _____ _____ _____

_____

☐ _____ _____ _____

_____

☐ _____ _____ _____

_____

☐ _____ _____ _____

_____

☐ _____ _____ _____
                                                 _____
☐ _____ _____ _____
                                                 _____
☐ _____ _____ _____
                                                 _____
☐ _____ _____ _____
                                                 _____
☐ _____ _____ _____
                                                 _____
☐ _____ _____ _____
                                                 _____
☐ _____ _____ _____
                                                 _____
☐ _____ _____ _____
                                                 _____
☐ _____ _____ _____
                                                 _____
☐ _____ _____ _____
                                                 _____
☐ _____ _____ _____
                                                 _____
☐ _____ _____ _____
                                                 _____

☐ _____ _____ _____

_____

☐ _____ _____ _____

_____

☐ _____ _____ _____

_____

☐ _____ _____ _____

_____

☐ _____ _____ _____

_____

☐ _____ _____ _____

_____

☐ _____ _____ _____

_____

☐ _____ _____ _____

_____

☐ _____ _____ _____

_____

☐ _____ _____ _____

_____

☐ _____ _____ _____

_____

☐ _____ _____ _____

_____

Class Aves: Birds

Order Anseriformes: Screamers, Ducks, Geese, and Swans

Family Anatidae: Ducks, Geese, and Swans
(North America: 52; World: 159)

☐ Black-bellied Whistling-Duck   *Dendrocygna autumnalis*   _____

_____

☐ Fulvous Whistling-Duck   *Dendrocygna bicolor*   _____

_____

☐ Bean Goose   *Anser fabalis*   _____

_____

☐ Greater White-fronted Goose   *Anser albifrons*   _____

_____

☐ Emperor Goose   *Chen canagica*   *   _____

_____

☐ Snow Goose   *Chen caerulescens*   _____

_____

☐ Ross's Goose   *Chen rossii*   _____

_____

☐ Brant   *Branta bernicla*   _____

_____

☐ Cackling Goose   *Branta hutchinsii*   _____

_____

☐ Canada Goose   *Branta canadensis*   _____

_____

☐ Trumpeter Swan   *Cygnus buccinator*   _____

_____

☐ Tundra Swan   *Cygnus columbianus*   _____

_____

☐ Whooper Swan   *Cygnus cygnus*   _____

_____

☐ American Pygmy-Goose   *Anabernicula gracilenta*   †P _____

_____

☐ Muscovy Duck   *Cairina moschata*   _____

_____

☐ Wood Duck   *Aix sponsa*   _____

_____

☐ Gadwall   *Anas strepera*   _____

_____

☐ Eurasian Wigeon   *Anas penelope*   _____

_____

☐ American Wigeon   *Anas americana*   _____

_____

☐ American Black Duck   *Anas rubripes*   _____

_____

☐ Mallard   *Anas platyrhynchos*   _____

_____

☐ Mottled Duck   *Anas fulvigula*   _____

_____

☐ Blue-winged Teal   *Anas discors*   _____

_____

☐ Cinnamon Teal   *Anas cyanoptera*   _____

_____

☐ Northern Shoveler   *Anas clypeata*   _____

_____

☐ Northern Pintail   *Anas acuta*   _____

_____

☐ Garganey   *Anas querquedula*   _____

_____

☐ Green-winged Teal   *Anas crecca*   _____

_____

☐ Canvasback   *Aythya valisineria*   _____

_____

☐ Redhead   *Aythya americana*   _____

_____

☐ Common Pochard   *Aythya ferina*   _____

_____

☐ Ring-necked Duck   *Aythya collaris*   _____

_____

☐ Tufted Duck   *Aythya fuligula*   _____

_____

☐ Greater Scaup   *Aythya marila*   _____

_____

☐ Lesser Scaup   *Aythya affinis*   _____

_____

☐ Steller's Eider   *Polysticta stelleri*   *   _____

_____

☐ Spectacled Eider   *Somateria fischeri*   *   _____

_____

☐ King Eider   *Somateria spectabilis*   _____

_____

☐ Common Eider   *Somateria mollissima*   _____

_____

☐ Harlequin Duck   *Histrionicus histrionicus*   _____

_____

☐ Labrador Duck   *Camptorhynchus labradorius* † _____

_____

☐ Surf Scoter   *Melanitta perspicillata*   _____

_____

☐ White-winged Scoter   *Melanitta fusca*   _____

_____

☐ Black Scoter   *Melanitta nigra*   _____

_____

☐ Flightless Scoter   *Chendytes lawi*   †P _____

_____

☐ Long-tailed Duck   *Clangula hyemalis*   _____

_____

☐ Bufflehead   *Bucephala albeola*   _____

_____

☐ Common Goldeneye   *Bucephala clangula*   _____

_____

☐ Barrow's Goldeneye   *Bucephala islandica*   _____

_____

☐ Smew   *Mergellus albellus*   _____

_____

☐ Hooded Merganser   *Lophodytes cucullatus*   _____

_____

☐ Common Merganser   *Mergus merganser*   _____

_____

☐ Red-breasted Merganser   *Mergus serrator*   _____

_____

☐ Masked Duck   *Nomonyx dominicus*   _____

_____

☐ Ruddy Duck   *Oxyura jamaicensis*   _____

_____

Order Galliformes: Gallinaceous Birds

**Family Cracidae: Curassows and Guans
(North America: 1; World: 50)**

☐ Plain Chachalaca   *Ortalis vetula*   _____

_____

**Family Phasianidae: Partridges, Grouse, Turkeys,
and Old World Quail (North America: 12; World: 175)**

☐ Ruffed Grouse   *Bonasa umbellus*   _____

_____

☐ Greater Sage-Grouse   *Centrocercus urophasianus*   _____

_____

☐ Gunnison Sage-Grouse   *Centrocercus minimus*   *   _____

_____

☐ Spruce Grouse   *Falcipennis canadensis*   _____

_____

☐ Willow Ptarmigan   *Lagopus lagopus*   _____

_____

☐ Rock Ptarmigan   *Lagopus muta*   _____

_____

☐ White-tailed Ptarmigan   *Lagopus leucura*   _____

_____

☐ Blue Grouse   *Dendragapus obscurus*   _____

_____

☐ Sharp-tailed Grouse   *Tympanuchus phasianellus*   _____

_____

☐ Greater Prairie-Chicken   *Tympanuchus cupido*   _____

_____

☐ Lesser Prairie-Chicken   *Tympanuchus pallidicinctus* *   _____

_____

☐ Wild Turkey   *Meleagris gallopavo*   _____

_____

☐ Lesser Turkey   *Meleagris crassipes*   †P _____

_____

**Family Odontophoridae: New World Quail
(North America: 6; World: 31)**

☐ Mountain Quail   *Oreortyx pictus*   _____

_____

☐ Scaled Quail   *Callipepla squamata*   _____

_____

☐ California Quail   *Callipepla californica*   _____

_____

☐ Gambel's Quail   *Callipepla gambelii*   _____

_____

☐ Northern Bobwhite   *Colinus virginianus*   _____

_____

☐ Montezuma Quail   *Cyrtonyx montezumae*   _____

_____

Order Gaviiformes: Loons

Family Gaviidae: Loons (North America: 5; World: 5)

☐ Red-throated Loon   *Gavia stellata*   _____

_____

☐ Arctic Loon *Gavia arctica* _____

_____

☐ Pacific Loon *Gavia pacifica* _____

_____

☐ Common Loon *Gavia immer* _____

_____

☐ Yellow-billed Loon *Gavia adamsii* _____

_____

Order Podicipediformes: Grebes

Family Podicipedidae: Grebes (North America: 7; World: 19)

☐ Least Grebe *Tachybaptus dominicus* _____

_____

☐ Pied-billed Grebe *Podilymbus podiceps* _____

_____

☐ Horned Grebe *Podiceps auritus* _____

_____

☐ Red-necked Grebe *Podiceps grisegena* _____

_____

☐ Eared Grebe *Podiceps nigricollis* _____

_____

☐ Western Grebe *Aechmophorus occidentalis* _____

_____

☐ Clark's Grebe *Aechmophorus clarkii* _____

_____

Order Procellariiformes: Tube-nosed Swimmers

Family Diomedeidae: Albatrosses (North America: 3; World: 14)

☐ Laysan Albatross *Phoebastria immutabilis* * _____

_____

☐ Black-footed Albatross   *Phoebastria nigripes*   * _____

_____

☐ Short-tailed Albatross   *Phoebastria albatrus*   * _____

_____

Family Procellariidae: Shearwaters and Petrels
(North America: 17; World: 75)

☐ Northern Fulmar   *Fulmarus glacialis*   _____

_____

☐ Herald Petrel   *Pterodroma arminjoniana*   _____

_____

☐ Murphy's Petrel   *Pterodroma ultima*   * _____

_____

☐ Mottled Petrel   *Pterodroma inexpectata*   * _____

_____

☐ Black-capped Petrel   *Pterodroma hasitata*   * _____

_____

☐ Fea's/Zino's Petrel   *Pterodroma feae/madeira*   * _____

_____

☐ Cook's Petrel   *Pterodroma cookii*   * _____

_____

☐ Cory's Shearwater   *Calonectris diomedea*   _____

_____

☐ Pink-footed Shearwater   *Puffinus creatopus*   * _____

_____

☐ Flesh-footed Shearwater   *Puffinus carneipes*   * _____

_____

☐ Greater Shearwater   *Puffinus gravis*   _____

_____

☐   Buller's Shearwater   *Puffinus bulleri*   *   _____

_____

☐   Sooty Shearwater   *Puffinus griseus*   _____

_____

☐   Short-tailed Shearwater   *Puffinus tenuirostris*   _____

_____

☐   Manx Shearwater   *Puffinus puffinus*   _____

_____

☐   Black-vented Shearwater   *Puffinus opisthomelas*   *   _____

_____

☐   Audubon's Shearwater   *Puffinus lherminieri*   _____

_____

**Family Hydrobatidae: Storm-Petrels
(North America: 7; World: 20)**

☐   Wilson's Storm-Petrel   *Oceanites oceanicus*   _____

_____

☐   Fork-tailed Storm-Petrel   *Oceanodroma furcata*   _____

_____

☐   Leach's Storm-Petrel   *Oceanodroma leucorhoa*   _____

_____

☐   Ashy Storm-Petrel   *Oceanodroma homochroa*   *   _____

_____

☐   Band-rumped Storm-Petrel *Oceanodroma castro*   _____

_____

☐   Black Storm-Petrel   *Oceanodroma melania*   *   _____

_____

☐   Least Storm-Petrel   *Oceanodroma microsoma*   *   _____

_____

Order Pelecaniformes: Totipalmate Birds

Family Phaethontidae: Tropicbirds (North America: 2; World: 3)

☐ White-tailed Tropicbird   *Phaethon lepturus*   _____

_____

☐ Red-billed Tropicbird   *Phaethon aethereus*   _____

_____

Family Sulidae: Boobies and Gannets (North America: 3; World: 10)

☐ Masked Booby   *Sula dactylatra*   _____

_____

☐ Brown Booby   *Sula leucogaster*   _____

_____

☐ Northern Gannet   *Morus bassanus*   _____

_____

Family Pelecanidae: Pelicans (North America: 2; World: 8)

☐ American White Pelican   *Pelecanus erythrorhynchos*   *   _____

_____

☐ Brown Pelican   *Pelecanus occidentalis*   _____

_____

Family Phalacrocoracidae: Cormorants (North America: 6; World: 39)

☐ Brandt's Cormorant   *Phalacrocorax penicillatus*   _____

_____

☐ Neotropic Cormorant   *Phalacrocorax brasilianus*   _____

_____

☐ Double-crested Cormorant   *Phalacrocorax auritus*   _____

_____

☐ Great Cormorant   *Phalacrocorax carbo*   _____

_____

☐ Red-faced Cormorant   *Phalacrocorax urile*   _____

_____

☐ Pelagic Cormorant   *Phalacrocorax pelagicus*   _____

_____

Family Anhingidae: Darters (North America: 1; World: 2)

☐ Anhinga   *Anhinga anhinga*   _____

_____

Family Fregatidae: Frigatebirds (North America: 1; World: 5)

☐ Magnificent Frigatebird   *Fregata magnificens*   _____

_____

Order Ciconiiformes: Herons, Ibises, Storks, New World Vultures, and Allies

**Family Ardeidae: Herons, Bitterns, and Allies
(North America: 12; World: 63)**

☐ American Bittern   *Botaurus lentiginosus*   _____

_____

☐ Least Bittern   *Ixobrychus exilis*   _____

_____

☐ Great Blue Heron   *Ardea herodias*   _____

_____

☐ Great Egret   *Ardea alba*   _____

_____

☐ Snowy Egret   *Egretta thula*   _____

_____

☐ Little Blue Heron   *Egretta caerulea*   _____

_____

☐ Tricolored Heron   *Egretta tricolor*   _____

_____

☐ Reddish Egret   *Egretta rufescens*   _____

_____

☐ Cattle Egret   *Bubulcus ibis*   _____

_____

☐ Green Heron   *Butorides virescens*   _____

_____

☐ Black-crowned Night-Heron   *Nycticorax nycticorax*   _____

_____

☐ Yellow-crowned Night-Heron   *Nyctanassa violacea*   _____

_____

**Family Threskiornithidae: Ibises and Spoonbills
(North America: 4; World: 33)**

☐ White Ibis   *Eudocimus albus*   _____

_____

☐ Glossy Ibis   *Plegadis falcinellus*   _____

_____

☐ White-faced Ibis   *Plegadis chihi*   _____

_____

☐ Roseate Spoonbill   *Platalea ajaja*   _____

_____

Family Ciconiidae: Storks (North America: 1; World: 19)

☐ Wood Stork   *Mycteria americana*   _____

_____

☐ North American Stork   *Ciconia maltha*   †P _____

_____

Family Teratornithidae: Teratorns (North America: 0; World: 0)

☐ Merriam's Teratorn   *Teratornis merriami*   †P _____

_____

☐ Giant Teratorn   *Teratornis incredibilis*   †P _____

_____

☐ Slender Teratorn   *Cathartornis gracilis*   †P _____

_____

Family Cathartidae: New World Vultures
(North America: 3; World: 7)

☐ Black Vulture   *Coragyps atratus*   _____

_____

☐ Turkey Vulture   *Cathartes aura*   _____

_____

☐ California Condor   *Gymnogyps californianus*   *   _____

_____

☐ La Brea Condor   *Breagyps clarki*   †P _____

_____

Order Phoenicopteriformes: Flamingos

Family Phoenicopteridae: Flamingos
(North America: 1; World: 5)

☐ Greater Flamingo   *Phoenicopterus ruber*   *   _____

_____

☐ Playa Flamingo   *Phoenicopterus minutus*   †P _____

_____

Order Falconiformes: Diurnal Birds of Prey

Family Accipitridae: Hawks, Kites, Eagles, and Allies
(North America: 24; World: 238)

☐ Osprey   *Pandion haliaetus*   _____

_____

☐ Hook-billed Kite   *Chondrohierax uncinatus*   _____

_____

☐ Swallow-tailed Kite   *Elanoides forficatus*   _____

_____

☐ White-tailed Kite   *Elanus leucurus*   _____

_____

☐ Snail Kite   *Rostrhamus sociabilis* _____

_____

☐ Mississippi Kite   *Ictinia mississippiensis* _____

_____

☐ Bald Eagle   *Haliaeetus leucocephalus* _____

_____

☐ American Vulture   *Neophrontops americanus*   †P _____

_____

☐ Errant Vulture   *Neogyps errans*   †P _____

_____

☐ Northern Harrier   *Circus cyaneus* _____

_____

☐ Sharp-shinned Hawk   *Accipiter striatus* _____

_____

☐ Cooper's Hawk   *Accipiter cooperii* _____

_____

☐ Northern Goshawk   *Accipiter gentilis* _____

_____

☐ Gray Hawk   *Asturina nitida* _____

_____

☐ Long-legged Eagle   *Wetmoregyps daggetti*   †P _____

_____

☐ Common Black-Hawk   *Buteogallus anthracinus* _____

_____

☐ Harris's Hawk   *Parabuteo unicinctus* _____

_____

☐ Red-shouldered Hawk   *Buteo lineatus* _____

_____

☐ Broad-winged Hawk   *Buteo platypterus*   _____

_____

☐ Short-tailed Hawk   *Buteo brachyurus*   _____

_____

☐ Swainson's Hawk   *Buteo swainsoni*   _____

_____

☐ White-tailed Hawk   *Buteo albicaudatus*   _____

_____

☐ Zone-tailed Hawk   *Buteo albonotatus*   _____

_____

☐ Red-tailed Hawk   *Buteo jamaicensis*   _____

_____

☐ Ferruginous Hawk   *Buteo regalis*   _____

_____

☐ Rough-legged Hawk   *Buteo lagopus*   _____

_____

☐ Woodward's Eagle   *Amplibuteo woodwardi*   †P _____

_____

☐ Golden Eagle   *Aquila chrysaetos*   _____

_____

☐ Northern Hawk-Eagle   *Spizaetus grinnelli*   †P _____

_____

Family Falconidae: Caracaras and Falcons
(North America: 7; World: 63)

☐ Crested Caracara   *Caracara cheriway*   _____

_____

☐ Yellow-headed Caracara   *Milvago chimachima*   øP _____

_____

☐ American Kestrel   *Falco sparverius*   _____

_____

☐ Merlin   *Falco columbarius*   _____

_____

☐ Aplomado Falcon   *Falco femoralis*   _____

_____

☐ Gyrfalcon   *Falco rusticolus*   _____

_____

☐ Peregrine Falcon   *Falco peregrinus*   _____

_____

☐ Prairie Falcon   *Falco mexicanus*   _____

_____

Order Gruiformes: Rails, Cranes, and Allies

**Family Rallidae: Rails, Gallinules, and Coots
(North America: 9; World: 134)**

☐ Yellow Rail   *Coturnicops noveboracensis*   _____

_____

☐ Black Rail   *Laterallus jamaicensis*   _____

_____

☐ Clapper Rail   *Rallus longirostris*   _____

_____

☐ King Rail   *Rallus elegans*   _____

_____

☐ Virginia Rail   *Rallus limicola*   _____

_____

☐ Sora   *Porzana carolina*   _____

_____

☐ Purple Gallinule   *Porphyrio martinica*   _____

_____

☐ Common Moorhen   *Gallinula chloropus* _____

☐ American Coot   *Fulica americana* _____

Family Aramidae: Limpkins (North America: 1; World: 1)

☐ Limpkin   *Aramus guarauna* _____

Family Gruidae: Cranes (North America: 2; World: 15)

☐ Sandhill Crane   *Grus canadensis* _____

☐ Whooping Crane   *Grus americana*   * _____

Family Phorusrhacidae: Terrorbirds (North America: 0; World: 0)

☐ Titan Terrorbird   *Titanis walleri*   †P _____

Order Charadriiformes: Shorebirds, Gulls, Auks, and Allies

Family Charadriidae: Lapwings and Plovers
(North America: 11; World: 66)

☐ Black-bellied Plover   *Pluvialis squatarola* _____

☐ American Golden-Plover   *Pluvialis dominica* _____

☐ Pacific Golden-Plover   *Pluvialis fulva* _____

☐ Lesser Sand-Plover   *Charadrius mongolus* _____

☐ Snowy Plover   *Charadrius alexandrinus* _____

☐ Wilson's Plover   *Charadrius wilsonia*   _____

_____

☐ Common Ringed Plover   *Charadrius hiaticula*   _____

_____

☐ Semipalmated Plover   *Charadrius semipalmatus*   _____

_____

☐ Piping Plover   *Charadrius melodus*   * _____

_____

☐ Killdeer   *Charadrius vociferus*   _____

_____

☐ Mountain Plover   *Charadrius montanus*   * _____

_____

Family Haematopodidae: Oystercatchers
(North America: 2; World: 11)

☐ American Oystercatcher   *Haematopus palliatus*   _____

☐ Black Oystercatcher   *Haematopus bachmani*   _____

_____

Family Recurvirostridae: Stilts and Avocets
(North America: 2; World: 10)

☐ Black-necked Stilt   *Himantopus mexicanus*   _____

_____

☐ American Avocet   *Recurvirostra americana*   _____

_____

Family Scolopacidae: Sandpipers, Phalaropes, and Allies
(North America: 50; World: 89)

☐ Common Greenshank   *Tringa nebularia*   _____

_____

☐ Greater Yellowlegs   *Tringa melanoleuca*   _____

_____

☐ Lesser Yellowlegs   *Tringa flavipes*   _____

_____

☐ Wood Sandpiper   *Tringa glareola*   _____

_____

☐ Solitary Sandpiper   *Tringa solitaria*   _____

_____

☐ Willet   *Catoptrophorus semipalmatus*   _____

_____

☐ Wandering Tattler   *Heteroscelus incanus*   _____

_____

☐ Gray-tailed Tattler   *Heteroscelus brevipes*   _____

_____

☐ Common Sandpiper   *Actitis hypoleucos*   _____

_____

☐ Spotted Sandpiper   *Actitis macularius*   _____

_____

☐ Terek Sandpiper   *Xenus cinereus*   _____

_____

☐ Upland Sandpiper   *Bartramia longicauda*   _____

_____

☐ Eskimo Curlew   *Numenius borealis*   †?_____

_____

☐ Whimbrel   *Numenius phaeopus*   _____

_____

☐ Bristle-thighed Curlew   *Numenius tahitiensis*   *_____

_____

☐ Long-billed Curlew   *Numenius americanus*   _____

_____

☐ Black-tailed Godwit   *Limosa limosa*   _____

_____

☐ Hudsonian Godwit   *Limosa haemastica*   _____

_____

☐ Bar-tailed Godwit   *Limosa lapponica*   _____

_____

☐ Marbled Godwit   *Limosa fedoa*   _____

_____

☐ Ruddy Turnstone   *Arenaria interpres*   _____

_____

☐ Black Turnstone   *Arenaria melanocephala*   _____

_____

☐ Surfbird   *Aphriza virgata*   _____

_____

☐ Red Knot   *Calidris canutus*   _____

_____

☐ Sanderling   *Calidris alba*   _____

_____

☐ Semipalmated Sandpiper   *Calidris pusilla*   _____

_____

☐ Western Sandpiper   *Calidris mauri*   _____

_____

☐ Red-necked Stint   *Calidris ruficollis*   _____

_____

☐ Temminck's Stint   *Calidris temminckii*   _____

_____

☐ Long-toed Stint   *Calidris subminuta*   _____

_____

☐ Least Sandpiper   *Calidris minutilla*   _____

_____

☐ White-rumped Sandpiper   *Calidris fuscicollis*   _____

_____

☐ Baird's Sandpiper   *Calidris bairdii*   _____

_____

☐ Pectoral Sandpiper   *Calidris melanotos*   _____

_____

☐ Sharp-tailed Sandpiper   *Calidris acuminata*   _____

_____

☐ Purple Sandpiper   *Calidris maritima*   _____

_____

☐ Rock Sandpiper   *Calidris ptilocnemis*   _____

_____

☐ Dunlin   *Calidris alpina*   _____

_____

☐ Curlew Sandpiper   *Calidris ferruginea*   _____

_____

☐ Stilt Sandpiper   *Calidris himantopus*   _____

_____

☐ Buff-breasted Sandpiper   *Tryngites subruficollis*   _____

_____

☐ Ruff   *Philomachus pugnax*   _____

_____

☐ Short-billed Dowitcher   *Limnodromus griseus*   _____

_____

☐ Long-billed Dowitcher   *Limnodromus scolopaceus*   _____

_____

☐ Wilson's Snipe   *Gallinago delicata*   _____

_____

☐ Common Snipe   *Gallinago gallinago*   _____

_____

☐ American Woodcock   *Scolopax minor*   _____

_____

☐ Wilson's Phalarope   *Phalaropus tricolor*   _____

_____

☐ Red-necked Phalarope   *Phalaropus lobatus*   _____

_____

☐ Red Phalarope   *Phalaropus fulicarius*   _____

_____

**Family Laridae: Skuas, Gulls, Terns, and Skimmers
(North America: 46; World: 105)**

☐ Great Skua   *Stercorarius skua*   _____

_____

☐ South Polar Skua   *Stercorarius maccormicki*   _____

_____

☐ Pomarine Jaeger   *Stercorarius pomarinus*   _____

_____

☐ Parasitic Jaeger   *Stercorarius parasiticus*   _____

_____

☐ Long-tailed Jaeger   *Stercorarius longicaudus*   _____

_____

☐ Laughing Gull   *Larus atricilla*   _____

_____

☐ Franklin's Gull   *Larus pipixcan*   _____

☐ Little Gull   *Larus minutus*   _____

_____

☐ Black-headed Gull   *Larus ridibundus*   _____

_____

☐ Bonaparte's Gull   *Larus philadelphia*   _____

_____

☐ Heermann's Gull   *Larus heermanni*   _____

_____

☐ Mew Gull   *Larus canus*   _____

_____

☐ Ring-billed Gull   *Larus delawarensis*   _____

_____

☐ California Gull   *Larus californicus*   _____

_____

☐ Herring Gull   *Larus argentatus*   _____

_____

☐ Thayer's Gull   *Larus thayeri*   _____

_____

☐ Iceland Gull   *Larus glaucoides*   _____

_____

☐ Lesser Black-backed Gull   *Larus fuscus*   _____

_____

☐ Slaty-backed Gull   *Larus schistisagus*   _____

_____

☐ Yellow-footed Gull   *Larus livens*   _____

_____

☐ Western Gull   *Larus occidentalis*   _____

_____

☐ Glaucous-winged Gull   *Larus glaucescens*   _____

_____

☐ Glaucous Gull   *Larus hyperboreus*   _____

_____

☐ Great Black-backed Gull   *Larus marinus*   _____

_____

☐ Sabine's Gull   *Xema sabini*   _____

_____

☐ Black-legged Kittiwake   *Rissa tridactyla*   _____

_____

☐ Red-legged Kittiwake   *Rissa brevirostris*   * _____

_____

☐ Ross's Gull   *Rhodostethia rosea*   * _____

_____

☐ Ivory Gull   *Pagophila eburnea*   _____

_____

☐ Gull-billed Tern   *Sterna nilotica*   _____

_____

☐ Caspian Tern   *Sterna caspia*   _____

_____

☐ Royal Tern   *Sterna maxima*   _____

_____

☐ Elegant Tern   *Sterna elegans*   * _____

_____

☐ Sandwich Tern   *Sterna sandvicensis*   _____

_____

☐ Roseate Tern   *Sterna dougallii*   _____

_____

☐ Common Tern   *Sterna hirundo*   _____

_____

☐ Arctic Tern   *Sterna paradisaea*   _____

_____

☐ Forster's Tern   *Sterna forsteri*   _____

_____

☐ Least Tern   *Sterna antillarum*   _____

_____

☐ Aleutian Tern   *Sterna aleutica*   _____

_____

☐ Bridled Tern   *Sterna anaethetus*   _____

_____

☐ Sooty Tern   *Sterna fuscata*   _____

_____

☐ Black Tern   *Chlidonias niger*   _____

_____

☐ Brown Noddy   *Anous stolidus*   _____

_____

☐ Black Noddy   *Anous minutus*   _____

_____

☐ Black Skimmer   *Rynchops niger*   _____

_____

**Family Alcidae: Auks, Murres, and Puffins
(North America: 20; World: 23)**

☐ Dovekie   *Alle alle*   _____

_____

☐ Common Murre   *Uria aalge*   _____

_____

☐ Thick-billed Murre   *Uria lomvia*   _____

_____

☐ Razorbill   *Alca torda*   _____

_____

☐ Great Auk   *Pinguinus impennis*   † _____

_____

☐ Black Guillemot   *Cepphus grylle*   _____

_____

☐ Pigeon Guillemot   *Cepphus columba*   _____

_____

☐ Marbled Murrelet   *Brachyramphus marmoratus* * _____

_____

☐ Kittlitz's Murrelet   *Brachyramphus brevirostris* * _____

_____

☐ Xantus's Murrelet   *Synthliboramphus hypoleucus* * _____

_____

☐ Craveri's Murrelet   *Synthliboramphus craveri* * _____

_____

☐ Ancient Murrelet   *Synthliboramphus antiquus*   _____

_____

☐ Cassin's Auklet   *Ptychoramphus aleuticus*   _____

_____

☐ Parakeet Auklet   *Aethia psittacula*   _____

_____

☐ Least Auklet   *Aethia pusilla*   _____

_____

☐ Whiskered Auklet   *Aethia pygmaea*   _____

_____

☐ Crested Auklet   *Aethia cristatella*

_____

_____

☐ Rhinoceros Auklet   *Cerorhinca monocerata*

_____

_____

☐ Atlantic Puffin   *Fratercula arctica*

_____

_____

☐ Horned Puffin   *Fratercula corniculata*

_____

_____

☐ Tufted Puffin   *Fratercula cirrhata*

_____

_____

Order Columbiformes: Pigeons and Doves

**Family Columbidae: Pigeons and Doves
(North America: 9; World: 308)**

☐ White-crowned Pigeon   *Patagioenas leucocephala*   *

_____

_____

☐ Red-billed Pigeon   *Patagioenas flavirostris*

_____

_____

☐ Band-tailed Pigeon   *Patagioenas fasciata*

_____

_____

☐ White-winged Dove   *Zenaida asiatica*

_____

_____

☐ Mourning Dove   *Zenaida macroura*

_____

_____

☐ Passenger Pigeon   *Ectopistes migratorius*   †

_____

_____

☐ Inca Dove   *Columbina inca*

_____

_____

☐ Common Ground-Dove   *Columbina passerina*

_____

_____

☐ Ruddy Ground-Dove   *Columbina talpacoti*

_____

_____

☐ White-tipped Dove   *Leptotila verreauxi*

_____

_____

Order Psittaciformes: Parrots

Family Psittacidae: Lories, Parakeets, Macaws, and Parrots (North America: 0; World: 333)

☐ Carolina Parakeet   *Conuropsis carolinensis*   †

_____

_____

Order Cuculiformes: Cuckoos and Allies

Family Cuculidae: Cuckoos, Roadrunners, and Anis (North America: 7; World: 138)

☐ Common Cuckoo   *Cuculus canorus*

_____

_____

☐ Black-billed Cuckoo   *Coccyzus erythropthalmus*

_____

_____

☐ Yellow-billed Cuckoo   *Coccyzus americanus*

_____

_____

☐ Mangrove Cuckoo   *Coccyzus minor*

_____

_____

☐ Greater Roadrunner   *Geococcyx californianus*

_____

_____

☐ Smooth-billed Ani   *Crotophaga ani*

_____

_____

☐ Groove-billed Ani   *Crotophaga sulcirostris*

_____

_____

Order Strigiformes: Owls

Family Tytonidae: Barn Owls (North America: 1; World: 16)

☐ Barn Owl   *Tyto alba*

_____

_____

Family Strigidae: Typical Owls (North America: 18; World: 190)

☐ Flammulated Owl   *Otus flammeolus*

_____

_____

☐ Western Screech-Owl   *Megascops kennicottii*

_____

_____

☐ Eastern Screech-Owl   *Megascops asio*

_____

_____

☐ Whiskered Screech-Owl   *Megascops trichopsis*

_____

_____

☐ Great Horned Owl   *Bubo virginianus*

_____

_____

☐ Snowy Owl   *Bubo scandiacus*

_____

_____

☐ Northern Hawk Owl   *Surnia ulula*

_____

_____

☐ Northern Pygmy-Owl   *Glaucidium gnoma*

_____

_____

☐ Ferruginous Pygmy-Owl   *Glaucidium brasilianum*

_____

_____

☐ Elf Owl   *Micrathene whitneyi*

_____

_____

☐ Burrowing Owl   *Athene cunicularia*

_____

_____

☐ Spotted Owl   *Strix occidentalis*   *

_____

_____

☐ Barred Owl   *Strix varia*

_____

_____

☐ Great Gray Owl   *Strix nebulosa*

_____

_____

☐ Long-eared Owl   *Asio otus*   _____

_____

☐ Short-eared Owl   *Asio flammeus*   _____

_____

☐ Boreal Owl   *Aegolius funereus*   _____

_____

☐ Northern Saw-whet Owl   *Aegolius acadicus*   _____

_____

Order Caprimulgiformes: Goatsuckers, Oilbirds, and Allies

Family Caprimulgidae: Nighthawks and Nightjars
(North America: 7; World: 89)

☐ Lesser Nighthawk   *Chordeiles acutipennis*   _____

_____

☐ Common Nighthawk   *Chordeiles minor*   _____

_____

☐ Antillean Nighthawk   *Chordeiles gundlachii*   _____

_____

☐ Common Pauraque   *Nyctidromus albicollis*   _____

_____

☐ Common Poorwill   *Phalaenoptilus nuttallii*   _____

_____

☐ Chuck-will's-widow   *Caprimulgus carolinensis*   _____

_____

☐ Whip-poor-will   *Caprimulgus vociferus*   _____

_____

Order Apodiformes: Swifts and Hummingbirds

Family Apodidae: Swifts (North America: 4; World: 99)

☐ Black Swift   *Cypseloides niger*   _____

_____

☐ Chimney Swift   *Chaetura pelagica*   _____

☐ Vaux's Swift   *Chaetura vauxi*   _____

_____

☐ White-throated Swift   *Aeronautes saxatalis*   _____

_____

Family Trochilidae: Hummingbirds
(North America: 16; World: 336)

☐ Broad-billed Hummingbird   *Cynanthus latirostris*   _____

_____

☐ White-eared Hummingbird   *Hylocharis leucotis*   _____

_____

☐ Berylline Hummingbird   *Amazilia beryllina*   _____

_____

☐ Buff-bellied Hummingbird   *Amazilia yucatanensis*   _____

_____

☐ Violet-crowned Hummingbird   *Amazilia violiceps*   _____

_____

☐ Blue-throated Hummingbird   *Lampornis clemenciae*   _____

_____

☐ Magnificent Hummingbird   *Eugenes fulgens*   _____

_____

☐ Lucifer Hummingbird   *Calothorax lucifer*   _____

_____

☐ Ruby-throated Hummingbird   *Archilochus colubris*   _____

_____

☐ Black-chinned Hummingbird   *Archilochus alexandri*   _____

_____

☐ Anna's Hummingbird   *Calypte anna*

_____

_____

☐ Costa's Hummingbird   *Calypte costae*

_____

_____

☐ Calliope Hummingbird   *Stellula calliope*

_____

_____

☐ Broad-tailed Hummingbird   *Selasphorus platycercus*

_____

_____

☐ Rufous Hummingbird   *Selasphorus rufus*

_____

_____

☐ Allen's Hummingbird   *Selasphorus sasin*

_____

_____

Order Trogoniformes: Trogons

Family Trogonidae: Trogons (North America: 1; World: 39)

☐ Elegant Trogon   *Trogon elegans*

_____

_____

Order Coraciiformes: Rollers, Motmots, Kingfishers, and Allies

Family Alcedinidae: Kingfishers (North America: 3; World: 93)

☐ Ringed Kingfisher   *Ceryle torquatus*

_____

_____

☐ Belted Kingfisher   *Ceryle alcyon*

_____

_____

☐ Green Kingfisher   *Chloroceryle americana*

_____

_____

Order Piciformes: Puffbirds, Jacamars, Toucans, Woodpeckers, and Allies

**Family Picidae: Woodpeckers and Allies
(North America: 23; World: 218)**

☐ Lewis's Woodpecker   *Melanerpes lewis*

_____

_____

☐ Red-headed Woodpecker *Melanerpes erythrocephalus* _____

_____

☐ Acorn Woodpecker *Melanerpes formicivorus* _____

_____

☐ Gila Woodpecker *Melanerpes uropygialis* _____

_____

☐ Golden-fronted Woodpecker *Melanerpes aurifrons* _____

_____

☐ Red-bellied Woodpecker *Melanerpes carolinus* _____

_____

☐ Williamson's Sapsucker *Sphyrapicus thyroideus* _____

_____

☐ Yellow-bellied Sapsucker *Sphyrapicus varius* _____

_____

☐ Red-naped Sapsucker *Sphyrapicus nuchalis* _____

_____

☐ Red-breasted Sapsucker *Sphyrapicus ruber* _____

_____

☐ Ladder-backed Woodpecker *Picoides scalaris* _____

_____

☐ Nuttall's Woodpecker *Picoides nuttallii* _____

_____

☐ Downy Woodpecker *Picoides pubescens* _____

_____

☐ Hairy Woodpecker *Picoides villosus* _____

_____

☐ Arizona Woodpecker *Picoides arizonae* _____

_____

☐ Red-cockaded Woodpecker   *Picoides borealis*   * _____

_____

☐ White-headed Woodpecker   *Picoides albolarvatus*   _____

_____

☐ American Three-toed Woodpecker   *Picoides dorsalis*   _____

_____

☐ Black-backed Woodpecker   *Picoides arcticus*   _____

_____

☐ Northern Flicker   *Colaptes auratus*   _____

_____

☐ Gilded Flicker   *Colaptes chrysoides*   _____

_____

☐ Pileated Woodpecker   *Dryocopus pileatus*   _____

_____

☐ Ivory-billed Woodpecker   *Campephilus principalis*   * _____

_____

Order Passeriformes: Passerine Birds

Family Tyrannidae: Tyrant Flycatchers (North America: 35; World: 436)

☐ Northern Beardless-Tyrannulet   *Camptostoma imberbe*   _____

_____

☐ Olive-sided Flycatcher   *Contopus cooperi*   _____

_____

☐ Greater Pewee   *Contopus pertinax*   _____

_____

☐ Western Wood-Pewee   *Contopus sordidulus*   _____

_____

☐ Eastern Wood-Pewee   *Contopus virens*   _____

_____

☐ Yellow-bellied Flycatcher   *Empidonax flaviventris*   _____

_____

☐ Acadian Flycatcher   *Empidonax virescens*   _____

_____

☐ Alder Flycatcher   *Empidonax alnorum*   _____

_____

☐ Willow Flycatcher   *Empidonax traillii*   _____

_____

☐ Least Flycatcher   *Empidonax minimus*   _____

_____

☐ Hammond's Flycatcher   *Empidonax hammondii*   _____

_____

☐ Gray Flycatcher   *Empidonax wrightii*   _____

_____

☐ Dusky Flycatcher   *Empidonax oberholseri*   _____

_____

☐ Pacific-slope Flycatcher   *Empidonax difficilis*   _____

_____

☐ Cordilleran Flycatcher   *Empidonax occidentalis*   _____

_____

☐ Buff-breasted Flycatcher   *Empidonax fulvifrons*   _____

_____

☐ Black Phoebe   *Sayornis nigricans*   _____

_____

☐ Eastern Phoebe   *Sayornis phoebe*   _____

_____

☐ Say's Phoebe   *Sayornis saya*   _____

_____

☐ Vermilion Flycatcher *Pyrocephalus rubinus* _____

_____

☐ Dusky-capped Flycatcher *Myiarchus tuberculifer* _____

_____

☐ Ash-throated Flycatcher *Myiarchus cinerascens* _____

_____

☐ Great Crested Flycatcher *Myiarchus crinitus* _____

_____

☐ Brown-crested Flycatcher *Myiarchus tyrannulus* _____

_____

☐ Great Kiskadee *Pitangus sulphuratus* _____

_____

☐ Sulphur-bellied Flycatcher *Myiodynastes luteiventris* _____

_____

☐ Tropical Kingbird *Tyrannus melancholicus* _____

_____

☐ Couch's Kingbird *Tyrannus couchii* _____

_____

☐ Cassin's Kingbird *Tyrannus vociferans* _____

_____

☐ Thick-billed Kingbird *Tyrannus crassirostris* _____

_____

☐ Western Kingbird *Tyrannus verticalis* _____

_____

☐ Eastern Kingbird *Tyrannus tyrannus* _____

_____

☐ Gray Kingbird *Tyrannus dominicensis* _____

_____

☐ Scissor-tailed Flycatcher   *Tyrannus forficatus*   _____

_____

☐ Rose-throated Becard   *Pachyramphus aglaiae*   _____

_____

Family Laniidae: Shrikes (North America: 2; World: 30)

☐ Loggerhead Shrike   *Lanius ludovicianus*   _____

_____

☐ Northern Shrike   *Lanius excubitor*   _____

_____

Family Vireonidae: Vireos (North America: 14; World: 52)

☐ White-eyed Vireo   *Vireo griseus*   _____

_____

☐ Bell's Vireo   *Vireo bellii*   _____

_____

☐ Black-capped Vireo   *Vireo atricapilla*   *   _____

_____

☐ Gray Vireo   *Vireo vicinior*   _____

_____

☐ Yellow-throated Vireo   *Vireo flavifrons*   _____

_____

☐ Plumbeous Vireo   *Vireo plumbeus*   _____

_____

☐ Cassin's Vireo   *Vireo cassinii*   _____

_____

☐ Blue-headed Vireo   *Vireo solitarius*   _____

_____

☐ Hutton's Vireo   *Vireo huttoni*   _____

_____

☐ Warbling Vireo   *Vireo gilvus*

_____

_____

☐ Philadelphia Vireo   *Vireo philadelphicus*

_____

_____

☐ Red-eyed Vireo   *Vireo olivaceus*

_____

_____

☐ Yellow-green Vireo   *Vireo flavoviridis*

_____

_____

☐ Black-whiskered Vireo   *Vireo altiloquus*

_____

_____

Family Corvidae: Crows and Jays (North America: 19; World: 119)

☐ Gray Jay   *Perisoreus canadensis*

_____

☐ Steller's Jay   *Cyanocitta stelleri*

_____

_____

☐ Blue Jay   *Cyanocitta cristata*

_____

_____

☐ Green Jay   *Cyanocorax yncas*

_____

_____

☐ Brown Jay   *Cyanocorax morio*

_____

_____

☐ Florida Scrub-Jay   *Aphelocoma coerulescens*   *

_____

_____

☐ Island Scrub-Jay   *Aphelocoma insularis*   *

_____

☐ Western Scrub-Jay   *Aphelocoma californica*

_____

_____

☐ Mexican Jay   *Aphelocoma ultramarina*   _____

                                                          _____

☐ Pinyon Jay   *Gymnorhinus cyanocephalus*   _____

                                                          _____

☐ Clark's Nutcracker   *Nucifraga columbiana*   _____

                                                          _____

☐ Black-billed Magpie *Pica hudsonia*   _____

                                                          _____

☐ Yellow-billed Magpie *Pica nuttalli*   _____

                                                          _____

☐ American Crow   *Corvus brachyrhynchos*   _____

                                                          _____

☐ Northwestern Crow   *Corvus caurinus*   _____

                                                          _____

☐ Tamaulipas Crow   *Corvus imparatus*   _____

                                                          _____

☐ Fish Crow   *Corvus ossifragus*   _____

                                                          _____

☐ Chihuahuan Raven   *Corvus cryptoleucus*   _____

                                                          _____

☐ Common Raven   *Corvus corax*   _____

                                                          _____

Family Alaudidae: Larks (North America: 1; World: 91)

☐ Horned Lark   *Eremophila alpestris*   _____

                                                          _____

Family Hirundinidae: Swallows (North America: 8; World: 90)

☐ Purple Martin   *Progne subis*   _____

                                                          _____

☐ Tree Swallow   *Tachycineta bicolor*

_____

_____

☐ Violet-green Swallow   *Tachycineta thalassina*

_____

_____

☐ Northern Rough-winged Swallow   *Stelgidopteryx serripennis*

_____

_____

☐ Bank Swallow   *Riparia riparia*

_____

_____

☐ Cliff Swallow   *Petrochelidon pyrrhonota*

_____

_____

☐ Cave Swallow   *Petrochelidon fulva*

_____

_____

☐ Barn Swallow   *Hirundo rustica*

_____

_____

**Family Paridae: Chickadees and Titmice
(North America: 12; World: 56)**

☐ Carolina Chickadee   *Poecile carolinensis*

_____

_____

☐ Black-capped Chickadee   *Poecile atricapillus*

_____

_____

☐ Mountain Chickadee   *Poecile gambeli*

_____

_____

☐ Mexican Chickadee   *Poecile sclateri*

_____

_____

☐ Chestnut-backed Chickadee   *Poecile rufescens*

_____

_____

☐ Boreal Chickadee   *Poecile hudsonica*

_____

_____

☐ Gray-headed Chickadee   *Poecile cincta*   _____

_____

☐ Bridled Titmouse   *Baeolophus wollweberi*   _____

_____

☐ Oak Titmouse   *Baeolophus inornatus*   _____

_____

☐ Juniper Titmouse   *Baeolophus ridgwayi*   _____

_____

☐ Tufted Titmouse   *Baeolophus bicolor*   _____

_____

☐ Black-crested Titmouse   *Baeolophus atricristatus*   _____

_____

**Family Remizidae: Penduline Tits and Verdins
(North America: 1; World: 13)**

☐ Verdin   *Auriparus flaviceps*   _____

_____

**Family Aegithalidae: Long-tailed Tits and Bushtits
(North America: 1; World: 8)**

☐ Bushtit   *Psaltriparus minimus*   _____

_____

Family Sittidae: Nuthatches (North America: 4; World: 24)

☐ Red-breasted Nuthatch   *Sitta canadensis*   _____

_____

☐ White-breasted Nuthatch   *Sitta carolinensis*   _____

_____

☐ Pygmy Nuthatch   *Sitta pygmaea*   _____

_____

☐ Brown-headed Nuthatch   *Sitta pusilla*   _____

_____

Family Certhiidae: Creepers (North America: 1; World: 7)

☐ Brown Creeper   *Certhia americana*   _____

_____

Family Troglodytidae: Wrens (North America: 9; World: 79)

☐ Cactus Wren   *Campylorhynchus brunneicapillus*   _____

_____

☐ Rock Wren   *Salpinctes obsoletus*   _____

_____

☐ Canyon Wren   *Catherpes mexicanus*   _____

_____

☐ Carolina Wren   *Thryothorus ludovicianus*   _____

_____

☐ Bewick's Wren   *Thryomanes bewickii*   _____

_____

☐ House Wren   *Troglodytes aedon*   _____

_____

☐ Winter Wren   *Troglodytes troglodytes*   _____

_____

☐ Sedge Wren   *Cistothorus platensis*   _____

_____

☐ Marsh Wren   *Cistothorus palustris*   _____

_____

Family Cinclidae: Dippers (North America: 1; World: 5)

☐ American Dipper   *Cinclus mexicanus*   _____

_____

Family Regulidae: Kinglets (North America: 2; World: 6)

☐ Golden-crowned Kinglet   *Regulus satrapa*   _____

_____

☐ Ruby-crowned Kinglet *Regulus calendula*
_____
_____

Family Sylviidae: Old World Warblers and Gnatcatchers (North America: 4; World: 301)

☐ Arctic Warbler *Phylloscopus borealis*
_____
_____

☐ Blue-gray Gnatcatcher *Polioptila caerulea*
_____
_____

☐ California Gnatcatcher *Polioptila californica* *
_____
_____

☐ Black-tailed Gnatcatcher *Polioptila melanura*
_____
_____

Family Turdidae: Thrushes (North America: 18; World: 175)

☐ Siberian Rubythroat *Luscinia calliope*
_____
_____

☐ Bluethroat *Luscinia svecica*
_____
_____

☐ Northern Wheatear *Oenanthe oenanthe*
_____
_____

☐ Eastern Bluebird *Sialia sialis*
_____
_____

☐ Western Bluebird *Sialia mexicana*
_____
_____

☐ Mountain Bluebird *Sialia currucoides*
_____
_____

☐ Townsend's Solitaire *Myadestes townsendi*
_____
_____

☐ Veery *Catharus fuscescens*
_____
_____

☐ Gray-cheeked Thrush   *Catharus minimus*   _____

_____

☐ Bicknell's Thrush   *Catharus bicknelli*   _____

_____

☐ Swainson's Thrush   *Catharus ustulatus*   _____

_____

☐ Hermit Thrush   *Catharus guttatus*   _____

_____

☐ Wood Thrush   *Hylocichla mustelina*   _____

_____

☐ Eyebrowed Thrush   *Turdus obscurus*   _____

_____

☐ Clay-colored Robin   *Turdus grayi*   _____

_____

☐ Rufous-backed Robin   *Turdus rufopalliatus*   _____

_____

☐ American Robin   *Turdus migratorius*   _____

_____

☐ Varied Thrush   *Ixoreus naevius*   _____

_____

Family Timaliidae: Babblers (North America: 1; World: 268)

☐ Wrentit   *Chamaea fasciata*   _____

_____

**Family Mimidae: Mockingbirds and Thrashers
(North America: 10; World: 35)**

☐ Gray Catbird   *Dumetella carolinensis*   _____

_____

☐ Northern Mockingbird   *Mimus polyglottos*   _____

_____

☐ Sage Thrasher   *Oreoscoptes montanus*   _____

_____

☐ Brown Thrasher   *Toxostoma rufum*   _____

_____

☐ Long-billed Thrasher   *Toxostoma longirostre*   _____

_____

☐ Bendire's Thrasher   *Toxostoma bendirei*   _____

_____

☐ Curve-billed Thrasher   *Toxostoma curvirostre*   _____

_____

☐ California Thrasher   *Toxostoma redivivum*   _____

_____

☐ Crissal Thrasher   *Toxostoma crissale*   _____

_____

☐ Le Conte's Thrasher   *Toxostoma lecontei*   *   _____

_____

Family Motacillidae: Wagtails and Pipits
(North America: 6; World: 62)

☐ Eastern Yellow Wagtail   *Motacilla tschutschensis*   _____

_____

☐ White Wagtail   *Motacilla alba*   _____

_____

☐ Olive-backed Pipit   *Anthus hodgsoni*   _____

_____

☐ Red-throated Pipit   *Anthus cervinus*   _____

_____

☐ American Pipit   *Anthus rubescens*   _____

_____

☐ Sprague's Pipit   *Anthus spragueii*   _____

_____

Family Bombycillidae: Waxwings (North America: 2; World: 3)

☐ Bohemian Waxwing   *Bombycilla garrulus*   _____

_____

☐ Cedar Waxwing   *Bombycilla cedrorum*   _____

_____

Family Ptilogonatidae: Silky-flycatchers (North America: 1; World: 4)

☐ Phainopepla   *Phainopepla nitens*   _____

_____

Family Peucedramidae: Olive Warbler (North America: 1; World: 1)

☐ Olive Warbler   *Peucedramus taeniatus*   _____

_____

Family Parulidae: Wood-Warblers (North America: 50; World: 118)

☐ Bachman's Warbler   *Vermivora bachmanii*   †   _____

_____

☐ Blue-winged Warbler   *Vermivora pinus*   _____

_____

☐ Golden-winged Warbler   *Vermivora chrysoptera*   _____

_____

☐ Tennessee Warbler   *Vermivora peregrina*   _____

_____

☐ Orange-crowned Warbler   *Vermivora celata*   _____

_____

☐ Nashville Warbler   *Vermivora ruficapilla*   _____

_____

☐ Virginia's Warbler   *Vermivora virginiae*   _____

_____

☐ Colima Warbler   *Vermivora crissalis*   * _____

_____

☐ Lucy's Warbler   *Vermivora luciae* _____

_____

☐ Northern Parula   *Parula americana* _____

_____

☐ Tropical Parula   *Parula pitiayumi* _____

_____

☐ Yellow Warbler   *Dendroica petechia* _____

_____

☐ Chestnut-sided Warbler   *Dendroica pensylvanica* _____

_____

☐ Magnolia Warbler   *Dendroica magnolia* _____

_____

☐ Cape May Warbler   *Dendroica tigrina* _____

_____

☐ Black-throated Blue Warbler   *Dendroica caerulescens* _____

_____

☐ Yellow-rumped Warbler   *Dendroica coronata* _____

_____

☐ Black-throated Gray Warbler   *Dendroica nigrescens* _____

_____

☐ Golden-cheeked Warbler   *Dendroica chrysoparia*   * _____

_____

☐ Black-throated Green Warbler   *Dendroica virens* _____

_____

☐ Townsend's Warbler   *Dendroica townsendi* _____

_____

☐ Hermit Warbler   *Dendroica occidentalis*   _____

_____

☐ Blackburnian Warbler   *Dendroica fusca*   _____

_____

☐ Yellow-throated Warbler   *Dendroica dominica*   _____

_____

☐ Grace's Warbler   *Dendroica graciae*   _____

_____

☐ Pine Warbler   *Dendroica pinus*   _____

_____

☐ Kirtland's Warbler   *Dendroica kirtlandii*   *   _____

_____

☐ Prairie Warbler   *Dendroica discolor*   _____

_____

☐ Palm Warbler   *Dendroica palmarum*   _____

_____

☐ Bay-breasted Warbler   *Dendroica castanea*   _____

_____

☐ Blackpoll Warbler   *Dendroica striata*   _____

_____

☐ Cerulean Warbler   *Dendroica cerulea*   _____

_____

☐ Black-and-white Warbler   *Mniotilta varia*   _____

_____

☐ American Redstart   *Setophaga ruticilla*   _____

_____

☐ Prothonotary Warbler   *Protonotaria citrea*   _____

_____

☐ Worm-eating Warbler   *Helmitheros vermivorum*   _____

_____

☐ Swainson's Warbler   *Limnothlypis swainsonii*   _____

_____

☐ Ovenbird   *Seiurus aurocapilla*   _____

_____

☐ Northern Waterthrush   *Seiurus noveboracensis*   _____

_____

☐ Louisiana Waterthrush   *Seiurus motacilla*   _____

_____

☐ Kentucky Warbler   *Oporornis formosus*   _____

_____

☐ Connecticut Warbler   *Oporornis agilis*   _____

_____

☐ Mourning Warbler   *Oporornis philadelphia*   _____

_____

☐ MacGillivray's Warbler   *Oporornis tolmiei*   _____

_____

☐ Common Yellowthroat   *Geothlypis trichas*   _____

_____

☐ Gray-crowned Yellowthroat   *Geothlypis poliocephala*   ø   _____

_____

☐ Hooded Warbler   *Wilsonia citrina*   _____

_____

☐ Wilson's Warbler   *Wilsonia pusilla*   _____

_____

☐ Canada Warbler   *Wilsonia canadensis*   _____

_____

☐ Red-faced Warbler   *Cardellina rubrifrons*   _____

_____

☐ Painted Redstart   *Myioborus pictus*   _____

_____

☐ Yellow-breasted Chat   *Icteria virens*   _____

_____

Family Thraupidae: Tanagers (North America: 4; World: 256)

☐ Hepatic Tanager   *Piranga flava*   _____

_____

☐ Summer Tanager   *Piranga rubra*   _____

_____

☐ Scarlet Tanager   *Piranga olivacea*   _____

_____

☐ Western Tanager   *Piranga ludoviciana*   _____

_____

Family Emberizidae: Emberizids (North America: 50; World: 321)

☐ White-collared Seedeater   *Sporophila torqueola*   _____

_____

☐ Olive Sparrow   *Arremonops rufivirgatus*   _____

_____

☐ Green-tailed Towhee   *Pipilo chlorurus*   _____

_____

☐ Spotted Towhee   *Pipilo maculatus*   _____

_____

☐ Eastern Towhee   *Pipilo erythrophthalmus*   _____

_____

☐ Canyon Towhee   *Pipilo fuscus*   _____

_____

☐ California Towhee   *Pipilo crissalis*   _____

_____

☐ Abert's Towhee   *Pipilo aberti*   *   _____

_____

☐ Rufous-winged Sparrow   *Aimophila carpalis*   _____

_____

☐ Cassin's Sparrow   *Aimophila cassinii*   _____

_____

☐ Bachman's Sparrow   *Aimophila aestivalis*   *   _____

_____

☐ Botteri's Sparrow   *Aimophila botterii*   _____

_____

☐ Rufous-crowned Sparrow   *Aimophila ruficeps*   _____

_____

☐ Five-striped Sparrow   *Aimophila quinquestriata*   _____

_____

☐ American Tree Sparrow   *Spizella arborea*   _____

_____

☐ Chipping Sparrow   *Spizella passerina*   _____

_____

☐ Clay-colored Sparrow   *Spizella pallida*   _____

_____

☐ Brewer's Sparrow   *Spizella breweri*   _____

_____

☐ Field Sparrow   *Spizella pusilla*   _____

_____

☐ Worthen's Sparrow   *Spizella wortheni*   ø   _____

_____

☐ Black-chinned Sparrow   *Spizella atrogularis*   _____

_____

☐ Vesper Sparrow   *Pooecetes gramineus*   _____

_____

☐ Lark Sparrow   *Chondestes grammacus*   _____

_____

☐ Black-throated Sparrow   *Amphispiza bilineata*   _____

_____

☐ Sage Sparrow   *Amphispiza belli*   _____

_____

☐ Lark Bunting   *Calamospiza melanocorys* _____

_____

☐ Savannah Sparrow   *Passerculus sandwichensis* _____

_____

☐ Grasshopper Sparrow   *Ammodramus savannarum*   _____

_____

☐ Baird's Sparrow   *Ammodramus bairdii*   _____

_____

☐ Henslow's Sparrow   *Ammodramus henslowii*   _____

_____

☐ Le Conte's Sparrow   *Ammodramus leconteii*   _____

_____

☐ Nelson's Sharp-tailed Sparrow   *Ammodramus nelsoni*   _____

_____

☐ Saltmarsh Sharp-tailed Sparrow   *Ammodramus caudacutus* _____

_____

☐ Seaside Sparrow   *Ammodramus maritimus*   _____

_____

☐ Fox Sparrow   *Passerella iliaca*

☐ Song Sparrow   *Melospiza melodia*

☐ Lincoln's Sparrow   *Melospiza lincolnii*

☐ Swamp Sparrow   *Melospiza georgiana*

☐ White-throated Sparrow   *Zonotrichia albicollis*

☐ Harris's Sparrow   *Zonotrichia querula*

☐ White-crowned Sparrow   *Zonotrichia leucophrys*

☐ Golden-crowned Sparrow   *Zonotrichia atricapilla*

☐ Dark-eyed Junco   *Junco hyemalis*

☐ Yellow-eyed Junco   *Junco phaeonotus*

☐ McCown's Longspur   *Calcarius mccownii*

☐ Lapland Longspur   *Calcarius lapponicus*

☐ Smith's Longspur   *Calcarius pictus*

☐ Chestnut-collared Longspur   *Calcarius ornatus*

☐   Rustic Bunting   *Emberiza rustica*   _____

_____

☐   Snow Bunting   *Plectrophenax nivalis*   _____

_____

☐   McKay's Bunting   *Plectrophenax hyperboreus* *   _____

_____

**Family Cardinalidae: Cardinals, Saltators, and Allies
(North America: 10; World: 43)**

☐   Northern Cardinal   *Cardinalis cardinalis*   _____

_____

☐   Pyrrhuloxia   *Cardinalis sinuatus*   _____

_____

☐   Rose-breasted Grosbeak *Pheucticus ludovicianus*   _____

_____

☐   Black-headed Grosbeak   *Pheucticus melanocephalus*   _____

_____

☐   Blue Grosbeak   *Passerina caerulea*   _____

_____

☐   Lazuli Bunting   *Passerina amoena*   _____

_____

☐   Indigo Bunting   *Passerina cyanea*   _____

_____

☐   Varied Bunting   *Passerina versicolor*   _____

_____

☐   Painted Bunting   *Passerina ciris*   _____

_____

☐   Dickcissel   *Spiza americana*   _____

_____

Family Icteridae: Blackbirds (North America: 21; World: 98)

☐ Bobolink *Dolichonyx oryzivorus*

☐ Red-winged Blackbird *Agelaius phoeniceus*

☐ Tricolored Blackbird *Agelaius tricolor* *

☐ Eastern Meadowlark *Sturnella magna*

☐ Western Meadowlark *Sturnella neglecta*

☐ Yellow-headed Blackbird *Xanthocephalus xanthocephalus*

☐ Rusty Blackbird *Euphagus carolinus*

☐ Brewer's Blackbird *Euphagus cyanocephalus*

☐ Common Grackle *Quiscalus quiscula*

☐ Boat-tailed Grackle *Quiscalus major*

☐ Great-tailed Grackle *Quiscalus mexicanus*

☐ California Mastodon-bird *Pandanaris convexa* †P

☐ New Mexico Mastodon-bird *Pyelorhamphus molothroides* †P

☐ Shiny Cowbird   *Molothrus bonariensis*   _____

_____

☐ Bronzed Cowbird   *Molothrus aeneus*   _____

_____

☐ Brown-headed Cowbird   *Molothrus ater*   _____

_____

☐ Orchard Oriole   *Icterus spurius*   _____

_____

☐ Hooded Oriole   *Icterus cucullatus*   _____

_____

☐ Bullock's Oriole   *Icterus bullockii*   _____

_____

☐ Altamira Oriole   *Icterus gularis*   _____

_____

☐ Audubon's Oriole   *Icterus graduacauda*   _____

_____

☐ Baltimore Oriole   *Icterus galbula*   _____

_____

☐ Scott's Oriole   *Icterus parisorum*   _____

_____

Family Fringillidae: Fringilline and Cardueline Finches and Allies (North America: 17; World: 136)

☐ Brambling   *Fringilla montifringilla*   _____

_____

☐ Gray-crowned Rosy-Finch   *Leucosticte tephrocotis*   _____

_____

☐ Black Rosy-Finch   *Leucosticte atrata*   _____

_____

☐ Brown-capped Rosy-Finch   *Leucosticte australis*   _____

_____

☐ Pine Grosbeak   *Pinicola enucleator*   _____

_____

☐ Purple Finch   *Carpodacus purpureus*   _____

_____

☐ Cassin's Finch   *Carpodacus cassinii*   _____

_____

☐ House Finch   *Carpodacus mexicanus*   _____

_____

☐ Red Crossbill   *Loxia curvirostra*   _____

_____

☐ White-winged Crossbill   *Loxia leucoptera*   _____

_____

☐ Common Redpoll   *Carduelis flammea*   _____

_____

☐ Hoary Redpoll   *Carduelis hornemanni*   _____

_____

☐ Pine Siskin   *Carduelis pinus*   _____

_____

☐ Lesser Goldfinch   *Carduelis psaltria*   _____

_____

☐ Lawrence's Goldfinch   *Carduelis lawrencei*   *   _____

_____

☐ American Goldfinch   *Carduelis tristis*   _____

_____

☐ Evening Grosbeak   *Coccothraustes vespertinus*   _____

_____

NON-ANNUAL VISITORS

Note: Species marked "OH?" have been positively identified in North America but it is uncertain whether they arrived with or without the aid of humans (see Robbins et al. 2003).

Order Anseriformes: Screamers, Ducks, Geese, and Swans
Family Anatidae: Ducks, Geese, and Swans

☐ Pink-footed Goose   *Anser brachyrhynchus*   _____

_____

☐ Lesser White-fronted Goose   *Anser erythropus*   _____

_____

☐ Barnacle Goose   *Branta leucopsis*   _____

_____

☐ Ruddy Shelduck   *Tadorna ferruginea*   OH? _____

_____

☐ Falcated Duck   *Anas falcata*   _____

_____

☐ Spot-billed Duck   *Anas poecilorhyncha*   _____

_____

☐ White-cheeked Pintail   *Anas bahamensis*   _____

_____

☐ Baikal Teal   *Anas formosa*   _____

_____

Order Procellariiformes: Tube-nosed Swimmers
Family Diomedeidae: Albatrosses

☐ Yellow-nosed Albatross   *Thalassarche chlororhynchos*   _____

_____

☐ Shy Albatross   *Thalassarche cauta*   _____

_____

☐ Black-browed Albatross   *Thalassarche melanophris*   _____

_____

☐ Light-mantled Albatross *Phoebetria palpebrata* OH? _____

_____

☐ Wandering Albatross *Diomedea exulans* _____

_____

Family Procellariidae: Shearwaters and Petrels

☐ Great-winged Petrel *Pterodroma macroptera* _____

_____

☐ Bermuda Petrel *Pterodroma cahow* * _____

_____

☐ Galapagos/Hawaiian Petrel *Pterodroma phaeopygia/* * _____
sandwichensis

☐ Stejneger's Petrel *Pterodroma longirostris* _____

_____

☐ Bulwer's Petrel *Bulweria bulwerii* _____

_____

☐ Streaked Shearwater *Calonectris leucomelas* _____

_____

☐ Wedge-tailed Shearwater *Puffinus pacificus* _____

_____

☐ Little Shearwater *Puffinus assimilis* _____

_____

Family Hydrobatidae: Storm-Petrels

☐ White-faced Storm-Petrel *Pelagodroma marina* _____

_____

☐ European Storm-Petrel *Hydrobates pelagicus* _____

_____

☐ Wedge-rumped Storm-Petrel *Oceanodroma tethys* _____

_____

Order Pelecaniformes: Totipalmate Birds
Family Phaethontidae: Tropicbirds

☐ Red-tailed Tropicbird *Phaethon rubricauda* _____

_____

Family Sulidae: Boobies and Gannets

☐ Blue-footed Booby *Sula nebouxii* _____

_____

☐ Red-footed Booby *Sula sula* _____

_____

Family Fregatidae: Frigatebirds

☐ Great Frigatebird *Fregata minor* _____

_____

☐ Lesser Frigatebird *Fregata ariel* _____

_____

Order Ciconiiformes: Herons, Ibises, Storks, New World Vultures, and Allies
Family Ardeidae: Herons, Bitterns, and Allies

☐ Yellow Bittern *Ixobrychus sinensis* _____

_____

☐ Chinese Egret *Egretta eulophotes* _____

_____

☐ Little Egret *Egretta garzetta* _____

_____

☐ Western Reef-Heron *Egretta gularis* _____

_____

☐ Chinese Pond-Heron *Ardeola bacchus* _____

_____

Family Threskiornithidae: Ibises and Spoonbills

☐ Scarlet Ibis *Eudocimus ruber* _____

_____

Family Ciconiidae: Storks

☐ Jabiru   *Jabiru mycteria*

Order Falconiformes: Diurnal Birds of Prey

Family Accipitridae: Hawks, Kites, Eagles, and Allies

☐ White-tailed Eagle   *Haliaeetus albicilla*

☐ Steller's Sea-Eagle   *Haliaeetus pelagicus*

☐ Crane Hawk   *Geranospiza caerulescens*

☐ Roadside Hawk   *Buteo magnirostris*

Family Falconidae: Caracaras and Falcons

☐ Collared Forest-Falcon   *Micrastur semitorquatus*

☐ Eurasian Kestrel   *Falco tinnunculus*

☐ Eurasian Hobby   *Falco subbuteo*

Order Gruiformes: Rails, Cranes, and Allies

Family Rallidae: Rails, Gallinules, and Coots

☐ Corn Crake   *Crex crex*

☐ Paint-billed Crake   *Neocrex erythrops*

☐ Spotted Rail   *Pardirallus maculatus*

☐ Eurasian Coot   *Fulica atra*   _____

_____

Family Gruidae: Cranes

☐ Common Crane   *Grus grus*   _____

_____

Order Charadriiformes: Shorebirds, Gulls, Auks, and Allies

Family Burhinidae: Thick-knees

☐ Double-striped Thick-knee   *Burhinus bistriatus*   _____

_____

Family Charadriidae: Lapwings and Plovers

☐ Northern Lapwing   *Vanellus vanellus*   _____

_____

☐ European Golden-Plover   *Pluvialis apricaria*   _____

_____

☐ Greater Sand-Plover   *Charadrius leschenaultii*   _____

_____

☐ Collared Plover   *Charadrius collaris*   _____

_____

☐ Little Ringed Plover   *Charadrius dubius*   _____

_____

☐ Eurasian Dotterel   *Charadrius morinellus*   _____

_____

Family Haematopodidae: Oystercatchers

☐ Eurasian Oystercatcher   *Haematopus ostralegus*   _____

_____

Family Recurvirostridae: Stilts and Avocets

☐ Black-winged Stilt   *Himantopus himantopus*   _____

_____

Family Jacanidae: Jacanas

☐ Northern Jacana   *Jacana spinosa*   _____

_____

Family Scolopacidae: Sandpipers, Phalaropes, and Allies

☐ Marsh Sandpiper   *Tringa stagnatilis*   _____

_____

☐ Common Redshank   *Tringa totanus*   _____

_____

☐ Spotted Redshank   *Tringa erythropus*   _____

_____

☐ Green Sandpiper   *Tringa ochropus*   _____

_____

☐ Little Curlew   *Numenius minutus*   _____

_____

☐ Far Eastern Curlew   *Numenius madagascariensis*   _____

_____

☐ Slender-billed Curlew   *Numenius tenuirostris*   _____

_____

☐ Eurasian Curlew   *Numenius arquata*   _____

_____

☐ Great Knot   *Calidris tenuirostris*   _____

_____

☐ Little Stint   *Calidris minuta*   _____

_____

☐ Spoon-billed Sandpiper   *Eurynorhynchus pygmeus*   _____

_____

☐ Broad-billed Sandpiper   *Limicola falcinellus*   _____

_____

☐ Jack Snipe   *Lymnocryptes minimus*   _____

_____

☐ Pin-tailed Snipe   *Gallinago stenura*   _____

_____

☐ Eurasian Woodcock   *Scolopax rusticola*   _____

_____

Family Glareolidae: Coursers and Pratincoles

☐ Oriental Pratincole   *Glareola maldivarum*   _____

_____

Family Laridae: Skuas, Gulls, Terns, and Skimmers

☐ Gray-hooded Gull   *Larus cirrocephalus*   _____

_____

☐ Belcher's Gull   *Larus belcheri*   _____

_____

☐ Black-tailed Gull   *Larus crassirostris*   _____

_____

☐ Yellow-legged Gull   *Larus cachinnans*   _____

_____

☐ Kelp Gull   *Larus dominicanus*   _____

_____

☐ Large-billed Tern   *Phaetusa simplex*   _____

_____

☐ White-winged Tern   *Chlidonias leucopterus*   _____

_____

☐ Whiskered Tern   *Chlidonias hybrida*   _____

_____

Family Alcidae: Auks, Murres, and Puffins

☐ Long-billed Murrelet   *Brachyramphus perdix*   _____

_____

Order Columbiformes: Pigeons and Doves

Family Columbidae: Pigeons and Doves

☐ Scaly-naped Pigeon   *Patagioenas squamosa*   _____

_____

☐ Oriental Turtle-Dove   *Streptopelia orientalis*   _____

_____

☐ Zenaida Dove   *Zenaida aurita*   _____

_____

☐ Key West Quail-Dove   *Geotrygon chrysia*   *   _____

_____

☐ Ruddy Quail-Dove   *Geotrygon montana*   _____

_____

Order Psittaciformes: Parrots

Family Psittacidae: Lories, Parakeets, Macaws, and Parrots

☐ Thick-billed Parrot   *Rhynchopsitta pachyrhyncha* *   _____

_____

Order Cuculiformes: Cuckoos and Allies

Family Cuculidae: Cuckoos, Roadrunners, and Anis

☐ Oriental Cuckoo   *Cuculus saturatus*   _____

_____

☐ Dark-billed Cuckoo   *Coccyzus melacoryphus*   OH? _____

_____

Order Strigiformes: Owls

Family Strigidae: Typical Owls

☐ Oriental Scops-Owl   *Otus sunia*   _____

_____

☐ Mottled Owl   *Ciccaba virgata*   _____

_____

☐ Stygian Owl   *Asio stygius*   _____

_____

Order Caprimulgiformes: Goatsuckers, Oilbirds, and Allies
Family Caprimulgidae: Nighthawks and Nightjars

☐ Buff-collared Nightjar   *Caprimulgus ridgwayi*

☐ Gray Nightjar   *Caprimulgus indicus*

Order Apodiformes: Swifts and Hummingbirds
Family Apodidae: Swifts

☐ White-collared Swift   *Streptoprocne zonaris*

☐ White-throated Needletail   *Hirundapus caudacutus*

☐ Common Swift   *Apus apus*

☐ Fork-tailed Swift   *Apus pacificus*

☐ Antillean Palm-Swift   *Tachornis phoenicobia*

Family Trochilidae: Hummingbirds

☐ Green Violet-ear   *Colibri thalassinus*

☐ Green-breasted Mango   *Anthracothorax prevostii*

☐ Xantus's Hummingbird   *Hylocharis xantusii*

☐ Cinnamon Hummingbird   *Amazilia rutila*

☐ Plain-capped Starthroat   *Heliomaster constantii*

☐ Bahama Woodstar   *Calliphlox evelynae*   _____

_____

☐ Bumblebee Hummingbird   *Atthis heloisa*   _____

_____

Order Trogoniformes: Trogons

Family Trogonidae: Trogons

☐ Eared Quetzal   *Euptilotis neoxenus*   *   _____

_____

Order Upupiformes: Hoopoes and Allies

Family Upupidae: Hoopoes

☐ Eurasian Hoopoe   *Upupa epops*   _____

_____

Order Piciformes: Puffbirds, Jacamars, Toucans, Woodpeckers, and Allies

Family Picidae: Woodpeckers and Allies

☐ Eurasian Wryneck   *Jynx torquilla*   _____

_____

☐ Great Spotted Woodpecker   *Dendrocopos major*   _____

_____

Order Passeriformes: Passerine Birds

Family Tyrannidae: Tyrant Flycatchers

☐ Greenish Elaenia   *Myiopagis viridicata*   _____

_____

☐ Caribbean Elaenia   *Elaenia martinica*   _____

_____

☐ Tufted Flycatcher   *Mitrephanes phaeocercus*   _____

_____

☐ Cuban Pewee   *Contopus caribaeus*   _____

_____

☐ Nutting's Flycatcher   *Myiarchus nuttingi*   _____

_____

☐ La Sagra's Flycatcher   *Myiarchus sagrae*   _____

_____

☐ Piratic Flycatcher   *Legatus leucophaius*   _____

_____

☐ Variegated Flycatcher   *Empidonomus varius*   _____

_____

☐ Fork-tailed Flycatcher   *Tyrannus savana*   _____

_____

☐ Masked Tityra   *Tityra semifasciata*   _____

_____

Family Laniidae: Shrikes

☐ Brown Shrike   *Lanius cristatus*   _____

_____

Family Vireonidae: Vireos

☐ Thick-billed Vireo   *Vireo crassirostris*   _____

_____

☐ Yucatan Vireo   *Vireo magister*   _____

_____

Family Corvidae: Crows and Jays

☐ Eurasian Jackdaw   *Corvus monedula*   _____

_____

Family Alaudidae: Larks

☐ Sky Lark   *Alauda arvensis*   _____

_____

Family Hirundinidae: Swallows

☐ Cuban Martin   *Progne cryptoleuca*

_____

☐ Gray-breasted Martin   *Progne chalybea*

_____

☐ Southern Martin   *Progne elegans*

_____

☐ Brown-chested Martin   *Progne tapera*

_____

☐ Mangrove Swallow   *Tachycineta albilinea*

_____

☐ Bahama Swallow   *Tachycineta cyaneoviridis*   *

_____

☐ Common House-Martin   *Delichon urbicum*

_____

Family Sylviidae: Old World Warblers and Gnatcatchers

☐ Middendorff's Grasshopper-Warbler   *Locustella ochotensis*

_____

☐ Lanceolated Warbler   *Locustella lanceolata*

_____

☐ Willow Warbler   *Phylloscopus trochilus*

_____

☐ Wood Warbler   *Phylloscopus sibilatrix*

_____

☐ Dusky Warbler   *Phylloscopus fuscatus*

_____

☐ Yellow-browed Warbler   *Phylloscopus inornatus*

_____

☐ Lesser Whitethroat   *Sylvia curruca*   _____

_____

☐ Black-capped Gnatcatcher   *Polioptila nigriceps*   _____

_____

Family Muscicapidae: Old World Flycatchers

☐ Narcissus Flycatcher   *Ficedula narcissina*   _____

_____

☐ Mugimaki Flycatcher   *Ficedula mugimaki*   _____

_____

☐ Red-breasted Flycatcher   *Ficedula parva*   _____

_____

☐ Dark-sided Flycatcher   *Muscicapa sibirica*   _____

_____

☐ Gray-streaked Flycatcher   *Muscicapa griseisticta*   _____

_____

☐ Asian Brown Flycatcher   *Muscicapa dauurica*   _____

_____

☐ Spotted Flycatcher   *Muscicapa striata*   _____

_____

Family Turdidae: Thrushes

☐ Blue Rock-Thrush   *Monticola solitarius*   OH? _____

_____

☐ Siberian Blue Robin   *Luscinia cyane*   _____

_____

☐ Red-flanked Bluetail   *Tarsiger cyanurus*   _____

_____

☐ Stonechat   *Saxicola torquatus*   _____

_____

☐ Orange-billed   *Catharus aurantiirostris*   _____
   Nightingale-Thrush
                                                                 _____

☐ Eurasian Blackbird   *Turdus merula*   _____

                                                                 _____

☐ Dusky Thrush   *Turdus naumanni*   _____

                                                                 _____

☐ Fieldfare   *Turdus pilaris*   _____

                                                                 _____

☐ Redwing   *Turdus iliacus*   _____

                                                                 _____

☐ White-throated Robin   *Turdus assimilis*   _____

                                                                 _____

☐ Aztec Thrush   *Ridgwayia pinicola*   _____

                                                                 _____

Family Mimidae: Mockingbirds and Thrashers

☐ Bahama Mockingbird   *Mimus gundlachii*   _____

                                                                 _____

☐ Blue Mockingbird   *Melanotis caerulescens*   _____

                                                                 _____

Family Prunellidae: Accentors

☐ Siberian Accentor   *Prunella montanella*   _____

                                                                 _____

Family Motacillidae: Wagtails and Pipits

☐ Citrine Wagtail   *Motacilla citreola*   _____

                                                                 _____

☐ Gray Wagtail   *Motacilla cinerea*   _____

                                                                 _____

☐ Tree Pipit   *Anthus trivialis*   _____

_____

☐ Pechora Pipit   *Anthus gustavi*   _____

_____

Family Ptilogonatidae: Silky-flycatchers

☐ Gray Silky-flycatcher   *Ptilogonys cinereus*   _____

_____

Family Parulidae: Wood-Warblers

☐ Crescent-chested Warbler   *Parula superciliosa*   _____

_____

☐ Slate-throated Redstart   *Myioborus miniatus*   _____

_____

☐ Fan-tailed Warbler   *Euthlypis lachrymosa*   _____

_____

☐ Golden-crowned Warbler   *Basileuterus culicivorus*   _____

_____

☐ Rufous-capped Warbler   *Basileuterus rufifrons*   _____

_____

Genus *incertae sedis* (placement uncertain)

☐ Bananaquit   *Coereba flaveola*   _____

_____

Family Thraupidae: Tanagers

☐ Flame-colored Tanager   *Piranga bidentata*   _____

_____

☐ Western Spindalis   *Spindalis zena*   _____

_____

Family Emberizidae: Emberizids

☐ Yellow-faced Grassquit   *Tiaris olivaceus*   _____

_____

☐ Black-faced Grassquit   *Tiaris bicolor*   _____

                                                  _____

☐ Pine Bunting   *Emberiza leucocephalos*   _____

                                                  _____

☐ Little Bunting   *Emberiza pusilla*   _____

                                                  _____

☐ Yellow-throated Bunting   *Emberiza elegans*   _____

                                                  _____

☐ Yellow-breasted Bunting   *Emberiza aureola*   _____

                                                  _____

☐ Gray Bunting   *Emberiza variabilis*   _____

                                                  _____

☐ Pallas's Bunting   *Emberiza pallasi*   _____

                                                  _____

☐ Reed Bunting   *Emberiza schoeniclus*   _____

                                                  _____

Family Cardinalidae: Cardinals, Saltators, and Allies

☐ Crimson-collared Grosbeak   *Rhodothraupis celaeno*   _____

                                                  _____

☐ Yellow Grosbeak   *Pheucticus chrysopeplus*   _____

                                                  _____

☐ Blue Bunting   *Cyanocompsa parellina*   _____

                                                  _____

Family Icteridae: Blackbirds

☐ Tawny-shouldered Blackbird   *Agelaius humeralis*   _____

                                                  _____

☐ Black-vented Oriole   *Icterus wagleri*   _____

                                                  _____

☐ Streak-backed Oriole *Icterus pustulatus* _____
_____

Family Fringillidae: Fringilline and Cardueline Finches and Allies

☐ Common Chaffinch *Fringilla coelebs* _____
_____

☐ Common Rosefinch *Carpodacus erythrinus* _____
_____

☐ Eurasian Siskin *Carduelis spinus* _____
_____

☐ Oriental Greenfinch *Carduelis sinica* _____
_____

☐ Eurasian Bullfinch *Pyrrhula pyrrhula* _____
_____

☐ Hawfinch *Coccothraustes coccothraustes* _____
_____

ALIEN BIRDS

Family Anatidae: Ducks, Geese, and Swans

☐ Mute Swan *Cygnus olor* _____
_____

Family Phasianidae: Partridges, Grouse, Turkeys, and Old World Quail

☐ Chukar *Alectoris chukar* _____
_____

☐ Himalayan Snowcock *Tetraogallus himalayensis* _____
_____

☐ Gray Partridge *Perdix perdix* _____
_____

☐ Ring-necked Pheasant *Phasianus colchicus* _____
_____

Family Columbidae: Pigeons and Doves

☐　Rock Pigeon　　　　　*Columba livia*　　　　　_____

_____

☐　Eurasian Collared-Dove　*Streptopelia decaocto*　_____

_____

☐　Spotted Dove　　　　*Streptopelia chinensis*　_____

_____

Family Psittacidae: Lories, Parakeets, Macaws, and Parrots

☐　Budgerigar　　　　　*Melopsittacus undulatus*　_____

_____

☐　Monk Parakeet　　　*Myiopsitta monachus*　　_____

_____

☐　Green Parakeet　　　*Aratinga holochlora*　　_____

_____

☐　White-winged Parakeet　*Brotogeris versicolurus*　_____

_____

☐　Yellow-chevroned Parakeet　*Brotogeris chiriri*　_____

_____

☐　Red-crowned Parrot　*Amazona viridigenalis*　_____

_____

Family Pycnonotidae: Bulbuls

☐　Red-whiskered Bulbul　*Pycnonotus jocosus*　　_____

_____

Family Sturnidae: Starlings

☐　European Starling　　*Sturnus vulgaris*　　　_____

_____

Family Icteridae: Blackbirds

☐　Spot-breasted Oriole　*Icterus pectoralis*　　_____

_____

Family Passeridae: Old World Sparrows

☐　House Sparrow　　　*Passer domesticus*　　　＿＿＿＿＿＿＿＿＿＿＿＿＿＿＿

＿＿＿＿＿＿＿＿＿＿＿＿＿＿＿

☐　Eurasian Tree Sparrow　*Passer montanus*　　　＿＿＿＿＿＿＿＿＿＿＿＿＿＿＿

＿＿＿＿＿＿＿＿＿＿＿＿＿＿＿

ADDITIONAL SPECIES

☐　＿＿＿＿＿＿＿＿＿　＿＿＿＿＿＿＿＿＿　＿＿＿＿＿＿＿＿＿＿＿＿＿＿＿

＿＿＿＿＿＿＿＿＿＿＿＿＿＿＿

☐　＿＿＿＿＿＿＿＿＿　＿＿＿＿＿＿＿＿＿　＿＿＿＿＿＿＿＿＿＿＿＿＿＿＿

＿＿＿＿＿＿＿＿＿＿＿＿＿＿＿

☐　＿＿＿＿＿＿＿＿＿　＿＿＿＿＿＿＿＿＿　＿＿＿＿＿＿＿＿＿＿＿＿＿＿＿

＿＿＿＿＿＿＿＿＿＿＿＿＿＿＿

☐　＿＿＿＿＿＿＿＿＿　＿＿＿＿＿＿＿＿＿　＿＿＿＿＿＿＿＿＿＿＿＿＿＿＿

＿＿＿＿＿＿＿＿＿＿＿＿＿＿＿

☐　＿＿＿＿＿＿＿＿＿　＿＿＿＿＿＿＿＿＿　＿＿＿＿＿＿＿＿＿＿＿＿＿＿＿

＿＿＿＿＿＿＿＿＿＿＿＿＿＿＿

☐　＿＿＿＿＿＿＿＿＿　＿＿＿＿＿＿＿＿＿　＿＿＿＿＿＿＿＿＿＿＿＿＿＿＿

＿＿＿＿＿＿＿＿＿＿＿＿＿＿＿

☐　＿＿＿＿＿＿＿＿＿　＿＿＿＿＿＿＿＿＿　＿＿＿＿＿＿＿＿＿＿＿＿＿＿＿

＿＿＿＿＿＿＿＿＿＿＿＿＿＿＿

☐　＿＿＿＿＿＿＿＿＿　＿＿＿＿＿＿＿＿＿　＿＿＿＿＿＿＿＿＿＿＿＿＿＿＿

＿＿＿＿＿＿＿＿＿＿＿＿＿＿＿

☐　＿＿＿＿＿＿＿＿＿　＿＿＿＿＿＿＿＿＿　＿＿＿＿＿＿＿＿＿＿＿＿＿＿＿

＿＿＿＿＿＿＿＿＿＿＿＿＿＿＿

☐　＿＿＿＿＿＿＿＿＿　＿＿＿＿＿＿＿＿＿　＿＿＿＿＿＿＿＿＿＿＿＿＿＿＿

＿＿＿＿＿＿＿＿＿＿＿＿＿＿＿

☐　＿＿＿＿＿＿＿＿＿　＿＿＿＿＿＿＿＿＿　＿＿＿＿＿＿＿＿＿＿＿＿＿＿＿

＿＿＿＿＿＿＿＿＿＿＿＿＿＿＿

☐ _____ _____ _____
_____

☐ _____ _____ _____
_____

☐ _____ _____ _____
_____

☐ _____ _____ _____
_____

☐ _____ _____ _____
_____

☐ _____ _____ _____
_____

☐ _____ _____ _____
_____

☐ _____ _____ _____
_____

☐ _____ _____ _____
_____

☐ _____ _____ _____
_____

☐ _____ _____ _____
_____

☐ _____ _____ _____
_____

☐ _____ _____ _____
_____

☐ _____ _____ _____
_____

☐ _____ _____ _____
_____

☐ _____ _____ _____
_____

☐ _____ _____ _____
_____

☐ _____ _____ _____
_____

☐ _____ _____ _____
_____

☐ _____ _____ _____
_____

☐ _____ _____ _____
_____

☐ _____ _____ _____
_____

☐ _____ _____ _____
_____

☐ _____ _____ _____
_____

☐ _____ _____ _____
_____

☐ _____ _____ _____
_____

☐ _____ _____ _____
_____

☐ _____ _____ _____
_____

☐ _____ _____ _____
_____

☐ _____ _____ _____
_____

☐ _____ _____ _____
_____

☐ _____ _____ _____
_____

☐ _____ _____ _____
_____

☐ _____ _____ _____
_____

☐ _____ _____ _____
_____

☐ _____ _____ _____
_____

☐ _____ _____ _____
_____

Class Reptilia: Reptiles

Order Squamata: Lizards, Amphisbaenians, and Snakes
Suborder Amphisbaenia: Worm Lizards

**Family Rhineuridae: North American Worm Lizards
(North America: 1; World: 1)**

☐ Florida Worm Lizard   *Rhineura floridana*   _____

_____

Suborder Sauria: Lizards

Family Iguanidae: Iguanid Lizards (North America: 2; World: 36)

☐ Desert Iguana   *Dipsosaurus dorsalis*   _____

_____

☐ Common Chuckwalla   *Sauromalus ater*   _____

_____

Family Polychrotidae: Anoles (North America: 1; World: 393)

☐ Green Anole   *Anolis carolinensis*   _____

_____

**Family Phrynosomatidae: Spiny Lizards
(North America: 43; World: 125)**

☐ Zebra-tailed Lizard   *Callisaurus draconoides*   _____

_____

☐ Greater Earless Lizard   *Cophosaurus texanus*   _____

_____

☐ Elegant Earless Lizard   *Holbrookia elegans*   _____

_____

☐ Spot-tailed Earless Lizard   *Holbrookia lacerata*   *   _____

_____

☐ Common Lesser Earless Lizard   *Holbrookia maculata*   _____

_____

☐ Keeled Earless Lizard   *Holbrookia propinqua*   *   _____

_____

☐ Banded Rock Lizard   *Petrosaurus mearnsi*   _____

_____

☐ Coast Horned Lizard   *Phrynosoma blainvillii*   _____

_____

☐ Texas Horned Lizard   *Phrynosoma cornutum*   _____

_____

☐ Pygmy Short-horned Lizard   *Phrynosoma douglasii*   _____

_____

☐ Greater Short-horned Lizard   *Phrynosoma hernandesi*   _____

_____

☐ Flat-tailed Horned Lizard   *Phrynosoma mcallii*   *   _____

_____

☐ Round-tailed Horned Lizard   *Phrynosoma modestum*   _____

_____

☐ Desert Horned Lizard   *Phrynosoma platyrhinos*   _____

_____

☐ Regal Horned Lizard   *Phrynosoma solare*   _____

_____

☐ Dunes Sagebrush Lizard   *Sceloporus arenicolus*   *   _____

_____

☐ Clark's Spiny Lizard   *Sceloporus clarkii*   _____

_____

☐ Prairie Lizard   *Sceloporus consobrinus*   _____

_____

☐ Southwestern Fence Lizard   *Sceloporus cowlesi*   _____

_____

☐ Blue Spiny Lizard   *Sceloporus cyanogenys*   _____

_____

☐ Common Sagebrush Lizard   *Sceloporus graciosus*   _____

_____

☐ Graphic Spiny Lizard   *Sceloporus grammicus*   _____

_____

☐ Yarrow's Spiny Lizard   *Sceloporus jarrovii*   _____

_____

☐ Desert Spiny Lizard   *Sceloporus magister*   _____

_____

☐ Canyon Lizard   *Sceloporus merriami*   _____

_____

☐ Western Fence Lizard   *Sceloporus occidentalis*   _____

_____

☐ Texas Spiny Lizard   *Sceloporus olivaceus*   _____

_____

☐ Granite Spiny Lizard   *Sceloporus orcutti*   _____

_____

☐ Crevice Spiny Lizard   *Sceloporus poinsettii*   _____

_____

☐ Slevin's Bunchgrass Lizard   *Sceloporus slevini*   _____

_____

☐ Plateau Lizard   *Sceloporus tristichus*   _____

_____

☐ Eastern Fence Lizard   *Sceloporus undulatus*   _____

_____

☐ Rose-bellied Lizard   *Sceloporus variabilis* _____

_____

☐ Striped Plateau Lizard   *Sceloporus virgatus* _____

_____

☐ Florida Scrub Lizard   *Sceloporus woodi*   * _____

_____

☐ Coachella Valley Fringe-toed Lizard   *Uma inornata*   * _____

_____

☐ Colorado Desert Fringe-toed Lizard   *Uma notata*   * _____

_____

☐ Yuman Desert Fringe-toed Lizard   *Uma rufopunctata* _____

_____

☐ Mojave Fringe-toed Lizard   *Uma scoparia*   * _____

_____

☐ Long-tailed Brush Lizard   *Urosaurus graciosus* _____

_____

☐ Baja California Brush Lizard   *Urosaurus nigricaudus* _____

_____

☐ Ornate Tree Lizard   *Urosaurus ornatus* _____

_____

☐ Common Side-blotched Lizard   *Uta stansburiana* _____

_____

Family Crotaphytidae: Collared Lizards and Leopard Lizards (North America: 8; World: 10)

☐ Great Basin Collared Lizard   *Crotaphytus bicinctores* _____

_____

☐ Eastern Collared Lizard   *Crotaphytus collaris* _____

_____

☐ Sonoran Collared Lizard *Crotaphytus nebrius* * _____

_____

☐ Reticulate Collared Lizard *Crotaphytus reticulatus* * _____

_____

☐ Baja California Collared Lizard *Crotaphytus vestigium* _____

_____

☐ Cope's Leopard Lizard *Gambelia copeii* _____

_____

☐ Blunt-nosed Leopard Lizard *Gambelia sila* * _____

_____

☐ Long-nosed Leopard Lizard *Gambelia wislizenii* _____

_____

Family Gekkonidae: Geckos (North America: 2; World: 1,026)

☐ Peninsular Leaf-toed Gecko *Phyllodactylus nocticolus* _____

_____

☐ Reef Gecko *Sphaerodactylus notatus* _____

_____

**Family Eublepharidae: Banded Geckos
(North America: 4; World: 21)**

☐ Texas Banded Gecko *Coleonyx brevis* _____

_____

☐ Reticulate Banded Gecko *Coleonyx reticulatus* * _____

_____

☐ Switak's Banded Gecko *Coleonyx switaki* _____

_____

☐ Western Banded Gecko *Coleonyx variegatus* _____

_____

Family Xantusiidae: Night Lizards
(North America: 5; World: 25)

☐   Bezy's Night Lizard   *Xantusia bezyi*   * _____

_____

☐   Sandstone Night Lizard   *Xantusia gracilis*   * _____

_____

☐   Granite Night Lizard   *Xantusia henshawi*   * _____

_____

☐   Island Night Lizard   *Xantusia riversiana*   * _____

_____

☐   Desert Night Lizard   *Xantusia vigilis*   _____

_____

Family Teiidae: Whiptails and Racerunners
(North America: 22; World: 121)

☐   Arizona Striped Whiptail   *Aspidoscelis arizonae*   * _____

_____

☐   Canyon Spotted Whiptail   *Aspidoscelis burti*   _____

_____

☐   Gray Checkered Whiptail   *Aspidoscelis dixoni*   * _____

_____

☐   Chihuahuan Spotted Whiptail   *Aspidoscelis exsanguis*   _____

_____

☐   Gila Spotted Whiptail   *Aspidoscelis flagellicauda*   _____

_____

☐   Eastern Spotted Whiptail   *Aspidoscelis gularis*   _____

_____

☐   Little White Whiptail   *Aspidoscelis gypsi*   _____

_____

☐ Orange-throated Whiptail *Aspidoscelis hyperythra* _____

                     _____

☐ Little Striped Whiptail *Aspidoscelis inornata* _____

                     _____

☐ Laredo Striped Whiptail *Aspidoscelis laredoensis* _____

                     _____

☐ Marbled Whiptail *Aspidoscelis marmorata* _____

                     _____

☐ New Mexico Whiptail *Aspidoscelis neomexicana* _____

                     _____

☐ Colorado Checkered Whiptail *Aspidoscelis neotesselata* * _____

                     _____

☐ Pai Striped Whiptail *Aspidoscelis pai* _____

                     _____

☐ Mexican Plateau Spotted Whiptail *Aspidoscelis septemvittata* _____

                     _____

☐ Six-lined Racerunner *Aspidoscelis sexlineata* _____

                     _____

☐ Sonoran Spotted Whiptail *Aspidoscelis sonorae* _____

                     _____

☐ Common Checkered Whiptail *Aspidoscelis tesselata* _____

                     _____

☐ Tiger Whiptail *Aspidoscelis tigris* _____

                     _____

☐ Desert Grassland Whiptail *Aspidoscelis uniparens* _____

                     _____

☐ Plateau Striped Whiptail *Aspidoscelis velox* _____

                     _____

☐   Red-backed Whiptail   *Aspidoscelis xanthonota*   _____

_____

Family Scincidae: Skinks (North America: 14; World: 1,305)

☐   Coal Skink   *Plestiodon anthracinus*   _____

_____

☐   Mountain Skink   *Plestiodon callicephalus*   _____

_____

☐   Mole Skink   *Plestiodon egregius*   _____

_____

☐   Common Five-lined Skink   *Plestiodon fasciatus*   _____

_____

☐   Gilbert's Skink   *Plestiodon gilberti*   _____

_____

☐   Southeastern Five-lined Skink   *Plestiodon inexpectatus*   _____

_____

☐   Broad-headed Skink   *Plestiodon laticeps*   _____

_____

☐   Many-lined Skink   *Plestiodon multivirgatus*   _____

_____

☐   Great Plains Skink   *Plestiodon obsoletus*   _____

_____

☐   Florida Sand Skink   *Plestiodon reynoldsi*   *   _____

_____

☐   Prairie Skink   *Plestiodon septentrionalis*   _____

_____

☐   Western Skink   *Plestiodon skiltonianus*   _____

_____

☐ Four-lined Skink   *Plestiodon tetragrammus*   _____

_____

☐ Little Brown Skink   *Scincella lateralis*   _____

_____

Family Anniellidae: North American Legless Lizards
(North America: 1; World: 2)

☐ California Legless Lizard   *Anniella pulchra*   *   _____

_____

Family Anguidae: Alligator Lizards and Glass Lizards
(North America: 9; World: 112)

☐ Northern Alligator Lizard   *Elgaria coerulea*   _____

_____

☐ Madrean Alligator Lizard   *Elgaria kingii*   _____

_____

☐ Southern Alligator Lizard   *Elgaria multicarinata*   _____

_____

☐ Panamint Alligator Lizard   *Elgaria panamintina*   *   _____

_____

☐ Texas Alligator Lizard   *Gerrhonotus infernalis*   _____

_____

☐ Slender Glass Lizard   *Ophisaurus attenuatus*   _____

_____

☐ Island Glass Lizard   *Ophisaurus compressus*   *   _____

_____

☐ Mimic Glass Lizard   *Ophisaurus mimicus*   *   _____

_____

☐ Eastern Glass Lizard   *Ophisaurus ventralis*   _____

_____

Family Helodermatidae: Venomous Lizards
(North America: 1; World: 2)

☐ Gila Monster   *Heloderma suspectum*

_____

_____

Suborder Serpentes: Snakes

Family Boidae: Boas and Pythons
(North America: 3; World: 74)

☐ Northern Rubber Boa   *Charina bottae*

_____

_____

☐ Southern Rubber Boa   *Charina umbratica*

_____

_____

☐ Rosy Boa   *Lichanura trivirgata*

_____

_____

Family Leptotyphlopidae: Threadsnakes
(North America: 3; World: 93)

☐ New Mexico Threadsnake   *Leptotyphlops dissectus*

_____

_____

☐ Texas Threadsnake   *Leptotyphlops dulcis*

_____

_____

☐ Western Threadsnake   *Leptotyphlops humilis*

_____

Family Colubridae: Colubrid Snakes
(North America: 115; World: 1,827)

☐ Glossy Snake   *Arizona elegans*

_____

_____

☐ Baja California Ratsnake   *Bogertophis rosaliae*

_____

_____

☐ Trans-Pecos Ratsnake   *Bogertophis subocularis*

_____

☐ Eastern Wormsnake   *Carphophis amoenus*   _____

_____

☐ Western Wormsnake   *Carphophis vermis*   _____

_____

☐ Scarletsnake   *Cemophora coccinea*   _____

_____

☐ Variable Sandsnake   *Chilomeniscus stramineus* _____

_____

☐ Western Shovel-nosed Snake   *Chionactis occipitalis*   _____

_____

☐ Sonoran Shovel-nosed Snake   *Chionactis palarostris*   * _____

_____

☐ Kirtland's Snake   *Clonophis kirtlandii*   * _____

_____

☐ Racer   *Coluber constrictor*   _____

_____

☐ Regal Black-striped Snake   *Coniophanes imperialis*   _____

_____

☐ Sharp-tailed Snake   *Contia tenuis*   _____

_____

☐ Ring-necked Snake   *Diadophis punctatus*   _____

_____

☐ Eastern Indigo Snake   *Drymarchon couperi*   * _____

_____

☐ Central American Indigo Snake   *Drymarchon melanurus*   _____

_____

☐ Speckled Racer   *Drymobius margaritiferus* _____

_____

☐ Red-bellied Mudsnake   *Farancia abacura*   _____

_____

☐ Rainbow Snake   *Farancia erytrogramma*   _____

_____

☐ Tamaulipan Hook-nosed Snake   *Ficimia streckeri*   _____

_____

☐ Chihuahuan Hook-nosed Snake   *Gyalopion canum*   _____

_____

☐ Thornscrub Hook-nosed Snake   *Gyalopion quadrangulare* _____

_____

☐ Dusty Hog-nosed Snake   *Heterodon gloydi*   _____

_____

☐ Mexican Hog-nosed Snake   *Heterodon kennerlyi*   _____

_____

☐ Western Hog-nosed Snake   *Heterodon nasicus*   _____

_____

☐ Eastern Hog-nosed Snake   *Heterodon platirhinos*   _____

_____

☐ Southern Hog-nosed Snake   *Heterodon simus*   *   _____

_____

☐ Nightsnake   *Hypsiglena torquata*   _____

_____

☐ Gray-banded Kingsnake   *Lampropeltis alterna*   _____

_____

☐ Yellow-bellied Kingsnake   *Lampropeltis calligaster*   _____

_____

☐ Common Kingsnake   *Lampropeltis getula*   _____

_____

☐ Sonoran Mountain Kingsnake   *Lampropeltis pyromelana*   _____

_____

☐ Milksnake   *Lampropeltis triangulum*   _____

_____

☐ California Mountain Kingsnake   *Lampropeltis zonata*   _____

_____

☐ Cat-eyed Snake   *Leptodeira septentrionalis*   _____

_____

☐ Sonoran Whipsnake   *Masticophis bilineatus*   _____

_____

☐ Coachwhip   *Masticophis flagellum*   _____

_____

☐ Baja California Coachwhip   *Masticophis fuliginosus*   _____

_____

☐ Striped Racer   *Masticophis lateralis*   _____

_____

☐ Schott's Whipsnake   *Masticophis schotti*   _____

_____

☐ Striped Whipsnake   *Masticophis taeniatus*   _____

_____

☐ Saltmarsh Snake   *Nerodia clarkii*   _____

_____

☐ Mississippi Green Watersnake   *Nerodia cyclopion*   _____

_____

☐ Plain-bellied Watersnake   *Nerodia erythrogaster*   _____

_____

☐ Southern Watersnake   *Nerodia fasciata*   _____

_____

☐ Florida Green Watersnake   *Nerodia floridana*

_____

_____

☐ Brazos River Watersnake   *Nerodia harteri*   *

_____

_____

☐ Concho Watersnake   *Nerodia paucimaculata*   *

_____

_____

☐ Diamond-backed Watersnake   *Nerodia rhombifer*

_____

_____

☐ Northern Watersnake   *Nerodia sipedon*

_____

_____

☐ Brown Watersnake   *Nerodia taxispilota*

_____

_____

☐ Rough Greensnake   *Opheodrys aestivus*

_____

_____

☐ Smooth Greensnake   *Opheodrys vernalis*

_____

_____

☐ Brown Vinesnake   *Oxybelis aeneus*

_____

_____

☐ Eastern Ratsnake   *Pantherophis alleghaniensis*

_____

_____

☐ Baird's Ratsnake   *Pantherophis bairdi*

_____

_____

☐ Great Plains Ratsnake   *Pantherophis emoryi*

_____

_____

☐ Eastern Foxsnake   *Pantherophis gloydi*   *

_____

_____

☐ Red Cornsnake   *Pantherophis guttata*

_____

_____

☐ Texas Ratsnake   *Pantherophis obsoleta*   _____

_____

☐ Slowinski's Cornsnake   *Pantherophis slowinskii*   _____

_____

☐ Gray Ratsnake   *Pantherophis spiloides*   _____

_____

☐ Western Foxsnake   *Pantherophis vulpina*   _____

_____

☐ Saddled Leaf-nosed Snake   *Phyllorhynchus browni*   _____

_____

☐ Spotted Leaf-nosed Snake   *Phyllorhynchus decurtatus*   _____

_____

☐ Gophersnake   *Pituophis catenifer*   _____

_____

☐ Pinesnake   *Pituophis melanoleucus*   _____

_____

☐ Louisiana Pinesnake   *Pituophis ruthveni*   *   _____

_____

☐ Striped Crayfish Snake   *Regina alleni*   _____

_____

☐ Graham's Crayfish Snake   *Regina grahamii*   _____

_____

☐ Glossy Crayfish Snake   *Regina rigida*   _____

_____

☐ Queen Snake   *Regina septemvittata*   _____

_____

☐ Pine Woods Littersnake   *Rhadinaea flavilata*   _____

_____

☐ Long-nosed Snake   *Rhinocheilus lecontei*   _____

                                                                         _____

☐ Eastern Patch-nosed Snake   *Salvadora grahamiae*   _____

                                                                         _____

☐ Western Patch-nosed Snake   *Salvadora hexalepis*   _____

                                                                         _____

☐ Black Swampsnake   *Seminatrix pygaea*   _____

                                                                         _____

☐ Green Ratsnake   *Senticolis triaspis*   _____

                                                                         _____

☐ Groundsnake   *Sonora semiannulata*   _____

                                                                         _____

☐ Short-tailed Snake   *Stilosoma extenuatum* *   _____

                                                                         _____

☐ DeKay's Brownsnake   *Storeria dekayi*   _____

                                                                         _____

☐ Red-bellied Snake   *Storeria occipitomaculata*_____

                                                                         _____

☐ Florida Brownsnake   *Storeria victa*   _____

                                                                         _____

☐ Mexican Black-headed Snake   *Tantilla atriceps*   *   _____

                                                                         _____

☐ Southeastern Crowned Snake   *Tantilla coronata*   _____

                                                                         _____

☐ Trans-Pecos Black-headed Snake   *Tantilla cucullata*   *   _____

                                                                         _____

☐ Flat-headed Snake   *Tantilla gracilis*   _____

                                                                         _____

☐ Smith's Black-headed Snake   *Tantilla hobartsmithi* _____

_____

☐ Plains Black-headed Snake   *Tantilla nigriceps* _____

_____

☐ Rim Rock Crowned Snake   *Tantilla oolitica*   * _____

_____

☐ Western Black-headed Snake   *Tantilla planiceps* _____

_____

☐ Florida Crowned Snake   *Tantilla relicta* _____

_____

☐ Chihuahuan Black-headed Snake   *Tantilla wilcoxi* _____

_____

☐ Yaqui Black-headed Snake   *Tantilla yaquia* _____

_____

☐ Aquatic Gartersnake   *Thamnophis atratus* _____

_____

☐ Short-headed Gartersnake   *Thamnophis brachystoma* _____

_____

☐ Butler's Gartersnake   *Thamnophis butleri* _____

_____

☐ Sierra Gartersnake   *Thamnophis couchii* _____

_____

☐ Black-necked Gartersnake   *Thamnophis cyrtopsis* _____

_____

☐ Terrestrial Gartersnake   *Thamnophis elegans* _____

_____

☐ Mexican Gartersnake   *Thamnophis eques*   * _____

_____

☐ Giant Gartersnake *Thamnophis gigas* * _____

_____

☐ Two-striped Gartersnake *Thamnophis hammondii* * _____

_____

☐ Checkered Gartersnake *Thamnophis marcianus* _____

_____

☐ Northwestern Gartersnake *Thamnophis ordinoides* _____

_____

☐ Western Ribbonsnake *Thamnophis proximus* _____

_____

☐ Plains Gartersnake *Thamnophis radix* _____

_____

☐ Narrow-headed Gartersnake *Thamnophis rufipunctatus* * _____

_____

☐ Eastern Ribbonsnake *Thamnophis sauritus* _____

_____

☐ Common Gartersnake *Thamnophis sirtalis* _____

_____

☐ Western Lyresnake *Trimorphodon biscutatus* _____

_____

☐ Chihuahuan Desert Lyresnake *Trimorphodon vilkinsonii* _____

_____

☐ Lined Snake *Tropidoclonion lineatum* _____

_____

☐ Rough Earthsnake *Virginia striatula* _____

_____

☐ Smooth Earthsnake *Virginia valeriae* _____

_____

**Family Elapidae: Coralsnakes and Seasnakes
(North America: 4; World: 138)**

☐ Sonoran Coralsnake   *Micruroides euryxanthus*   _____

_____

☐ Harlequin Coralsnake   *Micrurus fulvius*   _____

_____

☐ Texas Coralsnake   *Micrurus tener*   _____

_____

☐ Yellow-bellied Seasnake   *Pelamis platurus*   _____

_____

**Family Viperidae: Vipers and Pit Vipers
(North America: 18; World: 259)**

☐ Copperhead   *Agkistrodon contortrix*   _____

_____

☐ Cottonmouth   *Agkistrodon piscivorus*   _____

_____

☐ Eastern Diamond-backed   *Crotalus adamanteus*   _____
   Rattlesnake

_____

☐ Western Diamond-backed   *Crotalus atrox*   _____
   Rattlesnake

_____

☐ Sidewinder   *Crotalus cerastes*   _____

_____

☐ Timber Rattlesnake   *Crotalus horridus*   _____

_____

☐ Rock Rattlesnake   *Crotalus lepidus*   _____

_____

☐ Speckled Rattlesnake   *Crotalus mitchellii*   _____

_____

☐ Black-tailed Rattlesnake   *Crotalus molossus*   _____

_____

☐ Western Rattlesnake   *Crotalus oreganus*   _____

_____

☐ Twin-spotted Rattlesnake   *Crotalus pricei*   _____

_____

☐ Red Diamond Rattlesnake   *Crotalus ruber*   _____

_____

☐ Mohave Rattlesnake   *Crotalus scutulatus*   _____

_____

☐ Tiger Rattlesnake   *Crotalus tigris*   _____

_____

☐ Prairie Rattlesnake   *Crotalus viridis*   _____

_____

☐ Ridge-nosed Rattlesnake   *Crotalus willardi*   _____

_____

☐ Massasauga   *Sistrurus catenatus*   *   _____

_____

☐ Pygmy Rattlesnake   *Sistrurus miliarius*   _____

_____

Order Crocodylia: Crocodilians

**Family Alligatoridae: Alligators and Caimans
(North America: 1; World: 8)**

☐ American Alligator   *Alligator mississippiensis*   _____

_____

Family Crocodylidae: Crocodiles (North America: 1; World: 14)

☐ American Crocodile   *Crocodylus acutus*   *   _____

_____

Order Testudines: Turtles

Family Kinosternidae: Mud Turtles and Musk Turtles (North America: 10; World: 25)

☐ Arizona Mud Turtle   *Kinosternon arizonense*   _____

_____

☐ Striped Mud Turtle   *Kinosternon baurii*   _____

_____

☐ Yellow Mud Turtle   *Kinosternon flavescens*   _____

_____

☐ Rough-footed Mud Turtle   *Kinosternon hirtipes*   *   _____

_____

☐ Sonora Mud Turtle   *Kinosternon sonoriense*   _____

_____

☐ Eastern Mud Turtle   *Kinosternon subrubrum*   _____

_____

☐ Razor-backed Musk Turtle   *Sternotherus carinatus*   _____

_____

☐ Flattened Musk Turtle   *Sternotherus depressus*   *   _____

_____

☐ Loggerhead Musk Turtle   *Sternotherus minor*   _____

_____

☐ Stinkpot   *Sternotherus odoratus*   _____

_____

Family Chelydridae: Snapping Turtles (North America: 2; World: 3)

☐ Snapping Turtle   *Chelydra serpentina*   _____

_____

☐ Alligator Snapping Turtle   *Macrochelys temminckii*   *   _____

_____

Family Emydidae: Box Turtles and Water Turtles
North America: 33; World: 41)

☐ Pacific Pond Turtle   *Actinemys marmorata*   *   _____

_____

☐ Southern Painted Turtle   *Chrysemys dorsalis*   _____

_____

☐ Northern Painted Turtle   *Chrysemys picta*   _____

_____

☐ Spotted Turtle   *Clemmys guttata*   _____

_____

☐ Chicken Turtle   *Deirochelys reticularia*   _____

_____

☐ Blanding's Turtle   *Emydoidea blandingii*   _____

_____

☐ Wood Turtle   *Glyptemys insculpta*   _____

_____

☐ Bog Turtle   *Glyptemys muhlenbergii*   *   _____

_____

☐ Barbour's Map Turtle   *Graptemys barbouri*   *   _____

_____

☐ Cagle's Map Turtle   *Graptemys caglei*   *   _____

_____

☐ Escambia Map Turtle   *Graptemys ernsti*   *   _____

_____

☐ Yellow-blotched Map Turtle *Graptemys flavimaculata* *   _____

_____

☐ Northern Map Turtle   *Graptemys geographica*   _____

_____

☐ Pascagoula Map Turtle *Graptemys gibbonsi* * _____

_____

☐ Black-knobbed Map Turtle *Graptemys nigrinoda* * _____

_____

☐ Ringed Map Turtle *Graptemys oculifera* * _____

_____

☐ Ouachita Map Turtle *Graptemys ouachitensis* _____

_____

☐ False Map Turtle *Graptemys pseudogeographica* _____

_____

☐ Alabama Map Turtle *Graptemys pulchra* _____

_____

☐ Texas Map Turtle *Graptemys versa* _____

_____

☐ Diamond-backed Terrapin *Malaclemys terrapin* _____

_____

☐ Alabama Red-bellied Cooter *Pseudemys alabamensis* * _____

_____

☐ River Cooter *Pseudemys concinna* _____

_____

☐ Rio Grande Cooter *Pseudemys gorzugi* _____

_____

☐ Florida Red-bellied Cooter *Pseudemys nelsoni* _____

_____

☐ Peninsula Cooter *Pseudemys peninsularis* _____

_____

☐ Northern Red-bellied Cooter *Pseudemys rubriventris* _____

_____

☐ Suwannee Cooter   *Pseudemys suwanniensis*   _____

_____

☐ Texas River Cooter   *Pseudemys texana*   _____

_____

☐ Eastern Box Turtle   *Terrapene carolina*   _____

_____

☐ Ornate Box Turtle   *Terrapene ornata*   _____

_____

☐ Mexican Plateau Slider   *Trachemys gaigeae*   *   _____

_____

☐ Pond Slider   *Trachemys scripta*   _____

_____

Family Testudinidae: Tortoises (North America: 3; World: 51)

☐ Desert Tortoise   *Gopherus agassizii*   _____

_____

☐ Berlandier's Tortoise   *Gopherus berlandieri*   _____

_____

☐ Bolson Tortoise   *Gopherus flavomarginatus* øP   _____

_____

☐ Gopher Tortoise   *Gopherus polyphemus*   *   _____

_____

☐ North American Giant-Tortoise   *Hesperotestudo crassiscutata*   †P   _____

_____

☐ Smooth-shelled Tortoise   *Hesperotestudo equicomes*   †P   _____

_____

☐ Rough-shelled Tortoise   *Hesperotestudo incisa*   †P   _____

_____

☐ Plains Tortoise   *Hesperotestudo wilsoni*   †P _____

_____

Family Cheloniidae: Seaturtles (North America: 5; World: 6)

☐ Loggerhead Seaturtle   *Caretta caretta*   * _____

_____

☐ Green Seaturtle   *Chelonia mydas*   * _____

_____

☐ Hawksbill Seaturtle   *Eretmochelys imbricata*   * _____

_____

☐ Kemp's Ridley Seaturtle   *Lepidochelys kempii*   * _____

_____

☐ Olive Ridley Seaturtle   *Lepidochelys olivacea*   * _____

_____

Family Dermochelyidae: Leatherback Seaturtles (North America: 1; World: 1)

☐ Leatherback Seaturtle   *Dermochelys coriacea*   * _____

_____

Family Trionychidae: Softshells (North America: 3; World: 30)

☐ Florida Softshell   *Apalone ferox*   _____

_____

☐ Smooth Softshell   *Apalone mutica*   _____

_____

☐ Spiny Softshell   *Apalone spinifera*   _____

_____

ALIEN REPTILES, TURTLES, AND CROCODILLIANS

Family Iguanidae: Iguanid Lizards

☐ Western Spiny-tailed Iguana   *Ctenosaura pectinata*   _____

_____

☐ Common Green Iguana   *Iguana iguana*   _____

_____

Family Polychrotidae: Anoles

☐ Blue-green Anole   *Anolis chlorocyanus*   _____

_____

☐ Crested Anole   *Anolis cristatellus*   _____

_____

☐ Large-headed Anole   *Anolis cybotes*   _____

_____

☐ Bark Anole   *Anolis distichus*   _____

_____

☐ Knight Anole   *Anolis equestris*   _____

_____

☐ Jamaican Giant Anole   *Anolis garmani*   _____

_____

☐ Cuban Green Anole   *Anolis porcatus*   _____

_____

☐ Brown Anole   *Anolis sagrei*   _____

_____

☐ Brown Basilisk   *Basiliscus vittatus*   _____

_____

Family Phrynosomatidae: Spiny Lizards

☐ Northern Curly-tailed Lizard *Leiocephalus carinatus*   _____

_____

☐ Red-sided Curly-tailed Lizard *Leiocephalus schreibersii*   _____

_____

Family Gekkonidae: Geckos

☐ Flat-tailed House Gecko   *Cosymbotus platyurus*   _____

_____

☐ Rough-tailed Gecko   *Cyrtopodion scabrum*   _____

_____

☐ Stump-toed Gecko   *Gehyra mutilata*   _____

_____

☐ Tokay Gecko   *Gekko gecko*   _____

_____

☐ Yellow-headed Gecko   *Gonatodes albogularis*   _____

_____

☐ Common House Gecko   *Hemidactylus frenatus*   _____

_____

☐ Indo-Pacific Gecko   *Hemidactylus garnotii*   _____

_____

☐ Amerafrican House Gecko   *Hemidactylus mabouia*   _____

_____

☐ Mediterranean House Gecko   *Hemidactylus turcicus*   _____

_____

☐ Ocellated Gecko   *Sphaerodactylus argus*   _____

_____

☐ Ashy Gecko   *Sphaerodactylus elegans*   _____

_____

☐ Moorish Wall Gecko   *Tarentola mauritanica*   _____

_____

Family Teiidae: Whiptails and Racerunners

☐ Giant Ameiva   *Ameiva ameiva*   _____

_____

☐ Rainbow Whiptail *Cnemidophorus lemniscatus* _____

_____

Family Scincidae: Skinks

☐ Many-striped Mabuya *Mabuya multifasciata* _____

_____

Family Lacertidae: Lacertid Lizards

☐ Western Green Lizard *Lacerta bilineata* _____

_____

☐ Common Wall Lizard *Podarcis muralis* _____

_____

☐ Italian Wall Lizard *Podarcis sicula* _____

_____

Family Chamaeleonidae: Chameleons

☐ Jackson's Chameleon *Chamaeleo jacksonii* _____

_____

Family Typhlopidae: Blind Snakes

☐ Brahminy Blindsnake *Ramphotyphlops braminus* _____

_____

Family Alligatoridae: Alligators and Caimans

☐ Common Caiman *Caiman crocodilus* _____

_____

ADDITIONAL SPECIES

☐ _____   _____   _____

_____

☐ _____   _____   _____

_____

☐ _____   _____   _____

_____

☐ _____   _____   _____

_____

☐ _____   _____   _____

_____

☐ _____   _____   _____

_____

☐ _____   _____   _____

_____

☐ _____   _____   _____

_____

☐ _____   _____   _____

_____

☐ _____   _____   _____

_____

☐ _____   _____   _____

_____

☐ _____   _____   _____

_____

☐ _____ _____ _____
                                                          _____

☐ _____ _____ _____
                                                          _____

☐ _____ _____ _____
                                                          _____

☐ _____ _____ _____
                                                          _____

☐ _____ _____ _____
                                                          _____

☐ _____ _____ _____
                                                          _____

☐ _____ _____ _____
                                                          _____

☐ _____ _____ _____
                                                          _____

☐ _____ _____ _____
                                                          _____

☐ _____ _____ _____
                                                          _____

☐ _____ _____ _____
                                                          _____

☐ _____ _____ _____
                                                          _____

☐ _____ _____ _____
                                    _____
☐ _____ _____ _____
                                    _____
☐ _____ _____ _____
                                    _____
☐ _____ _____ _____
                                    _____
☐ _____ _____ _____
                                    _____
☐ _____ _____ _____
                                    _____
☐ _____ _____ _____
                                    _____
☐ _____ _____ _____
                                    _____
☐ _____ _____ _____
                                    _____
☐ _____ _____ _____
                                    _____
☐ _____ _____ _____
                                    _____
☐ _____ _____ _____
                                    _____
☐ _____ _____ _____
                                    _____

Class Amphibia: Amphibians

Order Anura: Frogs and Toads

Family Ascaphidae: Tailed Frogs (North America: 2; World: 2)

☐ Rocky Mountain Tailed Frog   *Ascaphus montanus*   _____

_____

☐ Coastal Tailed Frog   *Ascaphus truei*   _____

_____

**Family Rhinophrynidae: Burrowing Toads
(North America: 1; World: 1)**

☐ Mexican Burrowing Toad   *Rhinophrynus dorsalis*   _____

_____

**Family Scaphiopodidae: Spadefoots
(North America: 7; World: 7)**

☐ Couch's Spadefoot   *Scaphiopus couchii*   _____

_____

☐ Eastern Spadefoot   *Scaphiopus holbrookii*   _____

_____

☐ Hurter's Spadefoot   *Scaphiopus hurterii*   _____

_____

☐ Plains Spadefoot   *Spea bombifrons*   _____

_____

☐ Western Spadefoot   *Spea hammondii*   *   _____

_____

☐ Great Basin Spadefoot   *Spea intermontana*   _____

_____

Species Lifelist: Amphibians / 239

☐ Mexican Spadefoot   *Spea multiplicata*

_____

_____

**Family Leptodactylidae: Neotropical Frogs
(North America: 5; World: 1,256)**

☐ Barking Frog   *Eleutherodactylus augusti*

_____

_____

☐ Rio Grande Chirping Frog   *Eleutherodactylus cystignathoides*

_____

_____

☐ Spotted Chirping Frog   *Eleutherodactylus guttilatus*

_____

_____

☐ Cliff Chirping Frog   *Eleutherodactylus marnockii*

_____

_____

☐ Mexican White-lipped Frog   *Leptodactylus fragilis*

_____

_____

Family Bufonidae: True Toads (North America: 22; World: 478)

☐ Sonoran Desert Toad   *Bufo alvarius*

_____

_____

☐ American Toad   *Bufo americanus*

_____

_____

☐ Wyoming Toad   *Bufo baxteri*   *

_____

_____

☐ Western Toad   *Bufo boreas*

_____

_____

☐ Arroyo Toad   *Bufo californicus*   *

_____

_____

☐ Yosemite Toad   *Bufo canorus*   *

_____

_____

☐ Great Plains Toad   *Bufo cognatus*

_____

_____

☐ Green Toad   *Bufo debilis*   _____

_____

☐ Black Toad   *Bufo exsul*   *   _____

_____

☐ Fowler's Toad   *Bufo fowleri*   _____

_____

☐ Canadian Toad   *Bufo hemiophrys*   _____

_____

☐ Houston Toad   *Bufo houstonensis*   *   _____

_____

☐ Cane Toad   *Bufo marinus*   _____

_____

☐ Arizona Toad   *Bufo microscaphus*   *   _____

_____

☐ Gulf Coast Toad   *Bufo nebulifer*   _____

_____

☐ Amargosa Toad   *Bufo nelsoni*   *   _____

_____

☐ Red-spotted Toad   *Bufo punctatus*   _____

_____

☐ Oak Toad   *Bufo quercicus*   _____

_____

☐ Sonoran Green Toad   *Bufo retiformis*   *   _____

_____

☐ Texas Toad   *Bufo speciosus*   _____

_____

☐ Southern Toad   *Bufo terrestris*   _____

_____

☐ Woodhouse's Toad   *Bufo woodhousii*   _____

_____

Family Hylidae: Treefrogs, Chorus Frogs, and Cricket Frogs
(North America: 27; World: 808)

☐ Northern Cricket Frog   *Acris crepitans*   _____

_____

☐ Southern Cricket Frog   *Acris gryllus*   _____

_____

☐ Pine Barrens Treefrog   *Hyla andersonii*   _____

_____

☐ Canyon Treefrog   *Hyla arenicolor*   _____

_____

☐ Bird-voiced Treefrog   *Hyla avivoca*   _____

_____

☐ Cope's Gray Treefrog   *Hyla chrysoscelis*   _____

_____

☐ Green Treefrog   *Hyla cinerea*   _____

_____

☐ Pine Woods Treefrog   *Hyla femoralis*   _____

_____

☐ Barking Treefrog   *Hyla gratiosa*   _____

_____

☐ Squirrel Treefrog   *Hyla squirella*   _____

_____

☐ Gray Treefrog   *Hyla versicolor*   _____

_____

☐ Arizona Treefrog   *Hyla wrightorum*   _____

_____

☐ Mountain Chorus Frog *Pseudacris brachyphona* _____

_____

☐ Brimley's Chorus Frog *Pseudacris brimleyi* _____

_____

☐ California Treefrog *Pseudacris cadaverina* _____

_____

☐ Spotted Chorus Frog *Pseudacris clarkii* _____

_____

☐ Spring Peeper *Pseudacris crucifer* _____

_____

☐ Southeastern Chorus Frog *Pseudacris feriarum* _____

_____

☐ Boreal Chorus Frog *Pseudacris maculata* _____

_____

☐ Southern Chorus Frog *Pseudacris nigrita* _____

_____

☐ Little Grass Frog *Pseudacris ocularis* _____

_____

☐ Ornate Chorus Frog *Pseudacris ornata* _____

_____

☐ Pacific Treefrog *Pseudacris regilla* _____

_____

☐ Strecker's Chorus Frog *Pseudacris streckeri* _____

_____

☐ Western Chorus Frog *Pseudacris triseriata* _____

_____

☐ Lowland Burrowing Treefrog *Pternohyla fodiens* _____

_____

☐ Mexican Treefrog   *Smilisca baudinii*   _____

_____

**Family Microhylidae: Narrow-mouthed Frogs
(North America: 3; World: 427)**

☐ Eastern
Narrow-mouthed Toad   *Gastrophryne carolinensis*   _____

_____

☐ Great Plains
Narrow-mouthed Toad   *Gastrophryne olivacea*   _____

_____

☐ Sheep Frog   *Hypopachus variolosus*   _____

_____

Family Ranidae: True Frogs (North America: 28; World: 757)

☐ Crawfish Frog   *Rana areolata*   _____

_____

☐ Northern Red-legged Frog   *Rana aurora*   _____

_____

☐ Rio Grande Leopard Frog   *Rana berlandieri*   _____

_____

☐ Plains Leopard Frog   *Rana blairi*   _____

_____

☐ Foothill Yellow-legged Frog   *Rana boylii*   * _____

_____

☐ Gopher Frog   *Rana capito*   * _____

_____

☐ Cascades Frog   *Rana cascadae*   * _____

_____

☐ American Bullfrog   *Rana catesbeiana*   _____

_____

☐ Chiricahua Leopard Frog   *Rana chiricahuensis*   * _____

_____

☐ Green Frog   *Rana clamitans*   _____

_____

☐ California Red-legged Frog   *Rana draytonii*   _____

_____

☐ Vegas Valley Leopard Frog   *Rana fisheri*   †   _____

_____

☐ Pig Frog   *Rana grylio*   _____

_____

☐ River Frog   *Rana heckscheri*   _____

_____

☐ Columbia Spotted Frog   *Rana luteiventris*   _____

_____

☐ Mountain Yellow-legged Frog   *Rana muscosa*   *   _____

_____

☐ Florida Bog Frog   *Rana okaloosae*   *   _____

_____

☐ Relict Leopard Frog   *Rana onca*   *   _____

_____

☐ Pickerel Frog   *Rana palustris*   _____

_____

☐ Northern Leopard Frog   *Rana pipiens*   _____

_____

☐ Oregon Spotted Frog   *Rana pretiosa*   *   _____

_____

☐ Mink Frog   *Rana septentrionalis*   _____

_____

☐ Dusky Gopher Frog   *Rana sevosa*   *   _____

_____

☐ Southern Leopard Frog   *Rana sphenocephala*   _____

_____

☐ Ramsey Canyon   *Rana subaquavocalis*   * _____
    Leopard Frog

_____

☐ Wood Frog   *Rana sylvatica*   _____

_____

☐ Tarahumara Frog   *Rana tarahumarae*   * _____

_____

☐ Carpenter Frog   *Rana virgatipes*   _____

_____

☐ Lowland Leopard Frog   *Rana yavapaiensis*   _____

_____

Order Urodela: Salamanders

Family Cryptobranchidae: Hellbenders (North America: 1; World: 3)

☐ Hellbender   *Cryptobranchus alleganiensis*   * _____

_____

Family Sirenidae: Sirens (North America: 4; World: 4)

☐ Southern Dwarf Siren   *Pseudobranchus axanthus*   _____

_____

☐ Northern Dwarf Siren   *Pseudobranchus striatus*   _____

_____

☐ Lesser Siren   *Siren intermedia*   _____

_____

☐ Greater Siren   *Siren lacertina*   _____

_____

Family Salamandridae: Newts (North America: 6; World: 70)

☐ Black-spotted Newt   *Notophthalmus meridionalis*   * _____

_____

☐ Striped Newt   *Notophthalmus perstriatus* * _____

_____

☐ Eastern Newt   *Notophthalmus viridescens* _____

_____

☐ Rough-skinned Newt   *Taricha granulosa* _____

_____

☐ Red-bellied Newt   *Taricha rivularis* _____

_____

☐ California Newt   *Taricha torosa* _____

_____

Family Proteidae: Mudpuppies and Waterdogs
(North America: 5; World: 6)

☐ Blackwarrior Waterdog *Necturus alabamensis* * _____

_____

☐ Gulf Coast Waterdog   *Necturus beyeri* _____

_____

☐ Neuse River Waterdog   *Necturus lewisi* * _____

_____

☐ Mudpuppy   *Necturus maculosus* _____

_____

☐ Dwarf Waterdog   *Necturus punctatus* _____

_____

Family Amphiumidae: Amphiumas (North America: 3; World: 3)

☐ Two-toed Amphiuma   *Amphiuma means* _____

_____

☐ One-toed Amphiuma   *Amphiuma pholeter* * _____

_____

☐ Three-toed Amphiuma   *Amphiuma tridactylum* _____

_____

Family Ambystomatidae: Mole Salamanders
(North America: 14; World: 31)

☐ Ringed Salamander   *Ambystoma annulatum*   _____

_____

☐ Streamside Salamander   *Ambystoma barbouri*   _____

_____

☐ California Tiger Salamander *Ambystoma californiense*   *   _____

_____

☐ Flatwoods Salamander   *Ambystoma cingulatum*   *   _____

_____

☐ Northwestern Salamander   *Ambystoma gracile*   _____

_____

☐ Jefferson Salamander   *Ambystoma jeffersonianum*   _____

_____

☐ Blue-spotted Salamander   *Ambystoma laterale*   _____

_____

☐ Mabee's Salamander   *Ambystoma mabeei*   _____

_____

☐ Long-toed Salamander   *Ambystoma macrodactylum*   _____

_____

☐ Spotted Salamander   *Ambystoma maculatum*   _____

_____

☐ Marbled Salamander   *Ambystoma opacum*   _____

_____

☐ Mole Salamander   *Ambystoma talpoideum*   _____

_____

☐ Small-mouthed Salamander *Ambystoma texanum*   _____

_____

☐ Tiger Salamander   *Ambystoma tigrinum*   _____

_____

☐ Silvery Salamander   JJL   _____

_____

☐ Tremblay's Salamander   JLL   _____

_____

Family Dicamptodontidae: Pacific Giant Salamanders
(North America: 4; World: 4)

☐ Idaho Giant Salamander   *Dicamptodon aterrimus*   * _____

_____

☐ Cope's Giant Salamander   *Dicamptodon copei*   * _____

_____

☐ California Giant Salamander   *Dicamptodon ensatus*   * _____

_____

☐ Coastal Giant Salamander   *Dicamptodon tenebrosus*   _____

_____

Family Rhyacotritonidae: Torrent Salamanders
(North America: 4; World: 4)

☐ Cascade Torrent Salamander   *Rhyacotriton cascadae*   * _____

_____

☐ Columbia Torrent Salamander   *Rhyacotriton kezeri*   * _____

_____

☐ Olympic Torrent Salamander   *Rhyacotriton olympicus*   * _____

_____

☐ Southern Torrent Salamander   *Rhyacotriton variegatus*   * _____

_____

Family Plethodontidae: Lungless Salamanders
(North America: 138; World: 377)

☐ Green Salamander   *Aneides aeneus*   * _____

_____

☐ Clouded Salamander *Aneides ferreus* * _____

_____

☐ Black Salamander *Aneides flavipunctatus* _____

_____

☐ Sacramento Mountains *Aneides hardii* * _____
Salamander

_____

☐ Arboreal Salamander *Aneides lugubris* _____

_____

☐ Wandering Salamander *Aneides vagrans* _____

_____

☐ California Slender Salamander *Batrachoseps attenuatus* _____

_____

☐ Inyo Mountains Salamander *Batrachoseps campi* * _____

_____

☐ Hell Hollow Slender Salamander *Batrachoseps diabolicus* * _____

_____

☐ San Gabriel Mountains *Batrachoseps gabrieli* * _____
Slender Salamander

_____

☐ Gabilan Mountains *Batrachoseps* _____
Slender Salamander *gavilanensis*

_____

☐ Gregarious Slender Salamander *Batrachoseps gregarius* * _____

_____

☐ San Simeon Slender Salamander *Batrachoseps incognitus* * _____

_____

☐ Sequoia Slender Salamander *Batrachoseps kawia* * _____

_____

☐ Santa Lucia Mountains *Batrachoseps luciae* * _____
Slender Salamander

_____

☐ Garden Slender Salamander   *Batrachoseps major*   _____

_____

☐ Lesser Slender Salamander   *Batrachoseps minor*   * _____

_____

☐ Black-bellied Slender Salamander   *Batrachoseps nigriventris* _____

_____

☐ Channel Islands Slender Salamander   *Batrachoseps pacificus* _____

_____

☐ Kings River Slender Salamander   *Batrachoseps regius*   * _____

_____

☐ Relictual Slender Salamander   *Batrachoseps relictus*   * _____

_____

☐ Kern Plateau Salamander   *Batrachoseps robustus*   * _____

_____

☐ Kern Canyon Slender Salamander   *Batrachoseps simatus*   * _____

_____

☐ Tehachapi Slender Salamander   *Batrachoseps stebbinsi*   * _____

_____

☐ Oregon Slender Salamander   *Batrachoseps wrightorum*   * _____

_____

☐ Cumberland Dusky Salamander   *Desmognathus abditus*   * _____

_____

☐ Seepage Salamander   *Desmognathus aeneus*   * _____

_____

☐ Apalachicola Dusky Salamander   *Desmognathus apalachicolae*   * _____

_____

☐ Southern Dusky Salamander   *Desmognathus auriculatus* _____

_____

☐ Ouachita Dusky Salamander   *Desmognathus brimleyorum*   _____

_____

☐ Carolina Mountain
   Dusky Salamander   *Desmognathus carolinensis* _____

_____

☐ Spotted Dusky Salamander   *Desmognathus conanti*   _____

_____

☐ Dwarf Black-bellied Salamander *Desmognathus folkertsi* * _____

_____

☐ Northern Dusky Salamander   *Desmognathus fuscus*   _____

_____

☐ Imitator Salamander   *Desmognathus imitator* * _____

_____

☐ Shovel-nosed Salamander   *Desmognathus marmoratus*   _____

_____

☐ Seal Salamander   *Desmognathus monticola*   _____

_____

☐ Allegheny Mountain
   Dusky Salamander   *Desmognathus ochrophaeus*   _____

_____

☐ Ocoee Salamander   *Desmognathus ocoee*   _____

_____

☐ Blue Ridge Dusky Salamander   *Desmognathus orestes*   _____

_____

☐ Black-bellied Salamander   *Desmognathus quadramaculatus*   _____

_____

☐ Santeetlah Dusky Salamander *Desmognathus santeetlah* * _____

_____

☐ Black Mountain Salamander   *Desmognathus welteri*   _____

_____

☐ Pygmy Salamander   *Desmognathus wrighti* * _____

_____

☐ Ensatina   *Ensatina eschscholtzii* _____

_____

☐ Northern Two-lined Salamander   *Eurycea bislineata* _____

_____

☐ Chamberlain's Dwarf Salamander   *Eurycea chamberlaini* * _____

_____

☐ Salado Salamander   *Eurycea chisholmensis* * _____

_____

☐ Southern Two-lined Salamander   *Eurycea cirrigera* _____

_____

☐ Three-lined Salamander   *Eurycea guttolineata* _____

_____

☐ Junaluska Salamander   *Eurycea junaluska* * _____

_____

☐ Cascade Caverns Salamander   *Eurycea latitans* * _____

_____

☐ Long-tailed Salamander   *Eurycea longicauda* _____

_____

☐ Cave Salamander   *Eurycea lucifuga* _____

_____

☐ Many-ribbed Salamander   *Eurycea multiplicata* _____

_____

☐ San Marcos Salamander   *Eurycea nana* * _____

_____

☐ Georgetown Salamander   *Eurycea naufragia* * _____

_____

☐ Texas Salamander   *Eurycea neotenes*   * _____

_____

☐ Fern Bank Salamander   *Eurycea pterophila*   * _____

_____

☐ Dwarf Salamander   *Eurycea quadridigitata*   _____

_____

☐ Texas Blind Salamander   *Eurycea rathbuni*   * _____

_____

☐ Blanco Blind Salamander   *Eurycea robusta*   * †? _____

_____

☐ Barton Springs Salamander   *Eurycea sosorum*   * _____

_____

☐ Grotto Salamander   *Eurycea spelaeus*   _____

_____

☐ Jollyville Plateau Salamander   *Eurycea tonkawae*   * _____

_____

☐ Comal Blind Salamander   *Eurycea tridentifera*   * _____

_____

☐ Valdina Farms Salamander   *Eurycea troglodytes*   * _____

_____

☐ Oklahoma Salamander   *Eurycea tynerensis*   * _____

_____

☐ Austin Blind Salamander   *Eurycea waterlooensis*   * _____

_____

☐ Blue Ridge Two-lined Salamander   *Eurycea wilderae*   _____

_____

☐ Berry Cave Salamander   *Gyrinophilus gulolineatus*   * _____

☐ Tennessee Cave Salamander   *Gyrinophilus palleucus*   *   _____

_____

☐ Spring Salamander   *Gyrinophilus porphyriticus*   _____

_____

☐ West Virginia   *Gyrinophilus subterraneus*   *   _____
Spring Salamander

_____

☐ Georgia Blind Salamander   *Haideotriton wallacei*   *   _____

_____

☐ Four-toed Salamander   *Hemidactylium scutatum*   _____

_____

☐ Limestone Salamander   *Hydromantes brunus*   *   _____

_____

☐ Mount Lyell Salamander   *Hydromantes platycephalus*   *   _____

_____

☐ Shasta Salamander   *Hydromantes shastae*   *   _____

_____

☐ Red Hills Salamander   *Phaeognathus hubrichti*   *   _____

_____

☐ Catahoula Salamander   *Plethodon ainsworthi*   * †?_____

_____

☐ Western Slimy Salamander   *Plethodon albagula*   _____

_____

☐ Blue Ridge Gray-cheeked   *Plethodon amplus*   *   _____
Salamander

_____

☐ Ozark Salamander   *Plethodon angusticlavius*   _____

_____

☐ Scott Bar Salamander   *Plethodon asupak*   *   _____

_____

☐ Tellico Salamander   *Plethodon aureolus*   * _____

_____

☐ Caddo Mountain Salamander   *Plethodon caddoensis*   * _____

_____

☐ Chattahoochee Slimy
   Salamander   *Plethodon chattahoochee*   _____

_____

☐ Cheoah Bald Salamander   *Plethodon cheoah*   * _____

_____

☐ Atlantic Coast Slimy Salamander   *Plethodon chlorobryonis*   _____

_____

☐ Eastern Red-backed Salamander   *Plethodon cinereus*   _____

_____

☐ White-spotted Slimy Salamander   *Plethodon cylindraceus*   _____

_____

☐ Northern Zigzag Salamander   *Plethodon dorsalis*   _____

_____

☐ Dunn's Salamander   *Plethodon dunni*   _____

_____

☐ Northern Ravine Salamander   *Plethodon electromorphus* _____

_____

☐ Del Norte Salamander   *Plethodon elongatus*   _____

_____

☐ Fourche Mountain Salamander   *Plethodon fourchensis*   * _____

_____

☐ Northern Slimy Salamander   *Plethodon glutinosus*   _____

_____

☐ Southeastern Slimy Salamander *Plethodon grobmani*   _____

_____

☐ Valley and Ridge Salamander　　*Plethodon hoffmani*　　_____

_____

☐ Peaks of Otter Salamander　　*Plethodon hubrichti*　　*　_____

_____

☐ Coeur d'Alene Salamander　　*Plethodon idahoensis*　　_____

_____

☐ Red-cheeked Salamander　　*Plethodon jordani*　　*　_____

_____

☐ Cumberland Plateau Salamander　*Plethodon kentucki*　　_____

_____

☐ Kiamichi Slimy Salamander　　*Plethodon kiamichi*　　_____

_____

☐ Louisiana Slimy Salamander　　*Plethodon kisatchie*　　_____

_____

☐ Larch Mountain Salamander　　*Plethodon larselli*　　*　_____

_____

☐ South Mountain Gray-cheeked Salamander　　*Plethodon meridianus*　*　_____

_____

☐ Southern Gray-cheeked Salamander　　*Plethodon metcalfi*　　*　_____

_____

☐ Mississippi Slimy Salamander　　*Plethodon mississippi*　　_____

_____

☐ Northern Gray-cheeked Salamander　　*Plethodon montanus*　*　_____

_____

☐ Jemez Mountains Salamander　　*Plethodon neomexicanus*　*　_____

_____

☐ Cheat Mountain Salamander　　*Plethodon nettingi*　　*　_____

_____

☐ Ocmulgee Slimy Salamander   *Plethodon ocmulgee*   _____

_____

☐ Rich Mountain Salamander   *Plethodon ouachitae* *   _____

_____

☐ Pigeon Mountain Salamander   *Plethodon petraeus*   * _____

_____

☐ Cow Knob Salamander   *Plethodon punctatus* * _____

_____

☐ Southern Ravine Salamander   *Plethodon richmondi*   _____

_____

☐ Savannah Slimy Salamander   *Plethodon savannah*   _____

_____

☐ Sequoyah Slimy Salamander   *Plethodon sequoyah*   _____

_____

☐ Southern Red-backed Salamander   *Plethodon serratus*   _____

_____

☐ Shenandoah Salamander   *Plethodon shenandoah*   * _____

_____

☐ Big Levels Salamander   *Plethodon sherando*   _____

_____

☐ Red-legged Salamander   *Plethodon shermani* * _____

_____

☐ Siskiyou Mountains Salamander   *Plethodon stormi*   * _____

_____

☐ Southern Appalachian Salamander   *Plethodon teyahalee* * _____

_____

☐ Van Dyke's Salamander   *Plethodon vandykei* * _____

_____

☐ South Carolina   *Plethodon variolatus*
    Slimy Salamander

_____

☐ Western Red-backed   *Plethodon vehiculum*
    Salamander

_____

☐ Southern Zigzag   *Plethodon ventralis*
    Salamander

_____

☐ Shenandoah Mountain   *Plethodon virginia*   *
    Salamander

_____

☐ Webster's Salamander   *Plethodon websteri*   *

_____

☐ Wehrle's Salamander   *Plethodon wehrlei*

_____

☐ Weller's Salamander   *Plethodon welleri*   *

_____

☐ Yonahlossee Salamander   *Plethodon yonahlossee*

_____

☐ Mud Salamander   *Pseudotriton montanus*

_____

☐ Red Salamander   *Pseudotriton ruber*

_____

☐ Many-lined Salamander   *Stereochilus marginatus*

_____

ALIEN AMPHIBIANS

Family Leptodactylidae: Neotropical Frogs

☐ Coqui   *Eleutherodactylus coqui*

_____

☐ Greenhouse Frog   *Eleutherodactylus planirostris*

_____

Family Hylidae: Treefrogs

☐ Cuban Treefrog   *Osteopilus septentrionalis*   _____

_____

Family Pipidae: Tongueless Frogs

☐ African Clawed Frog   *Xenopus laevis*   _____

_____

ADDITIONAL SPECIES

☐ _____ _____ _____

☐ _____ _____ _____

☐ _____ _____ _____

☐ _____ _____ _____

☐ _____ _____ _____

☐ _____ _____ _____

☐ _____ _____ _____

☐ _____ _____ _____

☐ _____ _____ _____

☐ _____ _____ _____

☐ _____ _____ _____
_____

☐ _____ _____ _____
_____

☐ _____ _____ _____
_____

☐ _____ _____ _____
_____

☐ _____ _____ _____
_____

☐ _____ _____ _____
_____

☐ _____ _____ _____
_____

☐ _____ _____ _____
_____

☐ _____ _____ _____
_____

☐ _____ _____ _____
_____

☐ _____ _____ _____
_____

☐ _____ _____ _____
_____

☐ _____ _____ _____
_____

☐ _____ _____ _____
                                              _____

☐ _____ _____ _____
                                              _____

☐ _____ _____ _____
                                              _____

☐ _____ _____ _____
                                              _____

☐ _____ _____ _____
                                              _____

☐ _____ _____ _____
                                              _____

☐ _____ _____ _____
                                              _____

☐ _____ _____ _____
                                              _____

☐ _____ _____ _____
                                              _____

☐ _____ _____ _____
                                              _____

☐ _____ _____ _____
                                              _____

☐ _____ _____ _____
                                              _____

☐ _____ _____ _____
                                              _____

☐ _____ _____ _____

_____

☐ _____ _____ _____

_____

☐ _____ _____ _____

_____

☐ _____ _____ _____

_____

☐ _____ _____ _____

_____

☐ _____ _____ _____

_____

☐ _____ _____ _____

_____

☐ _____ _____ _____

_____

☐ _____ _____ _____

_____

Freshwater Fishes
Class Cephalaspidomorphi: Lampreys

Order Petromyzontiformes: Lampreys

Family Petromyzontidae: Lampreys
(North America: 18; World: 41)

☐ Ohio Lamprey   *Ichthyomyzon bdellium*   *   _____

_____

☐ Chestnut Lamprey   *Ichthyomyzon castaneus*   _____

_____

☐ Northern Brook Lamprey *Ichthyomyzon fossor*   _____

_____

☐ Southern Brook Lamprey *Ichthyomyzon gagei*   _____

_____

☐ Mountain Brook Lamprey *Ichthyomyzon greeleyi*   *   _____

_____

☐ Silver Lamprey   *Ichthyomyzon unicuspis*   _____

_____

☐ Least Brook Lamprey   *Lampetra aepyptera*   _____

_____

☐ American Brook Lamprey *Lampetra appendix*   _____

_____

☐ River Lamprey   *Lampetra ayresii*   _____

_____

☐ Arctic Lamprey   *Lampetra camtschatica*   _____

_____

☐ Kern Brook Lamprey   *Lampetra hubbsi*   *   _____

_____

☐ Pit-Klamath Brook Lamprey   *Lampetra lethophaga*   *   _____

_____

☐ Vancouver Lamprey   *Lampetra macrostoma*   *   _____

_____

☐ Miller Lake Lamprey   *Lampetra minima*   *   _____

_____

☐ Western Brook Lamprey   *Lampetra richardsoni*   _____

_____

☐ Klamath River Lamprey   *Lampetra similis*   *   _____

_____

☐ Pacific Lamprey   *Lampetra tridentata*   _____

_____

☐ Sea Lamprey   *Petromyzon marinus*   _____

_____

Class Chondrichthyes: Cartilaginous Fishes

Order Myliobatiformes: Stingrays, Mantas, and Allies

**Family Dasyatidae: Whiptail Stingrays
(North America: 1; World: 70)**

☐ Atlantic Stingray   *Dasyatis sabina*   _____

_____

Class Actinopterygii: Ray-finned Fishes

Order Acipenseriformes: Sturgeons and Paddlefishes

Family Acipenseridae: Sturgeons (North America: 8; World: 23)

☐ Shortnose Sturgeon   *Acipenser brevirostrum*   *   _____

_____

☐ Lake Sturgeon   *Acipenser fulvescens*   *   _____

_____

☐ Green Sturgeon   *Acipenser medirostris*   *   _____

_____

☐ Atlantic Sturgeon   *Acipenser oxyrinchus*   *   _____

_____

☐ White Sturgeon   *Acipenser transmontanus*   _____

_____

☐ Pallid Sturgeon   *Scaphirhynchus albus*   *   _____

_____

☐ Shovelnose Sturgeon   *Scaphirhynchus platorynchus*   _____

_____

☐ Alabama Sturgeon   *Scaphirhynchus suttkusi*   *   _____

_____

Family Polyodontidae: Paddlefishes (North America: 1; World: 2)

☐ Paddlefish   *Polyodon spathula*   _____

_____

Order Lepisosteiformes: Gars

Family Lepisosteidae: Gars (North America: 5; World: 7)

☐ Alligator Gar   *Atractosteus spatula*   *   _____

_____

☐ Spotted Gar   *Lepisosteus oculatus*   _____

_____

☐ Longnose Gar   *Lepisosteus osseus*   _____

_____

☐ Shortnose Gar   *Lepisosteus platostomus*   _____

_____

☐ Florida Gar   *Lepisosteus platyrhincus*   _____

_____

Order Amiiformes: Bowfins

Family Amiidae: Bowfins (North America: 1; World: 1)

☐   Bowfin   *Amia calva*   _____

_____

Order Hiodontiformes: Mooneyes

Family Hiodontidae: Mooneyes (North America: 2; World: 2)

☐   Goldeye   *Hiodon alosoides*   _____

_____

☐   Mooneye   *Hiodon tergisus*   _____

_____

Order Anguilliformes: Eels

Family Anguillidae: Freshwater Eels (North America: 1; World: 15)

☐   American Eel   *Anguilla rostrata*   _____

_____

Order Clupeiformes: Anchovies and Herrings

Family Engraulidae: Anchovies (North America: 1; World: 139)

☐   Bay Anchovy   *Anchoa mitchilli*   _____

_____

**Family Clupeidae: Herrings and Shads
(North America: 8; World: 216)**

☐   Blueback Herring   *Alosa aestivalis*   _____

_____

☐   Alabama Shad   *Alosa alabamae*   *   _____

_____

☐   Skipjack Herring   *Alosa chrysochloris*   _____

_____

☐   Hickory Shad   *Alosa mediocris*   _____

_____

☐   Alewife   *Alosa pseudoharengus*   _____

_____

☐ American Shad · · · · · · · · · · *Alosa sapidissima* · · · · · · · · · · _____

_____

☐ Gizzard Shad · · · · · · · · · · *Dorosoma cepedianum* · · · · · · · · · · _____

_____

☐ Threadfin Shad · · · · · · · · · · *Dorosoma petenense* · · · · · · · · · · _____

_____

Order Cypriniformes: Carps, Minnows, Suckers, and Loaches

Family Cyprinidae: Carps and Minnows
(North America: 257; World: 2,010)

☐ Chiselmouth · · · · · · · · · · *Acrocheilus alutaceus* · · · · · · · · · · _____

_____

☐ Longfin Dace · · · · · · · · · · *Agosia chrysogaster* · · · · · · · · · · _____

_____

☐ Central Stoneroller · · · · · · · · · · *Campostoma anomalum* · · · · · · · · · · _____

_____

☐ Largescale Stoneroller · · · · · · · · · · *Campostoma oligolepis* · · · · · · · · · · _____

_____

☐ Mexican Stoneroller · · · · · · · · · · *Campostoma ornatum* · · · · · · · · · · * · · · · · · · · · · _____

_____

☐ Bluefin Stoneroller · · · · · · · · · · *Campostoma pauciradii* · · · · · · · · · · _____

_____

☐ Redside Dace · · · · · · · · · · *Clinostomus elongatus* · · · · · · · · · · _____

_____

☐ Rosyside Dace · · · · · · · · · · *Clinostomus funduloides* · · · · · · · · · · _____

_____

☐ Lake Chub · · · · · · · · · · *Couesius plumbeus* · · · · · · · · · · _____

_____

☐ Satinfin Shiner · · · · · · · · · · *Cyprinella analostana* · · · · · · · · · · _____

_____

☐ Blue Shiner   *Cyprinella caerulea*   *   _____

_____

☐ Ocmulgee Shiner   *Cyprinella callisema*   *   _____

_____

☐ Alabama Shiner   *Cyprinella callistia*   _____

_____

☐ Bluestripe Shiner   *Cyprinella callitaenia*   *   _____

_____

☐ Bluntface Shiner   *Cyprinella camura*   _____

_____

☐ Greenfin Shiner   *Cyprinella chloristia*   _____

_____

☐ Beautiful Shiner   *Cyprinella formosa*   *   _____

_____

☐ Whitetail Shiner   *Cyprinella galactura*   _____

_____

☐ Tallapoosa Shiner   *Cyprinella gibbsi*   _____

_____

☐ Thicklip Chub   *Cyprinella labrosa*   _____

_____

☐ Bannerfin Shiner   *Cyprinella leedsi*   _____

_____

☐ Plateau Shiner   *Cyprinella lepida*   *   _____

_____

☐ Red Shiner   *Cyprinella lutrensis*   _____

_____

☐ Spotfin Chub   *Cyprinella monacha*   *   _____

_____

☐ Whitefin Shiner · *Cyprinella nivea* ·
_____

_____

☐ Proserpine Shiner · *Cyprinella proserpina* * ·
_____

_____

☐ Fieryblack Shiner · *Cyprinella pyrrhomelas* ·
_____

_____

☐ Spotfin Shiner · *Cyprinella spiloptera* ·
_____

_____

☐ Tricolor Shiner · *Cyprinella trichroistia* ·
_____

_____

☐ Blacktail Shiner · *Cyprinella venusta* ·
_____

_____

☐ Steelcolor Shiner · *Cyprinella whipplei* ·
_____

_____

☐ Altamaha Shiner · *Cyprinella xaenura* * ·
_____

_____

☐ Santee Chub · *Cyprinella zanema* ·
_____

_____

☐ Manantial Roundnose Minnow · *Dionda argentosa* * ·
_____

_____

☐ Devils River Minnow · *Dionda diaboli* * ·
_____

_____

☐ Roundnose Minnow · *Dionda episcopa* ·
_____

_____

☐ Guadalupe Roundnose Minnow · *Dionda nigrotaeniata* ·
_____

_____

☐ Nueces Roundnose Minnow · *Dionda serena* * ·
_____

_____

☐ Desert Dace   *Eremichthys acros* * _____

_____

☐ Slender Chub   *Erimystax cahni* * _____

_____

☐ Streamline Chub *Erimystax dissimilis* _____

_____

☐ Ozark Chub   *Erimystax harryi* * _____

_____

☐ Blotched Chub   *Erimystax insignis* * _____

_____

☐ Gravel Chub   *Erimystax x-punctatus* _____

_____

☐ Tonguetied Minnow *Exoglossum laurae* _____

_____

☐ Cutlip Minnow   *Exoglossum maxillingua* _____

_____

☐ Alvord Chub   *Gila alvordensis* * _____

_____

☐ Utah Chub   *Gila atraria* _____

_____

☐ Tui Chub   *Gila bicolor* _____

_____

☐ Borax Lake Chub *Gila boraxobius* * _____

_____

☐ Blue Chub   *Gila coerulea* * _____

_____

☐ Thicktail Chub   *Gila crassicauda* † _____

_____

☐ Humpback Chub   *Gila cypha*   * _____

_____

☐ Sonora Chub   *Gila ditaenia* _____

_____

☐ Bonytail   *Gila elegans*   * _____

_____

☐ Gila Chub   *Gila intermedia*   * _____

_____

☐ Headwater Chub   *Gila nigra* _____

_____

☐ Chihuahua Chub   *Gila nigrescens*   * _____

_____

☐ Arroyo Chub   *Gila orcuttii*   * _____

_____

☐ Rio Grande Chub   *Gila pandora*   * _____

_____

☐ Yaqui Chub   *Gila purpurea*   * _____

_____

☐ Roundtail Chub   *Gila robusta*   * _____

_____

☐ Virgin Chub   *Gila seminuda*   * _____

_____

☐ Flame Chub   *Hemitremia flammea*   * _____

_____

☐ California Roach   *Hesperoleucus symmetricus* _____

_____

☐ Rio Grande Silvery Minnow   *Hybognathus amarus*   * _____

_____

☐ Western Silvery Minnow   *Hybognathus argyritis*

_____

_____

☐ Brassy Minnow   *Hybognathus hankinsoni*

_____

_____

☐ Cypress Minnow   *Hybognathus hayi*

_____

_____

☐ Mississippi Silvery Minnow   *Hybognathus nuchalis*

_____

_____

☐ Plains Minnow   *Hybognathus placitus*

_____

_____

☐ Eastern Silvery Minnow   *Hybognathus regius*

_____

_____

☐ Bigeye Chub   *Hybopsis amblops*

_____

_____

☐ Pallid Shiner   *Hybopsis amnis*

_____

_____

☐ Highback Chub   *Hybopsis hypsinotus*

_____

_____

☐ Lined Chub   *Hybopsis lineapunctata*   *

_____

_____

☐ Rosyface Chub   *Hybopsis rubrifrons*

_____

_____

☐ Clear Chub   *Hybopsis winchelli*

_____

_____

☐ Least Chub   *Iotichthys phlegethontis*   *

_____

_____

☐ Hitch   *Lavinia exilicauda*

_____

_____

☐ White River Spinedace   *Lepidomeda albivallis*   * _____

_____

☐ Southern Leatherside Chub   *Lepidomeda aliciae*   * _____

_____

☐ Pahranagat Spinedace   *Lepidomeda altivelis*   † _____

_____

☐ Northern Leatherside Chub   *Lepidomeda copei*   * _____

_____

☐ Virgin Spinedace   *Lepidomeda mollispinis*   * _____

_____

☐ Little Colorado Spinedace   *Lepidomeda vittata*   * _____

_____

☐ White Shiner   *Luxilus albeolus* _____

_____

☐ Cardinal Shiner   *Luxilus cardinalis* _____

_____

☐ Crescent Shiner   *Luxilus cerasinus* _____

_____

☐ Striped Shiner   *Luxilus chrysocephalus* _____

_____

☐ Warpaint Shiner   *Luxilus coccogenis* _____

_____

☐ Common Shiner   *Luxilus cornutus* _____

_____

☐ Duskystripe Shiner   *Luxilus pilsbryi* _____

_____

☐ Bleeding Shiner   *Luxilus zonatus* _____

_____

☐ Bandfin Shiner   *Luxilus zonistius*   _____

_____

☐ Rosefin Shiner   *Lythrurus ardens*   _____

_____

☐ Blacktip Shiner   *Lythrurus atrapiculus*   _____

_____

☐ Pretty Shiner   *Lythrurus bellus*   _____

_____

☐ Scarlet Shiner   *Lythrurus fasciolaris*   _____

_____

☐ Ribbon Shiner   *Lythrurus fumeus*   _____

_____

☐ Mountain Shiner   *Lythrurus lirus*   _____

_____

☐ Pinewoods Shiner   *Lythrurus matutinus*   * _____

_____

☐ Cherryfin Shiner   *Lythrurus roseipinnis*   _____

_____

☐ Ouachita Mountain Shiner *Lythrurus snelsoni* * _____

_____

☐ Redfin Shiner   *Lythrurus umbratilis*   _____

_____

☐ Speckled Chub   *Macrhybopsis aestivalis* * _____

_____

☐ Prairie Chub   *Macrhybopsis australis* * _____

_____

☐ Sturgeon Chub   *Macrhybopsis gelida*   * _____

_____

☐ Shoal Chub   *Macrhybopsis hyostoma*   _____

_____

☐ Burrhead Chub   *Macrhybopsis marconis*   _____

_____

☐ Sicklefin Chub   *Macrhybopsis meeki*   *   _____

_____

☐ Silver Chub   *Macrhybopsis storeriana*   _____

_____

☐ Peppered Chub   *Macrhybopsis tetranema*   *   _____

_____

☐ Pearl Dace   *Margariscus margarita*   _____

_____

☐ Spikedace   *Meda fulgida*   *   _____

_____

☐ Moapa Dace   *Moapa coriacea*   *   _____

_____

☐ Peamouth   *Mylocheilus caurinus*   _____

_____

☐ Hardhead   *Mylopharodon conocephalus* *   _____

_____

☐ Redspot Chub   *Nocomis asper*   _____

_____

☐ Hornyhead Chub   *Nocomis biguttatus*   _____

_____

☐ Redtail Chub   *Nocomis effusus*   _____

_____

☐ Bluehead Chub   *Nocomis leptocephalus*   _____

_____

☐ River Chub   *Nocomis micropogon*   _____

_____

☐ Bigmouth Chub   *Nocomis platyrhynchus*   _____

_____

☐ Bull Chub   *Nocomis raneyi*   _____

_____

☐ Golden Shiner   *Notemigonus crysoleucas*   _____

_____

☐ Palezone Shiner   *Notropis albizonatus*   *   _____

_____

☐ Whitemouth Shiner   *Notropis alborus*   _____

_____

☐ Highfin Shiner   *Notropis altipinnis*   _____

_____

☐ Texas Shiner   *Notropis amabilis*   _____

_____

☐ Orangefin Shiner   *Notropis ammophilus*   _____

_____

☐ Comely Shiner   *Notropis amoenus*   _____

_____

☐ Pugnose Shiner   *Notropis anogenus*   *   _____

_____

☐ Popeye Shiner   *Notropis ariommus*   *   _____

_____

☐ Burrhead Shiner   *Notropis asperifrons*   _____

_____

☐ Emerald Shiner   *Notropis atherinoides*   _____

_____

☐ Blackspot Shiner   *Notropis atrocaudalis*   _____

_____

☐ Rough Shiner   *Notropis baileyi*   _____

_____

☐ Red River Shiner   *Notropis bairdi*   _____

_____

☐ Bridle Shiner   *Notropis bifrenatus*   *   _____

_____

☐ River Shiner   *Notropis blennius*   _____

_____

☐ Bigeye Shiner   *Notropis boops*   _____

_____

☐ Tamaulipas Shiner   *Notropis braytoni*   _____

_____

☐ Silverjaw Minnow   *Notropis buccatus*   _____

_____

☐ Smalleye Shiner   *Notropis buccula*   *   _____

_____

☐ Ghost Shiner   *Notropis buchanani*   _____

_____

☐ Cahaba Shiner   *Notropis cahabae*   *   _____

_____

☐ Silverside Shiner   *Notropis candidus*   _____

_____

☐ Ironcolor Shiner   *Notropis chalybaeus*   _____

_____

☐ Chihuahua Shiner   *Notropis chihuahua*   *   _____

_____

☐ Redlip Shiner   *Notropis chiliticus*   _____

_____

☐ Greenhead Shiner   *Notropis chlorocephalus*   _____

_____

☐ Rainbow Shiner   *Notropis chrosomus*   _____

_____

☐ Dusky Shiner   *Notropis cummingsae*   _____

_____

☐ Bigmouth Shiner   *Notropis dorsalis*   _____

_____

☐ Fluvial Shiner   *Notropis edwardraneyi*   _____

_____

☐ Arkansas River Shiner   *Notropis girardi*   *   _____

_____

☐ Wedgespot Shiner   *Notropis greenei*   _____

_____

☐ Redeye Chub   *Notropis harperi*   _____

_____

☐ Blackchin Shiner   *Notropis heterodon*   _____

_____

☐ Blacknose Shiner   *Notropis heterolepis*   _____

_____

☐ Spottail Shiner   *Notropis hudsonius*   _____

_____

☐ Highscale Shiner   *Notropis hypsilepis*   *   _____

_____

☐ Rio Grande Shiner   *Notropis jemezanus*   *   _____

_____

☐ Tennessee Shiner — *Notropis leuciodus* — _____

_____

☐ Longnose Shiner — *Notropis longirostris* — _____

_____

☐ Yellowfin Shiner — *Notropis lutipinnis* — _____

_____

☐ Taillight Shiner — *Notropis maculatus* — _____

_____

☐ Cape Fear Shiner — *Notropis mekistocholas* — * _____

_____

☐ Blackmouth Shiner — *Notropis melanostomus* — * _____

_____

☐ Highland Shiner — *Notropis micropteryx* — _____

_____

☐ Ozark Minnow — *Notropis nubilus* — _____

_____

☐ Phantom Shiner — *Notropis orca* — † _____

_____

☐ Kiamichi Shiner — *Notropis ortenburgeri* — * _____

_____

☐ Sharpnose Shiner — *Notropis oxyrhynchus* — * _____

_____

☐ Ozark Shiner — *Notropis ozarcanus* — * _____

_____

☐ Carmine Shiner — *Notropis percobromus* — _____

_____

☐ Peppered Shiner — *Notropis perpallidus* — * _____

_____

☐ Coastal Shiner   *Notropis petersoni*   _____

_____

☐ Silver Shiner   *Notropis photogenis*   _____

_____

☐ Chub Shiner   *Notropis potteri*   _____

_____

☐ Swallowtail Shiner   *Notropis procne*   _____

_____

☐ Yazoo Shiner   *Notropis rafinesquei*   _____

_____

☐ Rosyface Shiner   *Notropis rubellus*   _____

_____

☐ Saffron Shiner   *Notropis rubricroceus*   _____

_____

☐ Bedrock Shiner   *Notropis rupestris*   *   _____

_____

☐ Sabine Shiner   *Notropis sabinae*   _____

_____

☐ New River Shiner   *Notropis scabriceps*   _____

_____

☐ Sandbar Shiner   *Notropis scepticus*   _____

_____

☐ Roughhead Shiner   *Notropis semperasper*   *   _____

_____

☐ Silverband Shiner   *Notropis shumardi*   _____

_____

☐ Bluntnose Shiner   *Notropis simus*   *   _____

_____

☐ Sawfin Shiner   *Notropis* species

_____

☐ Mirror Shiner   *Notropis spectrunculus*

_____

☐ Silverstripe Shiner   *Notropis stilbius*

_____

☐ Sand Shiner   *Notropis stramineus*

_____

☐ Rocky Shiner   *Notropis suttkusi* *

_____

☐ Telescope Shiner   *Notropis telescopus*

_____

☐ Weed Shiner   *Notropis texanus*

_____

☐ Topeka Shiner   *Notropis topeka* *

_____

☐ Skygazer Shiner   *Notropis uranoscopus* *

_____

☐ Mimic Shiner   *Notropis volucellus*

_____

☐ Channel Shiner   *Notropis wickliffi*

_____

☐ Coosa Shiner   *Notropis xaenocephalus*

_____

☐ Pugnose Minnow   *Opsopoeodus emiliae*

_____

☐ Oregon Chub   *Oregonichthys crameri* *

_____

☐ Umpqua Chub   *Oregonichthys kalawatseti* * _____

_____

☐ Sacramento Blackfish   *Orthodon microlepidotus*   _____

_____

☐ Riffle Minnow   *Phenacobius catostomus*   _____

_____

☐ Fatlips Minnow   *Phenacobius crassilabrum* * _____

_____

☐ Suckermouth Minnow   *Phenacobius mirabilis*   _____

_____

☐ Kanawha Minnow   *Phenacobius teretulus*   * _____

_____

☐ Stargazing Minnow   *Phenacobius uranops*   _____

_____

☐ Blackside Dace   *Phoxinus cumberlandensis* * _____

_____

☐ Northern Redbelly Dace *Phoxinus eos*   _____

_____

☐ Southern Redbelly Dace *Phoxinus erythrogaster*   _____

_____

☐ Finescale Dace   *Phoxinus neogaeus*   _____

_____

☐ Mountain Redbelly Dace *Phoxinus oreas*   _____

_____

☐ Laurel Dace   *Phoxinus saylori*   * _____

_____

☐ Tennessee Dace   *Phoxinus tennesseensis*   * _____

_____

☐ Bluntnose Minnow   *Pimephales notatus* _____

_____

☐ Fathead Minnow   *Pimephales promelas* _____

_____

☐ Slim Minnow   *Pimephales tenellus* _____

_____

☐ Bullhead Minnow   *Pimephales vigilax* _____

_____

☐ Woundfin   *Plagopterus argentissimus* * _____

_____

☐ Flathead Chub   *Platygobio gracilis* _____

_____

☐ Clear Lake Splittail   *Pogonichthys ciscoides* † _____

_____

☐ Splittail   *Pogonichthys macrolepidotus* * _____

_____

☐ Broadstripe Shiner   *Pteronotropis euryzonus* * _____

_____

☐ Apalachee Shiner   *Pteronotropis grandipinnis* _____

_____

☐ Bluehead Shiner   *Pteronotropis hubbsi* * _____

_____

☐ Sailfin Shiner   *Pteronotropis hypselopterus* _____

_____

☐ Orangetail Shiner   *Pteronotropis merlini* _____

_____

☐ Metallic Shiner   *Pteronotropis metallicus* _____

_____

☐ Flagfin Shiner   *Pteronotropis signipinnis*   _____

_____

☐ Lowland Shiner   *Pteronotropis stonei*   _____

_____

☐ Bluenose Shiner   *Pteronotropis welaka*   * _____

_____

☐ Sacramento Pikeminnow   *Ptychocheilus grandis*   _____

_____

☐ Colorado Pikeminnow   *Ptychocheilus lucius*   * _____

_____

☐ Northern Pikeminnow   *Ptychocheilus oregonensis*   _____

_____

☐ Umpqua Pikeminnow   *Ptychocheilus umpquae*   _____

_____

☐ Relict Dace   *Relictus solitarius*   * _____

_____

☐ Eastern Blacknose Dace   *Rhinichthys atratulus*   _____

_____

☐ Longnose Dace   *Rhinichthys cataractae*   _____

_____

☐ Loach Minnow   *Rhinichthys cobitis*   * _____

_____

☐ Las Vegas Dace   *Rhinichthys deaconi*   † _____

_____

☐ Umpqua Dace   *Rhinichthys evermanni*   * _____

_____

☐ Leopard Dace   *Rhinichthys falcatus*   _____

_____

☐ Western Blacknose Dace   *Rhinichthys obtusus*

_____

_____

☐ Speckled Dace   *Rhinichthys osculus*

_____

_____

☐ Umatilla Dace   *Rhinichthys umatilla*

_____

_____

☐ Redside Shiner   *Richardsonius balteatus*

_____

_____

☐ Lahontan Redside   *Richardsonius egregius*

_____

_____

☐ Creek Chub   *Semotilus atromaculatus*

_____

_____

☐ Fallfish   *Semotilus corporalis*

_____

_____

☐ Sandhills Chub   *Semotilus lumbee*   *

_____

_____

☐ Dixie Chub   *Semotilus thoreauianus*

_____

_____

Family Catostomidae: Suckers (North America: 69; World: 75)

☐ River Carpsucker   *Carpiodes carpio*

_____

_____

☐ Quillback   *Carpiodes cyprinus*

_____

_____

☐ Highfin Carpsucker   *Carpiodes velifer*

_____

_____

☐ Utah Sucker   *Catostomus ardens*

_____

_____

☐ Yaqui Sucker   *Catostomus bernardini*

☐ Longnose Sucker   *Catostomus catostomus*

☐ Desert Sucker   *Catostomus clarkii*   *

☐ Bridgelip Sucker   *Catostomus columbianus*

☐ White Sucker   *Catostomus commersonii*

☐ Bluehead Sucker   *Catostomus discobolus*

☐ Owens Sucker   *Catostomus fumeiventris*   *

☐ Sonora Sucker   *Catostomus insignis*   *

☐ Flannelmouth Sucker   *Catostomus latipinnis*   *

☐ Largescale Sucker   *Catostomus macrocheilus*

☐ Modoc Sucker   *Catostomus microps*   *

☐ Sacramento Sucker   *Catostomus occidentalis*

☐ Mountain Sucker   *Catostomus platyrhynchus*

☐ Rio Grande Sucker   *Catostomus plebeius*   *

☐ Klamath Smallscale Sucker   *Catostomus rimiculus*

☐ Santa Ana Sucker   *Catostomus santaanae*   *

☐ Klamath Largescale Sucker   *Catostomus snyderi*   *

☐ Little Colorado River Sucker   *Catostomus* species

☐ Salish Sucker   *Catostomus* species

☐ Tahoe Sucker   *Catostomus tahoensis*

☐ Warner Sucker   *Catostomus warnerensis*   *

☐ Shortnose Sucker   *Chasmistes brevirostris*   *

☐ Cui-ui   *Chasmistes cujus*   *

☐ June Sucker   *Chasmistes liorus*   *

☐ Snake River Sucker   *Chasmistes muriei*   †

☐ Blue Sucker   *Cycleptus elongatus*   *

☐ Southeastern Blue Sucker   *Cycleptus meridionalis*   *

☐ Lost River Sucker   *Deltistes luxatus*   *

☐ Western Creek Chubsucker   *Erimyzon claviformis*   _____

_____

☐ Eastern Creek Chubsucker   *Erimyzon oblongus*   _____

_____

☐ Lake Chubsucker   *Erimyzon sucetta*   _____

_____

☐ Sharpfin Chubsucker   *Erimyzon tenuis*   _____

_____

☐ Alabama Hog Sucker   *Hypentelium etowanum*   _____

_____

☐ Northern Hog Sucker   *Hypentelium nigricans*   _____

_____

☐ Roanoke Hog Sucker   *Hypentelium roanokense*   _____

_____

☐ Smallmouth Buffalo   *Ictiobus bubalus*   _____

_____

☐ Bigmouth Buffalo   *Ictiobus cyprinellus*   _____

_____

☐ Black Buffalo   *Ictiobus niger*   _____

_____

☐ Spotted Sucker   *Minytrema melanops*   _____

_____

☐ Silver Redhorse   *Moxostoma anisurum*   _____

_____

☐ Bigeye Jumprock   *Moxostoma ariommum*   _____

_____

☐ Mexican Redhorse   *Moxostoma austrinum*   * _____

_____

☐ Smallmouth Redhorse   *Moxostoma breviceps*   _____

_____

☐ River Redhorse   *Moxostoma carinatum*   _____

_____

☐ Blacktip Jumprock   *Moxostoma cervinum*   _____

_____

☐ Notchlip Redhorse   *Moxostoma collapsum*   _____

_____

☐ Gray Redhorse   *Moxostoma congestum*   _____

_____

☐ Black Redhorse   *Moxostoma duquesnei*   _____

_____

☐ Golden Redhorse   *Moxostoma erythrurum*   _____

_____

☐ Copper Redhorse   *Moxostoma hubbsi*   *   _____

_____

☐ Harelip Sucker   *Moxostoma lacerum*   †   _____

_____

☐ Greater Jumprock   *Moxostoma lachneri*   _____

_____

☐ Shorthead Redhorse   *Moxostoma macrolepidotum*   _____

_____

☐ V-lip Redhorse   *Moxostoma pappillosum*   _____

_____

☐ Pealip Redhorse   *Moxostoma pisolabrum*   _____

_____

☐ Blacktail Redhorse   *Moxostoma poecilurum*   _____

_____

☐ Robust Redhorse   *Moxostoma robustum*   * _____

_____

☐ Striped Jumprock   *Moxostoma rupiscartes*   _____

_____

☐ Brassy Jumprock   *Moxostoma* species   _____

_____

☐ Grayfin Redhorse   *Moxostoma* species   _____

_____

☐ Greater Redhorse   *Moxostoma valenciennesi*   _____

_____

☐ Blackfin Sucker   *Thoburnia atripinnis*   * _____

_____

☐ Rustyside Sucker   *Thoburnia hamiltoni*   * _____

_____

☐ Torrent Sucker   *Thoburnia rhothoeca*   _____

_____

☐ Razorback Sucker   *Xyrauchen texanus*   * _____

_____

Order Characiformes: Characins

Family Characidae: Characins (North America: 1; World: 776)

☐ Mexican Tetra   *Astyanax mexicanus*   _____

_____

Order Siluriformes: Catfishes

**Family Ictaluridae: North American Catfishes
(North America: 40; World: 47)**

☐ Snail Bullhead   *Ameiurus brunneus*   _____

_____

☐ White Catfish   *Ameiurus catus*   _____

_____

☐ Black Bullhead   *Ameiurus melas*   _____

_____

☐ Yellow Bullhead   *Ameiurus natalis*   _____

_____

☐ Brown Bullhead   *Ameiurus nebulosus*   _____

_____

☐ Flat Bullhead   *Ameiurus platycephalus*   _____

_____

☐ Spotted Bullhead   *Ameiurus serracanthus*   *   _____

_____

☐ Blue Catfish   *Ictalurus furcatus*   _____

_____

☐ Headwater Catfish   *Ictalurus lupus*   *   _____

_____

☐ Yaqui Catfish   *Ictalurus pricei*   *   _____

_____

☐ Channel Catfish   *Ictalurus punctatus*   _____

_____

☐ Ozark Madtom   *Noturus albater*   _____

_____

☐ Smoky Madtom   *Noturus baileyi*   *   _____

_____

☐ Elegant Madtom   *Noturus elegans*   _____

_____

☐ Mountain Madtom   *Noturus eleutherus*   _____

_____

☐ Slender Madtom   *Noturus exilis*   _____

_____

☐ Checkered Madtom   *Noturus flavater*   * _____

_____

☐ Yellowfin Madtom   *Noturus flavipinnis*   * _____

_____

☐ Stonecat   *Noturus flavus*   _____

_____

☐ Black Madtom   *Noturus funebris*   _____

_____

☐ Carolina Madtom   *Noturus furiosus*   * _____

_____

☐ Orangefin Madtom   *Noturus gilberti*   * _____

_____

☐ Piebald Madtom   *Noturus gladiator*   * _____

_____

☐ Tadpole Madtom   *Noturus gyrinus*   _____

_____

☐ Least Madtom   *Noturus hildebrandi*   _____

_____

☐ Margined Madtom   *Noturus insignis*   _____

_____

☐ Ouachita Madtom   *Noturus lachneri*   * _____

_____

☐ Speckled Madtom   *Noturus leptacanthus*   _____

_____

☐ Brindled Madtom   *Noturus miurus*   _____

_____

☐ Frecklebelly Madtom   *Noturus munitus*   * _____

_____

☐ Freckled Madtom   *Noturus nocturnus* _____

_____

☐ Brown Madtom   *Noturus phaeus* _____

_____

☐ Neosho Madtom   *Noturus placidus*   * _____

_____

☐ Broadtail Madtom   *Noturus* species _____

_____

☐ Pygmy Madtom   *Noturus stanauli*   * _____

_____

☐ Northern Madtom   *Noturus stigmosus*   * _____

_____

☐ Caddo Madtom   *Noturus taylori*   * _____

_____

☐ Scioto Madtom   *Noturus trautmani*   † _____

_____

☐ Flathead Catfish   *Pylodictis olivaris* _____

_____

☐ Widemouth Blindcat   *Satan eurystomus*   * _____

_____

☐ Toothless Blindcat   *Trogloglanis pattersoni*   * _____

_____

Order Esociformes: Pikes and Mudminnows

Family Esocidae: Pikes (North America: 4; World: 5)

☐ Redfin Pickerel   *Esox americanus* _____

_____

☐ Northern Pike   *Esox lucius* _____

_____

☐ Muskellunge   *Esox masquinongy*   _____

_____

☐ Chain Pickerel   *Esox niger*   _____

_____

Family Umbridae: Mudminnows (North America: 4; World: 5)

☐ Alaska Blackfish   *Dallia pectoralis*   _____

_____

☐ Olympic Mudminnow *Novumbra hubbsi*   * _____

_____

☐ Central Mudminnow *Umbra limi*   _____

_____

☐ Eastern Mudminnow *Umbra pygmaea*   _____

_____

Order Salmoniformes: Smelts, Trouts, and Salmons

Family Osmeridae: Smelts (North America: 5; World: 13)

☐ Pond Smelt   *Hypomesus olidus*   _____

_____

☐ Delta Smelt   *Hypomesus transpacificus* * _____

_____

☐ Rainbow Smelt   *Osmerus mordax*   _____

_____

☐ Longfin Smelt   *Spirinchus thaleichthys* _____

_____

☐ Eulachon   *Thaleichthys pacificus*   _____

_____

**Family Salmonidae: Trouts and Salmons
(North America: 35; World: 66)**

☐ Cisco   *Coregonus artedi*   _____

_____

☐ Arctic Cisco   *Coregonus autumnalis*   _____

_____

☐ Lake Whitefish   *Coregonus clupeaformis*   _____

_____

☐ Bloater   *Coregonus hoyi*   _____

_____

☐ Atlantic Whitefish   *Coregonus huntsmani*   *   _____

_____

☐ Deepwater Cisco   *Coregonus johannae*   †   _____

_____

☐ Kiyi   *Coregonus kiyi*   *   _____

_____

☐ Bering Cisco   *Coregonus laurettae*   _____

_____

☐ Broad Whitefish   *Coregonus nasus*   _____

_____

☐ Blackfin Cisco   *Coregonus nigripinnis*   *   _____

_____

☐ Nipigon Cisco   *Coregonus nipigon*   _____

_____

☐ Humpback Whitefish   *Coregonus pidschian*   _____

_____

☐ Shortnose Cisco   *Coregonus reighardi*   †   _____

_____

☐ Least Cisco   *Coregonus sardinella*   _____

_____

☐ Shortjaw Cisco   *Coregonus zenithicus*   *   _____

_____

☐ Cutthroat Trout   *Oncorhynchus clarkii*

☐ Gila Trout   *Oncorhynchus gilae*   *

☐ Pink Salmon   *Oncorhynchus gorbuscha*

☐ Chum Salmon   *Oncorhynchus keta*

☐ Coho Salmon   *Oncorhynchus kisutch*

☐ Rainbow Trout   *Oncorhynchus mykiss*

☐ Sockeye Salmon   *Oncorhynchus nerka*

☐ Chinook Salmon   *Oncorhynchus tshawytscha*

☐ Bear Lake Whitefish   *Prosopium abyssicola*   *

☐ Pygmy Whitefish   *Prosopium coulterii*

☐ Round Whitefish   *Prosopium cylindraceum*

☐ Bonneville Cisco   *Prosopium gemmifer*   *

☐ Bonneville Whitefish   *Prosopium spilonotus*   *

☐ Mountain Whitefish   *Prosopium williamsoni*

□ Atlantic Salmon *Salmo salar* _____

_____

□ Arctic Char *Salvelinus alpinus* _____

_____

□ Bull Trout *Salvelinus confluentus* * _____

_____

□ Brook Trout *Salvelinus fontinalis* _____

_____

□ Dolly Varden *Salvelinus malma* _____

_____

□ Lake Trout *Salvelinus namaycush* _____

_____

□ Inconnu *Stenodus leucichthys* _____

_____

□ Arctic Grayling *Thymallus arcticus* _____

_____

Order Percopsiformes: Trout-perches, Pirate Perches, and Cavefishes

Family Percopsidae: Trout-perches (North America: 2; World: 2)

□ Trout-perch *Percopsis omiscomaycus* _____

_____

□ Sand Roller *Percopsis transmontana* _____

_____

Family Aphredoderidae: Pirate Perches (North America: 1; World: 1)

□ Pirate Perch *Aphredoderus sayanus* _____

_____

Family Amblyopsidae: Cavefishes (North America: 6; World: 6)

□ Ozark Cavefish *Amblyopsis rosae* * _____

_____

☐ Northern Cavefish   *Amblyopsis spelaea*

_____

☐ Swampfish   *Chologaster cornuta*

_____

☐ Spring Cavefish   *Forbesichthys agassizii*

_____

☐ Alabama Cavefish   *Speoplatyrhinus poulsoni*   *

_____

☐ Southern Cavefish   *Typhlichthys subterraneus*

_____

Order Gadiformes: Cods and Hakes

Family Gadidae: Cods (North America: 2; World: 22)

☐ Burbot   *Lota lota*

_____

☐ Atlantic Tomcod   *Microgadus tomcod*

_____

Order Mugiliformes: Mullets

Family Mugilidae: Mullets (North America: 1; World: 80)

☐ Striped Mullet   *Mugil cephalus*

_____

Order Atheriniformes: Silversides

**Family Atherinopsidae: New World Silversides
(North America: 4; World: 104)**

☐ Brook Silverside   *Labidesthes sicculus*

_____

☐ Mississippi Silverside   *Menidia audens*

_____

☐ Inland Silverside   *Menidia beryllina*

_____

☐ Waccamaw Silverside *Menidia extensa* * _____

_____

Order Beloniformes: Needlefishes
Family Belonidae: Needlefishes (North America: 1; World: 34)

☐ Atlantic Needlefish *Strongylura marina* _____

_____

Order Cyprinodontiformes: Rivulines, Topminnows, Livebearers, Goodeids, and Pupfishes
Family Aplocheilidae: Rivulines (North America: 1; World: 310)

☐ Mangrove Rivulus *Rivulus marmoratus* * _____

_____

Family Fundulidae: Topminnows (North America: 27; World: 48)

☐ Whiteline Topminnow *Fundulus albolineatus* † _____

_____

☐ Stippled Studfish *Fundulus bifax* * _____

_____

☐ Western Starhead Topminnow *Fundulus blairae* _____

_____

☐ Northern Studfish *Fundulus catenatus* _____

_____

☐ Golden Topminnow *Fundulus chrysotus* _____

_____

☐ Banded Topminnow *Fundulus cingulatus* _____

_____

☐ Marsh Killifish *Fundulus confluentus* _____

_____

☐ Banded Killifish *Fundulus diaphanus* _____

_____

☐ Starhead Topminnow *Fundulus dispar* _____

_____

☐ Russetfin Topminnow   *Fundulus escambiae*   _____

_____

☐ Broadstripe Topminnow   *Fundulus euryzonus*   *   _____

_____

☐ Barrens Topminnow   *Fundulus julisia*   *   _____

_____

☐ Northern Plains Killifish   *Fundulus kansae*   _____

_____

☐ Lined Topminnow   *Fundulus lineolatus*   _____

_____

☐ Blackstripe Topminnow   *Fundulus notatus*   _____

_____

☐ Bayou Topminnow   *Fundulus nottii*   _____

_____

☐ Blackspotted Topminnow   *Fundulus olivaceus*   _____

_____

☐ Bayou Killifish   *Fundulus pulvereus*   _____

_____

☐ Speckled Killifish   *Fundulus rathbuni*   _____

_____

☐ Redface Topminnow   *Fundulus rubrifrons*   _____

_____

☐ Plains Topminnow   *Fundulus sciadicus*   _____

_____

☐ Seminole Killifish   *Fundulus seminolis*   _____

_____

☐ Southern Studfish   *Fundulus stellifer*   _____

_____

☐ Waccamaw Killifish   *Fundulus waccamensis*   *   _____

_____

☐ Plains Killifish   *Fundulus zebrinus*   _____

_____

☐ Pygmy Killifish   *Leptolucania ommata*   _____

_____

☐ Bluefin Killifish   *Lucania goodei*   _____

_____

☐ Rainwater Killifish   *Lucania parva*   _____

_____

Family Poeciliidae: Livebearers (North America: 13; World: 293)

☐ Western Mosquitofish   *Gambusia affinis*   _____

_____

☐ Amistad Gambusia   *Gambusia amistadensis*   †   _____

_____

☐ San Felipe Gambusia   *Gambusia clarkhubbsi*   *   _____

_____

☐ Big Bend Gambusia   *Gambusia gaigei*   *   _____

_____

☐ Largespring Gambusia   *Gambusia geiseri*   _____

_____

☐ San Marcos Gambusia   *Gambusia georgei*   †   _____

_____

☐ Clear Creek Gambusia   *Gambusia heterochir*   *   _____

_____

☐ Eastern Mosquitofish   *Gambusia holbrooki*   _____

_____

☐ Pecos Gambusia   *Gambusia nobilis*   *   _____

_____

☐ Blotched Gambusia   *Gambusia senilis*   *   _____

_____

☐ Tex-Mex Gambusia   *Gambusia speciosa*   *   _____

_____

☐ Least Killifish   *Heterandria formosa*   _____

_____

☐ Amazon Molly   *Poecilia formosa*   _____

_____

☐ Sailfin Molly   *Poecilia latipinna*   _____

_____

☐ Gila Topminnow   *Poeciliopsis occidentalis*   *   _____

_____

Family Goodeidae: Goodeids (North America: 3; World: 40)

☐ White River Springfish   *Crenichthys baileyi*   *   _____

_____

☐ Railroad Valley Springfish   *Crenichthys nevadae*   *   _____

_____

☐ Pahrump Poolfish   *Empetrichthys latos*   *   _____

_____

☐ Ash Meadows Poolfish   *Empetrichthys merriami*   †   _____

_____

Family Cyprinodontidae: Pupfishes (North America: 14; World: 100)

☐ Santa Cruz Pupfish   *Cyprinodon arcuatus*   †   _____

_____

☐ Leon Springs Pupfish   *Cyprinodon bovinus*   *   _____

_____

☐ Devils Hole Pupfish   *Cyprinodon diabolis*   *   _____

_____

☐ Comanche Springs Pupfish   *Cyprinodon elegans*   * _____

_____

☐ Sonoyta Pupfish   *Cyprinodon eremus*   * _____

_____

☐ Conchos Pupfish   *Cyprinodon eximius*   * _____

_____

☐ Desert Pupfish   *Cyprinodon macularius*   * _____

_____

☐ Amargosa Pupfish   *Cyprinodon nevadensis*   * _____

_____

☐ Pecos Pupfish   *Cyprinodon pecosensis*   * _____

_____

☐ Owens Pupfish   *Cyprinodon radiosus*   * _____

_____

☐ Red River Pupfish   *Cyprinodon rubrofluviatilis*   _____

_____

☐ Salt Creek Pupfish   *Cyprinodon salinus*   * _____

_____

☐ White Sands Pupfish   *Cyprinodon tularosa*   * _____

_____

☐ Sheepshead Minnow   *Cyprinodon variegatus*   _____

_____

☐ Flagfish   *Jordanella floridae*   _____

_____

Order Gasterosteiformes: Sticklebacks and Pipefishes

Family Gasterosteidae: Sticklebacks (North America: 4; World: 7)

☐ Fourspine Stickleback   *Apeltes quadracus*   _____

_____

☐ Brook Stickleback   *Culaea inconstans*

_____

_____

☐ Threespine Stickleback   *Gasterosteus aculeatus*

_____

☐ Ninespine Stickleback   *Pungitius pungitius*

_____

_____

Family Syngnathidae: Pipefishes (North America: 1; World: 215)

☐ Gulf Pipefish   *Syngnathus scovelli*

_____

_____

Order Scorpaeniformes: Sculpins and Allies

Family Cottidae: Sculpins (North America: 29; World: 300)

☐ Coastrange Sculpin   *Cottus aleuticus*

_____

_____

☐ Prickly Sculpin   *Cottus asper*

_____

_____

☐ Rough Sculpin   *Cottus asperrimus*   *

_____

_____

☐ Black Sculpin   *Cottus baileyi*

_____

_____

☐ Mottled Sculpin   *Cottus bairdii*

_____

_____

☐ Paiute Sculpin   *Cottus beldingii*

_____

_____

☐ Malheur Sculpin   *Cottus bendirei*

_____

_____

☐ Blue Ridge Sculpin   *Cottus caeruleomentum*

_____

_____

☐ Banded Sculpin   *Cottus carolinae*

_____

☐ Slimy Sculpin   *Cottus cognatus*   _____

_____

☐ Shorthead Sculpin   *Cottus confusus*   _____

_____

☐ Utah Lake Sculpin   *Cottus echinatus*   † _____

_____

☐ Bear Lake Sculpin   *Cottus extensus*   * _____

_____

☐ Potomac Sculpin   *Cottus girardi*   _____

_____

☐ Shoshone Sculpin   *Cottus greenei*   * _____

_____

☐ Riffle Sculpin   *Cottus gulosus*   _____

_____

☐ Columbia Sculpin   *Cottus hubbsi*   _____

_____

☐ Ozark Sculpin   *Cottus hypselurus*   _____

_____

☐ Marbled Sculpin   *Cottus klamathensis*   _____

_____

☐ Wood River Sculpin   *Cottus leiopomus*   * _____

_____

☐ Margined Sculpin   *Cottus marginatus*   * _____

_____

☐ Pygmy Sculpin   *Cottus paulus*   * _____

_____

☐ Reticulate Sculpin   *Cottus perplexus*   _____

_____

☐ Pit Sculpin   *Cottus pitensis*   _____

_____

☐ Klamath Lake Sculpin   *Cottus princeps*   *   _____

_____

☐ Torrent Sculpin   *Cottus rhotheus*   _____

_____

☐ Spoonhead Sculpin   *Cottus ricei*   _____

_____

☐ Slender Sculpin   *Cottus tenuis*   *   _____

_____

☐ Fourhorn Sculpin   *Myoxocephalus quadricornis*   _____

_____

☐ Deepwater Sculpin   *Myoxocephalus thompsonii*   _____

_____

Order Perciformes: Snooks, Basses, Sunfishes, Perches, and Allies

Family Moronidae: Temperate Basses (North America: 4; World: 6)

☐ White Perch   *Morone americana*   _____

_____

☐ White Bass   *Morone chrysops*   _____

_____

☐ Yellow Bass   *Morone mississippiensis*   _____

_____

☐ Striped Bass   *Morone saxatilis*   _____

_____

Family Centrarchidae: Sunfishes and Basses (North America: 31; World: 31)

☐ Mud Sunfish   *Acantharchus pomotis*   _____

_____

☐ Shadow Bass   *Ambloplites ariommus*   _____

_____

☐ Roanoke Bass   *Ambloplites cavifrons*   *   _____

_____

☐ Ozark Bass   *Ambloplites constellatus*   _____

_____

☐ Rock Bass   *Ambloplites rupestris*   _____

_____

☐ Sacramento Perch   *Archoplites interruptus*   *   _____

_____

☐ Flier   *Centrarchus macropterus*   _____

_____

☐ Blackbanded Sunfish   *Enneacanthus chaetodon*   _____

_____

☐ Bluespotted Sunfish   *Enneacanthus gloriosus*   _____

_____

☐ Banded Sunfish   *Enneacanthus obesus*   _____

_____

☐ Redbreast Sunfish   *Lepomis auritus*   _____

_____

☐ Green Sunfish   *Lepomis cyanellus*   _____

_____

☐ Pumpkinseed   *Lepomis gibbosus*   _____

_____

☐ Warmouth   *Lepomis gulosus*   _____

_____

☐ Orangespotted Sunfish   *Lepomis humilis*   _____

_____

☐ Bluegill *Lepomis macrochirus* _____

_____

☐ Dollar Sunfish *Lepomis marginatus* _____

_____

☐ Longear Sunfish *Lepomis megalotis* _____

_____

☐ Redear Sunfish *Lepomis microlophus* _____

_____

☐ Northern Longear Sunfish *Lepomis peltastes* _____

_____

☐ Spotted Sunfish *Lepomis punctatus* _____

_____

☐ Bantam Sunfish *Lepomis symmetricus* _____

_____

☐ Shoal Bass *Micropterus cataractae* * _____

_____

☐ Redeye Bass *Micropterus coosae* _____

_____

☐ Smallmouth Bass *Micropterus dolomieu* _____

_____

☐ Suwannee Bass *Micropterus notius* * _____

_____

☐ Spotted Bass *Micropterus punctulatus* _____

_____

☐ Largemouth Bass *Micropterus salmoides* _____

_____

☐ Guadalupe Bass *Micropterus treculii* * _____

_____

☐ White Crappie   *Pomoxis annularis*   _____

_____

☐ Black Crappie   *Pomoxis nigromaculatus*   _____

_____

Family Percidae: Perches and Darters
(North America: 189; World: 206)

☐ Naked Sand Darter   *Ammocrypta beanii*   _____

_____

☐ Florida Sand Darter   *Ammocrypta bifascia*   _____

_____

☐ Western Sand Darter   *Ammocrypta clara*   *   _____

_____

☐ Southern Sand Darter   *Ammocrypta meridiana*   _____

_____

☐ Eastern Sand Darter   *Ammocrypta pellucida*   *   _____

_____

☐ Scaly Sand Darter   *Ammocrypta vivax*   _____

_____

☐ Crystal Darter   *Crystallaria asprella*   *   _____

_____

☐ Sharphead Darter   *Etheostoma acuticeps*   *   _____

_____

☐ Coppercheek Darter   *Etheostoma aquali*   *   _____

_____

☐ Redspot Darter   *Etheostoma artesiae*   _____

_____

☐ Mud Darter   *Etheostoma asprigene*   _____

_____

☐ Cumberland Snubnose Darter   *Etheostoma atripinne*   _____

_____

☐ Emerald Darter   *Etheostoma baileyi*   _____

_____

☐ Teardrop Darter   *Etheostoma barbouri*   _____

_____

☐ Splendid Darter   *Etheostoma barrenense*   _____

_____

☐ Corrugated Darter   *Etheostoma basilare*   _____

_____

☐ Warrior Darter   *Etheostoma bellator*   *   _____

_____

☐ Orangefin Darter   *Etheostoma bellum*   _____

_____

☐ Buffalo Darter   *Etheostoma bison*   _____

_____

☐ Greenside Darter   *Etheostoma blennioides*   _____

_____

☐ Blenny Darter   *Etheostoma blennius*   _____

_____

☐ Slackwater Darter   *Etheostoma boschungi*   *   _____

_____

☐ Holiday Darter   *Etheostoma brevirostrum* *   _____

_____

☐ Brook Darter   *Etheostoma burri*   _____

_____

☐ Rainbow Darter   *Etheostoma caeruleum*   _____

_____

☐ Bluebreast Darter   *Etheostoma camurum*

☐ Chickasaw Darter   *Etheostoma cervus*   *

☐ Vermilion Darter   *Etheostoma chermocki*   *

☐ Relict Darter   *Etheostoma chienense*   *

☐ Greenfin Darter   *Etheostoma chlorobranchium*

☐ Bluntnose Darter   *Etheostoma chlorosoma*

☐ Lipstick Darter   *Etheostoma chuckwachatte*   *

☐ Ashy Darter   *Etheostoma cinereum*   *

☐ Creole Darter   *Etheostoma collettei*

☐ Carolina Darter   *Etheostoma collis*   *

☐ Coastal Darter   *Etheostoma colorosum*

☐ Coosa Darter   *Etheostoma coosae*

☐ Crown Darter   *Etheostoma corona*   *

☐ Arkansas Darter   *Etheostoma cragini*   *

☐   Fringed Darter   *Etheostoma crossopterum*   _____

_____

☐   Choctawhatchee Darter   *Etheostoma davisoni*   _____

_____

☐   Golden Darter   *Etheostoma denoncourti*   * _____

_____

☐   Stone Darter   *Etheostoma derivativum*   _____

_____

☐   Coldwater Darter   *Etheostoma ditrema*   * _____

_____

☐   Tuskaloosa Darter   *Etheostoma douglasi*   * _____

_____

☐   Blackside Snubnose Darter   *Etheostoma duryi*   _____

_____

☐   Brown Darter   *Etheostoma edwini*   _____

_____

☐   Cherry Darter   *Etheostoma etnieri*   _____

_____

☐   Etowah Darter   *Etheostoma etowahae*   * _____

_____

☐   Arkansas Saddled Darter   *Etheostoma euzonum*   * _____

_____

☐   Iowa Darter   *Etheostoma exile*   _____

_____

☐   Fantail Darter   *Etheostoma flabellare*   _____

_____

☐   Saffron Darter   *Etheostoma flavum*   _____

_____

□ Fountain Darter   *Etheostoma fonticola*   *   _____

_____

□ Barrens Darter   *Etheostoma forbesi*   *   _____

_____

□ Strawberry Darter   *Etheostoma fragi*   _____

_____

□ Savannah Darter   *Etheostoma fricksium*   _____

_____

□ Swamp Darter   *Etheostoma fusiforme*   _____

_____

□ Slough Darter   *Etheostoma gracile*   _____

_____

□ Rio Grande Darter   *Etheostoma grahami*   *   _____

_____

□ Tuckasegee Darter   *Etheostoma gutselli*   _____

_____

□ Harlequin Darter   *Etheostoma histrio*   _____

_____

□ Christmas Darter   *Etheostoma hopkinsi*   _____

_____

□ Turquoise Darter   *Etheostoma inscriptum*   _____

_____

□ Blueside Darter   *Etheostoma jessiae*   _____

_____

□ Greenbreast Darter   *Etheostoma jordani*   _____

_____

□ Yoke Darter   *Etheostoma juliae*   _____

_____

☐ Kanawha Darter   *Etheostoma kanawhae*   _____

_____

☐ Highland Rim Darter   *Etheostoma kantuckeense*   _____

_____

☐ Stripetail Darter   *Etheostoma kennicotti*   _____

_____

☐ Tombigbee Darter   *Etheostoma lachneri*   _____

_____

☐ Headwater Darter   *Etheostoma lawrencei*   _____

_____

☐ Greenthroat Darter   *Etheostoma lepidum*   *   _____

_____

☐ Longfin Darter   *Etheostoma longimanum*   _____

_____

☐ Redband Darter   *Etheostoma luteovinctum*   _____

_____

☐ Brighteye Darter   *Etheostoma lynceum*   _____

_____

☐ Spotted Darter   *Etheostoma maculatum*   *   _____

_____

☐ Pinewoods Darter   *Etheostoma mariae*   *   _____

_____

☐ Smallscale Darter   *Etheostoma microlepidum*   *   _____

_____

☐ Least Darter   *Etheostoma microperca*   _____

_____

☐ Yellowcheek Darter   *Etheostoma moorei*   *   _____

_____

☐ Lollypop Darter   *Etheostoma neopterum*   *   _____

_____

☐ Niangua Darter   *Etheostoma nianguae*   *   _____

_____

☐ Blackfin Darter   *Etheostoma nigripinne*   _____

_____

☐ Johnny Darter   *Etheostoma nigrum*   _____

_____

☐ Watercress Darter   *Etheostoma nuchale*   *   _____

_____

☐ Barcheek Darter   *Etheostoma obeyense*   _____

_____

☐ Okaloosa Darter   *Etheostoma okaloosae*   *   _____

_____

☐ Dirty Darter   *Etheostoma olivaceum*   *   _____

_____

☐ Tessellated Darter   *Etheostoma olmstedi*   _____

_____

☐ Guardian Darter   *Etheostoma oophylax*   _____

_____

☐ Candy Darter   *Etheostoma osburni*   *   _____

_____

☐ Paleback Darter   *Etheostoma pallididorsum*   *   _____

_____

☐ Goldstripe Darter   *Etheostoma parvipinne*   _____

_____

☐ Duskytail Darter   *Etheostoma percnurum*   *   _____

_____

☐ Waccamaw Darter   *Etheostoma perlongum*   *

☐ Rush Darter   *Etheostoma phytophilum*   *

☐ Riverweed Darter   *Etheostoma podostemone*

☐ Cypress Darter   *Etheostoma proeliare*

☐ Egg-mimic Darter   *Etheostoma pseudovulatum* *

☐ Stippled Darter   *Etheostoma punctulatum*

☐ Firebelly Darter   *Etheostoma pyrrhogaster*   *

☐ Orangebelly Darter   *Etheostoma radiosum*

☐ Kentucky Snubnose Darter   *Etheostoma rafinesquei*

☐ Alabama Darter   *Etheostoma ramseyi*

☐ Yazoo Darter   *Etheostoma raneyi*   *

☐ Bayou Darter   *Etheostoma rubrum*   *

☐ Redline Darter   *Etheostoma rufilineatum*

☐ Rock Darter   *Etheostoma rupestre*

☐ Arrow Darter   *Etheostoma sagitta*   * _____

_____

☐ Bloodfin Darter   *Etheostoma sanguifluum*   _____

_____

☐ Cherokee Darter   *Etheostoma scotti*   * _____

_____

☐ Maryland Darter   *Etheostoma sellare*   † _____

_____

☐ Sawcheek Darter   *Etheostoma serrifer*   _____

_____

☐ Tennessee Snubnose Darter   *Etheostoma simoterum*   _____

_____

☐ Slabrock Darter   *Etheostoma smithi*   _____

_____

☐ Sunburst Darter   *Etheostoma* species   _____

_____

☐ Tennessee Darter   *Etheostoma* species   _____

_____

☐ Duck Darter   *Etheostoma* species   _____

_____

☐ Westrim Darter   *Etheostoma* species   _____

_____

☐ Eastrim Darter   *Etheostoma* species   _____

_____

☐ Orangethroat Darter   *Etheostoma spectabile*   _____

_____

☐ Spottail Darter   *Etheostoma squamiceps*   _____

_____

☐ Speckled Darter   *Etheostoma stigmaeum*

_____

_____

☐ Striated Darter   *Etheostoma striatulum*   *

_____

_____

☐ Gulf Darter   *Etheostoma swaini*

_____

_____

☐ Swannanoa Darter   *Etheostoma swannanoa*

_____

_____

☐ Tallapoosa Darter   *Etheostoma tallapoosae*

_____

_____

☐ Shawnee Darter   *Etheostoma tecumsehi*   *

_____

_____

☐ Missouri Saddled Darter   *Etheostoma tetrazonum*

_____

_____

☐ Seagreen Darter   *Etheostoma thalassinum*

_____

_____

☐ Tippecanoe Darter   *Etheostoma tippecanoe*   *

_____

_____

☐ Trispot Darter   *Etheostoma trisella*   *

_____

_____

☐ Tuscumbia Darter   *Etheostoma tuscumbia*   *

_____

_____

☐ Current Darter   *Etheostoma uniporum*

_____

_____

☐ Variegate Darter   *Etheostoma variatum*

_____

_____

☐ Striped Darter   *Etheostoma virgatum*

_____

_____

☐ Glassy Darter	*Etheostoma vitreum*		_____
			_____
☐ Wounded Darter	*Etheostoma vulneratum*	*	_____
			_____
☐ Boulder Darter	*Etheostoma wapiti*	*	_____
			_____
☐ Redfin Darter	*Etheostoma whipplei*		_____
			_____
☐ Banded Darter	*Etheostoma zonale*		_____
			_____
☐ Backwater Darter	*Etheostoma zonifer*	*	_____
			_____
☐ Bandfin Darter	*Etheostoma zonistium*		_____
			_____
☐ Yellow Perch	*Perca flavescens*		_____
			_____
☐ Amber Darter	*Percina antesella*	*	_____
			_____
☐ Tangerine Darter	*Percina aurantiaca*		_____
			_____
☐ Goldline Darter	*Percina aurolineata*	*	_____
			_____
☐ Pearl Darter	*Percina aurora*	*	_____
			_____
☐ Southern Logperch	*Percina austroperca*	*	_____
			_____
☐ Coal Darter	*Percina brevicauda*	*	_____
			_____

☐ Blotchside Logperch · *Percina burtoni* · *

_____

_____

☐ Logperch · *Percina caprodes*

_____

_____

☐ Texas Logperch · *Percina carbonaria*

_____

_____

☐ Channel Darter · *Percina copelandi*

_____

_____

☐ Piedmont Darter · *Percina crassa*

_____

_____

☐ Bluestripe Darter · *Percina cymatotaenia* · *

_____

_____

☐ Gilt Darter · *Percina evides*

_____

_____

☐ Appalachia Darter · *Percina gymnocephala*

_____

_____

☐ Conasauga Logperch · *Percina jenkinsi* · *

_____

_____

☐ Mobile Logperch · *Percina kathae*

_____

_____

☐ Freckled Darter · *Percina lenticula* · *

_____

_____

☐ Longhead Darter · *Percina macrocephala* · *

_____

_____

☐ Bigscale Logperch · *Percina macrolepida*

_____

_____

☐ Blackside Darter · *Percina maculata*

_____

☐ Longnose Darter   *Percina nasuta*   *   _____

_____

☐ Chesapeake Logperch   *Percina nebulosa*   _____

_____

☐ Chainback Darter   *Percina nevisense*   _____

_____

☐ Blackbanded Darter   *Percina nigrofasciata*   _____

_____

☐ Stripeback Darter   *Percina notogramma*   _____

_____

☐ Sharpnose Darter   *Percina oxyrhynchus*   _____

_____

☐ Bronze Darter   *Percina palmaris*   _____

_____

☐ Leopard Darter   *Percina pantherina*   *   _____

_____

☐ Shield Darter   *Percina peltata*   _____

_____

☐ Slenderhead Darter   *Percina phoxocephala*   _____

_____

☐ Roanoke Logperch   *Percina rex*   *   _____

_____

☐ Roanoke Darter   *Percina roanoka*   _____

_____

☐ Dusky Darter   *Percina sciera*   _____

_____

☐ River Darter   *Percina shumardi*   _____

_____

☐ Muscadine Darter   *Percina* species   _____

_____

☐ Coosa Bridled Darter   *Percina* species   _____

_____

☐ Warrior Bridled Darter   *Percina* species   _____

_____

☐ Olive Darter   *Percina squamata*   *   _____

_____

☐ Frecklebelly Darter   *Percina stictogaster*   _____

_____

☐ Gulf Logperch   *Percina suttkusi*   _____

_____

☐ Snail Darter   *Percina tanasi*   *   _____

_____

☐ Stargazing Darter   *Percina uranidea*   *   _____

_____

☐ Saddleback Darter   *Percina vigil*   _____

_____

☐ Sauger   *Sander canadensis*   _____

_____

☐ Walleye   *Sander vitreus*   _____

_____

Family Sciaenidae: Drums and Croakers
(North America: 1; World: 270)

☐ Freshwater Drum   *Aplodinotus grunniens*   _____

_____

Family Elassomatidae: Pygmy Sunfishes
(North America: 6; World: 6)

☐   Spring Pygmy Sunfish   *Elassoma alabamae*   *   _____

_____

☐   Carolina Pygmy Sunfish   *Elassoma boehlkei*   *   _____

_____

☐   Everglades Pygmy Sunfish   *Elassoma evergladei*   _____

_____

☐   Bluebarred Pygmy Sunfish   *Elassoma okatie*   *   _____

_____

☐   Okefenokee Pygmy Sunfish   *Elassoma okefenokee*   _____

_____

☐   Banded Pygmy Sunfish   *Elassoma zonatum*   _____

_____

Family Cichlidae: Cichlids (North America: 1; World: 1,300)

☐   Rio Grande Cichlid   *Cichlasoma cyanoguttatum*   _____

_____

Family Embiotocidae: Surfperches (North America: 1; World: 24)

☐   Tule Perch   *Hysterocarpus traskii*   _____

_____

Family Eleotridae: Sleepers (North America: 3; World: 150)

☐   Fat Sleeper   *Dormitator maculatus*   _____

_____

☐   Largescaled Spinycheek   *Eleotris amblyopsis*   _____
     Sleeper

_____

☐   Bigmouth Sleeper   *Gobiomorus dormitor*   _____

_____

Family Gobiidae: Gobies (North America: 12; World: 1,875)

☐ River Goby   *Awaous banana*   _____

_____

☐ Arrow Goby   *Clevelandia ios*   _____

_____

☐ Darter Goby   *Ctenogobius boleosoma*   _____

_____

☐ Blotchcheek Goby   *Ctenogobius fasciatus*   _____

_____

☐ Slashcheek Goby   *Ctenogobius pseudofasciatus*   _____

_____

☐ Freshwater Goby   *Ctenogobius shufeldti*   _____

_____

☐ Tidewater Goby   *Eucyclogobius newberryi*   *   _____

_____

☐ Longjaw Mudsucker   *Gillichthys mirabilis*   _____

_____

☐ Violet Goby   *Gobioides broussonetii*   _____

_____

☐ Naked Goby   *Gobiosoma bosc*   _____

_____

☐ Crested Goby   *Lophogobius cyprinoides*   _____

_____

☐ Clown Goby   *Microgobius gulosus*   _____

_____

Order Pleuronectiformes: Flounders and Soles

Family Achiridae: American Soles (North America: 1; World: 28)

☐ Hogchoker   *Trinectes maculatus*   _____

_____

NON-ANNUAL MARINE VISITORS

Class Chondrichthyes: Cartilaginous Fishes

Order Carcharhiniformes: Requiem Sharks
Family Carcharhinidae: Requiem Sharks

☐   Bull Shark   *Carcharhinus leucas*   _____

_____

Order Pristiformes: Sawfishes
Family Pristidae: Sawfishes

☐   Smalltooth Sawfish   *Pristis pectinata*   _____

_____

Class Actinopterygii: Ray-finned Fishes

Order Elopiformes: Tenpounders and Tarpons
Family Elopidae: Tenpounders

☐   Machete   *Elops affinis*   _____

_____

☐   Ladyfish   *Elops saurus*   _____

_____

Family Megalopidae: Tarpons

☐   Tarpon   *Megalops atlanticus*   _____

_____

Order Clupeiformes: Anchovies and Herrings
Family Clupeidae: Herrings and Shads

☐   Scaled Sardine   *Harengula jaguana*   _____

_____

☐   Atlantic Thread Herring   *Opisthonema oglinum*   _____

_____

Order Siluriformes: Catfishes

Family Ariidae: Sea Catfishes

☐ Hardhead Catfish   *Ariopsis felis*   _____

_____

Order Salmoniformes: Smelts, Trouts, and Salmons

Family Osmeridae: Smelts

☐ Surf Smelt   *Hypomesus pretiosus*   _____

_____

☐ Capelin   *Mallotus villosus*   _____

_____

Order Mugiliformes: Mullets

Family Mugilidae: Mullets

☐ Mountain Mullet   *Agonostomus monticola*   _____

_____

☐ White Mullet   *Mugil curema*   _____

_____

Order Atheriniformes: Silversides

Family Atherinopsidae: New World Silversides

☐ Rough Silverside   *Membras martinica*   _____

_____

Order Cyprinodontiformes: Rivulines, Topminnows, Livebearers, Goodeids, and Pupfishes

Family Fundulidae: Topminnows

☐ Gulf Killifish   *Fundulus grandis*   _____

_____

☐ Mummichog   *Fundulus heteroclitus*   _____

_____

☐ Saltmarsh Topminnow   *Fundulus jenkinsi*   _____

_____

☐ Spotfin Killifish *Fundulus luciae* _____

_____

☐ California Killifish *Fundulus parvipinnis* _____

_____

Family Poeciliidae: Livebearers

☐ Mangrove Gambusia *Gambusia rhizophorae* _____

_____

Order Gasterosteiformes: Sticklebacks and Pipefishes

Family Syngnathidae: Pipefishes

☐ Opossum Pipefish *Microphis brachyurus* _____

_____

Order Scorpaeniformes: Sculpins and Allies

Family Cottidae: Sculpins

☐ Sharpnose Sculpin *Clinocottus acuticeps* _____

_____

☐ Pacific Staghorn Sculpin *Leptocottus armatus* _____

_____

Order Perciformes: Snooks, Basses, Sunfishes, Perches, and Allies

Family Centropomidae: Snooks

☐ Swordspine Snook *Centropomus ensiferus* _____

_____

☐ Smallscale Fat Snook *Centropomus parallelus* _____

_____

☐ Tarpon Snook *Centropomus pectinatus* _____

_____

☐ Common Snook *Centropomus undecimalis* _____

_____

Family Lutjanidae: Snappers

☐ Gray Snapper   *Lutjanus griseus*   _____

_____

Family Gerreidae: Mojarras

☐ Irish Pompano   *Diapterus auratus*   _____

_____

☐ Tidewater Mojarra *Eucinostomus harengulus* _____

_____

☐ Striped Mojarra   *Eugerres plumieri*   _____

_____

Family Haemulidae: Grunts

☐ Pigfish   *Orthopristis chrysoptera* _____

_____

Family Sparidae: Porgies

☐ Sheepshead   *Archosargus probatocephalus* _____

_____

☐ Pinfish   *Lagodon rhomboides*   _____

_____

Family Sciaenidae: Drums and Croakers

☐ Silver Perch   *Bairdiella chrysoura* _____

_____

☐ Spotted Seatrout *Cynoscion nebulosus*   _____

_____

☐ Spot   *Leiostomus xanthurus* _____

_____

☐ Atlantic Croaker *Micropogonias undulatus* _____

_____

☐ Red Drum   *Sciaenops ocellatus*   _____

_____

Family Embiotocidae: Surfperches

☐ Shiner Perch   *Cymatogaster aggregata*   _____

_____

Family Eleotridae: Sleepers

☐ Smallscaled Spinycheek   *Eleotris perniger*   _____
Sleeper

_____

☐ Spotted Sleeper   *Eleotris picta*   _____

_____

☐ Guavina   *Guavina guavina*   _____

_____

Family Gobiidae: Gobies

☐ Mexican Goby   *Ctenogobius claytonii*   _____

_____

Order Pleuronectiformes: Flounders and Soles

Family Paralichthyidae: Sand Flounders

☐ Bay Whiff   *Citharichthys spilopterus*   _____

_____

☐ Southern Flounder   *Paralichthys lethostigma*   _____

_____

Family Pleuronectidae: Righteye Flounders

☐ Starry Flounder   *Platichthys stellatus*   _____

_____

ALIEN SPECIES

Family Notopteridae: Featherfin Knifefishes

☐ Clown Knifefish   *Chitala ornata*   _____

_____

Family Cyprinidae: Carps and Minnows

☐ Goldfish   *Carassius auratus*   _____

_____

☐ Grass Carp *Ctenopharyngodon idella* _____

☐ Common Carp *Cyprinus carpio* _____

☐ Silver Carp *Hypophthalmichthys molitrix* _____

☐ Bighead Carp *Hypophthalmichthys nobilis* _____

☐ Ide *Leuciscus idus* _____

☐ Bitterling *Rhodeus sericeus* _____

☐ Rudd *Scardinius erythrophthalmus* _____

☐ Tench *Tinca tinca* _____

Family Cobitidae: Loaches

☐ Oriental Weatherfish *Misgurnus anguillicaudatus* _____

Family Clariidae: Labyrinth Catfishes

☐ Walking Catfish *Clarias batrachus* _____

Family Doradidae: Thorny Catfishes

☐ Southern Striped Raphael *Platydoras armatulus* _____

Family Callichthyidae: Callichthyid Armored Catfishes

☐ Brown Hoplo *Hoplosternum littorale* _____

Family Loricariidae: Suckermouth Amored Catfishes

☐ unidentified suckermouth catfish   *Hypostomus* species

_____

_____

☐ Southern Sailfin Catfish   *Pterygoplichthys anisitsi*

_____

_____

☐ Vermiculated Sailfin Catfish   *Pterygoplichthys disjunctivus*

_____

_____

☐ Orinoco Sailfin Catfish   *Pterygoplichthys multiradiatus*

_____

_____

☐ Amazon Sailfin Catfish   *Pterygoplichthys pardalis*

_____

_____

Family Osmeridae: Smelts

☐ Wakasagi   *Hypomesus nipponensis*

_____

_____

Family Salmonidae: Trouts and Salmons

☐ Brown Trout   *Salmo trutta*

_____

_____

Family Aplocheilidae: Rivulines

☐ Giant Rivulus   *Rivulus hartii*

_____

_____

Family Poeciliidae: Livebearers

☐ Pike Killifish   *Belonesox belizanus*

_____

_____

☐ Shortfin Molly   *Poecilia mexicana*

_____

_____

☐ Guppy   *Poecilia reticulata*

_____

_____

☐ Mexican Molly   *Poecilia sphenops*

_____

_____

☐ Porthole Livebearer   *Poeciliopsis gracilis*   _____

_____

☐ Green Swordtail   *Xiphophorus hellerii*   _____

_____

☐ Southern Platyfish   *Xiphophorus maculatus*   _____

_____

☐ Variable Platyfish   *Xiphophorus variatus*   _____

_____

Family Synbranchidae: Swamp Eels

☐ Asian Swamp Eel   *Monopterus albus*   _____

_____

Family Percidae: Darters, Perches, Walleye, and Sauger

☐ Ruffe   *Gymnocephalus cernuus*   _____

_____

☐ Zander   *Sander lucioperca*   _____

_____

Family Sciaenidae: Drums and Croakers

☐ Bairdiella   *Bairdiella icistia*   _____

_____

☐ Orangemouth Corvina   *Cynoscion xanthulus*   _____

_____

Family Cichlidae: Cichlids

☐ Oscar   *Astronotus ocellatus*   _____

_____

☐ Butterfly Peacock Cichlid   *Cichla ocellaris*   _____

_____

☐ Black Acara   *Cichlasoma bimaculatum*   _____

_____

☐ Midas Cichlid   *Cichlasoma citrinellum*   _____

_____

☐ Jaguar Guapote   *Cichlasoma managuense*   _____

_____

☐ Firemouth   *Cichlasoma meeki*   _____

_____

☐ Convict Cichlid   *Cichlasoma nigrofasciatum*   _____

_____

☐ Jack Dempsey   *Cichlasoma octofasciatum*   _____

_____

☐ Yellowbelly Cichlid   *Cichlasoma salvini*   _____

_____

☐ Mayan Cichlid   *Cichlasoma urophthalmus*   _____

_____

☐ Redstriped Eartheater   *Geophagus surinamensis*   _____

_____

☐ African Jewelfish   *Hemichromis letourneuxi*   _____

_____

☐ Banded Cichlid   *Heros severus*   _____

_____

☐ Blue Tilapia   *Oreochromis aureus*   _____

_____

☐ Mozambique Tilapia   *Oreochromis mossambicus*   _____

_____

☐ Nile Tilapia   *Oreochromis niloticus*   _____

_____

☐ Wami Tilapia   *Oreochromis urolepis*   _____

_____

☐ Blackchin Tilapia   *Sarotherodon melanotheron* _____

_____

☐ Spotted Tilapia   *Tilapia mariae* _____

_____

☐ Redbelly Tilapia   *Tilapia zillii* _____

_____

Family Gobiidae: Gobies

☐ Yellowfin Goby   *Acanthogobius flavimanus* _____

_____

☐ Round Goby   *Neogobius melanostomus* _____

_____

☐ Tubenose Goby   *Proterorhinus marmoratus* _____

_____

☐ Shokihaze Goby   *Tridentiger barbatus* _____

_____

☐ Shimofuri Goby   *Tridentiger bifasciatus* _____

_____

Family Belontiidae: Gouramies

☐ Croaking Gourami   *Trichopsis vittata* _____

_____

Family Channidae: Snakeheads

☐ Bullseye Snakehead   *Channa marulius* _____

_____

ADDITIONAL SPECIES

☐ _____ _____ _____

_____

☐ _____ _____ _____

_____

☐ _____ _____ _____

_____

☐ _____ _____ _____

_____

☐ _____ _____ _____

_____

☐ _____ _____ _____

_____

☐ _____ _____ _____

_____

☐ _____ _____ _____

_____

☐ _____ _____ _____

_____

☐ _____ _____ _____

_____

☐ _____ _____ _____

_____

☐ _____ _____ _____

_____

☐ _____ _____ _____

_____

☐ _____ _____ _____

_____

☐ _____ _____ _____

_____

☐ _____ _____ _____

☐ _____ _____ _____

☐ _____ _____ _____

☐ _____ _____ _____

☐ _____ _____ _____

☐ _____ _____ _____

☐ _____ _____ _____

☐ _____ _____ _____

☐ _____ _____ _____

☐ _____ _____ _____

☐ _____ _____ _____

☐ _____ _____ _____

☐ _____ _____ _____

Order Lepidoptera: Butterflies

Family Papilionidae: Swallowtails and Parnassians
(North America: 23; World: 560)

SUBFAMILY PARNASSIINAE: PARNASSIANS

☐ Eversmann's Parnassian   *Parnassius eversmanni*   _____

_____

☐ Clodius Parnassian   *Parnassius clodius*   _____

_____

☐ Phoebus Parnassian   *Parnassius phoebus*   _____

_____

SUBFAMILY PAPILIONINAE: SWALLOWTAILS

☐ Pipevine Swallowtail   *Battus philenor*   _____

_____

☐ Polydamas Swallowtail   *Battus polydamas*   _____

_____

☐ Zebra Swallowtail   *Eurytides marcellus*   _____

_____

☐ Black Swallowtail   *Papilio polyxenes*   _____

_____

☐ Ozark Swallowtail   *Papilio joanae*   *   _____

_____

☐ Short-tailed Swallowtail   *Papilio brevicauda*   *   _____

_____

☐ Old World Swallowtail   *Papilio machaon*   _____

_____

☐ Anise Swallowtail   *Papilio zelicaon*

☐ Indra Swallowtail   *Papilio indra*

☐ Giant Swallowtail   *Papilio cresphontes*

☐ Schaus's Swallowtail   *Papilio aristodemus*   *

☐ Ornythion Swallowtail   *Papilio ornythion*

☐ Eastern Tiger Swallowtail   *Papilio glaucus*

☐ Canadian Tiger Swallowtail   *Papilio canadensis*

☐ Western Tiger Swallowtail   *Papilio rutulus*

☐ Two-tailed Swallowtail   *Papilio multicaudata*

☐ Pale Swallowtail   *Papilio eurymedon*

☐ Spicebush Swallowtail   *Papilio troilus*

☐ Palamedes Swallowtail   *Papilio palamedes*

☐ Ruby-spotted Swallowtail   *Papilio anchisiades*

Family Pieridae: Whites and Sulphurs (North America: 54; World: 1,100)

SUBFAMILY PIERINAE: WHITES

☐ Pine White   *Neophasia menapia*

☐ Chiricahua White   *Neophasia terlootii*   *

☐ Florida White   *Appias drusilla*

☐ Becker's White   *Pontia beckerii*

☐ Spring White   *Pontia sisymbrii*

☐ Checkered White   *Pontia protodice*

☐ Western White   *Pontia occidentalis*

☐ Mustard White   *Pieris napi*

☐ West Virginia White   *Pieris virginiensis*   *

☐ Great Southern White   *Ascia monuste*

☐ Giant White   *Ganyra josephina*

☐ Howarth's White   *Ganyra howarthii*

☐ Large Marble   *Euchloe ausonides*

☐ Green Marble   *Euchloe naina*   _____

_____

☐ Northern Marble   *Euchloe creusa*   _____

_____

☐ Pearly Marble   *Euchloe hyantis*   *   _____

_____

☐ Olympia Marble   *Euchloe olympia*   _____

_____

☐ Desert Orangetip   *Anthocharis cethura*   _____

_____

☐ Sara Orangetip   *Anthocharis sara*   _____

_____

☐ Falcate Orangetip   *Anthocharis midea*   _____

_____

☐ Gray Marble   *Anthocharis lanceolata*   *   _____

_____

SUBFAMILY COLIADINAE: SULPHURS

☐ Clouded Sulphur   *Colias philodice*   _____

_____

☐ Orange Sulphur   *Colias eurytheme*   _____

_____

☐ Western Sulphur   *Colias occidentalis*   *   _____

_____

☐ Christina's Sulphur   *Colias christina*   _____

_____

☐ Queen Alexandra's Sulphur   *Colias alexandra*   _____

_____

☐ Mead's Sulphur   *Colias meadii*   _____

_____

☐ Coppermine Sulphur   *Colias johanseni*   *   _____

_____

_____

☐ Canadian Sulphur   *Colias canadensis*   _____

_____

☐ Hecla Sulphur   *Colias hecla*   _____

_____

☐ Labrador Sulphur   *Colias nastes*   _____

_____

☐ Scudder's Sulphur   *Colias scudderi*   _____

_____

☐ Giant Sulphur   *Colias gigantea*   _____

_____

☐ Sierra Sulphur   *Colias behrii*   *   _____

_____

☐ Pelidne Sulphur   *Colias pelidne*   _____

_____

☐ Pink-edged Sulphur   *Colias interior*   _____

_____

☐ Palaeno Sulphur   *Colias palaeno*   _____

_____

☐ California Dogface   *Colias eurydice*   *   _____

_____

☐ Southern Dogface   *Colias cesonia*   _____

_____

☐ White Angled-Sulphur   *Anteos clorinde*   _____

_____

☐ Cloudless Sulphur   *Phoebis sennae*   _____

_____

☐ Orange-barred Sulphur   *Phoebis philea*

☐ Large Orange Sulphur   *Phoebis agarithe*

☐ Statira Sulphur   *Phoebis statira*

☐ Lyside Sulphur   *Kricogonia lyside*

☐ Barred Yellow   *Eurema daira*

☐ Boisduval's Yellow   *Eurema boisduvaliana*

☐ Mexican Yellow   *Eurema mexicana*

☐ Tailed Orange   *Eurema proterpia*

☐ Little Yellow   *Eurema lisa*

☐ Mimosa Yellow   *Eurema nise*

☐ Dina Yellow   *Eurema dina*

☐ Sleepy Orange   *Eurema nicippe*

☐ Dainty Sulphur   *Nathalis iole*

Family Lycaenidae: Gossamer-wing Butterflies
(North America: 112; World: 5,000)

☐ Harvester   *Feniseca tarquinius*   _____

_____

SUBFAMILY LYCAENINAE: COPPERS

☐ Tailed Copper   *Lycaena arota*   _____

_____

☐ American Copper   *Lycaena phlaeas*   _____

_____

☐ Lustrous Copper   *Lycaena cupreus*   _____

_____

☐ Great Copper   *Lycaena xanthoides*   _____

_____

☐ Gray Copper   *Lycaena dione*   _____

_____

☐ Edith's Copper   *Lycaena editha*   _____

_____

☐ Gorgon Copper   *Lycaena gorgon*   *   _____

_____

☐ Bronze Copper   *Lycaena hyllus*   _____

_____

☐ Ruddy Copper   *Lycaena rubidus*   _____

_____

☐ Blue Copper   *Lycaena heteronea*   _____

_____

☐ Bog Copper   *Lycaena epixanthe*   _____

_____

☐ Dorcas Copper   *Lycaena dorcas*   _____

_____

☐ Purplish Copper   *Lycaena helloides*

_____

_____

☐ Lilac-bordered Copper   *Lycaena nivalis*

_____

_____

☐ Mariposa Copper   *Lycaena mariposa*

_____

_____

☐ Hermes Copper   *Lycaena hermes*   *

_____

_____

SUBFAMILY THECLINAE: HAIRSTREAKS

☐ Colorado Hairstreak   *Hypaurotis crysalus*

_____

_____

☐ Golden Hairstreak   *Habrodais grunus*

_____

_____

☐ Atala   *Eumaeus atala*

_____

_____

☐ Great Purple Hairstreak   *Atlides halesus*

_____

_____

☐ Amethyst Hairstreak   *Chlorostrymon maesites*

_____

_____

☐ Silver-banded Hairstreak   *Chlorostrymon simaethis*

_____

_____

☐ Soapberry Hairstreak   *Phaeostrymon alcestis*

_____

_____

☐ Coral Hairstreak   *Satyrium titus*

_____

_____

☐ Behr's Hairstreak   *Satyrium behrii*

_____

_____

☐ Sooty Hairstreak   *Satyrium fuliginosa*

_____

_____

☐ Acadian Hairstreak   *Satyrium acadica*   _____

_____

☐ California Hairstreak   *Satyrium californica*   _____

_____

☐ Sylvan Hairstreak   *Satyrium sylvinus*   _____

_____

☐ Edwards's Hairstreak   *Satyrium edwardsii*   _____

_____

☐ Banded Hairstreak   *Satyrium calanus*   _____

_____

☐ Hickory Hairstreak   *Satyrium caryaevorum*   _____

_____

☐ King's Hairstreak   *Satyrium kingi*   *   _____

_____

☐ Striped Hairstreak   *Satyrium liparops*   _____

_____

☐ Gold-hunter's Hairstreak   *Satyrium auretorum*   _____

_____

☐ Mountain Mahogany Hairstreak   *Satyrium tetra*   _____

_____

☐ Hedgerow Hairstreak   *Satyrium saepium*   _____

_____

☐ Oak Hairstreak   *Satyrium favonius*   _____

_____

☐ Ilavia Hairstreak   *Satyrium ilavia*   _____

_____

☐ Poling's Hairstreak   *Satyrium polingi*   *   _____

_____

☐ Clench's Greenstreak   *Cyanophrys miserabilis*   _____

_____

☐ Goodson's Greenstreak   *Cyanophrys goodsoni*   _____

_____

☐ Bramble Hairstreak   *Callophrys dumetorum*   * _____

_____

☐ Sheridan's Hairstreak   *Callophrys sheridanii*   _____

_____

☐ Xami Hairstreak   *Callophrys xami*   _____

_____

☐ Sandia Hairstreak   *Callophrys mcfarlandi*   _____

_____

☐ Brown Elfin   *Callophrys augustinus*   _____

_____

☐ Desert Elfin   *Callophrys fotis*   * _____

_____

☐ Moss's Elfin   *Callophrys mossii*   _____

_____

☐ Hoary Elfin   *Callophrys polios*   _____

_____

☐ Frosted Elfin   *Callophrys irus*   * _____

_____

☐ Henry's Elfin   *Callophrys henrici*   _____

_____

☐ Bog Elfin   *Callophrys lanoraieensis*   * _____

_____

☐ Eastern Pine Elfin   *Callophrys niphon*   _____

_____

☐ Western Pine Elfin   *Callophrys eryphon*   _____

_____

☐ Thicket Hairstreak   *Callophrys spinetorum*   _____

_____

☐ Johnson's Hairstreak   *Callophrys johnsoni*   *   _____

_____

☐ Juniper Hairstreak   *Callophrys gryneus*   _____

_____

☐ Hessel's Hairstreak   *Callophrys hesseli*   *   _____

_____

☐ White M Hairstreak   *Parrhasius m-album*   _____

_____

☐ Gray Hairstreak   *Strymon melinus*   _____

_____

☐ Avalon Scrub-Hairstreak   *Strymon avalona*   *   _____

_____

☐ Red-crescent Scrub-Hairstreak   *Strymon rufofusca*   _____

_____

☐ Martial Scrub-Hairstreak   *Strymon martialis*   _____

_____

☐ Bartram's Scrub-Hairstreak   *Strymon acis*   _____

_____

☐ Lacey's Scrub-Hairstreak   *Strymon alea*   *   _____

_____

☐ Mallow Scrub-Hairstreak   *Strymon istapa*   _____

_____

☐ Lantana Scrub-Hairstreak   *Strymon bazochii*   _____

_____

☐ Ruddy Hairstreak   *Electrostrymon sangala*   _____

_____

☐ Muted Hairstreak   *Electrostrymon canus*   _____

_____

☐ Red-banded Hairstreak   *Calycopis cecrops*   _____

_____

☐ Dusky-blue Groundstreak   *Calycopis isobeon*   _____

_____

☐ Leda Ministreak   *Ministrymon leda*   _____

_____

☐ Clytie Ministreak   *Ministrymon clytie*   _____

_____

☐ Gray Ministreak   *Ministrymon azia*   _____

_____

☐ Early Hairstreak   *Erora laeta*   *   _____

_____

☐ Arizona Hairstreak   *Erora quaderna*   _____

_____

SUBFAMILY POLYOMMATINAE: BLUES

☐ Western Pygmy-Blue   *Brephidium exile*   _____

_____

☐ Eastern Pygmy-Blue   *Brephidium isophthalma*   _____

_____

☐ Cassius Blue   *Leptotes cassius*   _____

_____

☐ Marine Blue   *Leptotes marina*   _____

_____

☐ Cyna Blue   *Zizula cyna*   _____

_____

☐ Miami Blue   *Hemiargus thomasi*   *

_____

_____

☐ Nickerbean Blue   *Hemiargus ammon*

_____

_____

☐ Ceraunus Blue   *Hemiargus ceraunus*

_____

_____

☐ Reakirt's Blue   *Hemiargus isola*

_____

_____

☐ Eastern Tailed-Blue *Everes comyntas*

_____

_____

☐ Western Tailed-Blue *Everes amyntula*

_____

_____

☐ Spring Azure   *Celastrina ladon*

_____

_____

☐ Appalachian Azure   *Celastrina neglectamajor*

_____

_____

☐ Dusky Azure   *Celastrina nigra*

_____

_____

☐ Sonoran Blue   *Philotes sonorensis*   *

_____

_____

☐ Square-spotted Blue *Euphilotes battoides*

_____

_____

☐ Dotted Blue   *Euphilotes enoptes*

_____

_____

☐ Rita Blue   *Euphilotes rita*   *

_____

_____

☐ Spalding's Blue   *Euphilotes spaldingi*   *

_____

_____

☐ Small Blue   *Philotiella speciosa*   * _____

_____

☐ Arrowhead Blue   *Glaucopsyche piasus* _____

_____

☐ Silvery Blue   *Glaucopsyche lygdamus* _____

_____

☐ Xerces Blue   *Glaucopsyche xerces*   † _____

_____

☐ Northern Blue   *Lycaeides idas* _____

_____

☐ Melissa Blue   *Lycaeides melissa* _____

_____

☐ Greenish Blue   *Plebejus saepiolus* _____

_____

☐ San Emigdio Blue   *Plebejus emigdionis*   * _____

_____

☐ Boisduval's Blue   *Plebejus icarioides* _____

_____

☐ Shasta Blue   *Plebejus shasta* _____

_____

☐ Acmon Blue   *Plebejus acmon* _____

_____

☐ Lupine Blue   *Plebejus lupini* _____

_____

☐ Veined Blue   *Plebejus neurona*   * _____

_____

☐ Cranberry Blue   *Vacciniina optilete* _____

_____

☐ Arctic Blue   *Agriades glandon*   _____

_____

☐ Heather Blue   *Agriades cassiope*   *   _____

_____

Family Riodinidae: Metalmarks (North America: 16; World: 1,500)

SUBFAMILY: RIODININAE: METALMARKS

☐ Little Metalmark   *Calephelis virginiensis*   _____

_____

☐ Northern Metalmark   *Calephelis borealis*   *   _____

_____

☐ Fatal Metalmark   *Calephelis nemesis*   _____

_____

☐ Rounded Metalmark   *Calephelis perditalis*   *   _____

_____

☐ Wright's Metalmark   *Calephelis wrighti*   *   _____

_____

☐ Swamp Metalmark   *Calephelis mutica*   *   _____

_____

☐ Rawson's Metalmark   *Calephelis rawsoni*   _____

_____

☐ Arizona Metalmark   *Calephelis arizonensis*   *   _____

_____

☐ Red-bordered Metalmark   *Caria ino*   _____

_____

☐ Blue Metalmark   *Lasaia sula*   _____

_____

☐ Red-bordered Pixie   *Melanis pixe*   _____

_____

☐ Zela Metalmark   *Emesis zela* _____

_____

☐ Ares Metalmark   *Emesis ares* _____

_____

☐ Mormon Metalmark   *Apodemia mormo* _____

_____

☐ Palmer's Metalmark   *Apodemia palmeri* _____

_____

☐ Nais Metalmark   *Apodemia nais* _____

_____

Family Nymphalidae: Brushfooted Butterflies
(North America: 277; World: 5,000)

SUBFAMILY LIBYTHEINAE: SNOUTS

☐ American Snout   *Libytheana carinenta* _____

_____

SUBFAMILY HELICONIINAE: HELICONIANS AND FRITILLARIES

☐ Gulf Fritillary   *Agraulis vanillae* _____

_____

☐ Julia Heliconian   *Dryas iulia* _____

_____

☐ Zebra Heliconian   *Heliconius charithonia* _____

_____

☐ Variegated Fritillary   *Euptoieta claudia* _____

_____

☐ Mexican Fritillary   *Euptoieta hegesia* _____

_____

☐ Diana Fritillary   *Speyeria diana*   * _____

_____

☐ Great Spangled Fritillary   *Speyeria cybele*   _____

_____

☐ Aphrodite Fritillary   *Speyeria aphrodite*   _____

_____

☐ Regal Fritillary   *Speyeria idalia*   *   _____

_____

☐ Nokomis Fritillary   *Speyeria nokomis*   *   _____

_____

☐ Edwards's Fritillary   *Speyeria edwardsii*   _____

_____

☐ Coronis Fritillary   *Speyeria coronis*   _____

_____

☐ Zerene Fritillary   *Speyeria zerene*   _____

_____

☐ Callippe Fritillary   *Speyeria callippe*   _____

_____

☐ Great Basin Fritillary   *Speyeria egleis*   _____

_____

☐ Unsilvered Fritillary   *Speyeria adiaste*   *   _____

_____

☐ Atlantis Fritillary   *Speyeria atlantis*   _____

_____

☐ Hydaspe Fritillary   *Speyeria hydaspe*   _____

_____

☐ Mormon Fritillary   *Speyeria mormonia*   _____

_____

☐ Mountain Fritillary   *Boloria napaea*   _____

_____

☐   Bog Fritillary   *Boloria eunomia*   _____

_____

☐   Silver-bordered Fritillary   *Boloria selene*   _____

_____

☐   Meadow Fritillary   *Boloria bellona*   _____

_____

☐   Frigga Fritillary   *Boloria frigga*   _____

_____

☐   Dingy Fritillary   *Boloria improba*   _____

_____

☐   Relict Fritillary   *Boloria kriemhild*   *   _____

_____

☐   Pacific Fritillary   *Boloria epithore*   _____

_____

☐   Polaris Fritillary   *Boloria polaris*   _____

_____

☐   Freija Fritillary   *Boloria freija*   _____

_____

☐   Alberta Fritillary   *Boloria alberta*   *   _____

_____

☐   Astarte Fritillary   *Boloria astarte*   _____

_____

☐   Purplish Fritillary   *Boloria montinus*   _____

_____

☐   Arctic Fritillary   *Boloria chariclea*   _____

_____

☐   Cryptic Fritillary   *Boloria natazhati*   *   _____

_____

SUBFAMILY NYMPHALINAE: TRUE BRUSHFOOTS

☐ Dotted Checkerspot   *Poladryas minuta*   _____

_____

☐ Arachne Checkerspot   *Poladryas arachne*   _____

_____

☐ Theona Checkerspot   *Chlosyne theona*   _____

_____

☐ Chinati Checkerspot   *Chlosyne chinatiensis*   _____

_____

☐ Black Checkerspot   *Chlosyne cyneas*   _____

_____

☐ Fulvia Checkerspot   *Chlosyne fulvia*   _____

_____

☐ Leanira Checkerspot   *Chlosyne leanira*   _____

_____

☐ California Patch   *Chlosyne californica*   _____

_____

☐ Bordered Patch   *Chlosyne lacinia*   _____

_____

☐ Definite Patch   *Chlosyne definita*   *   _____

_____

☐ Banded Patch   *Chlosyne endeis*   _____

_____

☐ Crimson Patch   *Chlosyne janais*   _____

_____

☐ Gorgone Checkerspot   *Chlosyne gorgone*   _____

_____

☐ Silvery Checkerspot   *Chlosyne nycteis*   _____

_____

☐ Harris's Checkerspot   *Chlosyne harrisii*   _____

☐ Northern Checkerspot   *Chlosyne palla*   _____

☐ Rockslide Checkerspot   *Chlosyne whitneyi*   _____

☐ Sagebrush Checkerspot   *Chlosyne acastus*   _____

☐ Gabb's Checkerspot   *Chlosyne gabbii*   * _____

☐ Hoffmann's Checkerspot   *Chlosyne hoffmanni*   _____

☐ Tiny Checkerspot   *Dymasia dymas*   _____

☐ Elada Checkerspot   *Texola elada*   _____

☐ Texan Crescent   *Phyciodes texana*   _____

☐ Cuban Crescent   *Phyciodes frisia*   _____

☐ Vesta Crescent   *Phyciodes vesta*   _____

☐ Phaon Crescent   *Phyciodes phaon*   _____

☐ Pearl Crescent   *Phyciodes tharos*   _____

☐ Northern Crescent   *Phyciodes selenis*   _____

☐ Tawny Crescent   *Phyciodes batesii*   _____

_____

☐ Field Crescent   *Phyciodes campestris*   _____

_____

☐ Painted Crescent   *Phyciodes picta*   _____

_____

☐ California Crescent   *Phyciodes orseis*   *   _____

_____

☐ Pale Crescent   *Phyciodes pallida*   _____

_____

☐ Mylitta Crescent   *Phyciodes mylitta*   _____

_____

☐ Gillett's Checkerspot   *Euphydryas gillettii*   *   _____

_____

☐ Variable Checkerspot   *Euphydryas chalcedona*   _____

_____

☐ Edith's Checkerspot   *Euphydryas editha*   _____

_____

☐ Baltimore Checkerspot   *Euphydryas phaeton*   _____

_____

☐ Question Mark   *Polygonia interrogationis*   _____

_____

☐ Eastern Comma   *Polygonia comma*   _____

_____

☐ Satyr Comma   *Polygonia satyrus*   _____

_____

☐ Green Comma   *Polygonia faunus*   _____

_____

☐ Hoary Comma   *Polygonia gracilis*   _____

☐ Oreas Comma   *Polygonia oreas*   _____

☐ Gray Comma   *Polygonia progne*   _____

☐ Compton Tortoiseshell   *Nymphalis vaualbum*   _____

☐ California Tortoiseshell   *Nymphalis californica*   _____

☐ Mourning Cloak   *Nymphalis antiopa*   _____

☐ Milbert's Tortoiseshell   *Nymphalis milberti*   _____

☐ American Lady   *Vanessa virginiensis*   _____

☐ Painted Lady   *Vanessa cardui*   _____

☐ West Coast Lady   *Vanessa annabella*   _____

☐ Red Admiral   *Vanessa atalanta*   _____

☐ Common Buckeye   *Junonia coenia*   _____

☐ Mangrove Buckeye   *Junonia evarete*   _____

☐ Tropical Buckeye   *Junonia genoveva*   _____

☐ White Peacock   *Anartia jatrophae*

☐ Banded Peacock   *Anartia fatima*

☐ Malachite   *Siproeta stelenes*

SUBFAMILY LIMENITIDINAE: ADMIRALS AND ALLIES

☐ Red-spotted Admiral   *Limenitis arthemis*

☐ Viceroy   *Limenitis archippus*

☐ Weidemeyer's Admiral   *Limenitis weidemeyerii*

☐ Lorquin's Admiral   *Limenitis lorquini*

☐ Band-celled Sister   *Adelpha fessonia*

☐ California Sister   *Adelpha bredowii*

☐ Mexican Bluewing   *Myscelia ethusa*

☐ Dingy Purplewing   *Eunica monima*

☐ Florida Purplewing   *Eunica tatila*

☐ Common Mestra   *Mestra amymone*

☐ Gray Cracker   *Hamadryas februa*

☐ Many-banded Daggerwing   *Marpesia chiron* _____

☐ Ruddy Daggerwing   *Marpesia petreus* _____

SUBFAMILY CHARAXINAE: LEAFWINGS

☐ Tropical Leafwing   *Anaea aidea* _____

☐ Florida Leafwing   *Anaea floridalis* _____

☐ Goatweed Leafwing   *Anaea andria* _____

☐ Pale-spotted Leafwing   *Anaea pithyusa* _____

SUBFAMILY APATURINAE: EMPERORS

☐ Hackberry Emperor   *Asterocampa celtis* _____

☐ Empress Leilia   *Asterocampa leilia* _____

☐ Tawny Emperor   *Asterocampa clyton* _____

SUBFAMILY SATYRINAE: SATYRS

☐ Southern Pearly-eye   *Enodia portlandia* _____

☐ Northern Pearly-eye   *Enodia anthedon* _____

☐ Creole Pearly-eye   *Enodia creola*   * _____

☐ Eyed Brown   *Satyrodes eurydice* _____

☐ Appalachian Brown — *Satyrodes appalachia* _____

☐ Nabokov's Satyr — *Cyllopsis pyracmon* _____

☐ Canyonland Satyr — *Cyllopsis pertepida* _____

☐ Gemmed Satyr — *Cyllopsis gemma* _____

☐ Carolina Satyr — *Hermeuptychia sosybius* _____

☐ Georgia Satyr — *Neonympha areolata* _____

☐ Mitchell's Satyr — *Neonympha mitchellii* * _____

☐ Little Wood-Satyr — *Megisto cymela* _____

☐ Red Satyr — *Megisto rubricata* _____

☐ Pine Satyr — *Paramacera allyni* _____

☐ Hayden's Ringlet — *Coenonympha haydenii* _____

☐ Common Ringlet — *Coenonympha tullia* _____

☐ Common Wood-Nymph — *Cercyonis pegala* _____

☐ Mead's Wood-Nymph — *Cercyonis meadii* _____

☐ Great Basin Wood-Nymph   *Cercyonis sthenele*   _____

_____

☐ Small Wood-Nymph   *Cercyonis oetus*   _____

_____

☐ Vidler's Alpine   *Erebia vidleri*   _____

_____

☐ Ross's Alpine   *Erebia rossii*   _____

_____

☐ Disa Alpine   *Erebia disa*   _____

_____

☐ Taiga Alpine   *Erebia mancinus*   _____

_____

☐ Magdalena Alpine   *Erebia magdalena*   _____

_____

☐ Banded Alpine   *Erebia fasciata*   _____

_____

☐ Red-disked Alpine   *Erebia discoidalis*   _____

_____

☐ Theano Alpine   *Erebia theano*   _____

_____

☐ Four-dotted Alpine   *Erebia dabanensis*   _____

_____

☐ Common Alpine   *Erebia epipsodea*   _____

_____

☐ Colorado Alpine   *Erebia callias*   _____

_____

☐ Reddish Alpine   *Erebia kozhantshikovi*   _____

_____

☐ Eskimo Alpine   *Erebia occulta*

_____

_____

☐ Red-bordered Satyr   *Gyrocheilus patrobas*

_____

_____

☐ Ridings's Satyr   *Neominois ridingsii*

_____

_____

☐ Great Arctic   *Oeneis nevadensis*

_____

_____

☐ Macoun's Arctic   *Oeneis macounii*

_____

_____

☐ Chryxus Arctic   *Oeneis chryxus*

_____

_____

☐ Uhler's Arctic   *Oeneis uhleri*

_____

_____

☐ Alberta Arctic   *Oeneis alberta*

_____

_____

☐ White-veined Arctic   *Oeneis taygete*

_____

_____

☐ Jutta Arctic   *Oeneis jutta*

_____

_____

☐ Sentinel Arctic   *Oeneis alpina*   *

_____

_____

☐ Melissa Arctic   *Oeneis melissa*

_____

_____

☐ Polixenes Arctic   *Oeneis polixenes*

_____

_____

☐ Early Arctic   *Oeneis rosovi*   *

_____

_____

SUBFAMILY DANAINAE: MONARCHS

☐ Monarch   *Danaus plexippus*   _____

_____

☐ Queen   *Danaus gilippus*   _____

_____

☐ Soldier   *Danaus eresimus*   _____

_____

Family Hesperiidae: Skippers (North America: 217; World: 4,000)

SUBFAMILY PYRRHOPYGINAE: FIRETIPS

☐ Dull Firetip   *Pyrrhopyge araxes*   _____

_____

SUBFAMILY PYRGINAE: SPREAD-WING SKIPPERS

☐ Mangrove Skipper   *Phocides pigmalion*   _____

_____

☐ Guava Skipper   *Phocides polybius*   _____

_____

☐ Zestos Skipper   *Epargyreus zestos*   _____

_____

☐ Silver-spotted Skipper   *Epargyreus clarus*   _____

_____

☐ Hammock Skipper   *Polygonus leo*   _____

_____

☐ White-striped Longtail   *Chioides catillus*   _____

_____

☐ Zilpa Longtail   *Chioides zilpa*   _____

_____

☐ Gold-spotted Aguna   *Aguna asander*   _____

_____

☐ Short-tailed Skipper   *Zestusa dorus*   _____

_____

☐ Arizona Skipper   *Codatractus arizonensis*   _____

_____

☐ Valeriana Skipper   *Codatractus mysie*   _____

_____

☐ Long-tailed Skipper   *Urbanus proteus*   _____

_____

☐ Dorantes Longtail   *Urbanus dorantes*   _____

_____

☐ Teleus Longtail   *Urbanus teleus*   _____

_____

☐ Brown Longtail   *Urbanus procne*   _____

_____

☐ White-tailed Longtail   *Urbanus doryssus*   _____

_____

☐ Golden Banded-Skipper   *Autochton cellus*   _____

_____

☐ Sonoran Banded-Skipper   *Autochton pseudocellus*   *ø _____

_____

☐ Chisos Banded-Skipper   *Autochton cincta*   _____

_____

☐ Hoary Edge   *Achalarus lyciades*   _____

_____

☐ Desert Cloudywing   *Achalarus casica*   _____

_____

☐ Coyote Cloudywing   *Achalarus toxeus*   _____

_____

☐ Southern Cloudywing   *Thorybes bathyllus*   _____

_____

☐ Northern Cloudywing   *Thorybes pylades*   _____

_____

☐ Western Cloudywing   *Thorybes diversus*   * _____

_____

☐ Mexican Cloudywing   *Thorybes mexicanus*   _____

_____

☐ Confused Cloudywing   *Thorybes confusis*   _____

_____

☐ Drusius Cloudywing   *Thorybes drusius*   _____

_____

☐ Potrillo Skipper   *Cabares potrillo*   _____

_____

☐ Mimosa Skipper   *Cogia calchas*   _____

_____

☐ Acacia Skipper   *Cogia hippalus*   _____

_____

☐ Outis Skipper   *Cogia outis*   * _____

_____

☐ Gold-costa Skipper   *Cogia caicus*   _____

_____

☐ Golden-headed Scallopwing   *Staphylus ceos*   _____

_____

☐ Mazans Scallopwing   *Staphylus mazans*   _____

_____

☐ Hayhurst's Scallopwing   *Staphylus hayhurstii*   _____

_____

☐ Texas Powdered-Skipper   *Systasea pulverulenta*   _____

☐ Arizona Powdered-Skipper   *Systasea zampa*   _____

_____

☐ Sickle-winged Skipper   *Achlyodes thraso*   _____

_____

☐ Brown-banded Skipper   *Timochares ruptifasciatus*   _____

_____

☐ White-patched Skipper   *Chiomara asychis*   _____

_____

☐ False Duskywing   *Gesta gesta*   _____

_____

☐ Florida Duskywing   *Ephyriades brunneus*   _____

_____

☐ Dreamy Duskywing   *Erynnis icelus*   _____

_____

☐ Sleepy Duskywing   *Erynnis brizo*   _____

_____

☐ Juvenal's Duskywing   *Erynnis juvenalis*   _____

_____

☐ Rocky Mountain Duskywing   *Erynnis telemachus*   _____

_____

☐ Propertius Duskywing   *Erynnis propertius*   _____

_____

☐ Meridian Duskywing   *Erynnis meridianus*   _____

_____

☐ Scudder's Duskywing   *Erynnis scudderi*   _____

_____

☐ Horace's Duskywing   *Erynnis horatius*   _____

_____

☐ Mournful Duskywing   *Erynnis tristis*   _____

_____

☐ Mottled Duskywing   *Erynnis martialis*   * _____

_____

☐ Pacuvius Duskywing   *Erynnis pacuvius*   _____

_____

☐ Zarucco Duskywing   *Erynnis zarucco*   _____

_____

☐ Funereal Duskywing   *Erynnis funeralis*   _____

_____

☐ Columbine Duskywing   *Erynnis lucilius*   _____

_____

☐ Wild Indigo Duskywing   *Erynnis baptisiae*   _____

_____

☐ Afranius Duskywing   *Erynnis afranius*   _____

_____

☐ Persius Duskywing   *Erynnis persius*   _____

_____

☐ Grizzled Skipper   *Pyrgus centaureae*   _____

_____

☐ Two-banded Checkered-Skipper   *Pyrgus ruralis*   _____

_____

☐ Mountain Checkered-Skipper   *Pyrgus xanthus*   * _____

_____

☐ Small Checkered-Skipper   *Pyrgus scriptura*   _____

_____

☐ Common Checkered-Skipper *Pyrgus communis* _____

_____

☐ White Checkered-Skipper *Pyrgus albescens* _____

_____

☐ Tropical Checkered-Skipper *Pyrgus oileus* _____

_____

☐ Desert Checkered-Skipper *Pyrgus philetas* _____

_____

☐ Erichson's White-Skipper *Heliopetes domicella* _____

_____

☐ Northern White-Skipper *Heliopetes ericetorum* _____

_____

☐ Laviana White-Skipper *Heliopetes laviana* _____

_____

☐ Turk's-cap White-Skipper *Heliopetes macaira* _____

_____

☐ Common Streaky-Skipper *Celotes nessus* _____

_____

☐ Scarce Streaky-Skipper *Celotes limpia* * _____

_____

☐ Common Sootywing *Pholisora catullus* _____

_____

☐ Mexican Sootywing *Pholisora mejicana* _____

_____

☐ Mojave Sootywing *Hesperopsis libya* _____

_____

☐ Saltbush Sootywing *Hesperopsis alpheus* _____

_____

SUBFAMILY HETEROPTERINAE: SKIPPERLINGS

☐ Arctic Skipper   *Carterocephalus palaemon*   _____

_____

☐ Russet Skipperling   *Piruna pirus*   _____

_____

☐ Four-spotted Skipperling   *Piruna polingi*   *   _____

_____

☐ Many-spotted Skipperling   *Piruna cingo*   _____

_____

☐ Chisos Skipperling   *Piruna haferniki*   *   _____

_____

SUBFAMILY HESPERIINAE: GRASS-SKIPPERS

☐ Malicious Skipper   *Synapte malitiosa*   _____

_____

☐ Pale-rayed Skipper   *Vidius perigenes*   _____

_____

☐ Violet-patched Skipper   *Monca tyrtaeus*   _____

_____

☐ Swarthy Skipper   *Nastra lherminier*   _____

_____

☐ Julia's Skipper   *Nastra julia*   _____

_____

☐ Neamathla Skipper   *Nastra neamathla*   _____

_____

☐ Three-spotted Skipper   *Cymaenes tripunctus*   _____

_____

☐ Fawn-spotted Skipper   *Cymaenes odilia*   _____

_____

☐ Clouded Skipper   *Lerema accius*

_____

_____

☐ Double-dotted Skipper   *Decinea percosius*   *

_____

☐ Least Skipper   *Ancyloxypha numitor*

_____

_____

☐ Tropical Least Skipper *Ancyloxypha arene*

_____

_____

☐ Poweshiek Skipperling   *Oarisma poweshiek*   *

_____

_____

☐ Garita Skipperling   *Oarisma garita*

_____

_____

☐ Edwards's Skipperling   *Oarisma edwardsii*

_____

_____

☐ Orange Skipperling   *Copaeodes aurantiacus*

_____

_____

☐ Southern Skipperling   *Copaeodes minimus*

_____

_____

☐ Sunrise Skipper   *Adopaeoides prittwitzi*   *

_____

_____

☐ Fiery Skipper   *Hylephila phyleus*

_____

_____

☐ Alkali Skipper   *Pseudocopaeodes eunus*   *

_____

_____

☐ Morrison's Skipper   *Stinga morrisoni*

_____

_____

☐ Uncas Skipper   *Hesperia uncas*

_____

_____

☐ Juba Skipper — *Hesperia juba*

☐ Common Branded Skipper — *Hesperia comma*

☐ Apache Skipper — *Hesperia woodgatei* *

☐ Ottoe Skipper — *Hesperia ottoe* *

☐ Leonard's Skipper — *Hesperia leonardus*

☐ Pahaska Skipper — *Hesperia pahaska*

☐ Columbian Skipper — *Hesperia columbia* *

☐ Cobweb Skipper — *Hesperia metea*

☐ Green Skipper — *Hesperia viridis*

☐ Dotted Skipper — *Hesperia attalus* *

☐ Meske's Skipper — *Hesperia meskei* *

☐ Dakota Skipper — *Hesperia dacotae* *

☐ Lindsey's Skipper — *Hesperia lindseyi* *

☐ Indian Skipper — *Hesperia sassacus*

☐ Sierra Skipper   *Hesperia miriamae*   *   _____

                                                                _____

☐ Nevada Skipper   *Hesperia nevada*   _____

                                                                _____

☐ Rhesus Skipper   *Polites rhesus*   _____

                                                                _____

☐ Carus Skipper   *Polites carus*   _____

                                                                _____

☐ Peck's Skipper   *Polites peckius*   _____

                                                                _____

☐ Sandhill Skipper   *Polites sabuleti*   _____

                                                                _____

☐ Mardon Skipper   *Polites mardon*   *   _____

                                                                _____

☐ Draco Skipper   *Polites draco*   _____

                                                                _____

☐ Baracoa Skipper   *Polites baracoa*   _____

                                                                _____

☐ Tawny-edged Skipper   *Polites themistocles*   _____

                                                                _____

☐ Crossline Skipper   *Polites origenes*   _____

                                                                _____

☐ Long Dash   *Polites mystic*   _____

                                                                _____

☐ Sonoran Skipper   *Polites sonora*   _____

                                                                _____

☐ Whirlabout   *Polites vibex*   _____

                                                                _____

☐ Southern Broken-Dash   *Wallengrenia otho*   _____

☐ Northern Broken-Dash   *Wallengrenia egeremet*   _____

☐ Little Glassywing   *Pompeius verna*   _____

☐ Sachem   *Atalopedes campestris*   _____

☐ Arogos Skipper   *Atrytone arogos*   *   _____

☐ Delaware Skipper   *Anatrytone logan*   _____

☐ Byssus Skipper   *Problema byssus*   *   _____

☐ Rare Skipper   *Problema bulenta*   *   _____

☐ Woodland Skipper   *Ochlodes sylvanoides*   _____

☐ Rural Skipper   *Ochlodes agricola*   _____

☐ Yuma Skipper   *Ochlodes yuma*   _____

☐ Snow's Skipper   *Paratrytone snowi*   _____

☐ Mulberry Wing   *Poanes massasoit*   _____

☐ Hobomok Skipper   *Poanes hobomok*   _____

☐ Zabulon Skipper   *Poanes zabulon*

☐ Taxiles Skipper   *Poanes taxiles*

☐ Aaron's Skipper   *Poanes aaroni*

☐ Yehl Skipper   *Poanes yehl*

☐ Broad-winged Skipper   *Poanes viator*

☐ Umber Skipper   *Poanes melane*

☐ Common Mellana   *Quasimellana eulogius*

☐ Palmetto Skipper   *Euphyes arpa*   *

☐ Palatka Skipper   *Euphyes pilatka*   *

☐ Dion Skipper   *Euphyes dion*

☐ Bay Skipper   *Euphyes bayensis*   *

☐ Dukes's Skipper   *Euphyes dukesi*   *

☐ Black Dash   *Euphyes conspicua*

☐ Berry's Skipper   *Euphyes berryi*   *

☐ Two-spotted Skipper   *Euphyes bimacula*   _____

_____

☐ Dun Skipper   *Euphyes vestris*   _____

_____

☐ Dusted Skipper   *Atrytonopsis hianna*   _____

_____

☐ Deva Skipper   *Atrytonopsis deva*   * _____

_____

☐ Moon-marked Skipper   *Atrytonopsis lunus*   * _____

_____

☐ Viereck's Skipper   *Atrytonopsis vierecki*   _____

_____

☐ White-barred Skipper   *Atrytonopsis pittacus*   * _____

_____

☐ Python Skipper   *Atrytonopsis python*   * _____

_____

☐ Cestus Skipper   *Atrytonopsis cestus*   * _____

_____

☐ Sheep Skipper   *Atrytonopsis edwardsii*   * _____

_____

☐ Simius Roadside-Skipper   *Amblyscirtes simius*   _____

_____

☐ Large Roadside-Skipper   *Amblyscirtes exoteria*   _____

_____

☐ Cassus Roadside-Skipper   *Amblyscirtes cassus*   _____

_____

☐ Bronze Roadside-Skipper   *Amblyscirtes aenus*   _____

_____

☐ Linda's Roadside-Skipper   *Amblyscirtes linda*   *   _____

_____

☐ Oslar's Roadside-Skipper   *Amblyscirtes oslari*   _____

_____

☐ Pepper and Salt Skipper   *Amblyscirtes hegon*   _____

_____

☐ Elissa Roadside-Skipper   *Amblyscirtes elissa*   *   _____

_____

☐ Texas Roadside-Skipper   *Amblyscirtes texanae*   *   _____

_____

☐ Toltec Roadside-Skipper   *Amblyscirtes tolteca*   *   _____

_____

☐ Lace-winged Roadside-Skipper   *Amblyscirtes aesculapius*   *   _____

_____

☐ Carolina Roadside-Skipper   *Amblyscirtes carolina*   *   _____

_____

☐ Reversed Roadside-Skipper   *Amblyscirtes reversa*   *   _____

_____

☐ Slaty Roadside-Skipper   *Amblyscirtes nereus*   _____

_____

☐ Nysa Roadside-Skipper   *Amblyscirtes nysa*   _____

_____

☐ Dotted Roadside-Skipper   *Amblyscirtes eos*   _____

_____

☐ Common Roadside-Skipper   *Amblyscirtes vialis*   _____

_____

☐ Celia's Roadside-Skipper   *Amblyscirtes celia*   _____

_____

☐ Bell's Roadside-Skipper   *Amblyscirtes belli*   * _____

_____

☐ Dusky Roadside-Skipper   *Amblyscirtes alternata*   * _____

_____

☐ Orange-headed
Roadside-Skipper   *Amblyscirtes phylace* _____

_____

☐ Orange-edged
Roadside-Skipper   *Amblyscirtes fimbriata* _____

_____

☐ Eufala Skipper   *Lerodea eufala* _____

_____

☐ Violet-clouded Skipper   *Lerodea arabus* _____

_____

☐ Olive-clouded Skipper   *Lerodea dysaules* _____

_____

☐ Twin-spot Skipper   *Oligoria maculata* _____

_____

☐ Brazilian Skipper   *Calpodes ethlius* _____

_____

☐ Salt Marsh Skipper   *Panoquina panoquin* _____

_____

☐ Obscure Skipper   *Panoquina panoquinoides* _____

_____

☐ Wandering Skipper   *Panoquina errans* _____

_____

☐ Ocola Skipper   *Panoquina ocola* _____

_____

☐ Purple-washed Skipper   *Panoquina sylvicola* _____

_____

☐ Violet-banded Skipper   *Nyctelius nyctelius*   _____

   _____

SUBFAMILY MEGATHYMINAE: GIANT-SKIPPERS

☐ Orange Giant-Skipper   *Agathymus neumoegeni*

☐ Arizona Giant-Skipper   *Agathymus aryxna*

☐ Huachuca Giant-Skipper   *Agathymus evansi*   *

☐ Mary's Giant-Skipper   *Agathymus mariae*   *

☐ California Giant-Skipper   *Agathymus stephensi*   *

☐ Coahuila Giant-Skipper   *Agathymus remingtoni*

☐ Poling's Giant-Skipper   *Agathymus polingi*

☐ Mojave Giant-Skipper   *Agathymus alliae*

☐ Yucca Giant-Skipper   *Megathymus yuccae*

☐ Cofaqui Giant-Skipper   *Megathymus cofaqui*   *

☐ Strecker's Giant-Skipper   *Megathymus streckeri*

☐ Ursine Giant-Skipper   *Megathymus ursus*

☐ Manfreda Giant-Skipper   *Stallingsia maculosa*   *

NON-ANNUAL VISITORS
SUBFAMILY PAPILIONINAE: SWALLOWTAILS

☐ White-dotted Cattleheart   *Parides alopius*   _____

_____

☐ Dark Kite-Swallowtail   *Eurytides philolaus*   _____

_____

☐ Thoas Swallowtail   *Papilio thoas*   _____

_____

☐ Bahamian Swallowtail   *Papilio andraemon*   _____

_____

☐ Broad-banded Swallowtail   *Papilio astyalus*   _____

_____

☐ Androgeus Swallowtail   *Papilio androgeus*   _____

_____

☐ Three-tailed Swallowtail   *Papilio pilumnus*   _____

_____

☐ Magnificent Swallowtail   *Papilio garamas*   _____

_____

☐ Victorine Swallowtail   *Papilio victorinus*   _____

_____

☐ Pink-spotted Swallowtail   *Papilio pharnaces*   _____

_____

SUBFAMILY PIERINAE: WHITES

☐ Mexican Dartwhite   *Catasticta nimbice*   _____

_____

☐ Common Greeneyed-White   *Leptophobia aripa*   _____

_____

☐ Sonoran Marble   *Euchloe guaymasensis*   _____

_____

☐ Common Melwhite   *Melete lycimnia*

_____

_____

☐ Cross-barred White   *Itaballia demophile*

_____

_____

SUBFAMILY COLIADINAE: SULPHURS

☐ Yellow Angled-Sulphur   *Anteos maerula*

_____

_____

☐ Tailed Sulphur   *Phoebis neocypris*

_____

_____

☐ Orbed Sulphur   *Phoebis orbis*

_____

_____

☐ Ghost Yellow   *Eurema albula*

_____

_____

☐ Salome Yellow   *Eurema salome*

_____

_____

☐ Shy Yellow   *Eurema messalina*

_____

_____

SUBFAMILY DISMORPHIINAE: MIMIC-WHITES

☐ Costa-spotted Mimic-White   *Enantia albania*

_____

_____

SUBFAMILY THECLINAE: HAIRSTREAKS

☐ Strophius Hairstreak   *Allosmaitia strophius*

_____

_____

☐ Creamy Stripe-streak   *Arawacus jada*

_____

_____

☐ Gold-bordered Hairstreak   *Rekoa palegon*

_____

_____

☐ Marius Hairstreak   *Rekoa marius*

_____

_____

☐ Smudged Hairstreak *Rekoa stagira* _____

_____

☐ Black Hairstreak *Ocaria ocrisia* _____

_____

☐ Telea Hairstreak *Chlorostrymon telea* _____

_____

☐ Tropical Greenstreak *Cyanophrys herodotus* _____

_____

☐ Orange-crescent Groundstreak *Ziegleria guzanta* _____

_____

☐ Aquamarine Hairstreak *Oenomaus ortygnus* _____

_____

☐ Red-lined Scrub-Hairstreak *Strymon bebrycia* _____

_____

☐ Yojoa Scrub-Hairstreak *Strymon yojoa* _____

_____

☐ White Scrub-Hairstreak *Strymon albata* _____

_____

☐ Disguised Scrub-Hairstreak *Strymon limenia* _____

_____

☐ Tailless Scrub-Hairstreak *Strymon cestri* _____

_____

☐ Bromeliad Scrub-Hairstreak *Strymon serapio* _____

_____

☐ Red-spotted Hairstreak *Tmolus echion* _____

_____

☐ Pearly-gray Hairstreak *Siderus tephraeus* _____

_____

☐　Sonoran Hairstreak　　　*Hypostrymon critola*　　_____

_____

SUBFAMILY RIODININAE: METALMARKS

☐　Curve-winged Metalmark　　*Emesis emesia*　　_____

_____

☐　Falcate Metalmark　　　*Emesis tenedia*　　_____

_____

☐　Narrow-winged Metalmark　*Apodemia multiplaga*　　_____

_____

☐　Hepburn's Metalmark　　*Apodemia hepburni*　　_____

_____

☐　Walker's Metalmark　　　*Apodemia walkeri*　　_____

_____

☐　Crescent Metalmark　　　*Apodemia phyciodoides*　　_____

_____

SUBFAMILY HELICONIINAE: HELICONIANS AND FRITILLARIES

☐　Mexican Silverspot　　　*Dione moneta*　　_____

_____

☐　Banded Orange Heliconian　*Dryadula phaetusa*　　_____

_____

☐　Isabella's Heliconian　　*Eueides isabella*　　_____

_____

☐　Erato Heliconian　　　　*Heliconius erato*　　_____

_____

SUBFAMILY NYMPHALINAE: TRUE BRUSHFOOTS

☐　Rosita Patch　　　　　*Chlosyne rosita*　　_____

_____

☐　Red-spotted Patch　　　*Chlosyne marina*　　_____

_____

☐ Elf   *Microtia elva*   _____

_____

☐ Pale-banded Crescent   *Phyciodes tulcis*   _____

_____

☐ Black Crescent   *Phyciodes ptolyca*   _____

_____

☐ Chestnut Crescent   *Phyciodes argentea*   _____

_____

☐ Orange Mapwing   *Hypanartia lethe*   _____

_____

☐ Mimic   *Hypolimnas misippus*   _____

_____

☐ Cuban Peacock   *Anartia chrysopelea*   _____

_____

☐ Rusty-tipped Page   *Siproeta epaphus*   _____

_____

SUBFAMILY LIMENITIDINAE: ADMIRALS AND ALLIES

☐ Spot-celled Sister   *Adelpha basiloides*   _____

_____

☐ Common Banner   *Epiphile adrasta*   _____

_____

☐ Orange Banner   *Temensis laothoe*   _____

_____

☐ Blackened Bluewing   *Myscelia cyananthe*   _____

_____

☐ Blue-eyed Sailor   *Dynamine dyonis*   _____

_____

☐ Red Rim   *Biblis hyperia*   _____

_____

☐ Red Cracker *Hamadryas amphinome*

_____

_____

☐ Variable Cracker *Hamadryas feronia*

_____

_____

☐ Glaucous Cracker *Hamadryas glauconome*

_____

_____

☐ Pale Cracker *Hamadryas amphichloe*

_____

_____

☐ Guatemalan Cracker *Hamadryas guatemalena*

_____

_____

☐ Black-patched Cracker *Hamadryas atlantis*

_____

_____

☐ Orion Cecropian *Historis odius*

_____

_____

☐ Tailed Cecropian *Historis acheronta*

_____

_____

☐ Blomfild's Beauty *Smyrna blomfildia*

_____

_____

☐ Waiter Daggerwing *Marpesia coresia*

_____

_____

☐ Antillean Daggerwing *Marpesia eleuchea*

_____

_____

SUBFAMILY CHARAXINAE: LEAFWINGS

☐ Angled Leafwing *Anaea glycerium*

_____

_____

SUBFAMILY APATURINAE: EMPERORS

☐ Dusky Emperor *Asterocampa idyja*

_____

_____

☐ Pavon Emperor   *Doxocopa pavon*   _____

_____

☐ Silver Emperor   *Doxocopa laure*   _____

_____

SUBFAMILY ITHOMIINAE: CLEARWINGS

☐ Klug's Clearwing   *Dircenna klugii*   _____

_____

☐ Thick-tipped Greta   *Greta morgane*   _____

_____

SUBFAMILY DANAINAE: MONARCHS

☐ Tiger Mimic-Queen   *Lycorea cleobaea*   _____

_____

SUBFAMILY PYRGINAE: SPREAD-WING SKIPPERS

☐ Beautiful Beamer   *Phocides belus*   _____

_____

☐ Teal Beamer   *Phocides urania*   _____

_____

☐ Mercurial Skipper   *Proteides mercurius*   _____

_____

☐ Broken Silverdrop   *Epargyreus exadeus*   _____

_____

☐ Manuel's Skipper   *Polygonus manueli*   _____

_____

☐ Emerald Aguna   *Aguna claxon*   _____

_____

☐ Tailed Aguna   *Aguna metophis*   _____

_____

☐ Mottled Longtail   *Typhedanus undulatus*   _____

_____

☐ Mexican Longtail   *Polythrix mexicanus*   _____

☐ Eight-spotted Longtail   *Polythrix octomaculata*   _____

☐ White-crescent Longtail   *Codatractus alcaeus*   _____

☐ Pronus Longtail   *Urbanus pronus*   _____

☐ Esmeralda Longtail   *Urbanus esmeraldus*   _____

☐ Double-striped Longtail   *Urbanus belli*   _____

☐ Tanna Longtail   *Urbanus tanna*   _____

☐ Plain Longtail   *Urbanus simplicius*   _____

☐ Turquoise Longtail   *Urbanus evona*   _____

☐ Two-barred Flasher   *Astraptes fulgerator*   _____

☐ Small-spotted Flasher   *Astraptes egregius*   _____

☐ Frosted Flasher   *Astraptes alardus*   _____

☐ Gilbert's Flasher   *Astraptes gilberti*   _____

☐ Yellow-tipped Flasher   *Astraptes anaphus*   _____

☐ Skinner's Cloudywing   *Achalarus albociliatus*   _____

_____

☐ Jalapus Cloudywing   *Achalarus jalapus*   _____

_____

☐ Fritzgaertner's Flat   *Celaenorrhinus fritzgaertneri*   _____

_____

☐ Stallings's Flat   *Celaenorrhinus stallingsi*   _____

_____

☐ Falcate Skipper   *Spathilepia clonius*   _____

_____

☐ Starred Skipper   *Arteurotia tractipennis*   _____

_____

☐ Purplish-black Skipper   *Nisoniades rubescens*   _____

_____

☐ Glazed Pellicia   *Pellicia arina*   _____

_____

☐ Confused Pellicia   *Pellicia angra*   _____

_____

☐ Morning Glory Pellicia   *Pellicia dimidiata*   _____

_____

☐ Mottled Bolla   *Bolla clytius*   _____

_____

☐ Obscure Bolla   *Bolla brennus*   _____

_____

☐ Variegated Skipper   *Gorgythion begga*   _____

_____

☐ Blue-studded Skipper   *Sostrata bifasciata*   _____

_____

☐ Hoary Skipper   *Carrhenes canescens*   _____

_____

☐ Glassy-winged Skipper   *Xenophanes tryxus*   _____

_____

☐ White Spurwing   *Antigonus emorsus*   _____

_____

☐ Red-studded Skipper   *Noctuana stator*   _____

_____

☐ Pale Sicklewing   *Achlyodes pallida*   _____

_____

☐ Hermit Skipper   *Grais stigmatica*   _____

_____

☐ Common Bluevent   *Anastrus sempiternus*   _____

_____

☐ Slaty Skipper   *Chiomara mithrax*   _____

_____

☐ East-Mexican White-Skipper   *Heliopetes sublinea*   _____

_____

☐ Veined White-Skipper   *Heliopetes arsalte*   _____

_____

SUBFAMILY HETEROPTERINAE: SKIPPERLINGS

☐ Small-spotted Skipperling   *Piruna microstictus*   _____

_____

SUBFAMILY HESPERIINAE: GRASS-SKIPPERS

☐ Salenus Skipper   *Synapte salenus*   _____

_____

☐ Faceted Skipper   *Synapte syraces*   _____

_____

☐ Redundant Skipper   *Corticea corticea*

_____

_____

☐ Liris Skipper   *Lerema liris*

_____

_____

☐ Fantastic Skipper   *Vettius fantasos*

_____

_____

☐ Green-backed Ruby-eye   *Perichares philetes*

_____

_____

☐ Osca Skipper   *Rhinthon osca*

_____

_____

☐ Hidden-ray Skipper   *Conga chydaea*

_____

_____

☐ Glowing Skipper   *Anatrytone mazai*

_____

_____

☐ Hecebolus Skipper   *Panoquina hecebola*

_____

_____

☐ Evans's Skipper   *Panoquina fusina*

_____

_____

☐ Chestnut-marked Skipper   *Thespieus macareus*

_____

_____

ALIEN SPECIES
SUBFAMILY PIERINAE: WHITES

☐ Cabbage White   *Pieris rapae*

_____

_____

SUBFAMILY THECLINAE: HAIRSTREAKS

☐ Fulvous Hairstreak   *Electrostrymon angelia*

_____

_____

SUBFAMILY NYMPHALINAE: TRUE BRUSHFOOTS

☐ Small Tortoiseshell   *Nymphalis urticae*

_____

_____

SUBFAMILY HESPERIINAE: GRASS-SKIPPERS

☐ European Skipper   *Thymelicus lineola*   _____

_____

☐ Monk Skipper   *Asbolis capucinus*   _____

_____

ADDITIONAL SPECIES

☐ _____   _____   _____

_____

☐ _____   _____   _____

_____

☐ _____   _____   _____

_____

☐ _____   _____   _____

_____

☐ _____   _____   _____

_____

☐ _____   _____   _____

_____

☐ _____   _____   _____

_____

☐ _____   _____   _____

_____

☐ _____   _____   _____

_____

☐ _____   _____   _____

_____

☐ _____   _____   _____

_____

☐ _____ _____ _____

_____

☐ _____ _____ _____

_____

☐ _____ _____ _____

_____

☐ _____ _____ _____

_____

☐ _____ _____ _____

_____

☐ _____ _____ _____

_____

☐ _____ _____ _____

_____

☐ _____ _____ _____

_____

☐ _____ _____ _____

_____

☐ _____ _____ _____

_____

☐ _____ _____ _____

_____

☐ _____ _____ _____

_____

☐ _____ _____ _____

_____

☐ _____   _____   _____
                                       _____
☐ _____   _____   _____
                                       _____
☐ _____   _____   _____
                                       _____
☐ _____   _____   _____
                                       _____
☐ _____   _____   _____
                                       _____
☐ _____   _____   _____
                                       _____
☐ _____   _____   _____
                                       _____
☐ _____   _____   _____
                                       _____
☐ _____   _____   _____
                                       _____
☐ _____   _____   _____
                                       _____
☐ _____   _____   _____
                                       _____
☐ _____   _____   _____
                                       _____
☐ _____   _____   _____
                                       _____

☐ _____ _____ _____

☐ _____ _____ _____
_____

☐ _____ _____ _____
_____

☐ _____ _____ _____
_____

☐ _____ _____ _____
_____

☐ _____ _____ _____
_____

☐ _____ _____ _____
_____

☐ _____ _____ _____
_____

☐ _____ _____ _____
_____

☐ _____ _____ _____
_____

☐ _____ _____ _____
_____

☐ _____ _____ _____
_____

Order Odonata: Dragonflies and Damselflies

Suborder Zygoptera: Damselflies

**Family Calopterygidae: Broad-winged Damsels
(North America: 8; World: 160)**

☐ River Jewelwing   *Calopteryx aequabilis*   _____

_____

☐ Superb Jewelwing   *Calopteryx amata*   _____

_____

☐ Appalachian Jewelwing   *Calopteryx angustipennis*   _____

_____

☐ Sparkling Jewelwing   *Calopteryx dimidiata*   _____

_____

☐ Ebony Jewelwing   *Calopteryx maculata*   _____

_____

☐ American Rubyspot   *Hetaerina americana*   _____

_____

☐ Smoky Rubyspot   *Hetaerina titia*   _____

_____

☐ Canyon Rubyspot   *Hetaerina vulnerata*   _____

_____

Family Lestidae: Spreadwings (North America: 19; World: 154)

☐ California Spreadwing   *Archilestes californicus*   _____

_____

☐ Great Spreadwing   *Archilestes grandis*   _____

_____

☐ Plateau Spreadwing   *Lestes alacer*   _____

_____

☐ Southern Spreadwing   *Lestes australis*   _____

_____

☐ Spotted Spreadwing   *Lestes congener*   _____

_____

☐ Northern Spreadwing   *Lestes disjunctus*   _____

_____

☐ Emerald Spreadwing   *Lestes dryas*   _____

_____

☐ Amber-winged Spreadwing   *Lestes eurinus*   _____

_____

☐ Sweetflag Spreadwing   *Lestes forcipatus*   _____

_____

☐ Rainpool Spreadwing   *Lestes forficula*   _____

_____

☐ Elegant Spreadwing   *Lestes inaequalis*   _____

_____

☐ Slender Spreadwing   *Lestes rectangularis*   _____

_____

☐ Chalky Spreadwing   *Lestes sigma*   _____

_____

☐ Antillean Spreadwing   *Lestes spumarius*   _____

_____

☐ Black Spreadwing   *Lestes stultus*   _____

_____

☐ Blue-striped Spreadwing   *Lestes tenuatus*   _____

_____

☐ Lyre-tipped Spreadwing   *Lestes unguiculatus*   _____

_____

☐ Carolina Spreadwing   *Lestes vidua*   _____

_____

☐ Swamp Spreadwing   *Lestes vigilax*   _____

_____

Family Platystictidae: Shadowdamsels
(North America: 1; World: 173)

☐ Desert Shadowdamsel   *Palaemnema domina*   *   _____

_____

Family Protoneuridae: Threadtails (North America: 3; World: 247)

☐ Coral-fronted Threadtail   *Neoneura aaroni*   _____

_____

☐ Amelia's Threadtail   *Neoneura amelia*   _____

_____

☐ Orange-striped Threadtail   *Protoneura cara*   _____

_____

Family Coenagrionidae: Pond Damsels
(North America: 100; World: 1,070)

☐ Mexican Wedgetail   *Acanthagrion quadratum*   _____

_____

☐ Western Red Damsel   *Amphiagrion abbreviatum*   _____

_____

☐ Eastern Red Damsel   *Amphiagrion saucium*   _____

_____

☐ Black-and-white Damsel   *Apanisagrion lais*   _____

_____

☐ California Dancer   *Argia agrioides*   _____

_____

☐ Paiute Dancer · *Argia alberta* · _____

☐ Blue-fronted Dancer · *Argia apicalis* · _____

☐ Comanche Dancer · *Argia barretti* · _____

☐ Seepage Dancer · *Argia bipunctulata* · _____

☐ Coppery Dancer · *Argia cuprea* · _____

☐ Emma's Dancer · *Argia emma* · _____

☐ Spine-tipped Dancer · *Argia extranea* · _____

☐ Variable Dancer · *Argia fumipennis* · _____

☐ Lavender Dancer · *Argia hinei* · _____

☐ Kiowa Dancer · *Argia immunda* · _____

☐ Sierra Madre Dancer · *Argia lacrimans* · _____

☐ Leonora's Dancer · *Argia leonorae* · * _____

☐ Sooty Dancer · *Argia lugens* · _____

☐ Powdered Dancer · *Argia moesta* · _____

☐ Apache Dancer   *Argia munda*

_____

_____

☐ Aztec Dancer   *Argia nahuana*

_____

_____

☐ Fiery-eyed Dancer   *Argia oenea*

_____

_____

☐ Amethyst Dancer   *Argia pallens*

_____

_____

☐ Pima Dancer   *Argia pima*   *

_____

_____

☐ Springwater Dancer   *Argia plana*

_____

_____

☐ Golden-winged Dancer   *Argia rhoadsi*   *

_____

_____

☐ Sabino Dancer   *Argia sabino*   *

_____

_____

☐ Blue-ringed Dancer   *Argia sedula*

_____

_____

☐ Tarascan Dancer   *Argia tarascana*

_____

_____

☐ Tezpi Dancer   *Argia tezpi*

_____

_____

☐ Blue-tipped Dancer   *Argia tibialis*

_____

_____

☐ Tonto Dancer   *Argia tonto*

_____

_____

☐ Dusky Dancer   *Argia translata*

_____

_____

☐ Vivid Dancer   *Argia vivida*   _____

☐ Aurora Damsel   *Chromagrion conditum*   _____

☐ Lucifer Damsel   *Chrysobasis lucifer*   _____

☐ Prairie Bluet   *Coenagrion angulatum*   _____

☐ Subarctic Bluet   *Coenagrion interrogatum*   _____

☐ Taiga Bluet   *Coenagrion resolutum*   _____

☐ River Bluet   *Enallagma anna*   _____

☐ Northern Bluet   *Enallagma annexum*   _____

☐ Rainbow Bluet   *Enallagma antennatum*   _____

☐ Azure Bluet   *Enallagma aspersum*   _____

☐ Double-striped Bluet   *Enallagma basidens*   _____

☐ Boreal Bluet   *Enallagma boreale*   _____

☐ Tule Bluet   *Enallagma carunculatum*   _____

☐ Familiar Bluet   *Enallagma civile*   _____

☐ Alkali Bluet   *Enallagma clausum*   _____

_____

☐ Purple Bluet   *Enallagma coecum*   _____

_____

☐ Cherry Bluet   *Enallagma concisum*   _____

_____

☐ Attenuated Bluet   *Enallagma daeckii*   _____

_____

☐ Sandhill Bluet   *Enallagma davisi*   _____

_____

☐ Turquoise Bluet   *Enallagma divagans*   _____

_____

☐ Atlantic Bluet   *Enallagma doubledayi*   _____

_____

☐ Burgundy Bluet   *Enallagma dubium*   _____

_____

☐ Big Bluet   *Enallagma durum*   _____

_____

☐ Marsh Bluet   *Enallagma ebrium*   _____

_____

☐ Stream Bluet   *Enallagma exsulans*   _____

_____

☐ Skimming Bluet   *Enallagma geminatum*   _____

_____

☐ Hagen's Bluet   *Enallagma hageni*   _____

_____

☐ New England Bluet   *Enallagma laterale*   *   _____

_____

☐ Little Bluet   *Enallagma minusculum*   _____

_____

☐ Neotropical Bluet   *Enallagma novaehispaniae*   _____

_____

☐ Pale Bluet   *Enallagma pallidum*   _____

_____

☐ Scarlet Bluet   *Enallagma pictum*   *   _____

_____

☐ Florida Bluet   *Enallagma pollutum*   _____

_____

☐ Arroyo Bluet   *Enallagma praevarum*   _____

_____

☐ Pine Barrens Bluet   *Enallagma recurvatum*   *   _____

_____

☐ Claw-tipped Bluet   *Enallagma semicirculare*   *   _____

_____

☐ Orange Bluet   *Enallagma signatum*   _____

_____

☐ Golden Bluet   *Enallagma sulcatum*   _____

_____

☐ Slender Bluet   *Enallagma traviatum*   _____

_____

☐ Vernal Bluet   *Enallagma vernale*   _____

_____

☐ Vesper Bluet   *Enallagma vesperum*   _____

_____

☐ Blackwater Bluet   *Enallagma weewa*   _____

_____

☐ Painted Damsel — *Hesperagrion heterodoxum*

☐ Desert Forktail — *Ischnura barberi*

☐ Pacific Forktail — *Ischnura cervula*

☐ Plains Forktail — *Ischnura damula*

☐ Mexican Forktail — *Ischnura demorsa*

☐ Black-fronted Forktail — *Ischnura denticollis*

☐ Swift Forktail — *Ischnura erratica*

☐ San Francisco Forktail — *Ischnura gemina* *

☐ Citrine Forktail — *Ischnura hastata*

☐ Lilypad Forktail — *Ischnura kellicotti*

☐ Western Forktail — *Ischnura perparva*

☐ Fragile Forktail — *Ischnura posita*

☐ Furtive Forktail — *Ischnura prognata*

☐ Rambur's Forktail — *Ischnura ramburii*

☐ Eastern Forktail   *Ischnura verticalis*

☐ Cream-tipped Swampdamsel   *Leptobasis melinogaster*

☐ Sphagnum Sprite   *Nehalennia gracilis*

☐ Southern Sprite   *Nehalennia integricollis*

☐ Sedge Sprite   *Nehalennia irene*

☐ Tropical Sprite   *Nehalennia minuta*   *

☐ Everglades Sprite   *Nehalennia pallidula*   *

☐ Caribbean Yellowface   *Neoerythromma cultellatum*

☐ Duckweed Firetail   *Telebasis byersi*

☐ Desert Firetail   *Telebasis salva*

☐ Exclamation Damsel   *Zoniagrion exclamationis*

Suborder Anisoptera: Dragonflies

Family Petaluridae: Petaltails (North America: 2; World: 11)

☐ Gray Petaltail   *Tachopteryx thoreyi*

☐ Black Petaltail   *Tanypteryx hageni*

Family Aeshnidae: Darners (North America: 38; World: 433)

☐ Canada Darner   *Aeshna canadensis*   _____

_____

☐ Mottled Darner   *Aeshna clepsydra*   _____

_____

☐ Lance-tipped Darner   *Aeshna constricta*   _____

_____

☐ Lake Darner   *Aeshna eremita*   _____

_____

☐ Variable Darner   *Aeshna interrupta*   _____

_____

☐ Sedge Darner   *Aeshna juncea*   _____

_____

☐ Paddle-tailed Darner   *Aeshna palmata*   _____

_____

☐ Persephone's Darner   *Aeshna persephone*   *   _____

_____

☐ Azure Darner   *Aeshna septentrionalis*   _____

_____

☐ Zigzag Darner   *Aeshna sitchensis*   _____

_____

☐ Subarctic Darner   *Aeshna subarctica*   _____

_____

☐ Black-tipped Darner   *Aeshna tuberculifera*   _____

_____

☐ Shadow Darner   *Aeshna umbrosa*   _____

_____

☐ Green-striped Darner   *Aeshna verticalis*   _____

_____

☐ Walker's Darner   *Aeshna walkeri*   _____

_____

☐ Common Green Darner   *Anax junius*   _____

_____

☐ Comet Darner   *Anax longipes*   _____

_____

☐ Giant Darner   *Anax walsinghami*   _____

_____

☐ Springtime Darner   *Basiaeschna janata*   _____

_____

☐ Ocellated Darner   *Boyeria grafiana*   _____

_____

☐ Fawn Darner   *Boyeria vinosa*   _____

_____

☐ Blue-faced Darner   *Coryphaeschna adnexa*   _____

_____

☐ Regal Darner   *Coryphaeschna ingens*   _____

_____

☐ Mangrove Darner   *Coryphaeschna viriditas*   _____

_____

☐ Swamp Darner   *Epiaeschna heros*   _____

_____

☐ Taper-tailed Darner   *Gomphaeschna antilope*   _____

_____

☐ Harlequin Darner   *Gomphaeschna furcillata*   _____

_____

☐ Bar-sided Darner   *Gynacantha mexicana*   _____

_____

☐ Twilight Darner   *Gynacantha nervosa*   _____

_____

☐ Cyrano Darner   *Nasiaeschna pentacantha*   _____

_____

☐ Riffle Darner   *Oplonaeschna armata*   _____

_____

☐ Malachite Darner   *Remartinia luteipennis*   _____

_____

☐ California Darner   *Rhionaeschna californica*   _____

_____

☐ Arroyo Darner   *Rhionaeschna dugesi*   _____

_____

☐ Blue-eyed Darner   *Rhionaeschna multicolor*   _____

_____

☐ Spatterdock Darner   *Rhionaeschna mutata*   _____

_____

☐ Turquoise-tipped Darner   *Rhionaeschna psilus*   _____

_____

☐ Phantom Darner   *Triacanthagyna trifida*   _____

_____

Family Gomphidae: Clubtails (North America: 100; World: 951)

☐ Broad-striped Forceptail   *Aphylla angustifolia*   _____

_____

☐ Narrow-striped Forceptail   *Aphylla protracta*   _____

_____

☐ Two-striped Forceptail   *Aphylla williamsoni*   _____

_____

☐ Horned Clubtail   *Arigomphus cornutus*   _____

_____

☐ Lilypad Clubtail   *Arigomphus furcifer*

_____

☐ Stillwater Clubtail   *Arigomphus lentulus*

_____

☐ Bayou Clubtail   *Arigomphus maxwelli*

_____

☐ Gray-green Clubtail   *Arigomphus pallidus*

_____

☐ Jade Clubtail   *Arigomphus submedianus*

_____

☐ Unicorn Clubtail   *Arigomphus villosipes*

_____

☐ Southeastern Spinyleg   *Dromogomphus armatus*

_____

☐ Black-shouldered Spinyleg *Dromogomphus spinosus*

_____

☐ Flag-tailed Spinyleg   *Dromogomphus spoliatus*

_____

☐ White-belted Ringtail   *Erpetogomphus compositus*

_____

☐ Yellow-legged Ringtail   *Erpetogomphus crotalinus*

_____

☐ Eastern Ringtail   *Erpetogomphus designatus*

_____

☐ Blue-faced Ringtail   *Erpetogomphus eutainia*

_____

☐ Dashed Ringtail   *Erpetogomphus heterodon* *

_____

☐ Serpent Ringtail   *Erpetogomphus lampropeltis* _____

_____

☐ Spine-crowned Clubtail   *Gomphus abbreviatus* _____

_____

☐ Mustached Clubtail   *Gomphus adelphus* _____

_____

☐ Banner Clubtail   *Gomphus apomyius* _____

_____

☐ Clearlake Clubtail   *Gomphus australis* _____

_____

☐ Beaverpond Clubtail   *Gomphus borealis* _____

_____

☐ Sandhill Clubtail   *Gomphus cavillaris* _____

_____

☐ Cherokee Clubtail   *Gomphus consanguis*   * _____

_____

☐ Handsome Clubtail   *Gomphus crassus*   * _____

_____

☐ Harpoon Clubtail   *Gomphus descriptus* _____

_____

☐ Blackwater Clubtail   *Gomphus dilatatus* _____

_____

☐ Diminutive Clubtail   *Gomphus diminutus*   * _____

_____

☐ Lancet Clubtail   *Gomphus exilis* _____

_____

☐ Plains Clubtail   *Gomphus externus* _____

_____

☐ Midland Clubtail   *Gomphus fraternus*   _____

_____

☐ Twin-striped Clubtail   *Gomphus geminatus*   * _____

_____

☐ Tamaulipan Clubtail   *Gomphus gonzalezi*   * _____

_____

☐ Pronghorn Clubtail   *Gomphus graslinellus*   _____

_____

☐ Hodges's Clubtail   *Gomphus hodgesi*   * _____

_____

☐ Cocoa Clubtail   *Gomphus hybridus*   _____

_____

☐ Pacific Clubtail   *Gomphus kurilis*   _____

_____

☐ Splendid Clubtail   *Gomphus lineatifrons*   _____

_____

☐ Ashy Clubtail   *Gomphus lividus*   _____

_____

☐ Columbia Clubtail   *Gomphus lynnae*   * _____

_____

☐ Sulphur-tipped Clubtail   *Gomphus militaris*   _____

_____

☐ Cypress Clubtail   *Gomphus minutus*   _____

_____

☐ Gulf Coast Clubtail   *Gomphus modestus*   * _____

_____

☐ Oklahoma Clubtail   *Gomphus oklahomensis*   _____

_____

☐ Ozark Clubtail   *Gomphus ozarkensis*   _____

_____

☐ Piedmont Clubtail   *Gomphus parvidens*   _____

_____

☐ Rapids Clubtail   *Gomphus quadricolor*   _____

_____

☐ Sable Clubtail   *Gomphus rogersi*   _____

_____

☐ Tennessee Clubtail   *Gomphus sandrius*   *   _____

_____

☐ Septima's Clubtail   *Gomphus septima*   *   _____

_____

☐ Dusky Clubtail   *Gomphus spicatus*   _____

_____

☐ Cobra Clubtail   *Gomphus vastus*   _____

_____

☐ Skillet Clubtail   *Gomphus ventricosus*   *   _____

_____

☐ Green-faced Clubtail   *Gomphus viridifrons*   *   _____

_____

☐ Westfall's Clubtail   *Gomphus westfalli*   *   _____

_____

☐ Dragonhunter   *Hagenius brevistylus*   _____

_____

☐ Northern Pygmy Clubtail *Lanthus parvulus*   _____

_____

☐ Southern Pygmy Clubtail *Lanthus vernalis*   _____

_____

☐ Grappletail   *Octogomphus specularis*   _____

_____

☐ Acuminate Snaketail   *Ophiogomphus acuminatus* *   _____

_____

☐ Extra-striped Snaketail   *Ophiogomphus anomalus*   *   _____

_____

☐ Arizona Snaketail   *Ophiogomphus arizonicus* *   _____

_____

☐ Brook Snaketail   *Ophiogomphus aspersus*   _____

_____

☐ Southern Snaketail   *Ophiogomphus australis*   *   _____

_____

☐ Bison Snaketail   *Ophiogomphus bison*   _____

_____

☐ Riffle Snaketail   *Ophiogomphus carolus*   _____

_____

☐ Boreal Snaketail   *Ophiogomphus colubrinus*   _____

_____

☐ Edmund's Snaketail   *Ophiogomphus edmundo*   *   _____

_____

☐ Pygmy Snaketail   *Ophiogomphus howei*   *   _____

_____

☐ Appalachian Snaketail   *Ophiogomphus incurvatus* *   _____

_____

☐ Maine Snaketail   *Ophiogomphus mainensis*   _____

_____

☐ Great Basin Snaketail   *Ophiogomphus morrisoni*   _____

_____

☐ Sinuous Snaketail   *Ophiogomphus occidentis*   _____

_____

☐ Rusty Snaketail   *Ophiogomphus rupinsulensis*   _____

_____

☐ Pale Snaketail   *Ophiogomphus severus*   _____

_____

☐ Sioux Snaketail   *Ophiogomphus smithi*   _____

_____

☐ Wisconsin Snaketail   *Ophiogomphus susbehcha*   *   _____

_____

☐ Westfall's Snaketail   *Ophiogomphus westfalli*   *   _____

_____

☐ Ringed Forceptail   *Phyllocycla breviphylla*   _____

_____

☐ Five-striped Leaftail   *Phyllogomphoides albrighti*   _____

_____

☐ Four-striped Leaftail   *Phyllogomphoides stigmatus*   _____

_____

☐ Tawny Sanddragon   *Progomphus alachuensis*   _____

_____

☐ Belle's Sanddragon   *Progomphus bellei*   *   _____

_____

☐ Gray Sanddragon   *Progomphus borealis*   _____

_____

☐ Common Sanddragon   *Progomphus obscurus*   _____

_____

☐ Eastern Least Clubtail   *Stylogomphus albistylus*   _____

_____

☐ Interior Least Clubtail *Stylogomphus sigmastylus*

☐ Riverine Clubtail *Stylurus amnicola*

☐ Brimstone Clubtail *Stylurus intricatus*

☐ Shining Clubtail *Stylurus ivae*

☐ Laura's Clubtail *Stylurus laurae*

☐ Elusive Clubtail *Stylurus notatus* *

☐ Olive Clubtail *Stylurus olivaceus*

☐ Russet-tipped Clubtail *Stylurus plagiatus*

☐ Yellow-sided Clubtail *Stylurus potulentus* *

☐ Zebra Clubtail *Stylurus scudderi*

☐ Arrow Clubtail *Stylurus spiniceps*

☐ Townes's Clubtail *Stylurus townesi* *

Family Cordulegastridae: Spiketails
(North America: 9; World: 49)

☐ Brown Spiketail *Cordulegaster bilineata*

☐ Apache Spiketail   *Cordulegaster diadema*

_____

_____

☐ Delta-spotted Spiketail   *Cordulegaster diastatops*

_____

_____

☐ Pacific Spiketail   *Cordulegaster dorsalis*

_____

_____

☐ Tiger Spiketail   *Cordulegaster erronea*

_____

_____

☐ Twin-spotted Spiketail   *Cordulegaster maculata*

_____

_____

☐ Arrowhead Spiketail   *Cordulegaster obliqua*

_____

_____

☐ Say's Spiketail   *Cordulegaster sayi*   *

_____

_____

☐ Ouachita Spiketail   *Cordulegaster talaria*

_____

_____

Family Macromiidae: Cruisers (North America: 9; World: 122)

☐ Florida Cruiser   *Didymops floridensis*

_____

_____

☐ Stream Cruiser   *Didymops transversa*

_____

_____

☐ Allegheny River Cruiser   *Macromia alleghaniensis*

_____

_____

☐ Bronzed River Cruiser   *Macromia annulata*

_____

_____

☐ Swift River Cruiser   *Macromia illinoiensis*

_____

☐   Western River Cruiser   *Macromia magnifica*

_____

☐   Mountain River Cruiser   *Macromia margarita*   *

_____

☐   Gilded River Cruiser   *Macromia pacifica*

_____

☐   Royal River Cruiser   *Macromia taeniolata*

_____

Family Corduliidae: Emeralds (North America: 50; World: 238)

☐   American Emerald   *Cordulia shurtleffii*

_____

☐   Petite Emerald   *Dorocordulia lepida*

_____

☐   Racket-tailed Emerald   *Dorocordulia libera*

_____

☐   Beaverpond Baskettail   *Epitheca canis*

_____

☐   Stripe-winged Baskettail   *Epitheca costalis*

_____

☐   Common Baskettail   *Epitheca cynosura*

_____

☐   Dot-winged Baskettail   *Epitheca petechialis*

_____

☐   Prince Baskettail   *Epitheca princeps*

_____

☐   Mantled Baskettail   *Epitheca semiaquea*

_____

☐ Sepia Baskettail   *Epitheca sepia*

_____

_____

☐ Spiny Baskettail   *Epitheca spinigera*

_____

_____

☐ Robust Baskettail   *Epitheca spinosa*

_____

_____

☐ Florida Baskettail   *Epitheca stella*

_____

_____

☐ Selys's Sundragon   *Helocordulia selysii*

_____

_____

☐ Uhler's Sundragon   *Helocordulia uhleri*

_____

_____

☐ Alabama Shadowdragon   *Neurocordulia alabamensis*

_____

_____

☐ Broad-tailed Shadowdragon   *Neurocordulia michaeli*   *

_____

_____

☐ Smoky Shadowdragon   *Neurocordulia molesta*

_____

_____

☐ Umber Shadowdragon   *Neurocordulia obsoleta*

_____

_____

☐ Cinnamon Shadowdragon   *Neurocordulia virginiensis*

_____

_____

☐ Orange Shadowdragon   *Neurocordulia xanthosoma*

_____

_____

☐ Stygian Shadowdragon   *Neurocordulia yamaskanensis*

_____

_____

☐ Ringed Emerald   *Somatochlora albicincta*

_____

_____

☐ Quebec Emerald   *Somatochlora brevicincta*   *   _____

_____

☐ Calvert's Emerald   *Somatochlora calverti*   *   _____

_____

☐ Lake Emerald   *Somatochlora cingulata*   _____

_____

☐ Ski-tailed Emerald   *Somatochlora elongata*   _____

_____

☐ Plains Emerald   *Somatochlora ensigera*   _____

_____

☐ Fine-lined Emerald   *Somatochlora filosa*   _____

_____

☐ Forcipate Emerald   *Somatochlora forcipata*   _____

_____

☐ Delicate Emerald   *Somatochlora franklini*   _____

_____

☐ Coppery Emerald   *Somatochlora georgiana*   _____

_____

☐ Hine's Emerald   *Somatochlora hineana*   *   _____

_____

☐ Hudsonian Emerald   *Somatochlora hudsonica*   _____

_____

☐ Incurvate Emerald   *Somatochlora incurvata*   _____

_____

☐ Kennedy's Emerald   *Somatochlora kennedyi*   _____

_____

☐ Mocha Emerald   *Somatochlora linearis*   _____

_____

☐ Texas Emerald   *Somatochlora margarita*   *   _____

_____

☐ Ocellated Emerald   *Somatochlora minor*   _____

_____

☐ Ozark Emerald   *Somatochlora ozarkensis*   *   _____

_____

☐ Treetop Emerald   *Somatochlora provocans*   _____

_____

☐ Treeline Emerald   *Somatochlora sahlbergi*   _____

_____

☐ Mountain Emerald   *Somatochlora semicircularis*   _____

_____

☐ Muskeg Emerald   *Somatochlora septentrionalis*   _____

_____

☐ Clamp-tipped Emerald   *Somatochlora tenebrosa*   _____

_____

☐ Brush-tipped Emerald   *Somatochlora walshii*   _____

_____

☐ Whitehouse's Emerald   *Somatochlora whitehousei*   _____

_____

☐ Williamson's Emerald   *Somatochlora williamsoni*   _____

_____

☐ Ebony Boghaunter   *Williamsonia fletcheri*   _____

_____

☐ Ringed Boghaunter   *Williamsonia lintneri*   *   _____

_____

Family Libellulidae: Skimmers
(North America: 103; World: 966)

☐ Red-tailed Pennant   *Brachymesia furcata*

_____

☐ Four-spotted Pennant   *Brachymesia gravida*

_____

☐ Tawny Pennant   *Brachymesia herbida*

_____

☐ Pale-faced Clubskimmer   *Brechmorhoga mendax*

_____

☐ Masked Clubskimmer   *Brechmorhoga pertinax*

_____

☐ Gray-waisted Skimmer   *Cannaphila insularis*

_____

☐ Amanda's Pennant   *Celithemis amanda*

_____

☐ Red-veined Pennant   *Celithemis bertha*

_____

☐ Calico Pennant   *Celithemis elisa*

_____

☐ Halloween Pennant   *Celithemis eponina*

_____

☐ Banded Pennant   *Celithemis fasciata*

_____

☐ Martha's Pennant   *Celithemis martha*

_____

☐ Faded Pennant   *Celithemis ornata*

_____

☐ Double-ringed Pennant   *Celithemis verna*   _____

_____

☐ Checkered Setwing   *Dythemis fugax*   _____

_____

☐ Mayan Setwing   *Dythemis maya*   _____

_____

☐ Black Setwing   *Dythemis nigrescens*   _____

_____

☐ Swift Setwing   *Dythemis velox*   _____

_____

☐ Black Pondhawk   *Erythemis attala*   _____

_____

☐ Western Pondhawk   *Erythemis collocata*   _____

_____

☐ Pin-tailed Pondhawk   *Erythemis plebeja*   _____

_____

☐ Eastern Pondhawk   *Erythemis simplicicollis*   _____

_____

☐ Great Pondhawk   *Erythemis vesiculosa*   _____

_____

☐ Plateau Dragonlet   *Erythrodiplax basifusca*   _____

_____

☐ Seaside Dragonlet   *Erythrodiplax berenice*   _____

_____

☐ Black-winged Dragonlet   *Erythrodiplax funerea*   _____

_____

☐ Red-faced Dragonlet   *Erythrodiplax fusca*   _____

_____

☐ Little Blue Dragonlet   *Erythrodiplax minuscula*   _____

_____

☐ Band-winged Dragonlet   *Erythrodiplax umbrata*   _____

_____

☐ Metallic Pennant   *Idiataphe cubensis*   _____

_____

☐ Blue Corporal   *Ladona deplanata*   _____

_____

☐ White Corporal   *Ladona exusta*   _____

_____

☐ Chalk-fronted Corporal   *Ladona julia*   _____

_____

☐ Boreal Whiteface   *Leucorrhinia borealis*   _____

_____

☐ Frosted Whiteface   *Leucorrhinia frigida*   _____

_____

☐ Crimson-ringed Whiteface   *Leucorrhinia glacialis*   _____

_____

☐ Hudsonian Whiteface   *Leucorrhinia hudsonica*   _____

_____

☐ Dot-tailed Whiteface   *Leucorrhinia intacta*   _____

_____

☐ Canada Whiteface   *Leucorrhinia patricia*   _____

_____

☐ Belted Whiteface   *Leucorrhinia proxima*   _____

_____

☐ Golden-winged Skimmer   *Libellula auripennis*   _____

_____

☐ Bar-winged Skimmer   *Libellula axilena*

_____

_____

☐ Comanche Skimmer   *Libellula comanche*

_____

_____

☐ Bleached Skimmer   *Libellula composita*   *

_____

_____

☐ Neon Skimmer   *Libellula croceipennis*

_____

_____

☐ Spangled Skimmer   *Libellula cyanea*

_____

_____

☐ Yellow-sided Skimmer   *Libellula flavida*

_____

_____

☐ Eight-spotted Skimmer   *Libellula forensis*

_____

_____

☐ Slaty Skimmer   *Libellula incesta*

_____

_____

☐ Purple Skimmer   *Libellula jesseana*   *

_____

_____

☐ Widow Skimmer   *Libellula luctuosa*

_____

_____

☐ Needham's Skimmer   *Libellula needhami*

_____

_____

☐ Hoary Skimmer   *Libellula nodisticta*

_____

_____

☐ Twelve-spotted Skimmer   *Libellula pulchella*

_____

_____

☐ Four-spotted Skimmer   *Libellula quadrimaculata*

_____

_____

☐ Flame Skimmer   *Libellula saturata*   _____

_____

☐ Painted Skimmer   *Libellula semifasciata*   _____

_____

☐ Great Blue Skimmer   *Libellula vibrans*   _____

_____

☐ Marl Pennant   *Macrodiplax balteata*   _____

_____

☐ Ivory-striped Sylph   *Macrothemis imitans*   _____

_____

☐ Straw-colored Sylph   *Macrothemis inacuta*   _____

_____

☐ Jade-striped Sylph   *Macrothemis inequiunguis*   _____

_____

☐ Hyacinth Glider   *Miathyria marcella*   _____

_____

☐ Spot-tailed Dasher   *Micrathyria aequalis*   _____

_____

☐ Three-striped Dasher   *Micrathyria didyma*   _____

_____

☐ Thornbush Dasher   *Micrathyria hagenii*   _____

_____

☐ Elfin Skimmer   *Nannothemis bella*   _____

_____

☐ Carmine Skimmer   *Orthemis discolor*   _____

_____

☐ Roseate Skimmer   *Orthemis ferruginea*   _____

_____

☐ Antillean Skimmer   *Orthemis* species   _____

_____

☐ Blue Dasher   *Pachydiplax longipennis*   _____

_____

☐ Red Rock Skimmer   *Paltothemis lineatipes*   _____

_____

☐ Wandering Glider   *Pantala flavescens*   _____

_____

☐ Spot-winged Glider   *Pantala hymenaea*   _____

_____

☐ Slough Amberwing   *Perithemis domitia*   _____

_____

☐ Mexican Amberwing   *Perithemis intensa*   _____

_____

☐ Eastern Amberwing   *Perithemis tenera*   _____

_____

☐ Common Whitetail   *Plathemis lydia*   _____

_____

☐ Desert Whitetail   *Plathemis subornata*   _____

_____

☐ Filigree Skimmer   *Pseudoleon superbus*   _____

_____

☐ Blue-faced Meadowhawk   *Sympetrum ambiguum*   _____

_____

☐ Variegated Meadowhawk   *Sympetrum corruptum*   _____

_____

☐ Saffron-winged Meadowhawk   *Sympetrum costiferum*   _____

_____

☐   Black Meadowhawk   *Sympetrum danae*   _____

_____

☐   Cardinal Meadowhawk   *Sympetrum illotum*   _____

_____

☐   Cherry-faced Meadowhawk   *Sympetrum internum*   _____

_____

☐   Jane's Meadowhawk   *Sympetrum janeae*   _____

_____

☐   Red-veined Meadowhawk   *Sympetrum madidum*   _____

_____

☐   White-faced Meadowhawk   *Sympetrum obtrusum*   _____

_____

☐   Western Meadowhawk   *Sympetrum occidentale*   _____

_____

☐   Striped Meadowhawk   *Sympetrum pallipes*   _____

_____

☐   Ruby Meadowhawk   *Sympetrum rubicundulum*   _____

_____

☐   Band-winged Meadowhawk   *Sympetrum semicinctum*   _____

_____

☐   Spot-winged Meadowhawk   *Sympetrum signiferum*   * _____

_____

☐   Autumn Meadowhawk   *Sympetrum vicinum*   _____

_____

☐   Garnet Glider   *Tauriphila australis*   _____

_____

☐   Evening Skimmer   *Tholymis citrina*   _____

_____

☐ Vermilion Saddlebags   *Tramea abdominalis*   _____

_____

☐ Striped Saddlebags   *Tramea calverti*   _____

_____

☐ Carolina Saddlebags   *Tramea carolina*   _____

_____

☐ Antillean Saddlebags   *Tramea insularis*   _____

_____

☐ Black Saddlebags   *Tramea lacerata*   _____

_____

☐ Red Saddlebags   *Tramea onusta*   _____

_____

NON-ANNUAL VISITORS

Family Coenagrionidae: Pond Damsels

☐ Yaqui Dancer   *Argia carlcooki*   _____

_____

Family Aeshnidae: Darners

☐ Amazon Darner   *Anax amazili*   _____

_____

☐ Blue-spotted Comet Darner   *Anax concolor*   _____

_____

☐ Pale-green Darner   *Triacanthagyna septima*   _____

_____

Family Libellulidae: Skimmers

☐ Claret Pondhawk   *Erythemis mithroides*   _____

_____

☐ Flame-tailed Pondhawk   *Erythemis peruviana*   _____

_____

☐ Aztec Glider   *Tauriphila azteca*   _____

_____

☐ Sooty Saddlebags   *Tramea binotata*   _____

_____

ALIEN DRAGONFLIES AND DAMSELFLIES

Family Libellulidae: Skimmers

☐ Scarlet Skimmer   *Crocothemis servilia*   _____

_____

ADDITIONAL SPECIES

☐ _____   _____   _____

☐ _____   _____   _____

_____

☐ _____   _____   _____

_____

☐ _____   _____   _____

_____

☐ _____   _____   _____

_____

☐ _____   _____   _____

_____

☐ _____   _____   _____

_____

☐ _____   _____   _____

_____

☐ _____   _____   _____

☐ _____ _____ _____

_____

☐ _____ _____ _____

_____

☐ _____ _____ _____

_____

☐ _____ _____ _____

_____

☐ _____ _____ _____

_____

☐ _____ _____ _____

_____

☐ _____ _____ _____

_____

☐ _____ _____ _____

_____

☐ _____ _____ _____

_____

☐ _____ _____ _____

_____

☐ _____ _____ _____

_____

☐ _____ _____ _____

_____

☐ _____ _____ _____

_____

- [ ] _____ _____ _____
  _____
- [ ] _____ _____ _____
  _____
- [ ] _____ _____ _____
  _____
- [ ] _____ _____ _____
  _____
- [ ] _____ _____ _____
  _____
- [ ] _____ _____ _____
  _____
- [ ] _____ _____ _____
  _____
- [ ] _____ _____ _____
  _____
- [ ] _____ _____ _____
  _____
- [ ] _____ _____ _____
  _____
- [ ] _____ _____ _____
  _____
- [ ] _____ _____ _____
  _____
- [ ] _____ _____ _____

Appendix

Recent Taxonomic and Nomenclatural Changes

In science, each new point of view calls forth a revolution in nomenclature.
Friedrich Engels

Due to recent taxonomic and nomenclatural changes this book contains a number of English names, scientific names, and even species not found in any current field guide. Many of the name changes are relatively trivial or are easily understood by comparing both scientific and English names to the most recent field guides. The primary reasons for name changes, with examples, are the following:

1. Minor spelling changes in scientific or English name. Usually the new spellings are close enough to the original to not cause confusion.

Red Phalarope, *Phalaropus fulicaria* is now *Phalaropus fulicarius* (agreement of gender).

Pigmy Salamander is now Pygmy Salamander (to be consistent with the spelling of pygmy in the names of other animals).

2. Minor changes in the form of English names.

Common Garter Snake is now Common Gartersnake.

Longtail Salamander is now Long-tailed Salamander.

3. New genus name. This happens when new data, or new interpretations of old data, dictate moving a species from one genus to another, or when the previous name was found to be incorrect for nomenclatural reasons.

Snowy Owl, formerly *Nyctea scandiaca*, is now *Bubo scandiacus*, having been moved to the same genus as Great Horned Owl.

Blue Corporal, formerly *Libellula deplanata*, is now *Ladona deplanata*.

4. New species name (specific epithet). This indicates that a species has been split or lumped with another species, or the name has been changed for nomenclatural reasons.

Mountain Treefrog, formerly *Hyla eximia*, has been split, with North American populations now called Arizona Treefrog *Hyla wrightorum*.

Variable Sandsnake, formerly *Chilomeniscus cinctus*, has been synonymized with *C. punctatissimus* and *C. stramineus*. Since the latter name has priority (it was published first), the combined populations are now called *Chilomeniscus stramineus*.

5. Deletion of a species. A species is lumped with another species or is otherwise found to be invalid.

Brownback Salamander *Eurycea aquatica* is now included in Southern Two-lined Salamander *E. cirrigera*.

Mississippi Map Turtle *Graptemys kohnii* is now considered a subspecies of False Map Turtle *G. pseudogeographica*.

6. New English name. English names are changed to reflect taxonomic changes and for a variety of nomenclatural reasons (which vary with the group covered because each group has different rules).

Three-toed Woodpecker *Picoides tridactylus* is now American Three-toed Woodpecker *P. dorsalis* to reflect its split from populations in Eurasia, now called Eurasian Three-toed Woodpecker *P. tridactylus*.

White-spotted Salamander *Plethodon punctatus* is now Cow Knob Salamander because of its more prevalent usage, and because it eliminates confusion with White-spotted Slimy Salamander *P. cylindraceus*.

7. New species added. New species in the list are either former subspecies that have recently been elevated to full species status, a recently described species (usually from previously known populations of another species), or known species that had previously not been observed in North America.

Tuckasegee Darter *Etheostoma gutselli* was formerly treated as a subspecies of Greenside Darter *E. blennioides*.

Austin Blind Salamander *Eurycea waterlooensis* is a recently discovered species described in 2001.

Lucifer Damsel *Chrysobasis lucifer* is a tropical species first recorded in North America in Florida in 2000, and now known to breed there.

The differences between this book and selected recent field guides are listed and explained below. If no details are given for split species, assume that the split was the result of elevating subspecies to full species status, and that descriptions of those subspecies can be found in one of the field guides to which the lists in this book are compared. For example:

Henshaw's Night Lizard *Xantusia henshawi* is split into:

Sandstone Night Lizard *Xantusia gracilis*

Granite Night Lizard *Xantusia henshawi*

You can find descriptions of both in Stebbins (2003) as the subspecies *Xantusia henshawi gracilis* and *Xantusia henshawi henshawi*.

Newly described species, or species elevated from subspecies *not* described in current field guides, are provided with diagnostic characteristics, range, and references.

Mammals

As compared to:
Mammals of North America (Kays and Wilson 2002)

Taxonomic Changes

Bailey's Pocket Mouse *Chaetodipus baileyi* is split into:

Bailey's Pocket Mouse *Chaetodipus baileyi*

As now defined, restricted to populations east of the Colorado River.

Baja California Pocket Mouse *Chaetodipus rudinoris*

Has a darker pelage and more slender nasals than Bailey's Pocket Mouse (Elliot 1903).

Includes populations west of the Colorado River and south into Baja California (Riddle et al. 2000b).

Big-eared Kangaroo Rat *Dipodomys elephantinus*

Now treated as a subspecies of Narrow-faced Kangaroo Rat *Dipodomys venustus*.

Northern Collared Lemming *Dicrostonyx groenlandicus* is split into:

Nearctic Collared Lemming *Dicrostonyx groenlandicus*

Nelson's Collared Lemming *Dicrostonyx nelsoni*

Pelage is a uniform dull gray, without the grizzled black and dark red coloration seen on the upper foreparts of the nearest subspecies (*rubricatus*) of Nearctic Collared Lemming in northwestern and northern Alaska (Youngman 1975). Endemic to western Alaska from Seward Peninsula to Unimak Island in the Aleutian Islands and on Saint Lawrence Island (formerly *D. exsul*).

Ogilvie Mountains Collared Lemming *Dicrostonyx nunatakensis*

Differs from nearby collared lemmings by gray-brown dorsum (without any reddish tinge), gray rump, and pale venter. Restricted to rocky alpine tundra in the Ogilvie Mountains, Yukon Territory (Youngman 1967).

Unalaska Collared Lemming *Dicrostonyx unalascensis*

Probably because it lives in an oceanic climate, the Unalaska Collared Lemming is the only *Dicrostonyx* species that does not turn white or develop snow claws in winter. It is also larger than the other species. Restricted to Umnak and Unalaska islands of the Aleutian Archipelago, Alaska (Musser and Carleton 1993).

Mogollon Vole *Microtus mogollonensis*
   Now treated as a subspecies of Mexican Vole *Microtus mexicanus*.

White-throated Woodrat *Neotoma albigula* is split into:
   White-throated Woodrat *Neotoma albigula*
      Now consists of populations west of the Rio Grande and Rio Conchos, from southwestern Colorado
      to southern California, south into Mexico (Edwards et al. 2001).
   White-toothed Woodrat *Neotoma leucodon*
      Larger and darker than White-throated Woodrat with a larger, more robust skull (Goldman 1910).
      Includes populations of former *Neotoma albigula* east of the Rio Grande in New Mexico, Colorado,
      Oklahoma, and Texas, and east and south of the Rio Conchos in Mexico (Edwards et al. 2001).

Dusky-footed Woodrat *Neotoma fuscipes* is split into:
   Dusky-footed Woodrat *Neotoma fuscipes*
   Big-eared Woodrat *Neotoma macrotis*
      Differs from Dusky-footed Woodrat by having a larger vomer, narrower presphenoid relative to the
      basisphenoid, and a flowerlike (not oblong) phallus. Occupies (roughly) that portion of the formerly
      defined range of Dusky-footed Woodrat south of the North Fork of the American River in the Sierra
      Nevada; west of the Salinas River, San Juan Creek, and Carrizo Plain of the Coast Ranges; and south
      and west of central Ventura County, California (Matocq 2002).

Cactus Deermouse *Peromyscus eremicus* is split into:
   Cactus Deermouse *Peromyscus eremicus*
      Range now excludes southwestern California and Baja California (Riddle et al. 2000a.)
   Northern Baja Deermouse *Peromyscus fraterculus*
      Noticeably darker above (more reddish brown in summer, more blackish in winter), creamy or buff
      (not white) below as compared to Cactus Deermouse (Osgood 1909). Distributed from Ventura
      County, California, south into Baja California Sur (Riddle et al. 2000a).

North American Deermouse *Peromyscus maniculatus* is split into:
   North American Deermouse *Peromyscus maniculatus*
   Black-eared Deermouse *Peromyscus melanotis*
      Individuals not safely distinguished from North American Deermouse in the field. Primarily distrib-
      uted in Mexico but some populations are thought to occur at high elevations of mountains in south-
      eastern Arizona (Bowers 1974, but see Hoffmeister 1986).

Eastern Cottontail *Sylvilagus floridanus* is split into:
   Manzano Mountains Cottontail *Sylvilagus cognatus*
      Smaller skull with smaller bullae than in Robust Cottontail. Relatively longer ears, paler gray pelage,
      heavier winter coat, more thickly furred feet, and overall larger size than in most forms of Eastern
      Cottontail. Endemic to the Manzano Mountains of central New Mexico (Nelson 1909).
   Eastern Cottontail *Sylvilagus floridanus*
   Robust Cottontail *Sylvilagus robustus*
      Separated from Eastern and Mountain cottontails by larger size and cranial, mandibular, and dental
      characteristics. Occurs in the Guadalupe, Chisos, and Davis mountains of the Trans-Pecos region in
      New Mexico and Texas, and in the Sierra de la Madera of Mexico (Ruedas 1998). May be more endan-
      gered than The Nature Conservancy's vulnerable status would indicate. Also called Davis Mountains
      Cottontail.

Southern Short-tailed Shrew *Blarina carolinensis* is split into:
   Southern Short-tailed Shrew *Blarina carolinensis*

Everglades Short-tailed Shrew *Blarina peninsulae*
> Distinguished from Southern Short-tailed Shrew by uniform slate-black dorsum, lack of a sepia-brown tint, larger skull, teeth, and hind foot, and greater number of chromosomes. It may be more closely related to the Northern Short-tailed Shrew. Everglades Short-tailed Shrew is endemic to the southern half of peninsular Florida (Whitaker and Hamilton 1998).

Desert Shrew *Notiosorex crawfordi* is split into:
Cockrum's Desert Shrew *Notiosorex cockrumi*
> This recently described species (Baker et al. 2003b) is distinguished from Crawford's Desert Shrew only by genetics. Because so few specimens have been identified this way, the ranges of these two species are incompletely known. So far, Cockrum's Desert Shrew has been recorded from south central and southeastern Arizona to central Sonora, Mexico. It is sympatric with Crawford's Desert Shrew in southeastern Arizona.
Crawford's Desert Shrew *Notiosorex crawfordi*
> As now defined, it has been positively identified from Texas to southeastern Arizona (Baker et al. 2003b).

Water Shrew *Sorex palustris* is split into:
Glacier Bay Water Shrew *Sorex alaskanus*
> Similar in size and color to American Water Shrew, but the skull is shorter with a relatively shorter rostrum and it has more pronounced sagittal and lambdoidal crests (Jackson 1928). Known only from specimens collected in 1899 from Glacier Bay, Alaska.
American Water Shrew *Sorex palustris*

Cinereus Shrew *Sorex cinereus* is split into:
Cinereus Shrew *Sorex cinereus*
Saint Lawrence Island Shrew *Sorex jacksoni*
> Endemic to Saint Lawrence Island (Bering Sea, Alaska), where it is the only shrew on the island.

Montane Shrew *Sorex monticolus* is split into:
Dusky Shrew *Sorex monticolus*
New Mexico Shrew *Sorex neomexicanus*
> Differs from Dusky Shrew by larger size, dull brown dorsum with less reddish color, brown (not gray) venter, and by having a wider rostrum at the first unicuspid, and a longer unicuspid toothrow. Their ranges do not overlap. New Mexico Shrew is endemic to south central New Mexico in the Capitan and Sacramento mountains (Alexander 1996).

Alaska Tiny Shrew *Sorex yukonicus*
> In 1993 a specimen thought to be the Eurasian Tiny Shrew, *Sorex minutissimus*, was found in the University of Alaska Museum collection. It was subsequently determined to be of an undescribed species, Alaska Tiny Shrew, *Sorex yukonicus* (Dokuchaev 1997). This new species differs from Eurasian Tiny Shrew by having a narrower snout and generally smaller teeth. It is smaller than other Alaska shrews except American Pygmy Shrew, which has a much smaller third unicuspid and has bicolored, not slightly tricolored, pelage. Alaska Tiny Shrew is known only from central and southwestern Alaska.

Western Small-footed Myotis *Myotis ciliolabrum* is split into:
Western Small-footed Myotis *Myotis ciliolabrum*
> As now defined, found north and east of a line roughly from southwestern Oklahoma to northern Idaho (Holloway and Barclay 2001).

Dark-nosed Small-footed Myotis *Myotis melanorhinus*

> Compared to Western Small-footed Myotis, Dark-nosed Small-footed Myotis is buff (not white) below and a richer yellow above. Occupies the portion of the formerly defined range of *Myotis ciliolabrum*, which is west and south of a line running, roughly, from southwestern Oklahoma to northern Idaho (Holloway and Barclay 2001).

Little Brown Myotis *Myotis lucifugus* is split into:

Little Brown Myotis *Myotis lucifugus*

Arizona Myotis *Myotis occultus*

> Usually distinguished from Little Brown Myotis by the presence of a sagittal crest, larger skull and teeth, and longer toothrow (Findley and Jones 1967). Occurs in southern California, Arizona, New Mexico, southern Colorado, and Mexico (Piaggio et al. 2002).

Red Wolf *Canis rufus*

> Given its endangered status and the controversy concerning its validity as a full species, I err on the side of caution and include *Canis rufus*, following Baker et al. (2003a).

American Mink *Mustela vison* is moved to the genus *Neovison* and split into:

Sea Mink *Neovison macrodon*

> The Sea Mink was described, and is still scientifically known, only from bones found in Native American shell middens dated to within the last 5,100 years. It was hunted to extinction in historic times, probably sometime between 1860 and 1920. Sea Minks were up to twice as large as American Minks and had a more robust build (Mead et al. 2000). Their bones have been found in or near coastal and offshore island habitats from Massachusetts to the southern coasts of the Maritimes. However, archaeological evidence suggests that at least some Sea Mink bones found outside of Maine (that is, New Brunswick) were transported there by Native people (Black et al. 1998).

American Mink *Neovison vison*

American Hog-nosed Skunk *Conepatus leuconotus*

> The Western Hog-nosed Skunk (*Conepatus mesoleucus*) and Eastern Hog-nosed Skunk (*Conepatus leuconotus*) are now considered to be conspecific.

Moose *Alces alces* is split into:

Eurasian Elk *Alces alces*

> Only in Eurasia.

Moose *Alces americanus*

> The only *Alces* in North America, also found in northeastern Asia. Our Moose is darker with brown or gray (not white) legs, and has much larger antlers with two main lobes instead of one, and a longer dewlap (Geist 1998; Boyeskorov 1999).

Hector's Beaked Whale *Mesoplodon hectori* is split into:

Hector's Beaked Whale *Mesoplodon hectori*

> As now defined, this species is restricted to the southern hemisphere (Dalebout et al. 2002).

Perrin's Beaked Whale *Mesoplodon perrini*

> Separated from Hector's Beaked Whale by molecular characters and differences in the mandibles, teeth, and skull. Known and described from only five specimens stranded on the southern California coast. Four of the five were originally identified as Hector's Beaked Whales, the other as a Cuvier's Beaked Whale, but Dalebout et al. (2002) showed them to belong to a previously undescribed species.

Other Scientific Name Changes

Name in Kays and Wilson (2002)	Name in This Book
Clethrionomys (all three species)	*Myodes* (species names unchanged)
Erethizon dorsatum	*Erethizon dorsata*
Sorex bairdii	*Sorex bairdi*
Alopex lagopus	*Vulpes lagopus*
Phoca fasciata	*Histriophoca fasciata*
Phoca groenlandica	*Pagophilus groenlandicus*
Phoca hispida	*Pusa hispida*
Kogia simus	*Kogia sima*

Other English Name Changes

Name in Kays and Wilson (2002)	Name in This Book
Saxicolous Deermouse	Saxicoline Deermouse
Muskrat	Common Muskrat
Least Shrew	North American Least Shrew
Pygmy Shrew	American Pygmy Shrew
North American Long-nosed Bat	Lesser Long-nosed Bat
Island Gray Fox	Island Fox
Black Bear	American Black Bear
Northern River Otter	North American River Otter

Birds

As compared to:
Field Guide to the Birds of North America, 4th Edition (National Geographic Society 2002)

Taxonomic Changes

Canada Goose *Branta canadensis* is split into:
> Canada Goose *Branta canadensis*
>> Now restricted to large-bodied forms including the subspecies *Branta canadensis canadensis, interior, maxima, moffitti, parvipes, fulva,* and *occidentalis.*
>
> Cackling Goose *Branta hutchinsii*
>> This small-bodied form includes the subspecies formerly called *Branta canadensis hutchinsii, asiatica, leucopareia, taverneri,* and *minima.*

Labrador Duck *Camptorhynchus labradorius*
> Extinct. Last reported in 1878, Labrador Ducks were never very common and the cause of their rapid decline is unknown. Suggested (and speculative) reasons are hunting, human impacts on their molluscan prey, and localized breeding grounds that may have been vulnerable to human impacts. Males were distinctive with a white head, neck, and scapulars; a black body, crown stripe, and neck band; and an overall shape similar to a scoter or Harlequin Duck. Females were gray-brown with a white speculum and throat. Atlantic Coast from Labrador or farther north, south to possibly Virginia (see Fuller 2001, Alderfer 2006).

Common Snipe *Gallinago gallinago* is split into:
> Wilson's Snipe *Gallinago delicata*
>> First printing of NGS 2002 used *Gallinago gallinago* in error.
>
> Common Snipe *Gallinago gallinago*

Great Auk *Pinguinus impennis*

Extinct in 1844 due to overhunting and collection of eggs. In North America, Great Auks bred in colonies of up to 200,000 birds on Funk and Penguin islands, Newfoundland, and Bird Rocks in the Gulf of Saint Lawrence (other breeding colonies in the eastern Atlantic were in Iceland, the Faeroes, Saint Kilda, and Orkney Island). They wintered south to New England although their bones have been found in prehistoric middens in Florida. Great Auks were similar to Razorbills in plumage and bill shape but more like penguins in posture, size, and behavior. They were up to 31 inches long, weighed 10 pounds, and had tiny wings that were incapable of flight in air but very effective underwater (see Fuller 2001, Alderfer 2006).

Passenger Pigeon *Ectopistes migratorius*

Once the most abundant bird in North America, the Passenger Pigeon plummeted from billions to zero in one century due to overhunting and the destruction of its woodland habitat by humans. Extinct in the wild in 1900, the last captive bird (Martha) died at the Cincinnati Zoo in 1914. Like a large Mourning Dove with a long pointed tail; blue-gray head, wings, and back; a pinkish orange or rufous breast fading to a white belly; dark flight feathers; black marks on wing coverts; and white outer tail feathers. Eastern United States and southern Canada (see Fuller 2001, Alderfer 2006).

Carolina Parakeet *Conuropsis carolinensis*

The causes for the extinction of the Carolina Parakeet are not well understood, but they probably include overhunting and habitat loss. The last wild birds were observed in Florida in 1904. The last individual (Incas) died at the Cincinnati Zoo in 1918. Males and females were green with a yellow head, red-orange face, and a pale bill and eye ring. They had a long pointed tail and were about 13 inches long. Eastern United States west to central Colorado and north to Minnesota, Michigan, and New York (see Fuller 2001, Alderfer 2006).

Three-toed Woodpecker *Picoides tridactylus* is split into:

American Three-toed Woodpecker *Picoides dorsalis*

Eurasian Three-toed Woodpecker *Picoides tridactylus*

Not found in North America.

Yellow Wagtail *Motacilla flava* is split into:

Motacilla flava complex

May comprise more than one species but none have been recorded in North America.

Eastern Yellow Wagtail *Motacilla tschutschensis*

Includes *Motacilla flava tschutschensis* and *simillima*, that is, all North American populations of the former Yellow Wagtail.

Black-backed Wagtail *Motacilla lugens* is now a subspecies of White Wagtail *Motacilla alba*.

Other Scientific Name Changes

Name in National Geographic (2002)	Name in This Book
Actitis macularia	*Actitis macularius*
Ajaia ajaja	*Platalea ajaja*
Ceryle torquata	*Ceryle torquatus*
Columba fasciata	*Patagioenas fasciata*
Columba flavirostris	*Patagioenas flavirostris*
Columba leucocephala	*Patagioenas leucocephala*
Columba squamosa	*Patagioenas squamosa*
Delichon urbica	*Delichon urbicum*
Helmitheros vermivorus	*Helmitheros vermivorum*
Lagopus leucurus	*Lagopus leucura*

Lagopus mutus	*Lagopus muta*
Nyctea scandiaca	*Bubo scandiacus*
Otus asio	*Megascops asio*
Otus kennicottii	*Megascops kennicottii*
Otus trichopsis	*Megascops trichopsis*
Porphyrula martinica	*Porphyrio martinica*
Saxicola torquata	*Saxicola torquatus*
Tiaris olivacea	*Tiaris olivaceus*

Other English Name Changes

Name in National Geographic (2002)	Name in This Book
Mongolian Plover	Lesser Sand-Plover
Greater Sandplover	Greater Sand-Plover
Spoonbill Sandpiper	Spoon-billed Sandpiper
Band-tailed Gull	Belcher's Gull
Rock Dove	Rock Pigeon
Jungle Nightjar	Gray Nightjar
Siberian Flycatcher	Dark-sided Flycatcher
Gray-spotted Flycatcher	Gray-streaked Flycatcher

Reptiles

As compared to:

A Field Guide to the Reptiles and Amphibians: Eastern and Central North America (Conant and Collins 1998)

A Field Guide to Western Reptiles and Amphibians (Stebbins 2003).

Taxonomic Changes

Lesser Earless Lizard *Holbrookia maculata* is split into:

Elegant Earless Lizard *Holbrookia elegans*

Populations in the United States formerly recognized as *Holbrookia maculata thermophila* and the Mexican subspecies *Holbookia maculata elegans* are now treated together as a full species (*Holbrookia elegans*). In the United States, Elegant Earless Lizard is separated from Common Lesser Earless Lizard by very sharp (not blunt) points on the tail chevrons, bicolored breeding coloration in females, a colored gular patch (when present) that is an orange-red spot, and a lack of minute circumorbital scales. The illustration of a male *H. maculata* in Stebbins (2003, plate 28) would now be considered an illustration of *H. elegans*. Occurs in southeastern Arizona, extreme southwestern New Mexico, and Mexico (Axtell 1998 and pers. comm.).

Common Lesser Earless Lizard *Holbrookia maculata*

Coast Horned Lizard *Phrynosoma coronutum* is split into:

Coast Horned Lizard *Phrynosoma blainvillii*

three extralimital species (*Phrynosoma coronatum, cerroense,* and *wigginsi*) in Baja California

Sagebrush Lizard *Sceloporus graciosus* is split into:

Dunes Sagebrush Lizard *Sceloporus arenicolus*

Common Sagebrush Lizard *Sceloporus graciosus*

Mountain Spiny Lizard *Sceloporus jarrovii* is split into five species:
  Yarrow's Spiny Lizard *Sceloporus jarrovii* (formerly *Sceloporus jarrovii jarrovii*)
  four other species (*S. sugillatus*, *S. cyanostictus*, *S. oberon*, *S. minor*) endemic to Mexico

Blue Spiny Lizard *Sceloporus serrifer cyanogenys*
  Now recognized as a full species (*S. cyanogenys*).

Fence/Prairie/Plateau Lizard *Sceloporus undulatus* is split into four species:
  Prairie Lizard *Sceloporus consobrinus*
  Southwestern Fence Lizard *Sceloporus cowlesi*
  Plateau Lizard *Sceloporus tristichus*
  Eastern Fence Lizard *Sceloporus undulatus*

Colorado Desert Fringe-toed Lizard *Uma notata* is split into:
  Colorado Desert Fringe-toed Lizard *Uma notata*
    Now only includes populations in extreme southern California and adjacent Mexico.
  Yuman Desert Fringe-toed Lizard *Uma rufopunctata*
    Compared to *U. notata*, the sides of the belly of *U. rufopunctata* have narrower black bars and are often
    without any orange color. Occurs in sandy areas south of the Gila River in Yuma and Pima counties,
    Arizona, and adjacent Mexico (Arizona Game and Fish Department 2003). Populations from the
    Mohawk Dunes, Yuma County, Arizona, may represent an undescribed cryptic species (Trépanier
    and Murphy 2001).

Black-tailed Brush Lizard *Urosaurus nigricaudus*
  Now includes *Urosaurus microscutatus* so its range extends to southern tip of Baja California and the Eng-
  lish name is changed to Baja California Brush Lizard. Unfortunately, Stebbins (2003) uses the name Baja
  California Brush Lizard for *Urosaurus lahtelai*, a species confined to a small range (entirely within that of
  Urosaurus nigricaudus) near Cataviña, Baja California. Crother et al. (2003) suggest the name Cataviña
  Brush Lizard for *Urosaurus lahtelai*.

Leaf-toed Gecko *Phyllodactylus xanti* is split into:
  Peninsular Leaf-toed Gecko *Phyllodactylus nocticolus*
  Cape Leaf-toed Gecko *Phyllodactylus xanti* (endemic to Baja California, Mexico)

Henshaw's Night Lizard *Xantusia henshawi* is split into:
  Sandstone Night Lizard *Xantusia gracilis*
  Granite Night Lizard *Xantusia henshawi*

Desert Night Lizard *Xantusia vigilis* is split into:
  Bezy's Night Lizard *Xantusia bezyi*
    A new species described in 2001 (Papenfuss et al.) that is similar to Desert Night Lizard except it has
    larger dorsal blotches like those of Granite Night Lizard. Endemic to Arizona where it is known only
    from two sites southwest of Sunflower.
  Desert Night Lizard *Xantusia vigilis*

Little Striped Whiptail *Cnemidophorus inornatus* is moved to the genus *Aspidoscelis* and split into four species, based on subspecies described by Wright and Lowe (1993):
  Arizona Striped Whiptail *Aspidoscelis arizonae*
    Arizona Striped Whiptail has seven whitish dorsal stripes on a light bluish-gray dorsal ground color.
    It is now only found in Graham and Cochise counties, Arizona, although it was formerly present in
    New Mexico.

Little White Whiptail *Aspidoscelis gypsi*

> The Little White Whiptail is endemic to White Sands National Monument, New Mexico, rarely straying far from the dunes. Distinguished from others in this group by faint (sometimes absent) stripes on a white or whitish dorsal ground color.

Little Striped Whiptail *Aspidoscelis inornata*

> This taxon is now restricted to New Mexico, the Trans-Pecos of Texas, and parts of Mexico. Distinguished from others in this group by having at least eight stripes on a dark dorsal ground color (or no stripes near the type locality in Nuevo Leon, Mexico).

Pai Striped Whiptail *Aspidoscelis pai*

> Pai Striped Whiptail is distinguished from the above species by having six dorsal stripes, no mid-dorsal stripe on the nape, and a black dorsal ground color. Endemic to Arizona in the northwest (Grand Canyon, Coconino Plateau to the Navaho Reservation) and the Mazatzal Mountains of Gila County.

Western Whiptail *Cnemidophorus tigris* is moved to the genus *Aspidoscelis* and split into:

> Marbled Whiptail *Aspidoscelis marmorata*
> Tiger Whiptail *Aspidoscelis tigris*

Canyon Spotted Whiptail *Cnemidophorus burti* is moved to the genus *Aspidoscelis* and split into:

> Canyon Spotted Whiptail *Aspidoscelis burti*
> Red-backed Whiptail *Aspidoscelis xanthonota*

Texas Alligator Lizard *Gerrhonotus liocephalus* is split into:

> Texas Alligator Lizard *Gerrhonotus infernalis*
> extralimital Mexican species *Gerrhonotus liocephalus*

Rubber Boa *Charina bottae* is split into:

> Northern Rubber Boa *Charina bottae*
> Southern Rubber Boa *Charina umbratica*
>
> > Distinguished from Northern Rubber Boa by a combination of these scale characters: frontal scale shape more like a triangle (as opposed to a rectangle), 42 or more mid dorsal scale rows, and 197 or more full-sized ventral scales (Rodríguez-Robles et al. 2001). The ranges of the two species do not overlap. Southern Rubber Boa is restricted to southern California (San Bernardino and San Jacinto Mountains).

Texas Blind Snake *Leptotyphlops dulcis* is split into:

> New Mexico Threadsnake *Leptotyphlops dissectus*
> Texas Threadsnake *Leptotyphlops dulcis*

Variable Sandsnake *Chilomeniscus cinctus*

> Now synonymized with *C. punctatissimus* and *C. stramineus*. Since the latter name has priority (it was published first), the combined populations are now called Variable Sandsnake *Chilomeniscus stramineus*.

Indigo Snake *Drymarchon corais* is split into:

> South American Indigo Snake *Drymarchon corais*
> > Not found in North America.
> Eastern Indigo Snake *Drymarchon couperi*
> Central American Indigo Snake *Drymarchon melanurus*
> > Called Texas Indigo Snake (*Drymarchon corais erebennus*) in Conant and Collins (1998).

Corn Snake *Elaphe guttata* is split into three species (Burbrink 2002) and moved to *Pantherophis*:

Red Cornsnake *Pantherophis guttata*

The range of this redefined species is now restricted to areas east of the Mississippi River except in extreme southern Louisiana where it is found west to the Atchafalaya River (the original mouth of the Mississippi River). This species includes populations in the Florida Keys formerly known as *E. g. rosacea*.

Great Plains Ratsnake *Pantherophis emoryi*

Includes former subspecies *E. guttata emoryi*, *E. guttata meahllmorum*, and *E. guttata intermontanus*. The range includes that of all former *E. guttata* west of the Mississippi River except in eastern Texas and Louisiana. A small isolated population of Great Plains Ratsnake is found on the east side of the Mississippi River in southwestern Illinois.

Slowinski's Cornsnake *Pantherophis slowinskii*

A new species described in 2002. Includes members of the former *Elaphe guttata* that occur in southeastern Texas north of the Brazos River, and in Louisiana west of the Atchafalaya River. It lacks the bright red and yellow dorsal color pattern possessed by southern specimens of Red Cornsnake, and its dorsal blotches are dark red, maroon, or brownish, not dark gray or olive as in Great Plains Ratsnake.

Black/Yellow/Everglades/Gray/Texas Rat Snake *Elaphe obsoleta* is split into three species, none of which exactly match a previously described subspecies or group of subspecies, in spite of the fact that the newly delineated species use the names of former subspecies of *Elaphe obsoleta*. These snakes are highly variable with much overlap in characters, such as color patterns, that were previously used to separate the subspecies. The three newly delineated species differ in the averages of several measurements and scale counts, but the degree of overlap makes it more practical to identify the species by their range. Refer to Burbrink (2001) for individuals observed near range boundaries. These taxa are also moved to *Pantherophis*.

Eastern Ratsnake *Pantherophis alleghaniensis*

Occurs east of the Appalachian Mountains, the Chattahoochee River in Georgia, and the Apalachicola River in Florida, from New York to the Florida Keys.

Texas Ratsnake *Pantherophis obsoleta*

Occupies the portion of the range of former *E. obsoleta* that is west of the Mississippi River.

Gray Ratsnake *Pantherophis spiloides*

Ranges east of the Mississippi River to the Appalachian Mountains, the Chattahoochee River in Georgia, and the Apalachicola River in Florida.

Fox Snake *Elaphe vulpina* is split into:

Eastern Foxsnake *Pantherophis gloydi*

Western Foxsnake *Pantherophis vulpina*

Coachwhip *Masticophis flagellum* is split into:

Coachwhip *Masticophis flagellum*

Baja California Coachwhip *Masticophis fuliginosus*

Whipsnake *Masticophis taeniatus* is split into:

Schott's Whipsnake *Masticophis schotti*

Includes *Masticophis taeniatus schotti* and *Masticophis taeniatus ruthveni*.

Striped Whipsnake *Masticophis taeniatus*

Pine/Bull/Gopher Snake *Pituophis melanoleucus* is split into:

Gophersnake *Pituophis catenifer*

Pinesnake *Pituophis melanoleucus*

Louisiana Pinesnake *Pituophis ruthveni*

Big Bend Patch-nosed Snake *Salvadora deserticola*
  Now considered a subspecies of Western Patch-nosed Snake *Salvadora hexalepis*.

Blackhood/Devil's River Blackhead Snake *Tantilla rubra cucullata/Tantilla rubra diabola*
  Now treated as Trans-Pecos Black-headed Snake *Tantilla cucullata*.

Harter's Water Snake *Nerodia harteri* is split into:
  Brazos River Watersnake *Nerodia harteri*
  Concho Watersnake *Nerodia paucimaculata*

Brown Snake *Storeria dekayi* is split into:
  DeKay's Brownsnake *Storeria dekayi*
  Florida Brownsnake *Storeria victa*

Western Hognose Snake *Heterodon nasicus* is split into:
  Dusty Hog-nosed Snake *Heterodon gloydi*
  Mexican Hog-nosed Snake *Heterodon kennerlyi*
  Western Hognose Snake *Heterodon nasicus*

Western Lyre Snake *Trimorphodon biscutatus* is split into:
  Western Lyresnake *Trimorphodon biscutatus*
  Chihuahuan Desert Lyresnake *Trimorphodon vilkinsonii*

Eastern/Texas Coral Snake *Micrurus fulvius* is split into:
  Harlequin Coralsnake *Micrurus fulvius*
  Texas Coralsnake *Micrurus tener*

Western Rattlesnake *Crotalus viridis* is split into:
  Western Rattlesnake *Crotalus oreganus*
  Prairie Rattlesnake *Crotalus viridis*

Yellow Mud Turtle *Kinosternon flavescens* is split into:
  Arizona Mud Turtle *Kinosternon arizonense*
  Yellow Mud Turtle *Kinosternon flavescens*

Painted Turtle *Chrysemys picta* is split into:
  Southern Painted Turtle *Chrysemys dorsalis*
  Northern Painted Turtle *Chrysemys picta*

Alabama Map Turtle *Graptemys pulchra* is split into three species (Lovich and McCoy 1992):
  Escambia Map Turtle *Graptemys ernsti*
    Identified by having a vertical bar on each marginal scute, wide borders on the seams between the lower marginals, an interorbital blotch not connected to the postorbital blotches, and either two supraoccipital spots or bulbous anterior expansions of the first paramedian neck stripes. Found in the Pensacola Bay drainage (Conecuh, Escambia, Yellow, and Shoal rivers) in Alabama and Florida.
  Pascagoula Map Turtle *Graptemys gibbonsi*
    Identified by having a vertical bar on each marginal scute, narrow borders on the seams between the lower marginals, a lack of supraoccipital spots, no bulbous anterior expansions to the dorsal paramedian neck stripes, and a light interorbital blotch connected to the postorbital blotches. Occurs in the Pascagoula and Pearl river systems in Mississippi and Louisiana.

Alabama Map Turtle *Graptemys pulchra*
> Identified by having concentric yellow semicircles on each marginal scute, wide borders on the seams between the lower marginals, a light interorbital blotch connected to the post orbital blotches, no bulbous anterior expansions to the dorsal paramedian neck stripes, and no supraoccipital spots. This taxon is now considered to be restricted to populations in the Mobile Bay drainage.

False Map Turtle *Graptemys pseudogeographica* is split into:
> Ouachita Map Turtle *Graptemys ouachitensis*
> False Map Turtle *Graptemys pseudogeographica*

Mississippi Map Turtle *Graptemys kohnii*
> Treated as a full species in Conant and Collins (1998) but now considered a subspecies of False Map Turtle *G. pseudogeographica*.

Peninsula Cooter *Pseudemys floridana peninsularis*
> Elevated to full species status (*Pseudemys peninsularis*).

Florida Cooter *Pseudemys floridana floridana*
> Now considered a subspecies of River Cooter (*Pseudemys concinna*).

River Cooter *Pseudemys concinna* is split into:
> River Cooter *Pseudemys concinna*
> Suwannee Cooter *Pseudemys suwanniensis*

Other Scientific Name Changes

Name in Current Peterson Field Guides	Name in This Book
Charina trivirgata	*Lichanura trivirgata*
Clemmys insculpta	*Glyptemys insculpta*
Clemmys marmorata	*Actinemys marmorata*
Clemmys muhlenbergii	*Glyptemys muhlenbergii*
Cnemidophorus (all North American species)	*Aspidoscelis* (species names unchanged)
Elaphe (all North American species)	*Pantherophis* (species names unchanged)
Eumeces (all North American species)	*Plestiodon* (species names unchanged)
Neoseps reynoldsi	*Plestiodon reynoldsi*
Macroclemys temminckii	*Macrochelys temminckii*
Sauromalus obesus	*Sauromalus ater*
Trionyx ferox	*Apalone ferox*
Trionyx muticus	*Apalone mutica*
Trionyx spinifera	*Apalone spinifera*

Other English Name Changes

Name in Current Peterson Field Guides	Name in This Book
Big Bend Mud Turtle	Rough-footed Mud Turtle
Common Musk Turtle	Stinkpot
Western Pond Turtle	Pacific Pond Turtle
Common Map Turtle	Northern Map Turtle
Redbelly Turtle	Northern Red-bellied Cooter
Western Box Turtle	Ornate Box Turtle
Big Bend Slider	Mexican Plateau Slider
Texas Tortoise	Berlandier's Tortoise

Loggerhead	Loggerhead Seaturtle
Green Turtle	Green Seaturtle
Hawksbill	Hawksbill Seaturtle
Atlantic Ridley	Kemp's Ridley Seaturtle
Olive Ridley	Olive Ridley Seaturtle
Leatherback	Leatherback Seaturtle
Texas Earless Lizard	Greater Earless Lizard
Mountain Short-horned Lizard	Greater Short-horned Lizard
Mesquite Lizard	Graphic Spiny Lizard
Reticulated Gecko	Reticulate Banded Gecko
Barefoot Gecko	Switak's Banded Gecko
Common Spotted Whiptail	Eastern Spotted Whiptail
Five-lined Skink	Common Five-lined Skink
Sand Skink	Florida Sand Skink
Ground Skink	Little Brown Skink
Western Blind Snake	Western Threadsnake
Scarlet Snake	Scarletsnake
Mexican Hook-nosed Snake	Tamaulipan Hook-nosed Snake
Night Snake	Nightsnake
Milk Snake	Milksnake
California Whipsnake	Striped Racer
Brown Vine Snake	Brown Vinesnake
Mountain Patch-nosed Snake	Eastern Patch-nosed Snake
Black Swamp Snake	Black Swampsnake
Western Ground Snake	Groundsnake
Western Terrestrial Garter Snake	Terrestrial Gartersnake
Black-striped Snake	Regal Black-striped Snake
Mud Snake	Red-bellied Mudsnake
Pine Woods Snake	Pine Woods Littersnake
Yellow-bellied Sea Snake	Yellow-bellied Seasnake
all species of blackhead snake	black-headed snake
all species of garter snake	gartersnake
all species of ribbon snake	ribbonsnake
all species of rat snake	ratsnake
all species of worm snake	wormsnake
all species of water snake	watersnake
all species of green snake	greensnake
all species of pine snake	pinesnake
all species of earth snake	earthsnake

Amphibians

As compared to:

A Field Guide to Reptiles and Amphibians: Eastern and Central North America (Conant and Collins 1998)
A Field Guide to Western Reptiles and Amphibians (Stebbins 2003)

Taxonomic Changes

Tailed Frog *Ascaphus truei* is split into two species that exhibit much variation in color patterns that are cryptic and tend to match the local habitat. However their ranges are separated by at least 100 miles (Nielson et al. 2001).

Rocky Mountain Tailed Frog *Ascaphus montanus*
Restricted to the northern Rocky Mountains from extreme southeastern British Columbia to southern Idaho.

Coastal Tailed Frog *Ascaphus truei*
Restricted to the Cascades and coastal regions from British Columbia to northern California.

Eastern/Hurter's Spadefoot *Scaphiopus holbrookii* is split into:
Eastern Spadefoot *Scaphiopus holbrookii*
Hurter's Spadefoot *Scaphiopus hurterii*

Canadian Toad *Bufo hemiophrys* is split into:
Wyoming Toad *Bufo baxteri*
Restricted to Big Laramie and Little Laramie rivers within 15 miles of Laramie, Wyoming, over 400 miles from range of Canadian Toad. Distinguished from other local toads by its smaller adult size (to 2.2") and fused cranial crests. Highly endangered. Extinct in the wild in 1994, later reintroduced from captive breeding program.

Canadian Toad *Bufo hemiophrys*

Woodhouse's Toad *Bufo woodhousii* is split into:
Fowler's Toad *Bufo fowleri*
Woodhouse's Toad *Bufo woodhousii*

Gulf Coast Toad *Bufo valliceps* is split into:
Gulf Coast Toad *Bufo nebulifer*
a Mexican species *Bufo valliceps*

Mountain Treefrog *Hyla eximia* is split into:
Arizona Treefrog *Hyla wrightorum*
Mountain Treefrog *Hyla eximia* (only in Mexico)

Gray Treefrog *Hyla chrysoscelis* and *Hyla versicolor*
Treated as separate species in Conant and Collins (1998) but not given separate English names. They should be called Cope's Gray Treefrog *Hyla chrysoscelis* and Gray Treefrog *Hyla versicolor*.

Western Chorus Frog *Pseudacris triseriata* is split into:
Southeastern Chorus Frog *Pseudacris feriarum*
Boreal Chorus Frog *Pseudacris maculata*
Western Chorus Frog *Pseudacris triseriata*

Red-legged Frog *Rana aurora* is split into:
  Northern Red-legged Frog *Rana aurora*
  California Red-legged Frog *Rana draytonii*

Gopher Frog *Rana capito* is split into:
  Gopher Frog *Rana capito*
  Dusky Gopher Frog *Rana sevosa*

Relict Leopard Frog *Rana onca* is split into:
  Vegas Valley Leopard Frog *Rana fisheri*
      Extinct since 1942. Had fewer dorsal spots and shorter hind legs than Relict Leopard Frog (Linsdale 1940). Recorded only from type locality (Las Vegas, Nevada).
  Relict Leopard Frog *Rana onca*

Ramsey Canyon Leopard Frog *Rana subaquavocalis*
  A new species of the *R. pipiens* complex. Distinguished from other leopard frogs of Arizona by extensive mottling on the chin area, and by its unique behavior of producing all mating calls while underwater, usually deep enough (one meter) so that they are not audible above the surface. Known only from Ramsey, Brown, and Tinker canyons in the Huachuca Mountains of southeastern Arizona (Platz 1993; Platz et al. 1997).

Dwarf Siren *Pseudobranchus striatus* is split into:
  Southern Dwarf Siren *Pseudobranchus axanthus*
      Includes populations formerly regarded as *P. striatus axanthus* and *P. s. belli*. The Southern Dwarf Siren differs from *P. striatus* (now called Northern Dwarf Siren) by having 32 chromosomes instead of 24. External characters differ but the geographic variation has not been studied well enough to determine diagnostic characters. The two species occur in sympatry in north peninsular Florida although *P. axanthus* has not been found north of the Saint Johns River drainage. However, where they are sympatric, *P. axanthus* is usually found in open marsh or prairie ponds while *P. striatus* lives in cypress ponds located in acid pine flatwoods (Moler and Kezer 1993).
  Northern Dwarf Siren *Pseudobranchus striatus*
      Includes populations formerly regarded as *P. striatus lustricolus*, *P. s. spheniscus*, and *P. s. striatus*. See above.

Black-bellied Salamander *Desmognathus quadramaculatus* is split into two species (Camp et al. 2002):
  Dwarf Black-bellied Salamander *Desmognathus folkertsi*
      A new species described in 2002. Adults have a snout-vent length of 56 to 85 mm compared to 80 to 120 mm for Black-bellied Salamander. Dorsum of *D. folkertsi* is a mixture of brown and black in a vermiculate pattern or with irregular or alternating brown blotches. Known from two tributaries of the Nottely River, Union County, Georgia, where it is sympatric with Black-bellied Salamander.
  Black-bellied Salamander *Desmognathus quadramaculatus*
      Dorsum has a few irregular black spots on a uniform brown or dark green background. Young *D. quadrimaculatus* the size of large *D. folkertsi* are usually greenish above with a red tail-stripe.

Northern Dusky Salamander *Desmognathus fuscus* is split into:
  Spotted Dusky Salamander *Desmognathus conanti* (may represent two cryptic species)
  Northern Dusky Salamander *Desmognathus fuscus*

Mountain Dusky Salamander *Desmognathus ochrophaeus* is split into five species (Anderson and Tilley 2003; Tilley and Mahoney 1996; Petranka 1998):
  Cumberland Dusky Salamander *Desmognathus abditus*

Described in 2003. Differs from *D. ochrophaeus* by having distinct paired reddish dorsal spots or, in older individuals, wavy dorsolateral stripes. Differs from *D. ocoee* by dorsal pattern (usually no spots or outlines of spots in *D. ocoee*) and having no keel on the tail. Differs from other sympatric *Desmognathus* species by round tail. Endemic to the Cumberland Plateau of Tennessee from near Wartburg, Morgan County, south to near Tracy City, Grundy County.

Carolina Mountain Dusky Salamander *Desmognathus carolinensis*

A highly variable species that is most reliably separated from other members of the *D. ochrophaeus* complex by molecular data and geographic range. Found at elevations of 900 to 6,000 feet in the Blue Ridge, Black, Bald, and Unaka mountains, from McKinney Gap and the Doe River south to the Pigeon River, in eastern Tennessee and western North Carolina.

Allegheny Mountain Dusky Salamander *Desmognathus ochrophaeus*

Identified only by molecular data or geographic range when compared to other members of this complex. See range map of Mountain Dusky Salamander in Conant and Collins (1998), exclusive of ranges of *D. carolinensis*, *D. ocoee*, and *D. orestes* described here (or see Petranka 1998).

Ocoee Salamander *Desmognathus ocoee*

Identified only by molecular data or geographic range. Ocoee Salamander occurs at all elevations in the mountains of the conterminous corners of North Carolina (south of Pigeon River), South Carolina, Georgia, and Tennessee. A disjunct population occurs in northeastern Alabama.

Blue Ridge Dusky Salamander *Desmognathus orestes*

Safely separated only by molecular data or geographic range. Found from Mount Rogers in southwestern Virginia, southwest to Burke and Mitchell counties, North Carolina, and extreme northeastern Tennessee.

Brownback Salamander *Eurycea aquatica*

Now included in Southern Two-lined Salamander (*E. cirrigera*).

Longtail Salamander *Eurycea longicauda* is split into:
Three-lined Salamander *Eurycea guttolineata*
Long-tailed Salamander *Eurycea longicauda*

Texas Salamander *Eurycea neotenes* is currently split into eight species but as many as nine or more new species may soon be described. In addition to other populations mentioned below, the Comal Springs and Pedernales Springs populations may each be described as a new species. All information is from Chippindale et al. (2000) unless otherwise noted:

Salado Salamander *Eurycea chisholmensis*

A new and very rare species described in 2000. Unlike other spring-dwelling *Eurycea* north of the Colorado River in Texas, Salado Salamander has reduced eyes, a dark dorsal coloration, no dark eye ring, and no well-defined light and dark spots. Occurs only in Big Boiling and Robertson springs of Salado, Bell County, Texas, and possibly also in springs of nearby Buttermilk Creek.

Cascade Caverns Salamander *Eurycea latitans*

This species includes surface-dwelling and troglodytic forms distinguished from other species by molecular characters. It includes populations of the former *E. neotenes* complex found in Rebecca Creek Spring (Hays County); Cascade Caverns (Kendall County), and the following springs: Bear Creek, Cibolo Creek, Less Ranch, and Kneedeep Cave (Kendall County); Cherry Creek and Cloud Hollow (Kerr County); and Honey Creek Cave (Comal County), Texas.

Georgetown Salamander *Eurycea naufragia*

A new species described in 2000. See Jollyville Plateau Salamander. Georgetown Salamander is confined to springs in central and northern Williamson County, Texas, most of which are associated with the South, Middle, and North forks of the San Gabriel River system.

Texas Salamander *Eurycea neotenes*

Distinguished by molecular characters and range. This species is now considered to be restricted to

Helotes Creek Spring and Leon Springs in Bexar County, and Mueller's Spring in Kendall County, Texas.

Fern Bank Salamander *Eurycea pterophila*

Distinguished by allozymes and range. Restricted to springs and caves associated with the Blanco River, Texas.

Barton Springs Salamander *Eurycea sosorum*

A new species described in 1993. A permanently aquatic salamander of surface waters in the springs of the Barton Creek drainage in Austin, Texas. The Austin Blind Salamander (*Eurycea waterlooensis*) is the only other *Eurycea* in Barton Springs but it lacks eyes, has no pigmentation, and is only rarely flushed to the surface from underground (Chippindale et al. 1993).

Jollyville Plateau Salamander *Eurycea tonkawae*

A new species described in 2000. Differs from nearby Georgetown Salamander by having square or oblong (not rosette or starburst) light areas surrounding each dorsolateral iridophore, and irregular and chevron-shaped (not regular and complete) dark lateral margins of the yellow-orange dorsal tail fin coloration. Restricted to springs of the Jollyville Plateau of Travis County (north of the Colorado River) and southwestern Williamson County and Brushy Creek, Texas. The recently discovered populations of the Buttercup Creek Caves and Testudo Tube Cave may each represent an undescribed species.

Valdina Farms Salamander *Eurycea troglodytes*

This species complex currently includes all former members of *Eurycea neotenes* that occur west of extreme southeastern Kerr County, Texas. As many as five or more new species may eventually be described from these populations.

Dwarf Salamander *Eurycea quadridigitata* is split into:

Chamberlain's Dwarf Salamander *Eurycea chamberlaini*

A new species described in 2003 (Harrison III and Guttman). Like Dwarf Salamander in having four toes on front and hind limbs, but differs by having a bright yellow venter, distinct dorsolateral stripes, 16 or fewer costal grooves, a slightly smaller body size, and relatively longer limbs. Currently known from central and eastern North Carolina and central and western South Carolina. Sympatric with Dwarf Salamander at some sites.

Dwarf Salamander *Eurycea quadridigitata*

Austin Blind Salamander *Eurycea waterlooensis*

A newly described subterranian salamander of the Edwards Aquifer of central Texas. Occasionaly juveniles are accidentally flushed to surface outlets of Barton Springs, especially Sunken Gardens Spring, in Austin, Texas. Like Texas Blind Salamander (*E. rathbuni*) in general shape, limb structure, lack of external eyes, and having 12 costal grooves. It differs by having proportionally shorter limbs (when adpressed they do not overlap), weakly developed tail fins, and smaller gills. Known only from Barton Springs in Austin, Texas (Hillis et al. 2001).

Tennessee Cave Salamander *Gyrinophilus palleucus* is split into:

Berry Cave Salamander *Gyrinophilus gulolineatus*

Tennessee Cave Salamander *Gyrinophilus palleucus*

Catahoula Salamander *Plethodon ainsworthi*

Known from only two specimens collected in 1964, "discovered" in 1991 in a museum (having been erroneously labled *Plethodon glutinosus*), and described in 1998 after many fruitless searches for more specimens. May already be extinct. A very long-bodied *Plethodon*, most like Larch Mountain Salamander (*P. larselli*) in shape, with small legs, narrow head, and unpatterned blackish-brown coloration. Specimens were collected two miles south of Bay Springs, Mississippi, in springhead litter (Lazell 1998).

Scott Bar Salamander *Plethodon asupak*

A recently discovered species (Mead et al. 2005) that differs from the parapatric Del Norte and Siskiyou salamanders by having fewer than four intercostal folds between adpressed limbs. Scott Bar Salamander has a modal number of 17 costal grooves, while Del Norte Salamander has 18. Currently known only from a small area of Siskiyou County, California, from Walker Creek on the south side of the Klamath River to Mill Creek on the east side of Scott River.

Eastern Red-backed Salamander *Plethodon cinereus* is split into:

Eastern Red-backed Salamander *Plethodon cinereus*

Big Levels Salamander *Plethodon sherando*

Most similar to *P. cinereus* with which it is generally parapatric, but their ranges overlap in one small area. Big Levels Salamander has more white than gray on the venter (usually equal amounts in *P. cinereus*); usually 18 costal grooves (usually 20 in *P. cinereus* in the same region); and usually more than 5 costal interspaces between the toes of adpressed legs (usually 5 or fewer in *P. cinereus*). Big Levels Salamander was discovered in 2003 and is only known from above 1,900 feet in the Big Levels area of the Blue Ridge Mountains in Augusta County, Virginia (Highton 2004).

Zigzag Salamander *Plethodon dorsalis* is split into:

Ozark Salamander *Plethodon angusticlavius*

Northern Zigzag Salamander *Plethodon dorsalis*

Southern Zigzag Salamander *Plethodon ventralis*

Formerly included in *P. dorsalis dorsalis*. Overall, nearly identical to Northern Zigzag Salamander although in Kentucky, where their ranges meet, Southern Zigzag Salamander occurs only in the unstriped morph while Northern Zigzag Salamander is found in both striped and unstriped morphs. Otherwise separated only by genetics and range. Appalachians of southeastern Kentucky and southwestern Virginia, south to northeastern Mississippi and northwestern Georgia (Highton 1997).

Del Norte Salamander *Plethodon elongatus* is split into:

Del Norte Salamander *Plethodon elongatus*

Siskiyou Mountains Salamander *Plethodon stormi*

Valley and Ridge Salamander *Plethodon hoffmani* is split into:

Valley and Ridge Salamander *Plethodon hoffmani*

Shenandoah Mountain Salamander *Plethodon virginia*

These two species are morphologically identical. They differ genetically and have parapatric ranges in the Valley and Ridge Physiographic Province. Shenandoah Mountain Salamander occurs in a fairly small range that includes Shenandoah Mountain in eastern West Virginia and adjacent northwestern Virginia (Highton 1999).

Jordan's Salamander *Plethodon jordani* is split into seven species (Highton and Peabody 2000):

Blue Ridge Gray-cheeked Salamander *Plethodon amplus*

Gray cheeks and legs, large size, dark belly, without lateral spotting or brassy dorsal flecking. Indistinguishable from *P. meridianus* or southern populations of *P. metcalfi* except by range and genetics. Blue Ridge Mountains of Buncombe, Henderson, and Rutherford counties, North Carolina.

Cheoah Bald Salamander *Plethodon cheoah*

Red patches (smaller than in *P. shermani*) on legs, and lateral white or yellow spots. Endemic to Cheoah Bald in Graham and Swain counties, North Carolina.

Red-cheeked Salamander *Plethodon jordani*

This taxon is now restricted to populations with red cheek patches and a light belly. Range is now restricted to Great Smoky Mountains, Gregory Bald, and near Balsam, North Carolina.

South Mountain Gray-cheeked Salamander *Plethodon meridianus*

Gray cheeks and legs, large size and dark belly, without lateral spotting or brassy dorsal flecking. Indistinguishable from *P. amplus* and southern populations of *P. metcalfi* except by range and genetics. Endemic to South Mountains of Burke, Cleveland, and Rutherford counties, North Carolina.

Southern Gray-cheeked Salamander *Plethodon metcalfi*

Gray cheeks and legs, usually lacking lateral white spotting and dorsal brassy flecking, light belly in the north, dark belly in the south. Virtually indistinguishable from most other gray-cheeked salamanders except by range and genetics. Blue Ridge Mountains of southwestern North Carolina, extreme northeast Georgia, and extreme northwest South Carolina, and near Balsam and Cowee, North Carolina.

Northern Gray-cheeked Salamander *Plethodon montanus*

Gray cheeks and legs, lacks white and yellow on sides and legs, lighter belly than *P. amplus*, *P. meridianus*, and southern populations of *P. metcalfi*. It can only be separated from northern populations of *P. metcalfi* by geographic range and genetics. Valley and Ridge Province of Virginia and Blue Ridge Province of North Carolina, Tennessee, and Virginia. Essentially the portion of the range of Jordan's Salamander, as shown in Conant and Collins (1998), north of I-40.

Red-legged Salamander *Plethodon shermani*

Illustrated in Conant and Collins ("redleg" variation of Jordan's Salamander). Large red patches (larger than in *P. cheoah*) on legs except in Unicoi Mountains where it is separated from other members of the *P. jordani* complex by the combination of lateral white or yellow spots, and gray legs. Unicoi Mountains east to Wayah Bald and Standing Indian Mountain in extreme western North Carolina.

Ravine Salamander *Plethodon richmondi* is split into:

Northern Ravine Salamander *Plethodon electromorphus*

Morphologically identical to Southern Ravine Salamander. The two species can only be separated by genetics and range. Their ranges meet in extreme northern Kentucky, east along the Ohio River and Kanawha River in West Virginia (Highton 1999).

Southern Ravine Salamander *Plethodon richmondi*

Other Scientific Name Changes

Name in Current Peterson Field Guides	Name in This Book
Batrachoseps wrighti	*Batrachoseps wrightorum*
Hyla cadaverina	*Pseudacris cadaverina*
Hyla regilla	*Pseudacris regilla*
Leptodactylus labialis	*Leptodactylus fragilis*
Leurognathus marmoratus	*Desmognathus marmoratus*
Rana utricularia	*Rana sphenocephala*
Scaphiopus bombifrons	*Spea bombifrons*
Scaphiopus multiplicatus	*Spea multiplicata*
Syrrhophus (all three species)	*Eleutherodactylus* (species names unchanged)
Typhlomolge (both species)	*Eurycea* (species names unchanged)
Typhlotriton spelaeus	*Eurycea spelaeus*

Other English Name Changes

Name in Current Peterson Field Guides	Name in This Book
Giant Toad	Cane Toad
Northern Casque-headed Frog	Lowland Burrowing Treefrog
Alabama Waterdog	Blackwarrior Waterdog
Pacific Giant Salamander	Coastal Giant Salamander
Pigmy Salamander	Pygmy Salamander
Redback Salamander	Eastern Red-backed Salamander
White-spotted Salamander	Cow Knob Salamander

Freshwater Fishes

As compared to:

A Field Guide to Freshwater Fishes: North America North of Mexico (Page and Burr 1991).

Unfortunately, subspecies are not indexed in Page and Burr (1991). If no description follows a species below, look up the species from which it was split in Page and Burr (1991) and refer to the "remarks" section for descriptions of subspecies that are treated herein as full species.

Taxonomic Changes

Shovelnose Sturgeon *Scaphirhynchus platorynchus* is split into:

Shovelnose Sturgeon *Scaphirhynchus platorynchus*

Alabama Sturgeon *Scaphirhynchus suttkusi*

Differs from Shovelnose Sturgeon, with which it is allopatric, by its lack of sharp spines on the snout, and uniform brassy orangish-yellow coloration. Formerly widespread in the Mobile Basin in Alabama and Mississippi, it is now apparently only found in the Alabama River (Williams and Clemmer 1991; Mayden and Kuhajda 1996).

Roundnose Minnow *Dionda episcopa* is split into four species for which diagnostic characters have not yet been determined. However, they may be separated on the basis of range (Mayden et al. 1992).

Manantial Roundnose Minnow *Dionda argentosa*

Endemic to Texas in San Felipe Spring and Devil's River where it is sympatric with Devil's River Minnow *D. diaboli*.

Roundnose Minnow *Dionda episcopa*

Now considered to be restricted to the Rio Grande River system in Texas and New Mexico upstream of the Devil's River.

Guadalupe Roundnose Minnow *Dionda nigrotaeniata*

Endemic to the Guadalupe River drainage of Texas, mostly in springs.

Nueces Roundnose Minnow *Dionda serena*

Endemic to Texas in the Nueces and Frio river drainages

Streamline Chub *Erimystax dissimilis* is split into:

Streamline Chub *Erimystax dissimilis*

Ozark Chub *Erimystax harryi*

Now only found in the Saint Francis and White river drainages in Missouri and Arkansas.

Leatherside Chub *Gila copei* is split into two species (Johnson et al. 2004) and moved to *Lepidomeda*:

Southern Leatherside Chub *Lepidomeda aliciae*

Distinguished from Northern Leatherside Chub by longer snout, shallower head, and molecular characters, but most easily separated by range. Utah Lake and Sevier River systems, Utah.

Northern Leatherside Chub *Lepidomeda copei*

Bear Lake and Upper Snake River systems in Utah, Idaho, and Wyoming.

Roundtail Chub *Gila robusta* is split into four species (Minckley and DeMarais 2000; Sigler and Sigler 1996):

Gila Chub *Gila intermedia*

Gila Chub has thick, broadly overlapping scales, usually fewer than 70 lateral line scales, a dark (sometimes black) body, dark-outlined scales, and usually eight dorsal and anal fin rays. Occurs only in the Gila River basin of Arizona, New Mexico, and adjacent Mexico, usually associated with cover.

Headwater Chub *Gila nigra* (= *Gila grahami*)

Recognized by a combination of thin, narrowly overlapping scales, usually 73 to 83 lateral line scales, a dark gray or brown (not black) body coloration often with diffuse lateral stripes, and usually eight dorsal and anal fin rays. Restricted to the Gila River basin in Arizona and New Mexico, usually associated with cover.

Roundtail Chub *Gila robusta*

Has thin, narrowly overlapping scales, usually more than 78 lateral line scales, silvery sides (sometimes with dark, irregular dorsolateral blotches), transparent to translucent interradial fin membranes, and usually nine dorsal and anal fin rays. Found throughout the Colorado River basin from Wyoming and Colorado to Mexico, usually in more open areas of larger streams.

Virgin Chub *Gila seminuda*

Virgin Chub has 15 to 19 gill rakers, whereas Roundtail Chub has 12 to 15. Restricted to the Virgin and Muddy rivers of northwest Arizona, southeast Nevada, and southwest Utah. Does not overlap the ranges of the above three species.

Mississippi Silvery Minnow *Hybognathus nuchalis* is split into:

Rio Grande Silvery Minnow *Hybognathus amarus*

Only *Hybognathus* species in the Rio Grande river system.

Mississippi Silvery Minnow *Hybognathus nuchalis*

Rosefin Shiner *Lythrurus ardens* is split into:

Rosefin Shiner *Lythrurus ardens*

Scarlet Shiner *Lythrurus fasciolaris*

Speckled Chub *Extrarius aestivalis* is moved to the genus *Macrhybopsis* and split into five species (Eisenhour 1997):

Speckled Chub *Macrhybopsis aestivalis*

Speckled Chub is the only member of the *M. aestivalis* complex that has many scales with 20 to 30 tiny dots. It also has a single pair of barbels, no lateral stripe, no diamond pattern on the back and sides, and no tubercles on the head of breeding males. Endemic to the Rio Grande basin and Rio San Fernando drainage in New Mexico, Texas, and Mexico.

Prairie Chub *Macrhybopsis australis*

Has two long pairs of barbels as in Peppered Chub but usually only has seven anal fin rays, and the pectoral fins of adult males usually extend past the pelvic fin bases. Endemic to the Red River basin of Texas and Oklahoma upstream from Jefferson County, Oklahoma.

Shoal Chub *Macrhybopsis hyostoma*

Has larger eyes and shorter barbels than Prairie and Peppered chub, no tubercles on head of breeding males, and usually has a lateral stripe and dorsolateral diamond pattern. Ranges from the Lavaca River drainage in Texas to the Alabama River drainage in Alabama.

Burrhead Chub *Macrhybopsis marconis*

This is the only member of the *M. aestivalis* complex that has tubercles on the head of breeding males, and a well-defined lateral stripe from the operculum to the base of the tail. Also has a single pair of short barbels, and a diamond pattern on back and sides. Occurs in the Guadalupe and San Antonio river drainages, and the Edward's Plateau section of the Colorado River drainage in Texas.

Peppered Chub *Macrhybopsis tetranema*

Like Prairie Chub in having two pairs of long barbels. The longer, posterior barbels usually exceed orbit length, the shorter pair are over 50 percent of orbit length. Differs from Prairie Chub by usually having eight anal fin rays and, in adult males, pectoral fins that just reach the pelvic fin bases. Endemic to Great Plains streams of the Arkansas River basin from Pueblo, Colorado, to Tulsa County, Oklahoma. Currently survives only in the South Canadian River in New Mexico and Texas, the South Fork Ninnescah River in Kingman County, Kansas, and the Arkansas River in Sumner County, Kansas (Eisenhour 1999).

River Chub *Nocomis micropogon* is split into:
  River Chub *Nocomis micropogon*
  Bigmouth Chub *Nocomis platyrhynchus*

Yazoo Shiner *Notropis rafinesquei*
  Differs from the sympatric Sabine, Orangefin, and Longnose shiners by having an area of xanthic coloration (present all year but brightest during breeding) behind the opercle and, in males, extending above the opercle to the eye. Xanthic color is also concentrated at the base of all fins. Endemic to the upper Yazoo River system in Mississippi (Suttkus 1991).

Rosyface Shiner *Notropis rubellus* is split into four species:
  Highland Shiner *Notropis micropteryx*
    Differs from others in this group by coloration of breeding males: red-orange on the lower sides, jaws, and fin bases, and pale red on top of head with little or no contrast with nape (Page and Burr, forthcoming). Found only in the upland areas of the Green, Tennessee, and Cumberland (below Cumberland Falls) river systems in Tennessee and adjacent portions of Kentucky, Virginia, North Carolina, and Alabama (Wood et al. 2002).
  Carmine Shiner *Notropis percobromus*
    Cannot be distinguished from Rosyface Shiner by morphology (Page and Burr, forthcoming). Occurs in three separate regions: from Red River and upper Mississippi River basins in southern Manitoba southeast to central Indiana; southcentral Kansas and northeastern Oklahoma east through the Ozarks to eastern Missouri; and the Ouachita River in Arkansas (Wood et al. 2002).
  Rosyface Shiner *Notropis rubellus*
    As in Page and Burr (1991). Northeastern Wisconsin and Michigan east to the Hudson River drainage in Vermont, south to the Cumberland River (above Cumberland Falls) in Kentucky, and the James River system in Virginia (Wood et al. 2002).
  Rocky Shiner *Notropis suttkusi*
    Differs from Rosyface Shiner by having a lateral stripe of nearly uniform width (does not taper anteriorly), deeply decurved lateral line, more continuous red-orange pigment on sides, and dorsal scale margins usually obscured by dense pigmentation. It also has a deeper body and shorter snout. Endemic to the Ouachita Uplands from the Blue River in Oklahoma to the Cossatot River in Arkansas (Humphries and Cashner 1994).

Sawfin Shiner *Notropis* species
  Still formally undescribed.

Mimic Shiner *Notropis volucellus* is split into:
  Mimic Shiner *Notropis volucellus*
  Channel Shiner *Notropis wickliffi*

Oregon Chub *Oregonichthys crameri* is split into:
  Oregon Chub *Oregonichthys crameri*
  Umpqua Chub *Oregonichthys kalawatseti*
    Differs slightly from Oregon Chub by having a partly or completely unscaled breast and a slightly subterminal (not terminal) mouth. It is endemic to the Umpqua River system of western Oregon (Markle et al. 1991).

Laurel Dace *Phoxinus saylori*
  A new species described in 2001 (Skelton). Most similar to Tennessee Dace (*P. tennesseensis*) and Southern Redbelly Dace (*P. erythrogaster*). Laurel Dace differs by breeding males having uninterrupted black lateral stripes, and black on the underside of the head. Presently known from six streams (Youngs, Moc-

casin, Bumbee, Cupp, and Soddy creeks, and the Horn Branch of Rock Creek) on the Tennessee River side of Waldon Ridge, north of Chattanooga, Tennessee.

Sailfin Shiner *Pteronotropis hypselopterus* is split into five species (Suttkus and Mettee 2001; Suttkus et al. 2003):

Sailfin Shiner *Pteronotropis hypselopterus*
Differs from Apalachee and Orangetail shiners by having a round caudal spot and olive-yellow to olive-orange anal and caudal fins in breeding males. Inhabits the Gulf Coastal Plain from the Mobile Bay drainage in Alabama to the lower Choctawhatchee River and Saint Andrews Bay drainages in the Florida Panhandle.

Apalachee Shiner *Pteronotropis grandipinnis*
Differs from Sailfin and Orangetail shiners by having a vertically oval caudal spot, burnt-orange caudal and anal fins, and an anal fin that extends to near or beyond the base of the caudal fin in breeding males. Endemic to the Apalachicola River drainage including the Chipola River system to extreme southeastern Alabama, and the Flint River north to Taylor County, Georgia.

Orangetail Shiner *Pteronotropis merlini*
Differs from Sailfin and Apalachee shiners by breeding males having a chevron or crescent-shaped caudal spot, bright orange anal and caudal fins, and a deeper body. Endemic to southeastern Alabama in the Choctawhatchee and Pea rivers above their confluence.

Metallic Shiner *Pteronotropis metallicus*
Dorsal fin has black only in a crescent across most of lower half. Anal fin has a pale distal tip and overall less pigmentation. Ranges from the New River in the Florida Panhandle to Saint Marys River, Georgia.

Lowland Shiner *Pteronotropis stonei*
Distinguished from Apalachee Shiner by little or no caudal basal spot, dorsal and anal fins that are not greatly elevated, and relatively sharp (not diffuse) lower margin of lateral band. Has greater pigmentation in dorsal and anal fins than Metallic Shiner. Lower Piedmont and Coastal Plain from Little Lynches River system of the Pee Dee River drainage, South Carolina, to Satilla River, Georgia.

Cheat Minnow *Rhinichthys bowersi*
Now considered to be a hybrid (*Nocomis micropogon* X *Rhinichthys cataractae*).

Blacknose Dace *Rhinichthys atratulus* is split into two species (Matthews et al. 1982):

Eastern Blacknose Dace *Rhinichthys atratulus*
In breeding males the lower head and body are whitish to pale yellow. Scale counts are usually lower than in Western Blacknose Dace: scales across the back (23 to 26); caudal peduncle scales (11 to 14); lateral line scales (53 to 61). Atlantic slope drainages from the Maritimes to Virginia.

Western Blacknose Dace *Rhinichthys obtusus*
Includes some populations formerly called *Rhinichthys atratulus meleagris*. Best separated from Eastern Blacknose Dace by range and, in breeding males, orange to orange-red coloration of the lower head and body (like illustration of *R. a. meleagris* in Page and Burr 1991). In females and nonbreeding males check scale counts: scales across the back (26 to 33); caudal peduncle scales (13 to 16); and lateral line scales (57 to 70). Occurs from central Manitoba through the Great Lakes to western Lake Ontario and south through the upper Mississippi and Ohio river basins to northern Alabama and Georgia. Sympatric with Eastern Blacknose Dace only in Meadow Creek, upper James River drainage, Virginia.

Salish Sucker *Catostomus* species
Still formally undescribed.

Little Colorado River Sucker *Catostomus* species
Still formally undescribed.

Blue Sucker *Cycleptus elongatus* is split into:
> Blue Sucker *Cycleptus elongatus*
> Southeastern Blue Sucker *Cycleptus meridionalis*
>> Described in 1999 (Burr and Mayden). Differs from Blue Sucker by having less than 54 lateral line scales, less than 42 predorsal circumferential scales, and less than 19 caudal peduncle circumferential scales. Occurs in the Pearl and Pascagoula river drainages and the Mobile Basin in Louisiana, Alabama, and Mississippi.

Creek Chubsucker *Erimyzon oblongus* is split into:
> Western Creek Chubsucker *Erimyzon claviformis*
>> Has 9 to 11 dorsal rays (usually 10) compared to 11 to 14 (usually 12) in Eastern Creek Chubsucker. Otherwise, the two species are almost identical but their ranges do not overlap. Northern Illinois and southern Michigan south to the Gulf from eastern Texas to Alabama (Page and Burr, forthcoming).
> Eastern Creek Chubsucker *Erimyzon oblongus*
>> Maine and central New York south to eastern Georgia.

Shorthead Redhorse *Moxostoma macrolepidotum* is split into:
> Smallmouth Redhorse *Moxostoma breviceps*
> Shorthead Redhorse *Moxostoma macrolepidotum*
> Pealip Redhorse *Moxostoma pisolabrum*

Silver Redhorse *Moxostoma anisurum* is split into:
> Silver Redhorse *Moxostoma anisurum*
> Notchlip Redhorse *Moxostoma collapsum*
>> Like Silver Redhorse but has notches in the lower lip at the lateral corners. Atlantic slope drainages from southern Virginia to eastern Georgia (Nelson et al. 2004).

Smallfin Redhorse *Moxostoma robustum*
> After a century of confusion with another species, the fish originally described as *Moxostoma robustum* was rediscovered in the early 1990s. The characterization of Smallfin Redhorse *Moxostoma robustum* in Page and Burr (1991) actually applies to the Brassy Jumprock, an undescribed species of *Moxostoma*. The real *Moxostoma robustum* is the recently rediscovered Robust Redhorse (Jenkins and Burkhead 1994). This confusion persisted for over 100 years.

Robust Redhorse *Moxostoma robustum*
> The real Robust Redhorse (see previous entry) was rediscovered after 110 years in the Savannah, Pee Dee, and Oconee rivers of Georgia, North Carolina, and South Carolina. It is similar to River Redhorse (*M. carinatum*) but has 10 (not 9) pelvic rays (Jenkins and Burkhead 1994).

Brassy Jumprock *Moxostoma* species
> See Smallfin Redhorse above.

Grayfin Redhorse *Moxostoma* species
> Still formally undescribed.

Broadtail Madtom *Noturus* species
> Still formally undescribed.

Northern Madtom *Noturus stigmosus* is split into:
> Piebald Madtom *Noturus gladiator*
>> A new species (Thomas and Burr 2004) named for its bold markings. Differs from Northern Madtom by usually more distinct saddles and blotches; dark blotch on anal fin connected to third saddle; and a

much wider dark band that connects the caudal peduncle pigment to the mid-caudal crescent-shaped band. Known from eastern tributaries of the Mississippi River in western Tennessee and Mississippi, primarily in the Wolf, Hatchie, and upper Obion rivers.

Northern Madtom *Noturus stigmosus*

Pygmy Smelt *Osmerus spectrum*
  Now included in Rainbow Smelt *Osmerus mordax*.

Cisco *Coregonus artedi* is split into:
  Cisco *Coregonus artedi*
  Nipigon Cisco *Coregonus nipigon*
    Has more gill rakers (usually over 50) than Cisco or Shortjaw Cisco (Etnier and Skelton 2003). Lake Winnipeg, Manitoba across southern Canada and extreme northern Minnesota to northwestern Quebec.

Arctic Cisco *Coregonus autumnalis* is split into:
  Arctic Cisco *Coregonus autumnalis*
  Bering Cisco *Coregonus laurettae*

Shortjaw Cisco *Coregonus zenithicus* is split into:
  Deepwater Cisco *Coregonus johannae*
    Formerly endemic to lakes Michigan and Huron but not recorded since 1952. Presumed extinct due to overexploitation by commercial fishing, predation by exotic Sea Lamprey, and introgressive hybridization with other ciscos as it became rare. Deepwater Cisco lived at depths of 100 to 500 feet or more. Largest of all Great Lake ciscoes, it averaged about 11 inches in length. It was silvery with a pink iridescence, a green or blue back, and a long narrow head (Parker 1989).
  Shortjaw Cisco *Coregonus zenithicus*

Alaska Whitefish *Coregonus nelsoni*
  Now included in Lake Whitefish *Coregonus clupeaformis*.

Shortnose Cisco *Coregonus reighardi*
  Apparently extinct due to overfishing. Not recorded since 1985. Formerly occurerd in lakes Michigan, Ontario, and Huron. Compared to other *Coregonus* species it had a heavily pigmented short snout (NatureServe 2005).

Golden Trout *Oncorhynchus aguabonita*
  Now included in Rainbow Trout *Oncorhynchus mykiss*.

Angayukaksurak Char *Salvelinus anaktuvukensis*
  Now included in Dolly Varden *Salvelinus malma*.

Inland Silverside *Menidia beryllina* is split into two species (Suttkus and Thompson 2002):
  Mississippi Silverside *Menidia audens*
    Differs from Inland Silverside in having more than 19 predorsal scales, usually 40 or more lateral line scales, and a more elongate body. Recorded from Pearl River above Bogue Chitto River in Louisiana and Mississippi, Mississippi River near Memphis and Vicksburg, and the Big Black River at Edwards, Mississippi.
  Inland Silverside *Menidia beryllina*
    Now considered to be restricted to brackish and tidal waters.

Plains Killifish *Fundulus zebrinus* is split into:
    Northern Plains Killifish *Fundulus kansae*
    Plains Killifish *Fundulus zebrinus*

Banded Topminnow *Fundulus cingulatus* is split into two species (Gilbert et al. 1992):
    Banded Topminnow *Fundulus cingulatus*
        Now considered to occur in the Florida Panhandle east to the Ochlockonee River with a disjunct population in the Suwannee and Waccasassa river drainages. The ranges of Banded Topminnow and Redface Topminnow are in close proximity, if not sympatric, in the Santa Fe River system.
    Redface Topminnow *Fundulus rubrifrons*
        Differs from Banded Topminnow by having five preopercular pores (instead of six), and red pigment on the jaws and sides of the head in breeding males. Occurs in peninsular Florida north to the Okefenoke Swamp and the Altamaha River drainage of Georgia.

Mosquitofish *Gambusia affinis* is split into:
    Western Mosquitofish *Gambusia affinis*
    Eastern Mosquitofish *Gambusia holbrooki*

San Felipe Gambusia *Gambusia clarkhubbsi*
    Presumably, this species survived in low numbers and went undetected until its habitat was apparently improved by the initiation of stream bank protection and reduced nearby fertilizer use in 1997, and a 500-year magnitude flood that scoured the creek bed in 1998. Like Pecos Gambusia but lacks the teardrop mark and black margins of dorsal and caudal fins. Known only from San Felipe Creek, Del Rio, Texas, where the only other congener is the Tex-Mex Gambusia (Garrett and Edwards 2003).

Tex-Mex Gambusia *Gambusia speciosa*
    A member of the *Gambusia affinis* species group known from northern Mexico and recently reported from the Devil's River, Texas. Range is not clearly defined due to nomenclatural confusion within the *G. affinis* species group. Differs from similar *Gambusia* in the structure and shape of the gonopodium (Rauchenberger 1989).

Desert Pupfish *Cyprinodon macularius* is split into:
    Santa Cruz Pupfish *Cyprinodon arcuatus*
        The Santa Cruz Pupfish had a concave dorsal body surface posterior to the dorsal fin origin, and, in breeding males, no yellow orange on the caudal fin or peduncle. It was formerly distributed throughout the upper Santa Cruz River system in Arizona and Sonora. Human impacts to the system reduced its range to the Monkey Spring area. In 1971 the Santa Cruz Pupfish became extinct when the last individuals were eaten by introduced Largemouth Bass (Minckley et al. 2002).
    Sonoyta Pupfish *Cyprinodon eremus*
    Desert Pupfish *Cyprinodon macularius*

Mottled Sculpin *Cottus bairdi* is split into four species:
    Mottled Sculpin *Cottus bairdii*
        Populations other than those below.
    Malheur Sculpin *Cottus bendirei*
        Range and diagnostic characters not yet well defined and may vary with geographic location. In Oregon it is distinguished from Columbia Sculpin by having less than 30 prickles on the left side. Usually found in smaller tributaries and disconnected streams of the Pacific Northwest (Markle and Hill 2000).
    Blue Ridge Sculpin *Cottus caeruleomentum*
        Differs from Mottled Sculpin by having the caudal base band unnotched on one or both sides. There is little overlap in their ranges. Blue Ridge Sculpin occurs in Atlantic slope drainages from the lower

Susquehanna River system in Pennsylvania south to the Roanoke River system in Virginia, and in the Nanticoke River system in Maryland and Delaware (Kinziger et al. 2000).

Columbia Sculpin *Cottus hubbsi*

Range and diagnostic characters not yet well defined and may vary with geographic location. In Oregon it has more than 90 prickles on the left side. Usually found in river main stems of the Pacific Northwest (Markle and Hill 2000).

Longear Sunfish *Lepomis megalotis* is split into:

Longear Sunfish *Lepomis megalotis*

Northern Longear Sunfish *Lepomis peltastes*

Vermilion Darter *Etheostoma chermocki*

Differs from other snubnose darters of the Black Warrior River drainage by breeding males having a broad (not narrow) red band on each of the dorsal fins, two red-orange (not cream-colored) spots on the base of the caudal fin, and a red (not cream-colored) belly and ventral caudal peduncle. Females lack melanophores in the anal fin and do not have a solid band of melanophores below the medial lateral band. The only other *Etheostoma* darter in its range is the very different Redfin Darter. Formerly more widespread, the endangered Vermilion Darter is now restricted to only three miles of urban and suburban stream in the headwaters of Turkey Creek, Jefferson County, Alabama (Boschung et al. 1992).

Firebelly Darter *Etheostoma pyrrhogaster* is split into two species (Powers and Mayden 2003):

Chickasaw Darter *Etheostoma cervus*

Breeding male is straw-colored on the ventral part of the head (where Firebelly Darter has a greenish cast), and lacks the areas of turquoise color seen on the dorsal, anal, and pelvic fins of Firebelly Darter. Endemic to the upper reaches of the Forked Deer River system of western Tennessee.

Firebelly Darter *Etheostoma pyrrhogaster*

See Chickasaw Darter. As now defined, Firebelly Darter is endemic to the upper reaches of the Obion River system in western Tennessee and Kentucky.

Striped Darter *Etheostoma virgatum* is split into three species (Page et al. 2003):

Corrugated Darter *Etheostoma basilare*

All three of these species have multiple thin brown body stripes (most distinct in Corrugated Darter). Their ranges do not overlap. Corrugated Darter has black on first membrane of first dorsal fin, no dark blue margin on caudal and second dorsal fin, and no bright white spots on pectoral fin. Unlike Striped Darter, breeding male Corrugated Darter has yellow-gold spots on the cheek bar. Restricted to the Upper Caney Fork system of the Cumberland River drainage in central Tennessee.

Stone Darter *Etheostoma derivativum*

Unlike Corrugated and Striped darters, Stone Darter has no black (may be slightly dusky) on first membrane of first dorsal fin, and breeding male has dark blue margins on the caudal and second dorsal fins. Lower Cumberland River drainage from Red River system to West Fork Stones River, south-central Kentucky and north-central Tennessee.

Striped Darter *Etheostoma virgatum*

Distinguished from Stone Darter by black on first membrane of first dorsal fin and lack of dark blue margin on caudal and second dorsal fin. Differs from Corrugated Darter by having bright white spots on pectoral fin, and no yellow-gold spots on cheek bar of breeding male. Occurs in Rockcastle River, Buck Creek, and Beaver Creek systems of southeastern Kentucky.

Redfin Darter *Etheostoma whipplei* is split into:

Redspot Darter *Etheostoma artesiae*

Redfin Darter *Etheostoma whipplei*

Greenside Darter *Etheostoma blennioides* is split into:
>   Greenside Darter *Etheostoma blennioides*
>   Tuckasegee Darter *Etheostoma gutselli*

Orangethroat Darter *Etheostoma spectabile* is split into the eight species below (Ceas and Page 1997, unless otherwise noted). However, in the near future, the *E. spectabile* complex will be further divided because two subspecies will probably be elevated to full species status, and at least nine more species will soon be described (Ceas and Burr 2002). Among the undescribed species are the Sheltowee Darter (Dix River system, Kentucky), Ihiyo Darter (middle Cumberland and Caney Fork systems, Tennessee), Ozark Darter (White River system, Arkansas and Missouri), and Mamequit Darter (lower Cumberland River system, Kentucky and Tennessee).

>   Buffalo Darter *Etheostoma bison*
>
>   Breeding male Buffalo Darters are distinguished by having horizontal lines broken into long dashes, and a light tan color on their entire upper sides. Tributaries of the lower Duck and lower Tennessee rivers of Tennessee and (barely) Kentucky.
>
>   Brook Darter *Etheostoma burri*
>
>   Differs from other members of the *E. spectabile* complex by breeding males having an entirely deep red venter, and an alternating diamond and hourglass pattern in the posterior banding. Endemic to the upper Black River system in Missouri, from the headwaters to the Mississippi alluvial plain.
>
>   Strawberry Darter *Etheostoma fragi*
>
>   Breeding males differ from similar species by having orange chevrons on the belly, and a first dorsal fin in which the widest submarginal band is orange. Endemic to the headwaters of the Strawberry River in Missouri and Arkansas.
>
>   Highland Rim Darter *Etheostoma kantuckeense*
>
>   Breeding males have a powder-blue belly unlike any other members of the *E. spectabile* complex. Endemic to the upper Barren River system in Kentucky and Tennessee.
>
>   Headwater Darter *Etheostoma lawrencei*
>
>   Headwater Darter is the only member of the *E. spectabile* complex, besides Shawnee Darter, in which, in the breeding male, the orange on the belly connects to anterior orange interspaces and the alternating orange and blue transverse bars along the entire sides of the body. Differs from Shawnee Darter by molecular characters, usually 13 dorsal rays, and 30 or fewer pored lateral scales. Found in the Salt and upper Green river systems in Kentucky, and the Cumberland River system from Smith County, Tennessee, to near Cumberland Falls, Kentucky (Ceas and Burr 2002).
>
>   Orangethroat Darter *Etheostoma spectabile*
>
>   As defined by Ceas and Page (1997), differs from other members of the *E. spectabile* complex by breeding males having thin, continuous, dark horizontal lines along the body, and two oblong salmon-red patches on the belly.
>
>   Shawnee Darter *Etheostoma tecumsehi*
>
>   Shawnee Darter is the only member of the *E. spectabile* complex, besides Headwater Darter, in which, in the breeding male, the orange on the belly connects to anterior orange interspaces and the alternating orange and blue transverse bars along the entire sides of the body. Differs from Headwater Darter by molecular characters, usually 12 dorsal rays, and 30 or more pored lateral scales. Endemic to the upper Pond River tributaries in Christian, Todd, and Hopkins counties of western Kentucky.
>
>   Current Darter *Etheostoma uniporum*
>
>   Differs from other members of the *E. spectabile* complex in having one posterior infraorbital pore and, in breeding males, a suprabasal blue band in the first dorsal fin that is the widest, and iridescent turquoise transverse bars that nearly match the diagonal of the scales in their angle. Found in tributaries of the Black River system from Cane Creek in Butler County, Missouri, to Flat Creek in Lawrence County, Arkansas.

Lollypop Darter *Etheostoma neopterum* is split into four species (Page et al. 1992):

Relict Darter *Etheostoma chienense*

Separated from similar species by having two branches for each dorsal fin ray, and, in breeding males, small white knobs on the tip of each dorsal ray, and four or five rows of clear ovals on the second dorsal fin. Endemic to the Bayou de Chien, a small stream system in extreme western Kentucky.

Lollypop Darter *Etheostoma neopterum*

Range of redefined Lollypop Darter is now restricted to the Shoal Creek system of Alabama and Tennessee.

Guardian Darter *Etheostoma oophylax*

Breeding males are separated by the presence of two to four rows of large round clear spots or "windows" on the membranes between rays of the second dorsal fin. This species represents the largest portion of the former Lollypop Darter's range. Except for the Duck River system, it inhabits the lower Tennessee River system from Lick Creek, Decatur County, and Lick Creek, Perry County, Tennessee, north through Kentucky to the Ohio River.

Egg-mimic Darter *Etheostoma pseudovulatum*

Best identified by range and two or three yellow bars on each ray above the fin membrane on the second dorsal fin of breeding males. Restricted to Piney River, Beaverdam Creek, Happy Hollow Creek, and Little Piney Creek system—all tributaries of the Duck River in Tennessee.

Tippecanoe Darter *Etheostoma tippecanoe* is split into:

Golden Darter *Etheostoma denoncourti*

Differs from Tippecanoe Darter by having scales on the cheek, and a light line on the body anterior to the dorsal fin. Endemic to the Tennessee River drainage including the Duck, Buffalo, and Sequatchie river drainages in Tennessee, and the Clinch River drainage in Tennessee and Virginia (Kinziger et al. 2001; Stauffer and van Snik 1997; Skelton and Etnier 2000).

Tippecanoe Darter *Etheostoma tippecanoe*

Greenbreast Darter *Etheostoma jordani* is split into four species (Wood and Mayden 1993):

Tuskaloosa Darter *Etheostoma douglasi*

Separated from other members of the *E. jordani* species group by lack of red spots on the flanks, lack of opercular scales, and lack of red on the lips or anal fin. Occurs only in the upper Black Warrior River system in Alabama.

Greenbreast Darter *Etheostoma jordani*

Now considered to be restricted to populations in the Coosa, Cahaba, and Tallapoosa river systems below the Fall Line in Alabama, Georgia, and Tennessee.

Etowah Darter *Etheostoma etowahae*

Distinguished from other members of the *E. jordani* species group by lack of red spots on flanks, lack of red on anal fin or lips, and the presence of opercular scales. Found in the Upper Etowah River system (Upper Etowah River, Long Swamp and Amicalola creeks) in northern Georgia.

Lipstick Darter *Etheostoma chuckwachatte*

Compared to similar species in the *E. jordani* species group, Lipstick Darter has red spots on the flanks, a red band on the anal fin, red lips, and opercular scales. Known from the Tallapoosa River system above the Fall Line in Alabama and Georgia.

Barrens Darter *Etheostoma forbesi*

Populations of this species were formerly included in Spottail Darter or Dirty Darter. Separated from all similar species except Crown Darter by breeding males having a yellow margin on the second dorsal fin. The ranges of Crown and Barrens darters do not overlap. Barrens Darter is known only from the Caney Fork system of the Barren Fork Collins River in Cannon County, Tennessee, although hybrids between Barrens and Blackfin darters have been found in the adjacent upper Duck River system (Page et al. 1992).

Goldstripe Darter *Etheostoma parvipinne* is split into:
    Goldstripe Darter *Etheostoma parvipinne*
    Rush Darter *Etheostoma phytophilum*
        Distinguished from Goldstripe Darter by its less intense pigmentation of the brown areas and lateral stripe, and by having fewer than 48 lateral line scales, fewer than 14 transverse scales, and fewer than 23 caudal peduncle circumferential scales. Known from three widely separated locations in the upper Black Warrior River system above the Fall Line in Alabama (Bart and Taylor 1999).

Coosa Darter *Etheostoma coosae* is split into:
    Coosa Darter *Etheostoma coosae*
    Cherokee Darter *Etheostoma scotti*
        Differs from Coosa Darter by having a broad brick-red band (almost covering the entire fin), instead of a narrow red band, in the first dorsal fin of breeding males. Compared to the Holiday Darter (*E. brevirostrum*) the Cherokee Darter has a longer snout and no red band on the anal fin. Endemic to upland streams of the middle Etowah River system in northern Georgia. Range does not overlap that of Coosa and Holiday darters (Bauer et al. 1995).

Tennessee Snubnose Darter *Etheostoma simoterum* is split into six species (see www.wildlifelist.org for information on undescribed species):
    Cumberland Snubnose Darter *Etheostoma atripinne*
        Differs from Tennessee Snubsose Darter by more green and less orange below, and olive-green side blotches. Roaring River to Mansker Creek in the Nashville Basin, Tennessee (Page and Burr, forthcoming).
    Tennessee Snubnose Darter *Etheostoma simoterum*
    Tennessee Darter *Etheostoma* species
    Duck Darter *Etheostoma* species
    Westrim Darter *Etheostoma* species
    Eastrim Darter *Etheostoma* species

Coastal Plain Darter *Etheostoma* species is split into three allopatric species:
    Coastal Darter *Etheostoma colorosum*
        As now defined by Suttkus and Bailey (1993) Coastal Darter cannot be identified by the illustration of Coastal Plain Darter in Page and Burr (1991). Breeding male Coastal Darters are identified by the presence of orange to red-orange small spots running along the side, just above the lateral line brown blotches, from the base of the caudal fin to the base of the pectoral fin. Restricted to coastal drainages of southern Alabama and the adjacent portion of the Florida Panhandle (Perdido, Escambia, Blackwater, Yellow, and Choctawhatchee river drainages).
    Tombigbee Darter *Etheostoma lachneri*
        Identified by breeding males that have bright orange areas between slightly angled green bars on the sides and caudal peduncle. Restricted to the Tombigbee River system in Mississippi and Alabama (Suttkus et al. 1994a).
    Alabama Darter *Etheostoma ramseyi*
        Identified by male breeding coloration in which the side blotches and dorsal saddles are connected, and the orange areas of the sides of the belly extend upward between the posterior side blotches. Endemic, but widespread, within the Alabama River system, Alabama, mostly below the Fall Line but relatively common in headwater tributaries to the Cahaba River above the Fall Line (Suttkus et al. 1994a).

Sunburst Darter *Etheostoma* species
        Still formally undescribed.

Channel Darter *Percina copelandi* is split into three species (Suttkus et al. 1994b):

Pearl Darter *Percina aurora*

Differs from Channel Darter by its larger size (to 57 mm in females and 64 mm in males), lighter pigmentation, fully scaled cheeks, and lack of turbercles (in breeding males). Only known from the Pearl and Pascagoula river drainages in Mississippi and Louisiana.

Coal Darter *Percina brevicauda*

Differs from Channel Darter by having short fins with tubercular ridges, naked cheeks, and greater pigmentation. Endemic to Alabama where it is found in the Cahaba, Coosa, and Black Warrior river systems.

Channel Darter *Percina copelandi*

Logperch *Percina caprodes* is split into five species:

Southern Logperch *Percina austroperca*

Differs from similar *Percina* by usually having 15 pectoral fin rays, more than 87 lateral line scales, and more than 59 diagonal line scales (anal fin to first dorsal fin, plus anal fin to second dorsal fin, plus above lateral line). Found in the Choctawhatchee and Escambia river drainages of Florida and Alabama (Thompson 1995).

Logperch *Percina caprodes*

Mobile Logperch *Percina kathae*

Has a very wide red submarginal band on the first dorsal fin, and wide body bars. Looks most like Ozark and Texas logperches but it lacks the black breeding colors of the later species, and is distantly allopatric from both. Endemic to the Mobile Bay system, mostly above the Fall Line, in Mississippi, Alabama, Georgia, and extreme southeastern Tennessee (Thompson 1997b).

Chesapeake Logperch *Percina nebulosa*

See www.wildlifelist.org for information.

Gulf Logperch *Percina suttkusi*

Has a narrow red submarginal band in the first dorsal fin and narrow dark brown vertical bars on the sides. Most similar to the allopatric Southern Logperch but has fewer than 15 pectoral fin rays and fewer than 59 diagonal line scales (anal fin to first dorsal fin, plus anal fin to second dorsal fin, plus above lateral line). Found in Gulf Coast drainages from Lake Pontchartrain, Louisiana, through Mississippi to the Alabama River drainage in Alabama (Thompson 1997a).

Shield Darter *Percina peltata* is split into two species (Goodin et al. 1998):

Chainback Darter *Percina nevisense*

Most Chainback Darters have cheek scales, most Shield Darters do not. Chainback Darter inhabits the Roanoke-Chowan River drainage, Virginia, south to the Neuse River drainage, North Carolina.

Shield Darter *Percina peltata*

Now considered to occur only from the James River drainage, Virginia, north to the Hudson River drainage, New York.

Muscadine Darter *Percina* species is split into three species (see www.wildlifelist.org for more information):

Muscadine Darter *Percina* species

Only found in the upper Tallapoosa River drainage in Alabama and Georgia.

Coosa Bridled Darter *Percina* species

Endemic to the Coosa River drainage in Tennessee and Georgia.

Warrior Bridled Darter *Percina* species

Endemic to the upper Black Warrior River drainage in Alabama

Other Scientific Name Changes

Name in Page and Burr (1991)	Name in This Book
Acipenser oxyrhynchus	*Acipenser oxyrinchus*
Awaous tajasica	*Awaous banana*
Catostomus clarki	*Catostomus clarkii*
Catostomus commersoni	*Catostomus commersonii*
Cichlasoma severum	*Heros severus*
Cottus bairdi	*Cottus bairdii*
Cottus beldingi	*Cottus beldingii*
Cottus pygmaeus	*Cottus paulus*
Diapterus plumieri	*Eugerres plumieri*
Elassoma species (Spring Pygmy Sunfish)	*Elassoma alabamae*
Eleotris pisonis (misidentified)	*Eleotris amblyopsis*
Ericymba buccata	*Notropis buccatus*
Etheostoma beani	*Ammocrypta beanii*
Etheostoma bifascia	*Ammocrypta bifascia*
Etheostoma chlorosomum	*Etheostoma chlorosoma*
Etheostoma clarum	*Ammocrypta clara*
Etheostoma meridianum	*Ammocrypta meridiana*
Etheostoma pellucidum	*Ammocrypta pellucida*
Etheostoma species (Ellijay Darter)	*Etheostoma brevirostrum*
Etheostoma species (Duskytail Darter)	*Etheostoma percnurum*
Etheostoma species (Crown Darter)	*Etheostoma corona*
Etheostoma species (Yazoo Darter)	*Etheostoma raneyi*
Etheostoma species (Warrior Darter)	*Etheostoma bellator*
Etheostoma species (Tallapoosa Darter)	*Etheostoma tallapoosae*
Etheostoma vivax	*Ammocrypta vivax*
Forbesichthys agassizi	*Forbesichthys agassizii*
Fundulus notti	*Fundulus nottii*
Gila copei	*Lepidomeda copei*
Gila orcutti	*Gila orcuttii*
Gobioides broussoneti	*Gobioides broussonetii*
Gobionellus boleosoma	*Ctenogobius boleosoma*
Gobionellus shufeldti	*Ctenogobius shufeldti*
Hybopsis labrosa	*Cyprinella labrosa*
Hybopsis zanema	*Cyprinella zanema*
Hysterocarpus traski	*Hysterocarpus traskii*
Lampetra ayresi	*Lampetra ayresii*
Lampetra japonica	*Lampetra camtschatica*
Micropterus species (Shoal Bass)	*Micropterus cataractae*
Micropterus treculi	*Micropterus treculii*
Myoxocephalus thompsoni	*Myoxocephalus thompsonii*
Notropis ludibundus	*Notropis stramineus*
Notropis species (Palezone Shiner)	*Notropis albizonatus*
Notropis tristis	*Notropis topeka*
Oncorhynchus clarki	*Oncorhynchus clarkii*
Oostethus brachyurus	*Microphis brachyurus*
Percina ouachitae	*Percina vigil*
Percina species (Frecklebelly Darter)	*Percina stictogaster*
Prosopium coulteri	*Prosopium coulterii*
Prosopium gemmiferum	*Prosopium gemmifer*

Stizostedion canadense	*Sander canadensis*
Stizostedion vitreum	*Sander vitreus*
Tilapia zilli	*Tilapia zillii*
Xiphophorus helleri	*Xiphophorus hellerii*

Other English Name Changes

Name in Page and Burr (1991)	Name in This Book
Lake Lamprey	Vancouver Lamprey
Edwards Plateau Shiner	Plateau Shiner
Cutlips Minnow	Cutlip Minnow
Sacramento Squawfish	Sacramento Pikeminnow
Colorado Squawfish	Colorado Pikeminnow
Northern Squawfish	Northern Pikeminnow
Umpqua Squawfish	Umpqua Pikeminnow
West Mexican Redhorse	Mexican Redhorse
Black Jumprock	Blacktip Jumprock
Suckermouth Redhorse	V-lip Redhorse
Rivulus	Mangrove Rivulus
Northern Starhead Topminnow	Starhead Topminnow
Eastern Starhead Topminnow	Russetfin Topminnow
Southern Starhead Topminnow	Bayou Topminnow
Pahrump Killifish	Pahrump Poolfish
Ash Meadows Killifish	Ash Meadows Poolfish
Finescale Saddled Darter	Candy Darter
Ellijay Darter	Holiday Darter
Fat Snook	Smallscale Fat Snook
Snook	Common Snook
Radiated Ptero	Orinoco Sailfin Catfish
Peacock Cichlid	Butterfly Peacock Cichlid
Spinycheek Sleeper	Largescaled Spinycheek Sleeper

Marine Species Added or Removed from Freshwater List

Smalltooth Sawfish	*Pristis pectinata*	added
Capelin	*Mallotus villosus*	added
Rough Silverside	*Membras martinica*	added
Spotfin Killifish	*Fundulus luciae*	added
Bayou Killifish	*Fundulus pulvereus*	added
Mangrove Gambusia	*Gambusia rhizophorae*	added
Blackspotted Stickleback	*Gasterosteus wheatlandi*	removed
Irish Pompano	*Diapterus auratus*	added
Tidewater Mojarra	*Eucinostomus harengulus*	added
Spotfin Mojarra	*Eucinostomus argenteus*	removed
Shiner Perch	*Cymatogaster aggregata*	added
Pacific Fat Sleeper	*Dormitator latifrons*	removed
Mexican Goby	*Ctenogobius claytonii*	added
Slashcheek Goby	*Ctenogobius pseudofasciatus*	added
Green Goby	*Microgobius thalassinus*	removed
Code Goby	*Gobiosoma robustum*	removed
Chameleon Goby	*Tridentiger trigonocephalus*	removed

Alien Species Added or Removed from Freshwater List

Clown Knifefish	*Chitala ornata*	added
Silver Carp	*Hypophthalmichthys molitrix*	added
Bighead Carp	*Hypophthalmichthys nobilis*	added
Southern Striped Raphael	*Platydoras armatulus*	added
Brown Hoplo	*Hoplosternum littorale*	added
Southern Sailfin Catfish	*Pterygoplichthys anisitsi*	added
Vermiculated Sailfin Catfish	*Pterygoplichthys disjunctivus*	added
Amazon Sailfin Catfish	*Pterygoplichthys pardalis*	added
Giant Rivulus	*Rivulus hartii*	added
Mexican Molly	*Poecilia sphenops*	added
Asian Swamp Eel	*Monopterus albus*	added
Zander	*Sander lucioperca*	added
Orangemouth Corvina	*Cynoscion xanthulus*	added
Yellowbelly Cichlid	*Cichlasoma salvini*	added
Jewelfish	*Hemichromis bimaculatus*	removed
African Jewelfish	*Hemichromis letourneuxi*	added
Nile Tilapia	*Oreochromis niloticus*	added
Round Goby	*Neogobius melanostomus*	added
Tubenose Goby	*Proterorhinus marmoratus*	added
Shokihaze Goby	*Tridentiger barbatus*	added
Shimofuri Goby	*Tridentiger bifasciatus*	added
Bullseye Snakehead	*Channa marulius*	added

Butterflies

As compared to:

Butterflies of North America (Brock and Kaufman 2003). Note that this field guide was published two years after the NABA list, so a number of these differences may eventually be accepted by NABA.

Taxonomic Differences

Appalachian Tiger Swallowtail *Papilio appalachiensis*
   Not separated from Eastern Tiger Swallowtail on the NABA list.

Harford's Sulphur *Colias harfordii*
   Treated as *Colias alexandra harfordii*, a subspecies of Queen Alexandra's Sulphur, on the NABA list.

Booth's Sulphur *Colias tyche*
   Not treated as a species on the NABA list. It may be a hybrid between Hecla Sulphur (*C. hecla*) and Labrador Sulphur (*C. nastes*).

Xerces Blue *Glaucopsyche xerces*
   Extinct due to urbanization. Male was lilac-blue above, grayish-brown below with mostly round white dots or black dots with white rings. Females were brown above. Formerly inhabited coastal sand dunes now covered by San Francisco (see Pyle 1981).

Helicta Satyr *Neonympha helicta*
   Included in Georgia Satyr (*N. areolata*) on the NABA list.

Sonoran Banded-Skipper *Autochton pseudocellus*

Omitted in Brock and Kaufman (2003) because it has not been observed north of Mexico since 1936. Formerly occured in the Huachuca and Chiricahua mountains of southeastern Arizona. See Glassberg (2001) or Opler (1999).

Loammi Skipper *Atrytonopsis loammi*

Treated as *Atrytonopsis hianna loammi*, a subspecies of Dusted Skipper, in the NABA list.

Other Scientific Name Changes

Name in Brock and Kaufman (2003)	Name in This Book
Chlosyne melitaeoides	*Chlosyne marina*
Copaeodes aurantiaca	*Copaeodes aurantiacus*
Copaeodes minima	*Copaeodes minimus*
Cyclargus thomasi	*Hemiargus thomasi*
Cyclargus ammon	*Hemiargus ammon*
Ganyra howarthi	*Ganyra howarthii*
Heliopyrgus domicella	*Heliopetes domicella*
Phocides palemon	*Phocides polybius*
Polythrix mexicana	*Polythrix mexicanus*
Satyrium fuliginosum	*Satyrium fuliginosa*
Speyeria edwardsi	*Speyeria edwardsii*
Thessalia (all five species)	*Chlosyne* (species names unchanged)
Thorybes mexicana	*Thorybes mexicanus*

Dragonflies and Damselflies

As compared to:
Dragonflies Through Binoculars (Dunkle 2000).
At the time of writing there is no continent-wide field guide available for damselflies although at least one will be published soon. Some of the more recent changes, which may not be in your regional guide, are found below.

Fauna and Taxonomic Changes

Common Spreadwing *Lestes disjunctus* is split into:
Southern Spreadwing *Lestes australis*
Common Spreadwing *Lestes disjunctus*

Yaqui Dancer *Argia carlcooki*

Described in 1995 from Mexican specimens, it was recently found in Arizona.

Lucifer Damsel *Chrysobasis lucifer*

A tropical species recently found in Big Cypress National Preserve in southern Florida (Paulson 2000).

Northern Bluet *Enallagma cyathigerum* is split into:
Northern Bluet *Enallagma annexum*
a Eurasian species *Enallagma cyathigerum*
Vernal Bluet *Enallagma vernale*

Cream-tipped Swampdamsel *Leptobasis melinogaster*
> First described in 2002 from two specimens in southern Mexico. The only other known occurrence was recorded from southern Texas in 2004 (D. Paulson, pers. comm.).

Tropical Sprite *Nehalennia minuta*
> A tropical species recently found breeding on Big Pine Key in southern Florida (Paulson 2000).

Ringed Forceptail *Phyllocycla breviphylla*
> Recently recorded in south Texas.

Least Clubtail *Stylogomphus albistylus* is split into:
> Eastern Least Clubtail *Stylogomphus albistylus*
>> Now considered to range east of a line from northern Wisconsin to Ohio and northwestern Alabama (Cook and Laudermilk 2004).
>
> Interior Least Clubtail *Stylogomphus sigmastylus*
>> Compared to Eastern Least Clubtail, has cerci that are shorter and thicker at the base, and an epiproct that is wider than long and has a shallower, U-shaped (not V-shaped) median cleft. Mostly found west of the Appalachians mainly in Kentucky, Missouri, Arkansas, and Tennessee (Cook and Laudermilk 2004).

Ouachita Spiketail *Cordulegaster talaria*
> Discovered in 1990 and described in 2004 (Tennessen). Males are similar to those of Delta-spotted and Brown spiketails except that the dorsolateral yellow bands have an inward pointing dark yellow projection on abdominal segment two; and on abdominal segment four the anterolateral yellow area extends to the anterior margin of the segment. Females are like those of Delta-spotted Spiketail but have a flat (not convex) occipital crest when viewed from the front. So far, the Ouachita Spiketail is only known from the Ouachita Mountains of western Arkansas.

Stripe-winged Baskettail *Epitheca costalis* is split into:
> Stripe-winged Baskettail *Epitheca costalis*
> Dot-winged Baskettail *Epitheca petechialis*

Plateau Dragonlet *Erythrodiplax connata* is split into:
> a South American dragonlet species *Erythrodiplax connata* (Peru to Chile)
> Plateau Dragonlet *Erythrodiplax basifusca* (as described in Dunkle 2000)

Antillean Skimmer *Orthemis* species
> An undescribed or unidentified species common in southern Florida. The all-red males differ from male Roseate Skimmers in having red (not purple) face and eyes. Females have even (not irregular) stripes on the sides of the thorax, and lack dark spots on the thoracic venter (D. Paulson, pers. comm.).

Cherry-faced Meadowhawk *Sympetrum internum* is split into:
> Cherry-faced Meadowhawk *Sympetrum internum*
> Jane's Meadowhawk *Sympetrum janeae*

Band-winged Meadowhawk *Sympetrum semicinctum* is split into:
> Western Meadowhawk *Sympetrum occidentale*
> Band-winged Meadowhawk *Sympetrum semicinctum*

Other Scientific Name Changes

Name in Dunkle (2000)	Name in This Book
Aeshna californica	*Rhionaeschna californica*
Aeshna dugesi	*Rhionaeschna dugesi*
Aeshna multicolor	*Rhionaeschna multicolor*
Aeshna mutata	*Rhionaeschna mutata*
Aeshna psilus	*Rhionaeschna psilus*
Coryphaeschna luteipennis	*Remartinia luteipennis*
Ophiogomphus species (Sand Snaketail)	*Ophiogomphus smithi*
Libellula deplanata	*Ladona deplanata*
Libellula exusta	*Ladona exusta*
Libellula julia	*Ladona julia*
Libellula lydia	*Plathemis lydia*
Libellula subornata	*Plathemis subornata*
Neurocordulia species (Broad-tailed Shadowdragon)	*Neurocordulia michaeli*

Other English Name Changes

Name in Dunkle (2000)	Name in This Book
Sand Snaketail	Sioux Snaketail
Illinois River Cruiser	Swift River Cruiser
Narrow-winged Skimmer	Gray-waisted Skimmer
Red-waisted Whiteface	Belted Whiteface
Orange-bellied Skimmer	Carmine Skimmer
Yellow-legged Meadowhawk	Autumn Meadowhawk

Works Cited

Alderfer, J., editor. 2006. *Complete birds of North America*. Washington, D.C.: National Geographic Society.

Alexander, L. F. 1996. A morphometric analysis of geographic variation within *Sorex monticolus* (Insectivora: Soricidae). *University of Kansas Museum of Natural History Miscellaneous Publication* 88: 1–54.

American Birding Association (ABA). 2002. *ABA checklist: Birds of the continental United States and Canada*. 6th ed. Colorado Springs, Colo.: American Birding Association.

American Ornithologists' Union (AOU). 1998. *Check-list of North American birds*, 7th ed. Washington, D.C.: American Ornithologists' Union.

———. 2000. Forty-second supplement to the American Ornithologists' Union *Check-list of North American birds*. *Auk* 117: 847–58.

AmphibiaWeb. 2006. Information on amphibian biology and conservation. [web application]. Berkeley, Calif.: AmphibiaWeb. Available: http://amphibiaweb.org/. Accessed: 2006.

Anderson, E. 1984. Who's who in the Pleistocene: A mammalian bestiary. In *Quaternary extinctions: A prehistoric revolution*, ed. P. S. Martin and R. G. Klein, 40–89. Tucson: University of Arizona Press.

Anderson, J. A., and S. G. Tilley. 2003. Systematics of the *Desmognathus ochrophaeus* complex in the Cumberland Plateau of Tennessee. *Herpetological Monographs* 17: 75–110.

Arizona Game and Fish Department. 2003. *Uma notata rufopunctata*. Unpublished abstract compiled and edited by the Heritage Data Management System, Arizona Game and Fish Department, Phoenix, Ariz.

Axtell, R. W. 1998. Interpretive atlas of Texas lizards. No. 18, *Holbrookia maculata* Girard: 1–19. Privately published.

Baker, R. J., L. C. Bradley, R. D. Bradley, J. W. Dragoo, M. D. Engstrom, R. S. Hoffmann, C. A. Jones, F. Reid, D. W. Rice, and C. Jones. 2003a. Revised checklist of North American mammals north of Mexico, 2003. *Occasional Papers, The Museum of Texas Tech University* 229: 1–23.

Baker, R. J., M. B. O'Neill, and L. R. McAliley. 2003b. A new species of desert shrew, *Notiosorex*, based on nuclear and mitochondrial sequence data. *Occasional Papers, The Museum of Texas Tech University* 222: 1–12.

Banks, R. C., C. Cicero, J. L. Dunn, A. W. Kratter, P. C. Rasmussen, J. V. Remsen Jr., J. D. Rising, and D. F. Stotz. 2002. Forty-third supplement to the American Ornithologists' Union *Check-list of North American birds*. *Auk* 119: 897–906.

———. 2003. Forty-fourth supplement to the American Ornithologists' Union *Check-list of North American birds*. *Auk* 120: 923–31.

———. 2004. Forty-fifth supplement to the American Ornithologists' Union *Check-list of North American birds*. *Auk* 121(3): 985–95.

———. 2005. Forty-sixth supplement to the American Ornithologists' Union *Check-list of North American birds*. *Auk* 122(3): 1026–31.

Barlow, C. 2000. *The ghosts of evolution: Nonsensical fruit, missing partners, and other ecological anachronisms*. New York: Basic Books.

Bart, H. L., Jr., and M. S. Taylor. 1999. Systematic review of subgenus *Fuscatelum* of *Etheostoma* with description of a new species from the upper Black Warrior River system, Alabama. *Tulane Studies in Zoology and Botany* 31: 23–50.

Baskin, J. A. 1995. The giant flightless bird *Titanis walleri* (Aves: Phorusrhacidae) from the Pleistocene coastal plain of south Texas. *Journal of Vertebrate Paleontology* 15(4): 842–44.

Bauer, B. H., D. A. Etnier, and N. M. Burkhead. 1995. *Etheostoma* (*Ulocentra*) *scotti* (Osteichthyes: Percidae), a new darter from the Etowah River system in Georgia. *Bulletin of the Alabama Museum of Natural History* 17: 1–16.

BirdLife International. 2000. *Threatened birds of the world.* Barcelona and Cambridge, UK: Lynx Edicions and BirdLife International.

Black, D. W., J. E. Reading, and H. G. Savage. 1998. Archaeological records of the extinct Sea Mink, *Mustela macrodon* (Carnivora: Mustelidae), from Canada. *Canadian Field-Naturalist* 112: 45–49.

Boschung, H. T., R. L. Mayden, and J. R. Tomelleri. 1992. *Etheostoma chermocki*, a new species of darter (Teleostei: Percidae) from the Black Warrior River drainage of Alabama. *Bulletin of the Alabama Museum of Natural History* 13: 11–20.

Bowers, J. H. 1974. Genetic compatibility of *Peromyscus maniculatus* and *Peromyscus melanotis*, as indicated by breeding studies and morphometrics. *Journal of Mammalogy* 55(4): 720–37.

Boyeskorov, G. 1999. New data on Moose (*Alces*, Artiodactyla) systematics. *Saugetierkundliche Mitteilungen* 44(1): 3–13.

Briggs, J. C. 1986. Introduction to the zoogeography of North American fishes. In *The zoogeography of North American freshwater fishes*, ed. C. H. Hocutt and E. O. Wiley, 1–16. New York: John Wiley and Sons.

Brock, J. P., and K. Kaufman. 2003. *Butterflies of North America.* New York: Houghton Mifflin.

Broughton, J. M. 2004. Prehistoric human impacts on California birds: evidence from the Emeryville Shellmound avifauna. *Ornithological Monographs* 56: 1–90.

Brown, J. H., and M. V. Lomolino. 1998. *Biogeography.* 2nd ed. Sunderland, Mass.: Sinauer Associates.

Brunelle, P. 2000. A new species of *Neurocordulia* (Odonata: Anisoptera: Corduliidae) from eastern North America. *Canadian Entomologist* 132: 39–48.

Burbrink, F. T. 2001. Systematics of the Eastern Ratsnake complex (*Elaphe obsoleta*). *Herpetological Monographs* 15: 1–53.

———. 2002. Phylogeographic analysis of the Cornsnake (*Elaphe guttata*) complex as inferred from maximum likelihood and Bayesian analyses. *Molecular Phylogenetics and Evolution* 25: 465–76.

Burr, B. M., and R. L. Mayden. 1999. A new species of *Cycleptus* (Cypriniformes: Catostomidae) from Gulf Slope drainages of Alabama, Mississippi, and Louisiana, with a review of the distribution, biology, and conservation status of the genus. *Bulletin of the Alabama Museum of Natural History* 20: 19–57.

Byers, J. A. 1997. *The American Pronghorn: Social adaptations and the ghosts of predators past.* Chicago: University of Chicago Press.

Camp, C. D., S. G. Tilley, R. M. Austin Jr., and J. L. Marshall. 2002. A new species of black-bellied salamander (genus *Desmognathus*) from the Appalachian Mountains of Northern Georgia. *Herpetologica* 58(4): 471–84.

Caterino, M., J. Glassberg, and J. Heraty. 2003. Report of the NABA Names Committee. *American Butterflies* 11(2): 24–27.

Ceas, P. A., and B. M. Burr. 2002. *Etheostoma lawrencei*, a new species of darter in the *E. spectabile* species complex (Percidae: subgenus *Oligocephalus*), from Kentucky and Tennessee. *Ichthyological Exploration of Freshwaters* 13(3): 203–16.

Ceas, P. A., and L. M. Page. 1997. Systematic studies of the *Etheostoma spectabile* complex (Percidae; subgenus *Oligocephalus*), with descriptions of four new species. *Copeia* 1997(3): 496–522.

Chippindale, P. T., A. H. Price, and D. M. Hillis. 1993. A new species of perennibranchiate salamander (*Eurycea*: Plethodontidae) from Austin, Texas. *Herpetologica* 49: 248–59.

Chippindale, P. T., A. H. Price, J. J. Wiens, and D. M. Hillis. 2000. Phylogenetic relationships and systematic revision of central Texas hemidactyliine plethodontid salamanders. *Herpetological Monographs* 14: 1–80.

Churcher, C. S. 1984. *Sangamona*: The furtive deer. In *Contributions in Quaternary vertebrate paleontology: A volume in memorial to John E. Guilday*, ed. H. H. Genoways and M. R. Dawson, 233–40. Carnegie Museum of Natural History Special Publication 8.

Churcher, C. S., and R. L. Peterson. 1982. Chronologic and environmental implications of a new genus of fossil deer from late Wisconsin deposits at Toronto, Canada. *Quaternary Research* 18: 184–95.

Conant, R., and J. T. Collins. 1998. *A field guide to reptiles and amphibians: Eastern and central North America.* New York: Houghton Mifflin.

Cook, C., and E. L. Laudermilk. 2004. *Stylogomphus sigmastylus* sp. nov., a new North American dragonfly previously confused with *S. albistylus* (Odonata: Gomphidae). *International Journal of Odonatology* 7(1): 3–24.

Coyne, J. A., and H. A. Orr. 2004. *Speciation*. Sunderland, Mass.: Sinauer Associates.

Crother, B. I., J. Boundy, J. A. Campbell, K. DeQuieroz, D. Frost, D. M. Green, R. Highton, J. B. Iverson, R. W. McDiarmid, P. A. Meylan, T. W. Reeder, M. E. Seidel, J. W. Sites Jr., S. G. Tilley, and D. B. Wake. 2003. Scientific and standard English names of amphibians and reptiles of North America north of Mexico: update. *Herpetological Review* 34: 196–203.

Crother, B. I., J. Boundy, J. A. Campbell, K. DeQuieroz, D. Frost, R. Highton, J. B. Iverson, P. A. Meylan, T. W. Reeder, M. E. Seidel, J. W. Sites Jr., T. W. Taggart, S. G. Tilley, and D. B. Wake. 2000. Scientific and standard English names of amphibians and reptiles of North America north of Mexico, with comments regarding confidence in our understanding. *Society for the Study of Amphibians and Reptiles Herpetological Circular* 29.

Dalebout, M. L., J. G. Mead, C. S. Baker, A. N. Baker, and A. L. van Helden. 2002. A new species of beaked whale *Mesoplodon perrini* sp. n. (Cetacea: Ziphiidae) discovered through phylogenetic analyses of mitochondrial DNA sequences. *Marine Mammal Science* 18(3): 577–608.

Darwin, C. 1859. *On the origin of species by means of natural selection or the preservation of favored races in the struggle for life*. London: J. Murray.

Diamond, J. M. 1989. Quaternary megafaunal extinctions: variations on a theme by Paganini. *Journal of Archaeological Science* 16: 167–75.

Dickinson, E. C., ed. 2003. *The Howard and Moore complete checklist of the birds of the world*. Princeton, N.J.: Princeton University Press.

Dokuchaev, N. E. 1997. A new species of shrew (Soricidae, Insectivora) from Alaska. *Journal of Mammalogy* 78(3): 811–17.

Domning, D. P. 1970. Sirenian evolution in the North Pacific and the origin of Steller's sea cow. *Proc. 7th ann. conf. biol., sonar and diving mammals*, Stanford Res. Inst. 970: 217–20.

Donlan, J., H. W. Greene, J. Berger, C. E. Bock, J. H. Bock, D. A. Burney, J. A. Estes, D. Foreman, P. S. Martin, G. W. Roemer, F. A. Smith, M. E. Soulé. 2005. Re-wilding North America. *Nature* 436: 913–14.

Dragonfly Society of the Americas. 2005. The Odonata of North America <www.ups.edu/biology/museum/NAdragons>, accessed September 2005.

Dudley, J. P. 1996. Mammoths, gomphotheres, and the Great American Faunal Interchange. In *The Proboscidea: Evolution and palaeoecology of elephants and their relatives*, ed. J. Shoshani and P. Tassy, 289–95. New York: Oxford University Press.

Duellman, W. E., and S. S. Sweet. 1999. Distribution patterns of amphibians in the Nearctic Region of North America. In *Patterns of distribution of amphibians: A global perspective*, ed. W. E. Duellman, 31–109. Baltimore: Johns Hopkins University Press.

Dunkle, S. W. 2000. *Dragonflies through binoculars: A field guide to dragonflies of North America*. New York: Oxford University Press.

———. 2004. Critical species of Odonata in North America. *International Journal of Odonatology* 7(2): 149–62.

Edwards, C. W., C. F. Fulhorst, and R. D. Bradley. 2001. Molecular phylogenetics of the *Neotoma albigula* species group: further evidence of a paraphyletic assemblage. *Journal of Mammalogy* 82(2): 267–79.

Eisenhour, D. J. 1997. Systematics, variation, and speciation of the *Macrhybopsis aestivalis* complex (Cypriniformes: Cyprinidae) west of the Mississippi River. Unpublished Ph.D. Dissertation, Southern Illinois University, Carbondale.

———. 1999. Systematics of *Macrhybopsis tetranema* (Cypriniformes: Cyprinidae). *Copeia* 1999(4): 969–80.

Elliot, D. G. 1903. Description of apparently new species and subspecies of mammals from California, Oregon, the Kenai Peninsula, Alaska, and Lower California, Mexico. *Field Columbian Museum Publication* 74, Zoological Serial 3: 153–73.

Emslie, S. D. 1998. Avian community, climate, and sea-level changes in the Plio-Pleistocene of the Florida peninsula. *Ornithological Monographs* no. 50.

Etnier, D. A., and C. E. Skelton. 2003. Analysis of three cisco forms (*Coregonus*, Salmonidae) from Lake Saganaga and adjacent lakes near the Minnesota/Ontario border. *Copeia* 2003(4): 739–49.

Findley, J. S., and C. Jones. 1967. Taxonomic relationships of bats of the species *Myotis fortidens*, *M. lucifugus*, and *M. occultus*. *Journal of Mammalogy* 48(3): 429–44.

Fisher, D. C. 1996. Testing late Pleistocene extinction mechanisms with data on mastodon and mammoth life history. *Society of Vertebrate Paleontology Abstracts* 16(3): 34a.

———. 1997. Extinctions of Proboscideans in North America. In *The Proboscidea: Evolution and palaeoecology of elephants and their relatives*, ed. J. Shoshani and P. Tassy, 296–315. New York: Oxford University Press.

Flannery, T. 2001. *The eternal frontier: An ecological history of North America and its peoples*. New York: Grove Press.

Fuller, E. 2001. *Extinct birds*. Ithaca, N.Y.: Cornell University Press.

Fletcher, D. E., E. E. Dakin, B. A. Porter, and J. C. Avise. 2004. Spawning behavior and genetic parentage in the Pirate Perch (*Aphredoderus sayanus*), a fish with an enigmatic reproductive morphology. *Copeia* 2004(1): 1–10.

Gao, K.-Q., and N. H. Shubin. 2001. Late Jurassic salamanders from northern China. *Nature* 410: 574–77.

———. 2003. Earliest known crown-group salamanders. *Nature* 422: 424–28.

Garrett, G. P., and R. J. Edwards. 2003. New species of *Gambusia* (Cyprinodontiformes: Poeciliidae) from Del Rio, Texas. *Copeia* 2003(4): 783–88.

Geist, V. 1998. *Deer of the world: Their evolution, behavior, and ecology*. Mechanicsburg, Pa.: Stackpole Books.

Gilbert, C. R., R. C. Cashner, and E. O. Wiley. 1992. Taxonomic and nomenclatural status of the Banded Topminnow, *Fundulus cingulatus* (Cyprinodontiformes: Cyprinodontidae). *Copeia* 1992(3): 747–59.

Glassberg, J. 1999. *Butterflies through binoculars: The East*. New York: Oxford University Press.

———. 2001. *Butterflies through binoculars: The West*. New York: Oxford University Press.

Goldman, E. A. 1910. Revision of the wood rats of the genus *Neotoma*. *North American Fauna* 31: 124.

Goodin, J. T., E. G. Maurakis, E. S. Perry, and W. S. Woolcott. 1998. Species recognition for *Percina nevisense* Cope (Actinopterygii: Percidae). *Virginia Journal of Science* 49(3): 183–94.

Graham, R. W. 2003. Pleistocene tapir from Hill Top Cave, Trigg County, Kentucky, and a review of Plio-Pleistocene tapirs of North America and their paleoecology. In *Ice age cave faunas of North America*, ed. B. W. Schubert, J. I. Mead, and R. W. Graham, 87–118. Bloomington, Ind.: Indiana University Press.

Grayson, D. K., and D. J. Meltzer. 2003. A requiem for North American overkill. *Journal of Archaeological Science* 30: 585–93.

Gunnell, G. F., and A. Foral. 1994. New species of *Bretzia* (Cervidae: Artiodactyla) from the latest Pleistocene or earliest Holocene of Nebraska and South Dakota. *Journal of Mammalogy* 75(2): 378–81.

Guthrie, R. D. 1990. *Frozen fauna of the Mammoth Steppe: The story of Blue Babe*. Chicago: University of Chicago Press.

Harris, A. H. 1990. Taxonomic status of the Pleistocene Ringtail *Bassariscus sonoitensis* (Carnivora). *Southwestern Naturalist* 35(3): 343–46.

Harrison III, J. R., and S. I. Guttman. 2003. A new species of *Eurycea* (Caudata: Plethodontidae) from North and South Carolina. *Southeastern Naturalist* 2(2): 159–78.

Heaton, T. H. 1985. Quaternary paleontology and paleoecology of Crystal Ball Cave, Millard County, Utah: With emphasis on mammals and description of a new species of fossil skunk. *Great Basin Naturalist* 45(3): 337–90.

Hertel, F. 1994. Diversity in body size and feeding morphology within past and present vulture assemblages. *Ecology* 75(4): 1074–84.

Highton, R. 1997. Geographic protein variation and speciation in the *Plethodon dorsalis* complex. *Herpetologica* 53: 345–56.

———. 1999. Geographic protein variation and speciation in the salamanders of the *Plethodon cinereus* group with the description of two new species. *Herpetologica* 55(1): 43–90.

———. 2004. A new species of woodland salamander of the *Plethodon cinereus* group from the Blue Ridge Mountains of Virginia. *Jeffersoniana* no. 14: 1–22.

Highton, R., and R. B. Peabody. 2000. Geographic protein variation and speciation in salamanders of the *Plethodon jordani* and *Plethodon glutinosus* complexes in the southern Appalachian Mountains with the description of four new species. In *The biology of Plethodontid salamanders*, ed. R. C. Bruce, R. G. Jaeger, and L. D. Houck, 31–93. New York: Kluwer Academic/Plenum Publishers.

Hillis, D. M., D. A. Chamberlain, T. P. Wilcox, and P. T. Chippindale. 2001. A new species of subterranean blind salamander (Plethodontidae: Hemidactyliini: *Eurycea*: *Typhlomolge*) from Austin, Texas, and a systematic revision of central Texas paedomorphic salamanders. *Herpetologica* 57(3): 266–80.

Hoffmeister, D. F. 1986. *Mammals of Arizona*. Tucson: University of Arizona Press.

Holloway, G. L., and R.M.R. Barclay. 2001. *Myotis ciliolabrum*. *Mammalian Species* no. 670: 1–5.

Holman, J. A. 1995. *Pleistocene amphibians and reptiles in North America*. New York: Oxford University Press.

Howard, H. 1935. A new species of eagle from a Quarternary cave deposit in eastern Nevada. *Condor* 37: 206–9.

———. 1964. A new species of the "Pigmy Goose," *Anabernicula*, from the Oregon Pleistocene, with a discussion of the genus. *American Museum Novitates* no. 2200: 1–14.

Hulbert, R. C., Jr., ed. 2001. *The fossil vertebrates of Florida*. Gainesville: University Press of Florida.

Humphries, J. M., and R. C. Cashner. 1994. *Notropis suttkusi*, a new Cyprinid from the Ouachita Uplands of Oklahoma and Arkansas, with comments on the status of Ozarkian populations of *N. rubellus*. *Copeia* 1994(1): 82–90.

International Union for the Conservation of Nature (IUCN), Conservation International, and NatureServe. 2004. Global Amphibian Assessment. <www.globalamphibians.org>, accessed November 2004.

Jackson, H.H.T. 1928. A taxonomic review of the American long-tailed shrews (genera *Sorex* and *Microsorex*). *North American Fauna* 51: 1–238.

Jenkins, R. E., and N. M. Burkhead. 1994. *Freshwater fishes of Virginia*. Bethesda, Md.: American Fisheries Society.

Johnson, J. B., T. E. Dowling, and M. C. Belk. 2004. Neglected taxonomy of rare desert fishes: Congruent evidence for two species of leatherside chub. *Systematic Biology* 53(6): 841–55.

Kays, R. W., and D. E. Wilson. 2002. *Mammals of North America*. Princeton, N.J.: Princeton University Press.

Kinziger, A. P., R. L. Raesly, and D. A. Neely. 2000. New species of *Cottus* (Teleostei: Cottidae) from the middle Atlantic eastern United States. *Copeia* 2000(4): 1007–18.

Kinziger, A. P., R. M. Wood, and S. A. Welsh. 2001. Systematics of *Etheostoma tippecanoe* and *Etheostoma denoncourti* (Perciformes: Percidae). *Copeia* 2001: 235–39.

Kurtén, B., and E. Anderson. 1980. *Pleistocene mammals of North America*. New York: Columbia University Press.

Lazell, J. 1998. New salamander of the genus *Plethodon* from Mississippi. *Copeia* 1998(4): 967–70.

Linsdale, J. 1940. Amphibians and reptiles in Nevada. *Proceedings of the American Academy of Arts and Sciences* 73:197-257.

Lorion, C., D. F. Markle, S. B. Reid, and M. F. Docker. 2000. Redescription of the presumed-extinct Miller Lake Lamprey, *Lampetra minima*. *Copeia* 2000(4): 1019–28.

Lovich, J. E., and C. J. McCoy. 1992. Review of the *Graptemys pulchra* group (Reptilia: Testudines: Emydidae), with descriptions of two new species. *Annals of the Carnegie Museum* 61(4): 293–315.

MacPhee, R.D.E., and C. Flemming. 1999. Requiem Æternam: The last five hundred years of mammalian species extinctions. In *Extinctions in near time*, ed. R.D.E. MacPhee, 333–70. New York: Kluwer Academic/Plenum Publishers.

Mares, M., and J. Braun. 2000. *Graomys*, the genus that ate South America: A reply to Steppam and Sullivan. *Journal of Mammalogy* 81(1):271–76.

Markle, D. F., and D. L. Hill Jr. 2000. Taxonomy and distribution of the Malheur Mottled Sculpin, *Cottus bendirei*. *Northwest Science* 74(3): 202–11.

Markle, D. F., T. N. Pearsons, and D. T. Bills. 1991. Natural history of *Oregonichthys* (Pices: Cyprinidae), with a description of a new species from the Umpqua River of Oregon. *Copeia* 1991(2): 227–93.

Marshall, L. G. 1985. Geochronology and land-mammal biochronology of the transamerican faunal interchange. In *The Great American Biotic Interchange*, ed. F. G. Stehli and S. D. Webb, 49–85. New York: Plenum Press.

Martin, P. S. 1984. Prehistoric overkill: The global model. In *Quaternary extinctions: A prehistoric revolution*, ed. P. S. Martin and R. G. Klein, 354–403. Tucson: University of Arizona Press.

———. 1990. 40,000 years of extinctions on the "planet of doom." *Palaeogeography, Palaeoclimatology, Palaeoecology* (Global and Planetary change Section) 82: 187–201.

Martin, P. S., and D. A. Burney. 1999. Bring back the elephants! *Wild Earth* 9(1): 57–64.

Martin, P. S., and D. W. Steadman. 1999. Prehistoric extinctions on islands and continents. In *Extinctions in near time*, ed. R.D.E. MacPhee, 17–55. New York: Kluwer Academic/Plenum Publishers.

Matocq, M. D. 2002. Morphological and molecular analysis of a contact zone in the *Neotoma fuscipes* species complex. *Journal of Mammalogy* 83(3): 866–83.

Matthews, W. J., R. E. Jenkins, and J. T. Styron Jr. 1982. Systematics of two forms of Blacknose Dace, *Rhinichthys atratulus* (Pices: Cyprinidae) in a zone of syntopy, with a review of the species group. *Copeia* 1982(4): 902–20.

Mayden, R. L., and B. R. Kuhajda. 1996. Systematics, taxonomy, and conservation status of the endangered Alabama Sturgeon, *Scaphirhynchus suttkusi* Williams and Clemmer (Actinopterygii, Acipenseridae). *Copeia* 1996(2): 241–73.

Mayden, R. L., R. H. Matson, and D. M. Hillis. 1992. Speciation in the North American genus *Dionda* (Teleostei: Cypriniformes). In *Systematics, historical ecology, and North American freshwater fishes*, ed. R. L. Mayden, 710–46. Stanford, Calif.: Stanford University Press.

Mayr, E. 2001. *What evolution is*. New York: Basic Books.

McDonald, J. N., and C. E. Ray. 1989. The autochthonous North American musk oxen *Bootherium*, *Symbos*, and *Gidleya* (Mammalia: Artiodactyla: Bovidae). *Smithsonian Contributions to Paleobiology* 66.

Mead, J. I., A. E. Spiess, and K. D. Sobolik. 2000. Skeleton of extinct North American Sea Mink (*Mustela macrodon*). *Quaternary Research* 53(2): 247–62.

Mead, L. S., D. R. Clayton, R. S. Nauman, D. H. Olson, and M. E. Pfrender. 2005. Newly discovered populations of salamanders from Siskiyou County, California represent a species distinct from *Plethodon stormi*. *Herpetologica* 61(2): 158–77.

Meylan, P. A., and W. Sterrer. 2000. *Hesperotestudo* (Testudines: Testudinidae) from the Pleistocene of Bermuda, with comments on the phylogenetic position of the genus. *Zoological Journal of the Linnean Society* 128: 51–76.

Miller, R. R. 1966. Geographic distribution of Central American freshwater fishes. *Copeia* 1966(4): 773–802.

Minckley, W. L., and B. D. DeMarais. 2000. Taxonomy of chubs (Teleostei, Cyprinidae, genus *Gila*) in the American southwest with comments on conservation. *Copeia* 2000(1): 251–56.

Minckley, W. L., R. R. Miller, and S. M. Norris. 2002. Three new pupfish species, *Cyprinodon* (Teleostei, Cyprinodontidae), from Chihuahua, Mexico, and Arizona, USA. *Copeia* 2002: 687–705.

Moler, P. E., and J. Kezer. 1993. Karyology and systematics of the salamander genus *Pseudobranchus* (Sirenidae). *Copeia* 1993 (1): 39–47.

Morejohn, G. V. 1976. Evidence of the survival to Recent times of the extinct flightless duck *Chendytes lawi* Miller. In *Collected papers in avian paleontology honoring the 90th birthday of Alexander Wetmore*, ed. S. L. Olson, 207–11. Smithsonian Contributions in Paleobiology, no. 27.

Musser, G. G., and M. D. Carleton. 1993. Family Muridae. In *Mammal species of the world*, ed. D. E. Wilson and D. M. Reeder, 501–755. 2nd ed. Washington, D.C.: Smithsonian Institution Press.

National Geographic Society. 2002. *Field guide to the birds of North America*, 4th ed. Washington, D.C.: National Geographic Society.

NatureServe. 2005. NatureServe Explorer: An online encyclopedia of life. Version 3.1. <http://www.natureserve.org/explorer>, accessed March, 2005.

Nelson, E. W. 1909. The rabbits of North America. *North American Fauna* 29: 1–238.

Nelson, J. S., E. J. Crossman, H. Espinosa-Pérez, L. T. Findley, C. R. Gilbert, R. N. Lea, and J. D. Williams. 2004. *Common and scientific names of fishes from the United States, Canada, and Mexico*. 6th ed. Bethesda, Md.: American Fisheries Society, Special Publication 29.

Nielson, M., K. Lohman, and J. Sullivan. 2001. Phylogeography of the Tailed Frog (*Ascaphus truei*): Implications for the biogeography of the Pacific Northwest. *Evolution* 55(1): 147–60.

North American Butterfly Association (NABA). 2001. *Checklist and English names of North American butterflies*. Morristown, N.J.: NABA.

Noss, R. F., E. T. LaRoe III, and J. M. Scott. 1995. *Endangered ecosystems of the United States: A preliminary assessment of loss and degradation*. Biological report 28. Washington, D.C.: U.S. Department of Interior, National Biological Service.

Opler, P. A., and A. D. Warren. 2003. Butterflies of North America. 2. Scientific names list for butterfly species of North America, north of Mexico. Contributions of the Gillette Museum of Arthropod Biodiversity, May 2003 online version. <www.biology.ualberta.ca/old_site/uasm//Opler&Warren.pdf>, accessed December 2004.

Opler, P. A., and A. B. Wright. 1999. *A field guide to western butterflies*. 2nd ed. New York: Houghton Mifflin.

Osgood, W. H. 1909. Revision of the mice of the American genus *Peromyscus*. *North American Fauna* 28: 1–285.

Page, L. M., and B. M. Burr. 1991. *A field guide to freshwater fishes: North America north of Mexico*. Boston: Houghton Mifflin.

———. Forthcoming. *A field guide to freshwater fishes: North America north of Mexico*. 2nd ed. Boston: Houghton Mifflin

Page, L. M., P. A. Ceas, D. L. Swofford, and D. G. Buth. 1992. Evolutionary relationships within the *Etheostoma squamiceps* complex (Percidae: subgenus *Catonotus*) with descriptions of five new species. *Copeia* 1992(3): 615–46.

Page, L. M., M. Hardman, and T. J. Near. 2003. Phylogenetic relationships of barcheek darters (Percidae: *Etheostoma*, Subgenus *Catonotus*) with descriptions of two new species. *Copeia* 2003(3): 512–30.

Papenfuss, T. J., J. R. Macey, and J. A. Schulte II. 2001. A new lizard species in the genus *Xantusia* from Arizona. *Scientific Papers of the Natural History Museum, The University of Kansas*, 23: 1–9.

Parejko, K. 2003. Pliny the Elder's silphium: First recorded species extinction. *Conservation Biology* 17(3): 925–27.

Parker, B. J. 1989. Status of the Deepwater Cisco, *Coregonus johannae*, in Canada. *Canadian Field-Naturalist* 103: 168–70.

Paulson, D. R. 2000. First records of two tropical damselflies from the United States. *Argia* 12(1): 12.

Paulson, D. R., and S. W. Dunkle. 1999. A checklist of North American Odonata, including English name, etymology, type locality, and distribution. *Occasional Papers of the Slater Museum of Natural History*, no. 56. Tacoma, Wash.: University of Puget Sound.

Petranka, J. W. 1998. *Salamanders of the United States and Canada*. Washington, D.C.: Smithsonian Institution Press.

Piaggio, A. J., E. W. Valdez, M. A. Bogan, and G. S. Spicer. 2002. Systematics of *Myotis occultus* (Chiroptera: Vespertilionidae) inferred from sequences of two mitochondrial genes. *Journal of Mammalogy* 83(2): 386–95.

Platz, J. E. 1993. *Rana subaquavocalis*, a remarkable new species of leopard frog (*Rana pipiens* complex) from southeastern Arizona that calls under water. *Journal of Herpetology* 27(2): 154–62.

Platz, J. E., A. Lathrop, L. Hofbauer, and M. Vradenburg. 1997. Age distribution and longevity in the Ramsey Canyon leopard frog, *Rana subaquavocalis*. *Journal of Herpetology* 31: 552–57.

Powers, S. L., and R. L. Mayden. 2003. *Etheostoma cervus*: A new species from the Forked Deer River system in western Tennessee with comparison to *Etheostoma pyrrhogaster* (Percidae: Subgenus *Ulocentra*). *Copeia* 2003(3): 576–82.

Pyle, R. 1981. *The Audubon Society field guide to North American butterflies*. New York: Knopf.

Quammen, D. 1996. *The song of the Dodo: Island biogeography in an age of extinctions*. New York: Scribner.

Rauchenberger, M. 1989. Systematics and biogeography of the Genus *Gambusia* (Cyprinodontiformes: Poeciliidae). *American Museum Novitates* 2951.

Rea, A. M. 1980. Late Pleistocene and Holocene turkeys in the southwest. *Contributions of the Science and Natural History Museum of Los Angeles County* 330: 209–24.

Ricketts, T., D. Dinerstein, D. Olson, C. Loucks, W. Eichbaum, K. Kavanagh, P. Hedao, P. Hurley, K. Carney, R. Abell, and S. Walters. 1999. *A conservation assessment of the terrestrial ecosystems of North America*. Vol. 1 of *The United States and Canada*. Washington, D.C.: Island Press.

Riddle, B. R., D. J. Hafner, and L. F. Alexander. 2000a. Phylogeography and systematics of the *Peromyscus eremicus* species group and the historical biogeography of North American warm regional deserts. *Molecular Phylogenetics and Evolution* 17(2): 145–60.

Riddle, B. R., D. J. Hafner, and L. F. Alexander. 2000b. Comparative phylogeography of Bailey's Pocket Mouse (*Chaetodipus baileyi*) and the *Peromyscus eremicus* species group: Historical vicariance of the Baja California peninsular desert. *Molecular Phylogenetics and Evolution* 17(2): 161–72.

Robbins, C. S., D. Bystrak, and P. H. Geissler. 1986. *The breeding bird survey: Its first fifteen years, 1965–1979*. Resource Publication 157. Washington, D.C.: U.S. Fish and Wildlife Service.

Robbins, M. B., D. L. Dittmann, J. L. Dunn, K. L. Garrett, S. Heinl, A. W. Kratter, G. Lasley, and B. Mactavish. 2003. ABA checklist committee 2002 annual report. *Birding* 35(2): 138–44.

———. 2004. ABA checklist committee 2003 annual report. *Birding* 36(1): 38–41.

Robbins, R. K., and P. A. Opler. 1997. Butterfly diversity and a preliminary comparison with bird and mammal diversity. In *Biodiversity II: Understanding and protecting our biological resources*, ed. M. L. Reaka-Kudla, D. E. Wilson, and E. O. Wilson, 69–82. Washington, D.C.: Joseph Henry Press.

Rodríguez-Robles, J. A., G. R. Stewart, and T. J. Papenfuss. 2001. Mitochondrial DNA-based phylogeography of North American Rubber Boas, *Charina bottae* (Serpentes: Boidae). *Molecular Phylogenetics and Evolution* 18(2): 227–37.

Roth, L. 1996. Pleistocene dwarf elephants of the California Islands. In *The Proboscidea: Evolution and palaeoecology of elephants and their relatives*, ed. J. Shoshani and P. Tassy, 249–53. New York: Oxford University Press.

Ruedas, L. A. 1998. Systematics of *Sylvilagus* Gray, 1867 (Lagomorpha: Leporidae) from southwestern North America. *Journal of Mammalogy* 79(4): 1355–78.

Russell, B. D., and A. H. Harris. 1986. A new leporine (Lagomorpha: Leporidae) from Wisconsinan deposits of the Chihuahuan Desert. *Journal of Mammalogy* 67(4): 632–39.

Schorr, M., M. Lindeboom, and D. Paulson. 2004. List of Odonata of the world: An online reference. Electronic database available at <www.ups.edu/biology/museum/worldodonates.>, accessed September 2004.

Sigler, W. F., and J. W. Sigler. 1996. *Fishes of Utah: A natural history*. Salt Lake City: University of Utah Press.

Skelton, C. E. 2001. New dace of the genus *Phoxinus* (Cyprinidae: Cypriniformes) from the Tennessee River drainage, Tennessee. *Copeia* 2001(1): 118–28.

Skelton, C. E., and D. A. Etnier. 2000. Taxonomic status of *Etheostoma denoncourti* Stauffer and van Snik. *Copeia* 2000(4): 1097–1103.

Smith, C. L. 1994. *Fish watching: An outdoor guide to freshwater fishes*. Ithaca, N.Y.: Cornell University Press.

Stauffer, J. R., Jr., and E. S. van Snik. 1997. New species of *Etheostoma* (Teleostei: Percidae) from the upper Tennessee River. *Copeia* 1997(1): 116–22.

Steadman, D. W. 1995. Prehistoric extinctions of Pacific island birds: Biodiversity meets zooarchaeology. *Science* 267: 1123–31.

Steadman, D. W., and P. S. Martin. 1984. Extinctions of birds in the late Pleistocene of North America. In *Quaternary extinctions: A prehistoric revolution*, ed. P. S. Martin and R. G. Klein, 466–77. Tucson: University of Arizona Press.

Stebbins, R. C. 2003. *A field guide to western reptiles and amphibians*. New York: Houghton Mifflin.

Stein, B. A., L. S. Kutner, and J. S. Adams, eds. 2000. *Precious heritage: The status of biodiversity in the United States*. New York: Oxford University Press.

Stolzenburg, W. 1996. Extinction for the record. *Nature Conservancy*. May/June: 6.

Suttkus, R. D. 1991. *Notropis rafinesquei*, a new cyprinid fish from the Yazoo River system in Mississippi. *Bulletin of the Alabama Museum of Natural History* 10: 1–9.

Suttkus, R. D., and R. M. Bailey. 1993. *Etheostoma colorosum* and *E. bellator*, two new darters, subgenus *Ulocentra*, from the southeastern United States. *Tulane Studies in Zoology and Botany* 29: 1–28.

Suttkus, R. D., R. M. Bailey, and H. L. Bart Jr. 1994a. Three new species of *Etheostoma*, subgenus *Ulocentra*, from the Gulf Coastal Plain of southeastern United States. *Tulane Studies in Zoology and Botany* 29: 97–126.

Suttkus, R. D., and M. F. Mettee. 2001. Analysis of four species of *Notropis* included in the subgenus *Pteronotropis* Fowler, with comments on relationships, origin, and dispersion. *Geological Survey of Alabama Bulletin* 170: 1–50.

Suttkus, R. D., B. A. Porter, and B. J. Freeman. 2003. The status and infraspecific variation of *Notropis stonei* Fowler. *Proceedings of the American Philosophical Society* 147(4): 354–76.

Suttkus, R. D., and B. A. Thompson. 2002. The rediscovery of the Mississippi silverside, *Menidia audens*, in the Pearl River drainage in Mississippi and Louisiana. *Southeastern Fishes Council Proceedings* 44: 6–10.

Suttkus, R. D., B. A. Thompson, and H. L. Bart Jr. 1994b. Two new darters, *Percina* (Cottogaster), from the southeastern United States, with a review of the subgenus. *Occasional Papers of the Tulane Museum of Natural History* 4: 1–46.

Tennessen, K. J. 2004. *Cordulegaster talaria*, n. sp. (Odonata: Cordulegasteridae) from west-central Arkansas. *Proceedings of the Entomological Society of Washington* 106(4): 830–39.

Thomas, M. R., and B. M. Burr. 2004. *Noturus gladiator*, a new species of madtom (Siluriformes: Ictaluridae) from Coastal Plain streams of Tennessee and Mississippi. *Ichthyological Exploration of Freshwaters* 15(4): 351–68.

Thompson, B. A. 1995. *Percina austroperca*: A new species of logperch (Percidae, Subgenus *Percina*) from the Choctawhatchee and Escambia rivers in Alabama and Florida. *Louisiana State University Occasional Papers of the Museum of Natural Sciences* 69: 1–19.

———. 1997a. *Percina suttkusi*, a new species of logperch (subgenus *Percina*), from Louisiana, Mississippi, and Alabama (Perciformes, Percidae, Etheostomatini). *Louisiana State University Occasional Papers of the Museum of Natural Science* 72: 1–27.

———. 1997b. *Percina kathae*, a new logperch endemic to the Mobile Basin in Mississippi, Alabama, Georgia, and Tennessee (Percidae, Etheostomatini). *Louisiana State University Occasional Papers of the Museum of Natural Science* 73: 1–33.

Tilley, S. G., and M. J. Mahoney. 1996. Patterns of genetic differentiation in salamanders of the *Desmognathus ochrophaeus* complex (Amphibia: Plethodontidae). *Herpetological Monographs* 10: 1–41.

Trépanier, T. L., and R. W. Murphy. 2001. The Coachella Valley Fringe-toed Lizard (*Uma inornata*): Genetic diversity and phylogenetic relationships of an endangered species. *Molecular Phylogenetics and Evolution* 18(3): 327–34.

Turgeon, J., A. Estoup, and L. Bernatchez. 1999. Species flock in the North American Great Lakes: Molecular ecology of Lake Nipigon ciscoes (Teleostei: Coregonidae: *Coregonus*). *Evolution* 53(6): 1857–71.

Turner, A. 1997. *The big cats and their fossil relatives: An illustrated guide to their evolution and natural history*. New York: Columbia University Press.

Udvardy, M.D.F. 1975. A classification of the biogeographical provinces of the world. *IUCN Occasional Paper* no. 18.

Uetz, P. 2005. The European Molecular Biology Laboratory Reptile Database. Electronic database available at <www.embl-heidelberg.de/~uetz/LivingReptiles.html>, accessed March, 2005.

Van Devender, T. R., and G. W. Bradley. 1994. Late Quaternary amphibians and reptiles from Maravillas Canyon Cave, Texas, with discussion of the biogeography and evolution of the Chihuahuan Desert herpetofauna. In *Herpetology of the North American deserts: Proceedings of a symposium*, ed. P. R. Brown and J. W. Wright, 23–53. Southwest Herpetological Society Special Publication 5.

Vanzolini, P. E., and W. R. Heyer. 1985. The American herpetofauna and the interchange. In *The Great American Biotic Interchange*, ed. F. G. Stehli and S. D. Webb, 475–87. New York: Plenum Press.

Vuilleumier, F. 1985. Fossil and Recent avifaunas and the interamerican interchange. In *The Great American Biotic Interchange*, ed. F. G. Stehli and S. D. Webb, 387–424. New York: Plenum Press.

Warren, M. L., Jr., B. M. Burr, S. J. Walsh, H. L. Bart Jr., R. C. Cashner, D. A. Etnier, B. J. Freeman, B. R. Kuhajda, R. L. Mayden, H. W. Robison, S. T. Ross, and W. C. Starnes. 2000. Diversity, distribution, and conservation status of the native freshwater fishes of the southern United States. *Fisheries* 25(10): 7–31.

Watson, W., and H. J. Walker Jr. 2004. The world's smallest vertebrate, *Schindleria brevipinguis*, a new paedomorphic species in the family Schindleriidae (Perciformes: Gobioidei). *Records of the Australian Museum* 56: 139–42.

Werdelin, L. 1985. Small Pleistocene felines of North America. *Journal of Vertebrate Paleontology* 5(3): 194–210.

Wheeler, Q. D., and N. I. Platnick. 2000. The Phylogenetic Species Concept (*sensu* Wheeler and Platnick). In *Species concepts and phylogenetic theory*, ed. Q. D. Wheeler and R. Meier, 55–69. New York: Columbia University Press.

Whitaker, J. O., Jr., and W. J. Hamilton Jr. 1998. *Mammals of the eastern United States*. 3rd ed. Ithaca, N.Y.: Cornell University Press.

Wilcove, D. S. 1999. *The condor's shadow: The loss and recovery of wildlife in America*. New York: Freeman and Co.

Wilcove, D. S., D. Rothstein, J. Dubow, A. Phillips, and E. Losos. 2000. Leading threats to biodiversity:

What's imperiling U.S. Species. In *Precious heritage: The status of biodiversity in the United States*, ed. B. A. Stein, L. S. Kutner, and J. S. Adams, 239–54. New York: Oxford University Press.

Wiley, E. O. 1978. The evolutionary species concept reconsidered. *Systematic Zoology* 27: 17–26.

Williams, J. D., and G. H. Clemmer. 1991. *Scaphirhynchus suttkusi*, a new sturgeon (Pisces: Acipenseridae) from the Mobile Basin of Alabama and Mississippi. *Bulletin of Alabama Museum Natural History* 10: 17–31.

Wilson, D. E., and D. M. Reeder, eds. 2005. *Mammal species of the world: A taxonomic and geographic reference*. 3rd ed. Baltimore: Johns Hopkins University Press.

Winans, M. C. 1985. Revision of North American fossil species of the genus *Equus* (Mammalia: Perissodactyla: Equidae). Unpublished Ph.D. dissertation, University of Texas, Austin.

———. 1989. A quantitative study of the North American fossil species of the genus *Equus*. In *The evolution of Perissodactyls*, ed. D. R. Prothero and R. M. Schoch, 262–97. New York: Oxford University Press.

Wood, R. M., and R. L. Mayden. 1993. Systematics of the *Etheostoma jordani* species group (Teleostei: Percidae), with descriptions of three new species. *Bulletin of Alabama Museum of Natural History* 16: 31–46.

Wood, R. M., R. L. Mayden, R. H. Matson, B. R. Kuhajda, and S. R. Layman. 2002. Systematics and biogeography of the *Notropis rubellus* species group (Teleostei: Cyprinidae). *Bulletin of the Alabama Museum of Natural History* 22: 37–80.

Wright, J. W., and C. H. Lowe. 1993. Synopsis of the subspecies of the Little Striped Whiptail Lizard, *Cnemidophorus inornatus* Baird. *Journal of the Arizona-Nevada Academy of Science* 27: 129–57.

Youngman, P. M. 1967. A new subspecies of varying lemming, *Dicrostonyx torquatus* (Pallas), from Yukon Territory (Mammalia, Rodentia). *Proceedings of the Biological Society of Washington* 80: 31–34.

———. 1975. *Mammals of the Yukon Territory*. National Museum of Natural Sciences (Canada) Publications in Zoology, no. 10.

Youngman, P. M., and F. W. Schueler. 1991. *Martes nobilis* is a synonym of *Martes americana*, not an extinct Pleistocene-Holocene species. *Journal of Mammalogy* 72(3): 567–77.

Index to Scientific Names

The letter code following the page number refers to the type of wildlife: M = Mammal, B = Bird, R = Reptile, A = Amphibian, F = Fish, L (for Lepidoptera) = Butterfly, D = Dragonfly or Damselfly.

Ambystoma, 247 A
Ambystomatidae, 247 A
Ameiurus, 290 F
Ameiva, 233 R
ameiva, Ameiva, 233 R
amelia, Neoneura, 397 D
americana, Anas, 129 B
   Antilocapra, 117 M
   Aythya, 130 B
   Certhia, 169 B
   Chloroceryle, 159 B
   Fulica, 144 B
   Grus, 144 B
   Hetaerina, 395 D
   Martes, 113 M
   Morone, 306 F
   Mycteria, 139 B
   Parula, 174 B
   Recurvirostra, 145 B
   Spiza, 181 B
americanum, Mammut, 69, 83 M
americanus, Alces, 116, 435 M
   Bufo, 239 A
   Coccyzus, 155 B
   Esox, 293 F
   Lepus, 101 M
   Neophrontops, 80, 141 M
   Numenius, 146 B
   Oreamnos, 117 M
   Ursus, 112 M
Amia, 266 F
Amiidae, 266 F
amistadensis, Gambusia, 301 F
Ammocrypta, 309 F
Ammodramus, 179 B
ammon, Cyclargus, 466 L
   Hemiargus, 349, 466 L
ammophilus, Notropis, 276 F
Ammospermophilus, 85 M
Ammotragus, 124 M
amnicola, Felis, 69 M
   Stylurus, 414 D
amnis, Hybopsis, 272 F
amoena, Passerina, 181 B
amoenus, Carphophis, 217 R
   Notropis, 276 F
   Tamias, 88 M
Amphiagrion, 397 D
amphichloe, Hamadryas, 385 L
amphinome, Hamadryas, 385 L
Amphispiza, 179 B
Amphiuma, 246 A
Amphiumidae, 246 A
Amplibuteo, 80, 142 B
amplus, Perognathus, 92 M
   Plethodon, 254, 449 A
ampullatus, Hyperoodon, 121 M
amymone, Mestra, 359 L
amyntula, Everes, 349 L
Anabernicula, 78, 129 B
Anaea, 360, 385 L

anaethetus, Sterna, 152 B
anaktuvukensis, Salvelinus, 456 F
analostana, Cyprinella, 267 F
anaphus, Astraptes, 387 L
Anartia, 359, 384 L
Anas, 129, 185 B
Anastrus, 389 L
Anatidae, 128, 185, 201 B
Anatrytone, 374, 390 L
Anax, 406, 427 D
anchisiades, Papilio, 338 L
Anchoa, 266 F
Ancyloxypha, 371 L
andersonii, Hyla, 241 A
andraemon, Papilio, 380 L
andria, Anaea, 360 L
androgeus, Papilio, 380 L
Aneides, 248 A
angelia, Electrostrymon, 390 L
angra, Pellicia, 388 L
Anguidae, 215 R
Anguilla, 266 F
anguillicaudatus, Misgurnus, 330 F
Anguillidae, 266 F
angulatum, Coenagrion, 400 D
angusticlavius, Plethodon, 254, 449 A
angustifolia, Aphylla, 407 D
angustipennis, Calopteryx, 395 D
angustirostris, Mirounga, 113 M
Anhinga, 138 B
anhinga, Anhinga, 138 B
Anhingidae, 138 B
ani, Crotophaga, 155 B
anisitsi, Pterygoplichthys, 331, 465 F
anisurum, Moxostoma, 288, 455 F
anna, Calypte, 159 B
   Enallagma, 400 D
annabella, Vanessa, 358 L
annexum, Enallagma, 400, 466 D
Anniella, 215 R
Anniellidae, 215 R
annularis, Pomoxis, 309 F
annulata, Macromia, 415 D
annulatum, Ambystoma, 247 A
anogenus, Notropis, 276 F
Anolis, 207, 232 R
anomalum, Campostoma, 267 F
anomalus, Ophiogomphus, 412 D
Anous, 152 B
Anser, 128, 185 B
antennatum, Enallagma, 400 D
Anteos, 341, 381 L
antesella, Percina, 319 F
anthedon, Enodia, 360 L
Anthocharis, 340 L
anthracinus, Buteogallus, 141 B
   Plestiodon, 214 R
Anthracothorax, 193 B
Anthus, 172, 199 B
Antigonus, 389 L
antillarum, Sterna, 152 B

jordani, Etheostoma, 313, 460 F
    Plethodon, 256, 449 A
josephina, Ganyra, 339 L
juba, Hesperia, 372 L
jubatus, Eumetopias, 112 M
julia, Ladona, 422, 468 D
    Libellula, 468 D
    Nastra, 370 L
juliae, Etheostoma, 313 F
julisia, Fundulus, 300 F
junaluska, Eurycea, 252 A
juncea, Aeshna, 405 D
Junco, 180 B
junius, Anax, 406 D
Junonia, 358 L
jutta, Oeneis, 363 L
juvenalis, Erynnis, 367 L
Jynx, 194 B

kalawatseti, Oregonichthys, 282, 453 F
kanawhae, Etheostoma, 314 F
kansae, Fundulus, 300, 457 F
kantuckeense, Etheostoma, 314, 459 F
kathae, Percina, 320, 462 F
kawia, Batrachoseps, 249 A
keeni, Peromyscus, 99 M
keenii, Myotis, 109 M
kellicotti, Ischnura, 403 D
kempii, Lepidochelys, 231 R
kennedyi, Somatochlora, 418 D
kennerlyi, Heterodon, 218, 442 R
kennicotti, Etheostoma, 314 F
kennicottii, Megascops, 156, 438 B
    Otus, 438 B
kentucki, Plethodon, 256 A
keta, Oncorhynchus, 296 F
kezeri, Rhyacotriton, 248 A
kiamichi, Plethodon, 256 A
kingi, Satyrium, 345 L
kingii, Elgaria, 215 R
Kinosternidae, 227 R
Kinosternon, 227 R
kirtlandii, Clonophis, 217 R
    Dendroica, 175 B
kisatchie, Plethodon, 256 A
kisutch, Oncorhynchus, 296 F
kiyi, Coregonus, 295 F
klamathensis, Cottus, 305 F
klugii, Dircenna, 386 L
knoxjonesi, Geomys, 93 M
Kogia, 121 M
kohnii, Graptemys, 443 R
kozhantshikovi, Erebia, 362 L
Kricogonia, 342 L
kriemhild, Boloria, 354 L
kurilis, Gomphus, 410 D

labialis, Leptodactylus, 450 A
Labidesthes, 298 F
labradorius, Camptorhynchus, 131, 436 B
labrosa, Cyprinella, 268, 463 F

Hybopsis, 463 F
lacerata, Holbrookia, 207 R
    Tramea, 427 D
Lacerta, 234 R
Lacertidae, 234 R
lacertina, Siren, 245 A
lacerum, Moxostoma, 289 F
lachneri, Etheostoma, 314, 461 F
    Moxostoma, 289 F
    Noturus, 292 F
lachrymosa, Euthlypis, 199 B
lacinia, Chlosyne, 355 L
lacrimans, Argia, 398 D
ladon, Celastrina, 349 L
Ladona, 422 D
laeta, Erora, 348 L
laevis, Xenopus, 259 A
Lagenodelphis, 119 M
Lagenorhynchus, 119 M
Lagodon, 328 F
Lagopus, 132 B
lagopus, Alopex, 436 M
    Buteo, 142 B
    Lagopus, 132 B
    Vulpes, 111, 436 M
lais, Apanisagrion, 397 D
Lampetra, 263 F
Lampornis, 158 B
Lampropeltis, 218 R
lampropeltis, Erpetogomphus, 409 D
lanceolata, Anthocharis, 340 L
    Locustella, 196 B
Laniidae, 164, 195 B
Lanius, 164, 195 B
lanoraieensis, Callophrys, 346 L
Lanthus, 411 D
laothoe, Temensis, 384 L
lapponica, Limosa, 147 B
lapponicus, Calcarius, 180 B
laredoensis, Aspidoscelis, 213 R
largha, Phoca, 113 M
Laridae, 149, 191 B
larselli, Plethodon, 256 A
Larus, 149, 191 B
Lasaia, 351 L
Lasionycteris, 108 M
Lasiurus, 108 M
laterale, Ambystoma, 247 A
    Enallagma, 401 D
lateralis, Masticophis, 219 R
    Scincella, 215 R
    Spermophilus, 87 M
Laterallus, 78, 143 B
laticeps, Plestiodon, 214 R
latifrons, Bison, 77 M
    Cervalces, 76, 116 M
    Dormitator, 464 F
latimanus, Scapanus, 106 M
latipinna, Poecilia, 302 F
latipinnis, Catostomus, 286 F
latirostris, Cynanthus, 158 B

Oryx, 124 M
oryzivorus, Dolichonyx, 182 B
Oryzomys, 98 M
osburni, Etheostoma, 315 F
osca, Rhinthon, 390 L
osculus, Rhinichthys, 285 F
oslari, Amblyscirtes, 377 L
Osmeridae, 294, 326, 331 F
Osmerus, 294 F
osseus, Lepisosteus, 265 F
ossifragus, Corvus, 166 B
Osteopilus, 259 A
ostralegus, Haematopus, 189 B
Otariidae, 112 M
otho, Wallengrenia, 374 L
othus, Lepus, 102 M
ottoe, Hesperia, 372 L
Otus, 156, 192 B
otus, Asio, 157 B
ouachitae, Percina, 463 F
      Plethodon, 257 A
ouachitensis, Graptemys, 229, 443 R
outis, Cogia, 366 L
Ovibos, 118 M
Ovis, 118, 124 M
Oxybelis, 220 R
oxyrhynchus, Acipenser, 463 F
      Notropis, 279 F
      Percina, 321 F
oxyrinchus, Acipenser, 265, 463 F
Oxyura, 132 B
ozarcanus, Notropis, 279 F
ozarkensis, Gomphus, 411 D
      Somatochlora, 419 D

Pachydiplax, 425 D
Pachyramphus, 164 B
pachyrhyncha, Rhynchopsitta, 192 B
pacifica, Gavia, 134 B
      Macromia, 416 D
pacificus, Apus, 193 B
      Batrachoseps, 250 A
      Puffinus, 186 B
      Sorex, 105 M
      Thaleichthys, 294 F
pacuvius, Erynnis, 368 L
Pagophila, 151 B
Pagophilus, 113 M
pahaska, Hesperia, 372 L
pai, Aspidoscelis, 213, 440 R
Palaemnema, 397 D
palaemon, Carterocephalus, 370 L
palaeno, Colias, 341 L
Palaeolama, 76, 116 M
palamedes, Papilio, 338 L
palarostris, Chionactis, 217 R
palegon, Rekoa, 381 L
palemon, Phocides, 466 L
palla, Chlosyne, 356 L
pallasi, Emberiza, 200 B
pallens, Argia, 399 D

palleucus, Gyrinophilus, 254, 448 A
palliatus, Haematopus, 145 B
pallida, Achlyodes, 389 L
      Phyciodes, 357 L
      Spizella, 178 B
pallidicinctus, Tympanuchus, 133 B
pallididorsum, Etheostoma, 315 F
pallidula, Nehalennia, 404 D
pallidum, Enallagma, 402 D
pallidus, Antrozous, 107 M
      Arigomphus, 408 D
      Microdipodops, 92 M
pallipes, Sympetrum, 426 D
palmaris, Percina, 321 F
palmarum, Dendroica, 175 B
palmata, Aeshna, 405 D
palmeri, Apodemia, 352 L
      Tamias, 89 M
palpebrata, Phoebetria, 186 B
Paltothemis, 425 D
palustris, Cistothorus, 169 B
      Oryzomys, 98 M
      Rana, 244 A
      Sorex, 105, 434 M
      Sylvilagus, 102 M
Pampatheriidae, 84 M
panamintina, Elgaria, 215 R
panamintinus, Dipodomys, 92 M
      Tamias, 89 M
Pandanaris, 81, 182 B
Pandion, 140 B
pandora, Gila, 271 F
panoquin, Panoquina, 378 L
Panoquina, 378, 390 L
panoquinoides, Panoquina, 378 L
Pantala, 425 D
Panthera, 73, 110 M
pantherina, Percina, 321 F
Pantherophis, 220, 443 R
Papilio, 337, 380 L
Papilionidae, 337 L
pappillosum, Moxostoma, 289 F
Parabuteo, 141 B
paradisaea, Sterna, 152 B
Paralichthyidae, 329 F
Paralichthys, 329 F
parallelus, Centropomus, 327 F
Paramacera, 361 L
Paramylodon, 71, 84 M
Parascalops, 106 M
parasiticus, Stercorarius, 149 B
Paratrytone, 374 L
pardalis, Leopardus, 110 M
      Pterygoplichthys, 331, 465 F
Pardirallus, 188 B
parellina, Cyanocompsa, 200 B
Paridae, 167 B
Parides, 380 L
parisorum, Icterus, 183 B
Parnassius, 337 L
Parrhasius, 347 L

Sylvilagus, 102, 433 M
rogersi, Gomphus, 411 D
rosae, Amblyopsis, 297 F
rosaliae, Bogertophis, 216 R
rosea, Rhodostethia, 151 B
roseipinnis, Lythrurus, 274 F
rosita, Chlosyne, 383 L
rosmarus, Odobenus, 112 M
rosovi, Oeneis, 363 L
rossii, Chen, 128 B
    Erebia, 362 L
rostrata, Anguilla, 266 F
Rostrhamus, 141 B
rubellus, Notropis, 280, 453 F
ruber, Crotalus, 226 R
    Eudocimus, 187 B
    Phoenicopterus, 140 B
    Pseudotriton, 258 A
    Sphyrapicus, 160 B
rubescens, Anthus, 172 B
    Nisoniades, 388 L
rubicundulum, Sympetrum, 426 D
rubidus, Lycaena, 343 L
rubinus, Pyrocephalus, 163 B
rubra, Piranga, 177 B
    Tantilla, 442 R
rubricata, Megisto, 361 L
rubricauda, Phaethon, 187 B
rubricroceus, Notropis, 280 F
rubrifrons, Cardellina, 177 B
    Fundulus, 300, 457 F
    Hybopsis, 272 F
rubripes, Anas, 129 B
rubriventris, Pseudemys, 229 R
rubrofluviatilis, Cyprinodon, 303 F
rubrum, Etheostoma, 316 F
rudinoris, Chaetodipus, 91, 432 M
rufa, Aplodontia, 85 M
rufescens, Egretta, 138 B
    Poecile, 167 B
ruficapilla, Vermivora, 173 B
ruficaudus, Tamias, 89 M
ruficeps, Aimophila , 178 B
ruficollis, Calidris, 147 B
rufifrons, Basileuterus, 199 B
rufilineatum, Etheostoma, 316 F
rufipunctatus, Thamnophis, 224 R
rufivirgatus, Arremonops, 177 B
rufofusca, Strymon, 347 L
rufopalliatus, Turdus, 171 B
rufopunctata, Uma, 210, 439 R
rufum, Toxostoma, 172 B
rufus, Canis, 111, 435 M
    Lynx, 110 M
    Selasphorus, 159 B
    Tamias, 89 M
rupestre, Etheostoma, 316 F
rupestris, Ambloplites, 307 F
    Notropis, 280 F
rupinsulensis, Ophiogomphus, 413 D

rupiscartes, Moxostoma, 290 F
ruptifasciatus, Timochares, 367 L
ruralis, Pyrgus, 368 L
rusconi, Eremotherium, 71 M
rustica, Emberiza, 181 B
    Hirundo, 167 B
rusticola, Scolopax, 191 B
rusticolus, Falco, 143 B
ruthveni, Pituophis, 221, 441 R
ruticilla, Setophaga, 175 B
rutila, Amazilia, 193 B
rutilus, Myodes, 97 M
rutulus, Papilio, 338 L
Rynchops, 152 B

sabina, Dasyatis, 264 F
sabinae, Notropis, 280 F
sabini, Xema, 151 B
sabino, Argia, 399 D
sabrinus, Glaucomys, 85 M
sabuleti, Polites, 373 L
saepiolus, Plebejus, 350 L
saepium, Satyrium, 345 L
sagitta, Etheostoma, 317 F
sagrae, Myiarchus, 195 B
sagrei, Anolis, 232 R
sahlbergi, Somatochlora, 419 D
Saiga, 78, 118 M
Salamandridae, 245 A
salar, Salmo, 297 F
salenus, Synapte, 389 L
salinus, Cyprinodon, 303 F
Salmo, 297, 331 F
salmoides, Micropterus, 308 F
Salmonidae, 294, 331 F
salome, Eurema, 381 L
Salpinctes, 169 B
salva, Telebasis, 404 D
Salvadora, 222 R
Salvelinus, 297 F
salvini, Cichlasoma, 333, 465 F
Sander, 322, 332 F
sandrius, Gomphus, 411 D
sandvicensis, Sterna, 151 B
sandwichensis, Passerculus, 179 B
    Pterodroma, 186 B
sangala, Electrostrymon, 348 L
Sangamona, 69 M
sanguifluum, Etheostoma, 317 F
santaanae, Catostomus, 287 F
santeetlah, Desmognathus, 251 A
sapidissima, Alosa, 267 F
sapiens, Homo, 85 M
sara, Anthocharis, 340 L
sardinella, Coregonus, 295 F
Sarotherodon, 334 F
sasin, Selasphorus, 159 B
sassacus, Hesperia, 372 L
Satan, 293 F
satrapa, Regulus, 169 B

Index to Common Names

Whit Bronaugh is a professional nature photographer and writer. His natural history articles and photographs have appeared in a wide range of publications including *Wildlife Conservation*, *National Geographic*, *Natural History*, and *Smithsonian* magazines.